To Paul and Janet,
My dear friends,

Very fondly,

Hanna

Jerusalem, 23.XI.01

THE SEEDS OF TRIUMPH
Church and State in Gomułka's Poland

THE SEEDS OF TRIUMPH

Church and State in Gomułka's Poland

Hanna Diskin

Central European University Press

Published in 2001 by
Central European University Press

Nádor utca 15
H-1015 Budapest
Hungary

400 West 59th Street
New York NY 10019
USA

An imprint of the
Central European University Share Company

Distributed in the United Kingdom and Western Europe by
Plymbridge Distributors Ltd., Estover Road,
Plymouth PL6 7PZ, United Kingdom

ISBN 963 9241 16 4 Cloth

Library of Congress Cataloging-in-Publication Data
A CIP catalog record for this book is available upon request

Printed in Hungary by
Akadémiai Nyomda, Martonvásár

In memory of my parents

Felicja ('Fela') and Moshe ('Mietek')
Grynbaum who taught me to love my
homeland, to love the country where I
was born and to love humanity for its
very humanity.

TABLE OF CONTENTS

LIST OF TABLES

PREFACE

This book does not, I believe, reflect the usual type of research enquiry. The subject with which the book deals has accompanied me throughout most of my adult life and, to a great extent, has dictated my way of life and daily routine for over two decades. My dedication to the exploration of religio-political relations in Poland is no accident. It is the result of a decision taken early on, and I have treated it accordingly as the years passed. Naturally, such a decision has imposed certain limitations both regarding other research activities as well as in other areas of my life. The reader will judge whether this investment was worthwhile and whether it was justified.

My interest in Poland clearly has personal and historical origins. For hundreds of years Poland provided refuge for my people. We should not minimize the importance of this fact, despite the complex nature of Polish–Jewish relations across the generations. Sadly, the vast majority of Polish Jewry was annihilated during the Second World War. Among the few survivors were my own parents, although most members of their families did not survive the Holocaust. My parents returned to Poland under the repatriation agreement with the Soviet Union after the war. Thus, I was born in Poland (in 'the liberated territories'), which is where I spent my early years. Although my parents emigrated from Poland, I nevertheless consider Polish to be my mother tongue and have remained attached to Polish culture throughout my life. My interest in religion generally, and the Catholic Church in particular, seems to be linked to my family's experiences and to different contacts I have had since my childhood.

This book deals with Poland, the Polish Roman Catholic Church and the relationship between religion and state in Poland. Nevertheless, I hope that its lessons will resonate beyond the Polish and Eastern European arena and teach us something about relations between state and religion in other countries, about how to analyze and understand conflicts, and perhaps even how to resolve them in other settings. Personally, I have been able to apply conclusions drawn from the theoretical framework, the analytical tools and the scrutiny of the Polish case to other circumstances. I trust that others will find this book useful in areas unrelated to this specific case.

I hope that this book will appeal to scholars of Eastern European and Slavic studies, those interested in the Catholic Church, and those whose field is the broader context of contemporary history, comparative politics, conflict analysis, public administration and other political science disciplines.

In writing this book, I have tried to be as 'scientific' as possible. An attempt has been made to maximize the objectivity of the analysis and description. I believe that these reflect a lack of bias or critical prejudice toward one ideology or another. In order to substantiate the hypotheses and arguments, I have attempted to furnish abundant evidence and multiple, detailed examples. This, despite the fact that the book—including its epilogue—deals in fact with a period spanning over half a century. On the other hand, a consistent effort has been made to understand reasons, trends and dynamics and to present general conclusions carrying theoretical implications. In this regard, the material might sometimes seem relatively 'dry'. I have chosen this style of writing in preference to the more dramatic and colorful style of analysis, which although perhaps more popular, tends to err through inaccuracy.

Emotively speaking, there is nothing easier than painting positions that you oppose in bleak colors and those that you support in a flattering light. In principle, I find it difficult to believe in value systems, ideologies and forms of regime that purport to be an unequivocal representation of what is right and just. My own view is that humanity—in its very humanity—stands at the center of all human experience, including the political and social experience. Human helplessness before human distress is incomprehensible and saddening when compared with the human capacity for progress in other spheres such as technology.

Throughout the many years that I studied the actions of the book's two main 'protagonists', Stefan Wyszyński and Władysław Gomułka, I learned to appreciate them despite their antagonism and differences and despite their limitations and shortcomings. I also learned greatly from their actions.

One does not have to be a devout Catholic to appreciate—and perhaps even to like—Wyszyński, whose modest exterior belies his great merits, and who is revealed as a superior person in terms of his wisdom and allegiance to his beliefs. There are those who portray Gomułka one-sidedly, even mockingly, tending to detract from his stature and to emphasize qualities denoting gray mediocrity. However, sides exist to his personality, leadership and actions that are worthy of respect and recognition even from opponents of Communism. We can find several lines of similarity between the two personalities despite the disparities dividing them. Both exhibited tenacity toward goals, beliefs and their adopted way of life. Both were victims of the Stalinist period in Poland. Both were markedly patriotic Poles, albeit in very different ways. Needless to say, I have not allowed my own identification with the torturous path of one or the other to affect the nature of the inquiry or the depth of my analysis.

Studying the conduct and deeds of the two confronting personalities (Wyszyński and Gomułka) and systems (the Roman Catholic Church and the Communist regime), and of contemporary Poland and other political systems, has led to the conclusion that no one side can ever claim a monopoly on the truth. This conclusion reinforces the need for tolerant, democratic societies that enable the coexistence of different faiths while striving toward acknowledgment of differences and to conciliation and moderation—and applies to Poland as everywhere else.

Contrary to popular conception, we find that the Polish Church remained extremely powerful throughout the entire Communist period, and, as what is sometimes called a 'quasi-independent civil society', it prepared the ground for dramatic changes later on. On the other hand, we learn that when the church believed the path before it to be clear, and when it attempted to impose its own brand of truth on society—both during the Communist era and, in a different way, after the collapse of Communism—someone was there to block its way.

Earlier on, I referred to the difficulties involved in researching this book. With this in mind, I would like first and foremost to express my thanks to my family—to my husband Bertie (Professor Abraham Diskin) for his confidence, support and love, and to our children, Tommer, Ronnie, Inbal and Eyal for their encouragement, understanding and limitless patience. A special thanks also to Mr. Richárd Rados of the CEU Press for his pertinent and helpful contribution to the publication, to Mrs. Zsófia Nagy, and everyone at the CEU Press who has helped to bring this work to fruition.

I am greatly indebted to the three readers, Professor Barbara Falk (York University, Toronto), Dr. Dariusz Stola (Institute of Political Studies, Polish Academy of Sciences, Warsaw), and, last but not least, Professor Arieh Unger (The Hebrew University of Jerusalem). Of my academic colleagues who often lent me their advice over the years, the friendship, support and wisdom of Professor Paul Abramson (Michigan State University, East Lansing), Yair Abramski (Abramski Books, Leicester), and Professor Larry Black (Carleton University, Ottawa), were a tremendous help. The Ars Polona publishing house (Warsaw) and its industrious staff were a great help to me in obtaining material. Many of the individuals I interviewed helped me considerably to understand the issues. I would like to offer a special thanks to Professor Paweł Śpiewak (University of Warsaw) for allowing me an interview and for the material he so generously and kindly gave to me. Mr. J. F. Brown, former director and distinguished scholar at the RFE Research Institute, Munich, and his colleague at the institute, the late Antoni Kuczmierczyk, were extremely helpful in the early stages of my research. I would also like to thank Ms. Ruth Freedman, Mr. Reuven Kaminer, Mr. Michael Dahan, Mr. Gal Feinstein and Dr. Idan Yaron for their valued assistance and comments regarding the linguistic contents and technical elements of the draft. Without the assistance of everyone listed above, this book would not have been published.

The book is being published in the centenary year of Cardinal Stefan Wyszyński's birth. Following a cross-partisan consensus, the Sejm agreed to dedicate 2001 to his memory. The fact that this book is to be published in this particular year is highly significant to me, too, and I am delighted by the coincidence.

LIST OF ABBREVIATIONS

AK: Armia Krajowa (Home Army, Organization for Military Resistance), 1942–1945.

'Akcja': Akcja Wyborcza Katolicka (also WAK) (Catholic Electoral Action), 1991.

AWS: Akcja Wyborcza Solidarność (Electoral Action Solidarity), 1996.

CPSU: Communist Party of the Soviet Union.

Dz. Urz. Min. Finansów: Dziennik Urzędowy Ministerstwa Finansów (Official gazette of the Ministry of Finance).

Dz. Urz. Min. Oświaty: Dziennik Urzędowy Ministerstwa Oświaty (Official gazette of the Ministry of Education).

Dz. Us.: Dziennik Ustaw (Official gazette announcing current legislation).

EU: European Union.

FAZ: *Frankfurter Allgemeine Zeitung*.

FJN: Front Jedności Narodowej (National Unity Front), 1956–1989.

GUS: Główny Urząd Statystyczny (Central Statistical Office).

KC: Komitet Centralny (Central Committee).

KOR: Komitet Obrony Robotników (Workers' Defense Committee), September 1976–1977 (1980).

KPP: Komunistyczna Partia Polski (Communist Party of Poland), 1926–1938.

KRN: Krajowa Rada Narodowa (National Home Council), 1944.

KSS (KOR): Komitet Samoobrony Społecznej (Committee for Social Self-Defense), 1977–1980.

KUL: Katolicki Uniwersytet Lubelski (Catholic University of Lublin), 1918– .

NATO: North Atlantic Treaty Organization, 1949– .
NKVD: Soviet Secret Police.
NYT: *New York Times.*
PAN: Polska Akademia Nauk (Polish Academy of Sciences), 1951– .
PAP: Polska Agencja Prasowa (Polish News Agency).
Pers. File: Personality File, RFE.
Pers. File (Gom.): Personality File (Gomułka), RFE.
PKWN: Polski Komitet Wyzwolenia Narodowego (Polish Committee for National Liberation), July 1944.
PPR: Polska Partia Robotnicza (Polish Workers' Party), 1942–1948.
PPS: Polska Partia Socjalistyczna (Polish Socialist Party), 1892–1948.
PPS (RFE): Polish Press Survey, RFE.
PRL: Polska Rzeczpospolita Ludowa (The People's Republic of Poland), 1945–1989.
PSL: Polskie Stronnictwo Ludowe (Polish People's/Peasant Movement/Party), 1895–1947; 1990– .
PZPR: Polska Zjednoczona Partia Robotnicza (Polish United Workers' Party), 1948–1990.
RFE: Radio Free Europe.
SD: Stronnictwo Demokratyczne (Democratic Movement/Party), 1938–1990.
SDI: Strategic Defense Initiative ('Star Wars' Project).
SLD: Sojusz Lewicy Demokratycznej (Alliance of the Democratic Left), 1991– .
S/R (RFE): Situation Report (RFE).
SSP: Studia Socjologiczno-Polityczne (Socio-Political studies).
TPD: Towarzystwo Przyjaciół Dzieci (Association/Society of Friends of the Children).
UB: Urząd Bezpieczeństwa (Security Office/Services).
UdSW: Urząd do Spraw Wyznań (Department/Bureau of Religious Affairs).
USSR: Union of Soviet Socialist Republics.
UW: Unia Wolności (Freedom Union), 1994– .
ZBoWiD: Związek Bojowników o Wolności i Demokracji (Association of Fighters for Freedom and Democracy).
ZPP: Związek Patriotów Polskich (Polish Patriots' Union), 1942.
ZSL: Zjednoczone Stronnictwo Ludowe (United People's/Peasant Movement/Party), 1949–1990.

INTRODUCTION

The power struggle between the Roman Catholic Church and the Polish government in Communist Poland played a central role in shaping world politics over the last few decades. The impact of this struggle exceeded the boundaries of the Polish arena and had a decisive impact on the fate of Europe and the new international order. The Polish Church was in fact the main force behind the opposition movement in Poland and Eastern Europe, and despite suffering a series of serious blows and retreats, the opposition movement increased its power over the decades until its dramatic victory in 1989. Even during periods of repression, the Polish Church increased its potential power. It was against this background that a Polish pope appeared and made a major contribution to the 1989 revolution in Eastern Europe, the collapse of Communism and the emergence of the post-Communist regimes. One can discern that the Polish experience has guided the pope since his election, doubtless serving him in the numerous struggles he has conducted in different parts of the world.

Unique influence should be attributed to Cardinal Wyszyński, the Polish primate, a guide and a teacher of the present pope, who originally assigned and trained him to serve as his successor. The personality, activity and leadership of that prominent figure played a key role in the election of the Polish pope, Karol Wojtyła, as St. Peter's successor in Rome.

The new Poland enters the third millennium with great expectations. The church in Communist Poland, under Cardinal Wyszyński, was instrumental in the construction of a civil society that granted Poland a uniquely advantageous 'point of exit'. This, combined with other factors, paved the way towards democracy and integration in Europe in the

1990s, placing Poland in the lead within the community of East Central European countries.

This book analyzes the power struggle between the church and the Communist regime. It compares the characteristics and consequences of the struggle during three different periods—the first period of Gomułka's rule; the 'Stalinist' era; and the second period of Gomułka's rule—with emphasis on the two Gomułka periods. In each of these periods 'policy environments' are confronted with the ruling elite. We will examine the balance of power while focusing on the question of the degree to which the church and the other 'environments' influenced government policy making. The very nature of this examination contradicts the popularly held theory of the time, namely that internal environments played only a very marginal role in the process. The investigation of the 'environments' includes analyses of the Polish Roman Catholic Church, the Polish population, Pax and the Patriotic Priests, the Vatican and the Soviet Union. The analysis of the regime's policies focuses on the legal background, general policy, specific policies implemented during the period, and Gomułka's personal policy.

Some approaches in political science, in particular various versions of the 'systems approach' (Easton, 1965; Deutsch, 1963) but also points of view that are theoretically divorced from it (Laswell and Kaplan, 1950), have generally viewed the concept of *policy* as the product of four factors:

1. The key players in the political system—those who determine policy, whom we may call the *leadership* or the *policy makers* in the broad sense of these terms.

2. The *environment*—those elements that do not directly participate in policy making but are influenced by the process and/or influence it indirectly (e.g., the population, pressure groups, foreign countries and organizations).

3. The system of *mutual relationships* that exists among policy makers, and stands between them and their environments. The *output* (policy, decisions, and actions) of the political system affects its environment, while the *input* (i.e., demands and support from the environmental spheres) affects the policy makers.

4. The historical development of the system, including its policy—a factor that relates to the role of *feedback*, that is, the circular process by which the system's outputs are affected by its inputs and vice versa.

This study deviates from the pattern outlined above in two key respects.

First, with regard to the complex of elements involved in determining policy, the present examination does not concentrate on policy alone nor simply on an assessment of the power possessed by various policy-shaping factors, as in the generally accepted approach. It focuses on discerning the *balance of power between the policy makers and the environmental factors.*

Second, particular emphasis is placed on feedback mechanisms, that is, the comparison between the periods in question and the *subordination of the policy in the later periods to the lessons learned from the policy-making processes and from the implementation of the policy of the earlier periods.* This emphasis stems from the belief that the impact of the historical processes must be thoroughly examined. Thus, in contrast to a popular tendency at the time, to characterize political decisions in Communist systems as breakthrough types of decision making, here we maintain that such decisions possess an incremental character in those systems as well.

On the theoretical level, these two deviations distinguish the present study from other research.

We accept Blau's definition of the concept of *political power* (Blau, 1964), which has been broadened in keeping with the implications of Lehman's interpretation (Lehman, 1969). The wider definition deals both with the primary focal points of the system and with its peripheral and environmental spheres.

Some scholars tend to link the concept of power to the process of decision making in general, and in particular to the process of policy making. This analytical link between policy making on the one hand, and policy makers' power on the other, has sometimes been exaggerated to a point where the two are considered identical. It could be argued that this tendency is even more applicable to regimes such as those in Eastern Europe during the Communist era. Although this study tends to accept this approach, we should note that policy *per se* cannot be considered as an exclusive measure for power. As is well known, one should also refer to its implementation. It should also be remembered that policies are not only the outcome of the power of policy makers, but also of the environments. In other words, policy and its implementation are the outcome of the balance of power.

With respect to 'Gomułka's policy', we shall be dealing with the *systemic policy*, in other words, the policies of the ruling elite during

Gomułka's period. We will concentrate on some of the personal aspects
of the policy only after examining the policy of the elite. In any event,
the book does not discuss Gomułka's personality and life at length. This
subject has been addressed by numerous sources, no small number of
which are referred to in the bibliography. Another important differentiation of policy levels is that between the strictly formal policy, reflected
by the legal background and ideological dogmas on the one hand, and
the day-to-day, practical decisions and activities on the other. Both
levels need to be considered, particularly in the Eastern European context. Approaches that focus on pragmatic considerations only, and claim
that in such systems ideology carries no weight in the policy-making
process, appear fruitless and misleading. A further distinction will be
made between the elite's policy of *concessions and rewards* on the one
hand, and its policy of *restrictions and demands* on the other. It is this
combination of policy and power concepts that will guide us.

   The developments in the Soviet Union and Eastern Europe following Stalin's death led to the adoption of the 'conflict model'. In contrast
to the 'totalitarian school', the 'conflict model' accentuates the internal
struggles within the ruling elite—a phenomenon that dictates the necessity to examine policies within the context of factionalism (Conquest,
1962; Leonhard, 1962; Linden, 1967; Skilling, 1964, 1966, 1967).

   A corresponding approach *vis-à-vis* the Polish scene after Stalin's
death is presented by Nowak (1958). Bieńkowski (1969, 1971) demonstrates an extreme version of the 'conflict model', which minimizes the
leader's maneuverability in the face of factional pressures. At the same
time, Bieńkowski implicitly attributes considerable importance to the
impact of the 'environments' in Poland's post-1956 political system.
Nevertheless, the growing recognition, post-Stalin, regarding the in-
applicability of the 'totalitarian model' to Polish reality, has not produced an explicitly solid approach capable of ascribing adequate weight
to the environments and of assessing their 'active' input to the policies of
the elite. In fact, many observers failed to recognize the impact of the
'environments' until 1989. They ignored the substantial changes and
signals during the 1970s and the 1980s. Therefore, it is no wonder that
the fall of Communism took them by surprise.

   Moreover, even after 1989, Dudek (1995), for instance, continues to
examine Polish politics (PZPR's policy towards the church as well as its
policies in other areas) by applying the 'totalitarian model', thus un-

derestimating the power of the church and over-emphasizing its defensive activity.

The present study assumes that in the Polish framework under discussion one can locate environmental spheres that clearly exerted substantial influence upon the policies of the elite. Our aim is to investigate the degree to which these environmental spheres were influential.

The influence of the different environments in Communist Poland is epitomized by the concept of 'the Polish path to socialism'. This path is mainly expressed in two policy areas: policy towards the church and religious affairs, and policy in the agricultural sphere.

The concept of 'environment' is used here in its broadest sense. Hence, we refer not only to environments that can also be defined as organizational sub-systems, or to the real power of these environments, but also to the 'natural surroundings' (e.g. the Korean War, weather conditions, birth rate) and to the 'psychological environments' (the policy makers' subjective perception of the environments).

Both periods of Władysław Gomułka's rule in Poland (1945–1948 and 1956–1970) provide an historic opportunity, unique in the context of non-democratic governments, particularly in Communist Eastern Europe, for testing the following two universally intertwined problems of the role of the leader in history, and the problem of change and stability in systemic and personal policy over time. In addition to the two periods of Gomułka's rule (hereafter also referred to as 'the first period' or 'period A' and the 'second period' or 'period B'), the interval between the two periods is also examined. This interim period is referred to as both the 'Stalinist period' and the 'Bierut period'. It should be noted that 1959, and in particular the decisions adopted by the Third Congress of the PZPR (March 1959), marks the point of entry for the policies of the 1960s. In other words, processes and trends rooted in developments that took place in the late 1950s were sharpened and intensified during the last decade of Gomułka's rule.

Our main hypothesis concerning the time dimension is that post-1956 policy is strongly affected by overlapping feedback of the first Gomułka period and the Stalinist period. In 'dialectical' terms, the analysis scheme is as follows: the 'thesis' is the general pattern of the years 1945 to 1948; its 'antithesis' is the Stalinist period; while the policy after 1956 constitutes a kind of 'synthesis' of policies of the previous periods.

We will try to answer the following key questions derived from the above:

1. To what degree were policies influenced by the balance of power between the environmental spheres and the leadership?
2. What was Gomułka's role in terms of policy setting compared to Cardinal Wyszyński's role within the main 'environment' of the Roman Catholic Church?
3. What distinguished the two periods of Gomułka's rule and to what extent is the second period affected by developments in previous years?
4. What characterizes relationships between the policy makers and their environments?

The research is based on a wide spectrum of primary, secondary, early and late sources. Empirical data has been systematically integrated and the sources compared, with the intention of providing reliable evidence.

In fact, a satisfactory solution to the well-known problem of partial, biased sources, which characterized the Communist period in Eastern Europe, was not forthcoming in the years that followed 1989. This is especially true with regard to government and Communist Party archives. The opening of archives after 1989 indeed resulted in new data regarding church/state relations during Gomułka's period. However, access to new materials remained incomplete and limited. The newly emerged documents provided no dramatic or revolutionary understanding, but basically provided confirmatory and supplementary evidence. In fact, the new material served to amplify conclusions drawn from earlier testimony. Furthermore, some observers (e.g., Śpiewak, 11.11.97) claim that during Mazowiecki's premiership, certain functionaries did all in their power to destroy existing archives. In any case, the most important archives are those of the Ministry of the Interior, which remain inaccessible. It is safe to say that some of them were destroyed by the Communists.

One exception was the archive handed to Primate Glemp exposing those priests who had worked for the secret services—spies of the Communist regime.

The available materials and documents are mainly to be found at the Department of Religious Affairs (UdSW) and in the 'local branches' (e.g. the State Archive of Kraków.)

As for the church, even after 1989 it continues to maintain its confidential norms, particularly with regard to certain archives. Under these circumstances, the importance of Andrzej Micewski's most reliable book (1982) is especially noteworthy, owing to the fact that Micewski possessed an insider's view while enjoying access to the archives of the church.

Among the primary sources available during the Communist era, most prominent is the collection of Gomułka's speeches and articles written during his incumbency. Critics such as Raina, who have questioned the authenticity of this collection, may be lightly dismissed since it is clear that Gomułka stood behind this writing, even though ghostwriters did play a certain role. From this collection one can learn not only of the policies of Gomułka and the regime, but also of the basic features of the environments and the environmental difficulties. This additional contribution is especially important in cases of informational lacunae. A special mention should also be made of the publications of other leaders, including Bieńkowski's famous documents or Bierut's and Cyrankiewicz's papers. Polish newspapers, partisan or non-partisan, general or specific, constitute a most valuable source. Among these we can include various Catholic newspapers. Official Polish publications, such as the Statistical Bulletin, the Statistical Yearbook and the legal code (Dz. Us.) are also used extensively. Other primary sources are ecclesiastical documents, such as essays and pastoral letters of the church leaders (*inter alia*: Wyszyński, 1966, 1981 and 1983), documents published by the Inter Catholic Press Agency; the collection of legal documents on which the policy towards religion and church is based (Małkiewicz and Podemski, 1960), and the official reports on church–state affairs in Poland during 1945 to 1959 issued by the French government (Secrétariat Général du Gouvernement, 1959).

The documents included in Raina (1995)—protocols and reports from Archbishop Dąbrowski's archive—are most illuminating, although most of them cover the post-Gomułka era. Dąbrowski served as the secretary of the Polish Episcopate during the years 1969 to 1992. The documents include reports on almost all the important conversations held between him and senior government representatives. Also important are the supplementary documents to Dudek (1995) dealing with the 1960s. Another notable collection of sources is included in Kozub-Ciembroniewicz and Majchrowski (1993).

Two major problems concerning the secondary sources relevant to the subject of the present study are, first, the tendency of many such publications to be either biased or incomplete and non-systematic, and secondly, the lack of research based on inter-periodic comparisons. Nowak's work (1958) is exceptional in this respect. Nevertheless, his analysis is incomplete and limited. Moreover, given the date of publication, the historical perspective is obviously deficient.

Among the research dealing with the church prior to 1989, quite remarkable are Frank Dinka's comprehensive dissertation (1963), and the works by Nowak (1951), Zawadski (1953), Chrypiński (1958, 1989), Staron (1969), Michnik (1977, 1983), Raina (1979) and Micewski (1982).

Recent works that should be noted are Raina's additional studies on the Polish Church and his series of books on Wyszyński (1993, 1994, 1995), Dudek's documented research (1995), Gowin's excellent book (1995) (the insider's view of a Catholic liberal dealing with the 1990s), and Casanova's important research (1994) in which Poland is only one of four countries examined. In addition, one should mention the works of Jarocki (1990), Kisielewski (1990), Lipski (1994), Michnik et al. (1995), Kuroń (1990), Jasiukiewicz (1993), Garlicki (1993), Krukowski (1993), Weigel (1995), Ambrosini (1995) and Stehle (1993).

Furthermore, there are numerous important secondary Polish émigré sources, for example, the Historical Notebooks (*Zeszyty Historyczne*) of the Parisian *Kultura*. As is well known, the latter also distributed several valuable collections of documents (such as Bieńkowski's, mentioned above). Among the Western sources used in this study are newspapers and specifically emigration newspapers.

Outstanding collections of both primary and intermediate sources were found in several archives and libraries. In preliminary stages of the research the following were used extensively: the library of the University of Michigan, Ann Arbor; The East European Institute, Munich; and especially the archives of Radio Free Europe, Munich. Among the archives of the last, most valuable were the classified archives of Michael Gamarnikow and the institute's personal card index.

Over the years I have also conducted a long series of interviews with individuals who were involved either directly or indirectly in the processes investigated in this book.

1. THE FIRST PERIOD OF GOMUŁKA'S RULE

1.1 POLICY AREA ENVIRONMENTS

1.1.1 THE ROMAN CATHOLIC CHURCH

1.1.1.1. The Historical Power of the Church

As a central force in Poland's political culture, the Roman Catholic Church forced government leaders to pay serious attention to its positions and needs in formulating general policies, and even more so, in the case of policies directly affecting the church. It is impossible to understand the unique power of the church and its role without acknowledging the accumulated historical impact of its influence—the origins of which date from the beginnings of written Polish history—or without taking into account the factors that have constantly shaped its role and importance.

The church played an integral role in the history of the Polish people and state, and was characterized by unity and stability, in contrast to the Polish state, whose unity and continuity were frequently disrupted throughout history. Against precisely a history such as this, the relative importance of the church is impressive. The unity and stability of church organization and activity made it an almost exclusive alternative for evoking national feeling and unifying the country at times of internal and external crisis[1] when the political organization had lost its ability to fulfill its role. Under normal circumstances, these qualities encouraged the church to promote cooperation with the state on behalf of the national cause. By traveling this historical path, the church succeeded in striking deep roots among the Polish people and expanding its influence through all walks of life. This gave rise to a tremendous overlap between the Catholic faith on the one hand, and Polish nationalism and patriotism on the other. The church, in the eyes of the Poles, became a spiritual fortress and symbol of Polish independence, its links with Rome lending Poland its Western orientation. The church's sense of responsibility and mission contributed directly to its role as a moral authority, its status being further enhanced by the martyrdom which it experienced.[2]

The Roman Catholic Church extended its influence and burgeoned between the two world wars.[3] The concordat signed between the Polish state and the Vatican in 1925 granted special privileges to the church compared to other religions. The new regime installed after Piłsudski's coup d'état, and the rule of the colonels, witnessed an expansion of the church's sphere of influence, not only as the central spiritual authority but also as a political elite.

The heavy blows absorbed by the church during the Second World War reduced it from the zenith of its influence to a low point, where its very physical existence was threatened for the first time in its history. In contrast with the stereotypical version, according to which the church accommodated the Nazis, or, at the least, refrained from encouraging opposition (a version that was with foundation in many cases), we also find evidence of many instances in which the church demonstrated a determination not to collaborate. At any rate, as we shall see, the perception of the Polish people, which is a decisive point of view in terms of our purposes, rejected that stereotyped version. The church was also an active player in the resistance movement, granting full support to nationalist underground organizations. It is possible to learn about the active role of the church from the high price it paid during the war. The priesthood lost approximately 20 percent of its members.[4] A total of 3,599 Catholic priests were killed during the war, while many of the priests who managed to avoid death suffered greatly. There were 1,682 priests in Dachau, 849 of whom were killed. The monastic priesthood was not exempt from the bloodletting, which claimed 521 priests and functionaries. This balance sheet of losses must include those priests who found themselves driven out of Poland as a result of political developments, deportations, and the war. Of the 1,622 Roman Catholic priests who were active in the territories ceded to the Soviet Union after the war, 350 never returned to Poland.[5] The severance of the eastern territories wreaked even greater damage on the other Catholic churches, such as the Greek and the Armenian. Damage of another kind resulted from the paralysis imposed on the church in all that touched on the training of new novices for the priesthood. With the exception of the secret seminar conducted by Archbishop Adam Sapieha in Kraków, no theological seminars operated in Poland during the war.

There is a tendency to stress the post-war demographic effects of the border changes on the power of the Roman Catholic Church, but it would be a mistake to ignore the severe blows that the church had suffered previously. On the other hand, its conduct and martyrological record during the war definitely added another dimension to its prestige at the beginning of the new era that opened with the end of the war.

1.1.1.2 Post-War Church Reorganization

The early post-war years were marked by intensive efforts on the part of the church to rebuild its organization. This was particularly difficult in light of the manpower shortage, which the church had suffered even before the war and which had intensified during wartime. In 1946 it numbered 10,344 priests, and by 1947 there was evidence of a considerable increase in manpower at the church's disposal. During that year the overall number of priests reached 10,528. In response to the overall shortage of Roman Catholic priests, illustrated by the fact that in Poland in 1946 there was only one priest for every 2,063 believers, theological seminaries began to sprout up all over Poland. By the end of 1948 there were 23 seminaries, with 1,754 seminary students.[6]

The church's actions were guided, naturally, by its will for self-preservation and reconstruction. But, on the other hand, the church joined in urgent national tasks as before. It mobilized resources to organize the parishes, mainly in the western (and northern) territories (also called the liberated territories, German land prior to the Second World War), to perform charitable activities, and to extend aid to those suffering deprivation (through Caritas). It also introduced a host of Catholic educational and cultural projects. It was by these means that the church was able to contribute to the process of normalization after the war. Even so, it must be understood that all these actions, whether directly aimed at the church's reconstruction or whether prominently integrated into the national effort, contributed, in the final analysis, to an increase in church power and size of organization. Faced with this renewed demonstration of the church's strength, the new rulers of Poland could not remain indifferent. Their response will be discussed later.

The Polish episcopate, which had suffered serious damage during the war and which had toiled to complete its reconstruction during the first two post-war years, took the lead in the church's organizational efforts. In 1946 it numbered, all in all, 39 staff under the leadership of two cardinals and three 'ordinary archbishops' (*Arcybiskupów Ordynariuszy*). The episcopate met in June 1945 for the first time in nearly six years. From that date it held twice-yearly conferences on a more or less regular basis. In this context, Cardinal August Hlond made a unique contribution to the activity of the episcopate and the church. Hlond, the Polish primate, who enjoyed special authority in the church hierarchy, had been the leader of the church since 1926, when he was appointed archbishop of Gniezno and Poznań and primate, and had accumulated immense political experience in this capacity.[7] Hlond died on 22 October 1948, at the age of 67.[8] During his time in office, he was assisted by Adam Stefan Sapieha, the archbishop of Kraków, who enjoyed tremendous moral prestige, due, to a large degree, to his heroic role under Nazi occupation. Sapieha was appointed cardinal in 1946 and died in July 1951.[9]

Just as the roots of the church's power stem from its historical past, until 1948 its leader, Hlond, drew his strength from his earlier, rich political experience. Under Piłsudski, Hlond, showing a great interest in social issues, had initiated reforms designed to eliminate the gap between religious duty and daily life. At the onset of the German occupation, Cardinal Hlond had accompanied the Polish government to Romania, continuing on to Rome, at the government's request, in order to establish contact with the Holy See. There he sharply denounced the Nazi occupation in Poland and exposed Nazi crimes in the country. During the war he was arrested and imprisoned in a monastery near Paderborn, from which he was released by the US army on 1 April 1945. On 20 July 1945, Cardinal Hlond returned to Poland as head of the ecclesiastical administration, with an exceptionally broad mandate from the Vatican for the reorganization of the church. In addition to his designation as the Polish primate, he was granted the title of Metropolitan

Archbishop for Gniezno-Warsaw, a title that allowed him to transfer the primate's seat from Poznań to Warsaw. Equipped with this mandate from the Holy See, Hlond launched an intensive campaign designed to ensure the reconstruction of the church in formerly held Polish territory and to introduce church organization into the liberated territories.

Church activities in the western territories were clearly of special importance, in that they corresponded with the then national goals. As early as 15 August 1945, two weeks after the conclusion of the Potsdam conference and less than a month after his return to Poland, Cardinal Hlond established an interim ecclesiastical administration in those territories. The primate appointed five apostolic administrators, in Gdańsk, Olsztyn, Gorzów, Wrocław, and Opole, who received the status of resident bishops and began work on 1 September 1945. The work of the apostolic administrators in the liberated territories involved extraordinary organizational effort. The dearth of priests and material resources faced them with even greater challenges in these territories. Under such circumstances the apostolic administrators appealed for the mobilization of priests from other parts of Poland. Though the response was limited, due to the fact that the rest of Poland was also experiencing similar problems, church activity in the western territories was highly successful and made a genuine contribution to the settlement project in these territories and to the re-establishment of their Polish character.

1.1.1.3 Value Base and Positions on Current Issues

The radical antagonism that exists between the Catholic faith and Communist doctrine, and the inability to reconcile the two, needs no special clarification. The Catholic Church in Poland was profoundly aware of the situation and made no effort to conceal it. Moreover, as we shall demonstrate, the church even emphasized this position on several occasions. Two main factors determined the church's uncompromising stance and its total opposition to the competing ideology: the church could coexist with secular ideologies which did not negate Catholicism, but could not coexist with an atheistic and materialist Marxism which totally negated Catholicism and the existence of God. This second factor relates to the all-encompassing and mutually exclusive nature of both doctrines in that they competed to mobilize the same forces, their goals

and interests were in conflict, and they were in competition for resources and means. Thus the Polish Church, while enjoying the full
backing of the regime, spearheaded the battle against Communism in
the period between the two world wars and preached against the spread
of atheistic Communism. The church maintained this position during
the Nazi occupation, opposed the Communist underground, and was
extremely hostile to the Soviet Union, in contrast to its previously mentioned support for the nationalist underground organizations.

In post-war Poland, it was Cardinal Hlond who expressed the inevitable conflict stemming from the competing goals of Catholics and
Communists in their respective perception of their social role and exclusive right to represent the people: "The church is the Lord of the
people, its guide in good times and bad and its constant mentor. It is the
church which shows people today the ways of Divine Providence, which
in turn leads to universal moral regeneration and provides the necessary
preparation for new times."[10] There was an even clearer exposition of
this very intensive controversy in the first joint pastoral letter, issued by
the bishops in March 1946: "Neither the church, nor Catholic culture,
nor Christian national traditions ever came out against progress towards
a better life; on the contrary, we will always support progress, science,
and the healthy evolution of life...from a position different from that of
materialism which competes with Christianity on the meaning of the
principles of life and demands the exclusive right to educate future generations. The goal of this approach is the construction of a materialist
culture, which transcends religion and ethical norms. Poland cannot be
irreligious; Poland cannot be Communist. Poland must remain Catholic."[11]

1.1.1.4 The Communist Regime

Although the church in Poland was fully aware that the struggle with
Communism was inevitable, it preferred to delay the confrontation, distinguishing between ideological questions and practical matters and
adopting a cautious, restrained position on the practical sphere. The
church hierarchy was aware of the privileged status of the church compared with other non-Communist institutions and organizations, including other religious organizations in Poland, and compared with equiva-

lent organizations in other bloc countries, and was apprehensive about the threat to this status. In the pastoral letter published in April 1947, Cardinal Hlond described the situation of the Catholic Church in Poland in the following terms: "After the defeat of Hitler, the internal state of the church is calm and strong, but under a cloud, externally."[12] A powerful sense of responsibility, the need to act with caution, and a sense of anxiety regarding the future all expressed themselves in the first pastoral letter, published after the Russian penetration, by Archbishop Sapieha, dated 16 July 1945: "In any event, we must be conscious of the heavy responsibility we bear. Our future depends on how we behave today. We need, precisely now, discretion and complete maturity..."[13] In the same vein, towards the end of the period under discussion the bishops' pastoral letters call for calm behavior from the population: "Let us act with trust and tranquillity, let us feel a sense of national and Catholic pride. Let no one succumb to incitement and foolish acts by dark forces, which desire to weaken the people's vitality...the people must remain strong and vigorous..."[14] Thus the church refrained from a head-on clash with the regime, neither coming out against it explicitly nor attacking its legitimacy.[15]

There were, nevertheless, several groups among the priesthood that were slow to recognize the new reality and that refused to accept the role of foreign forces within the establishment. They argued that the agrarian reform and nationalization were opposed to the teachings of the church. Together with others, they opposed the first steps towards secularization, the cancellation of the concordat and the attacks by the Communist and socialist press against the pope and Vatican policy. However, the position of the Polish episcopate was based, at the very least, on non-opposition to the party's pragmatic economic and social policies. Moreover, the church hierarchy recognized the need for agrarian reform and related positively to central reforms such as the nationalization of heavy industry. The episcopate was willing to support the regime actively and to assist it in achieving different goals on behalf of the Polish people and the Polish state. This policy was built around a number of positive joint formulations, which facilitated cooperation and initiative with a national, patriotic orientation.[16]

Accordingly, in the previously mentioned pastoral letter, dated 23 September 1948, the episcopate joined the call for skilled effort and hard work to advance the reconstruction of the country in all areas of life. As we have already hinted, these efforts were especially prominent in the liberated territories. This can be learned, *inter alia*, from Cardinal Hlond's letter on the eve of his death. His firm patriotic attachment to these territories and his clear rejection of any attempt to accuse the church of doubts regarding Poland's future in them is clear from the text.[17] In this context it is worth mentioning that the interim (as opposed to permanent) appointment of apostolic administrators for the liberated territories supplied the regime's propaganda organs with ammunition for questioning the church's national devotion to the territories. However, the facts confirm the version of the Polish episcopate on this issue.[18] Otherwise, it is impossible to explain projects such as the reconstruction of the cathedral in Wrocław by the primate's curia at a cost of one million zloty. Historical perspective provides additional facts which support this version.

1.1.1.5 Elections and Parties

The social and national mission of the Polish Church was such that the church did not remain indifferent to the sharp political struggle at the beginning of the period under discussion, between the Communist-socialist camp on the one hand, and Mikołajczyk's party on the other, despite its nature as an institution that required abstention from participation in the electoral process as a party. In fact, there were no religious parties in Poland between the two world wars either, although during this period most of the parties were clearly Catholic in nature. After the war, the church withdrew its support for the 'Christian Labor Party' when its cadres were penetrated by government-backed elements. In a communiqué published by the Catholic bishops at the conference in Częstochowa in September 1946, the church hierarchy protested the party's 'reorganization', making it clear that, in its present composition, the party no longer enjoyed its blessing.[19] For one minority section of the priesthood, political involvement included assisting the nationalist underground movements, which continued to fight against the establishment of a Communist regime in Poland.

Sentimentally, the priesthood's tendency to support Mikołajczyk's party and to long for its victory was clear, despite his known anticlericalism in the pre-war period. However, in keeping with the church's policy of restraint it moderated its support for one camp and limited its opposition to the other, while usually avoiding the adoption of unequivocal, militant positions. The conclusions by Hiscocks (1963) and Dinka (1963), to the effect that church support for Mikołajczyk's Peasant Party and its opposition to the Communist Party was explicit and unequivocal, ignore the sophisticated tactics adopted by the church leadership. The church made its real position clear to the voters while avoiding any overt provocation of the Communists for fear of their possible success. The aim was to deny them any possible excuse for repressing the church in the event of a Communist victory. This cautious position expressed itself in abstention from the use of the elections as a battlefield. As the elections neared, the hierarchy adopted an ambiguous position. It came out, in some of its statements, against the regime's exploitation of religion for political propaganda,[20] rejected advances from the leaders of the regime, and refused to succumb to pressure.[21] However, it did accede, in part, to the demands of the United Democratic Front by not putting itself at the disposal of any party. However, there is also evidence of other, far less cautious activity. The pastoral letters of April and June 1946 explicitly declare: "Tell the believers that materialist styles of life, advocated by the Communist spokesmen, are opposed to Poland's traditions and historical role." These letters were confiscated by the censor but were nevertheless promulgated from the church pulpits.[22]

The 'Announcement on the Elections to the Sejm', read out in the churches on 20 October 1946, is of special interest. The announcement states that the church is not indifferent and directs the attention of the believers to the fact that they are morally obliged to vote. It notes that although the church did not conduct an election campaign it did have a list of moral principles, which the parties needed to honor if they sought Catholic votes. It clearly calls "not to vote for organizations or parties whose principles are opposed to Christianity and strive to undermine the ethical foundations of Christian teachings."[23] The pastoral letter, parts of which were approved for publication in *Tygodnik Powszechny*, 10 November 1946, was written in a similar spirit. Although it is not difficult to understand the allusion in a comment of this nature, it seems that Dinka's assertion (1963), that this announcement was tantamount to unequivocal support for the Peasant Party and denunciation of the Communists as enemies of the Catholic voter, is imprecise.

1.1.1.6 Demands from the Government and Modes of Struggle

Despite the caution and discretion of its leaders, the church was neither passive nor submissive; this was certainly so on the ideological level, but also true in terms of the tactical response to current political and social developments. On the contrary, the church, believing in the special mission of Catholic Poland in post-war Europe, was determined to preserve its traditional achievements.[24] Furthermore, church policy and activity between 1945 and 1948 bear witness to a militant church, with Cardinal Hlond emerging as the architect and main advocate of this policy. This was also the way the church perceived its character. This militancy was limited by elements of political realism, the interests of the people, and by the desire to avoid a doomed confrontation. But the militancy did find frequent and consistent expression in different modes of activity, mainly in the intensive and efficient use of pastoral letters[25] and church sermons, and by its use of memoranda to the regime, demonstrations, and other acts of protest. This was the nature, for example, of the large nationalist and religious demonstration organized by the episcopate in Częstochowa on 8 September 1946.[26]

We may describe church activity, using Staar's terms, as a semi-political pressure group. The church's demands centered on a call to honor its rights and freedom as an organization, in accordance with respect for civil rights and by anchoring these rights in the constitution. The church demanded freedom of faith and ritual in the widest sense, including jurisdiction over religious activity, Catholic education in schools, guarantees for church property, Catholic parliamentary representation, and a revision of the new law regarding marriage and divorce. Moreover, the church demanded a new agreement with the state, which would serve as a stable juridical foundation for the relations between them. The church also appealed for the establishment of a committee, which would liaise with the state and replace the previous arrangement of a single representative from each side—Bishop Choromański, the episcopate secretary, representing the church, and Wolski, the state representative. (See *Tygodnik Powszechny*, 22 September 1946, in which the episcopate communiqué at the conference on 9 and 10 September was published. The communiqué also noted support for Catholics' rights to parliamentary representation; see also *Tygodnik Powszechny*, 20 April 1947, in which appears the episcopate's memorandum, dated 14 March

1947, against the background of the Sejm discussion of the new constitution.)

One important device employed by the church in its struggle with the state was its deliberate emphasis on the ideological conflict between itself and the authorities. This emphasis often appeared when circumstances allowed, in response to restrictive policies initiated by the regime. Thus Hlond wrote in a pastoral letter, published on 23 April 1947 against a background of strained relations following the January 1947 elections: "A new paganism is currently casting its shadow over the globe...this modern paganism is not a religion and does not even aspire to be such. It is characterized by militant atheism, which not only denies God...but even dares to insult and declare war on Him."[27] The church clarified more explicitly that its policy of observing events from a distance did not mean abstention from its duty to articulate its position on matters of faith, morality, and public affairs, and on behalf of individual rights[28] These statements came in response to Cyrankiewicz's attacks.

Church militancy in the struggle to educate and recruit youth was of special significance. In 1948, in the face of rising threats to the rights of the church in this vital area,[29] the episcopate published two pastoral letters directed at Polish youth and its education. The first, which was published on 15 April 1948 following the Bishops' Conference in Kraków and directed to the youth of Katowice, attacked materialist doctrine and the propaganda techniques employed by the regime to win over the youth: "...materialism does not recognize the Word of God, the eternal laws of morality, or Christian ethics...this ideology wants to snare your soul by any means at its disposal—propaganda, literature and the press...beware and protect your soul from the attempts by materialism to snare your souls and fear not!"[30] On the other hand, the letter includes a call to "honor the good intentions of those materialists who work for a better future for the workers..."

The second pastoral letter, published in Wrocław on 23 September 1948, was directed, first and foremost, to parents, and reminded them of their duty to provide their children with a religious education. This letter also dwells on the conflict between Christianity and materialism regarding the education of the younger generation: "Education has become the fundamental issue of Poland's tomorrow...your holy duty as parents...to bestow our grand Catholic heritage...on your children."[31]

1.1.1.7 Attitude towards the Vatican

Despite the obvious bond, which exists according to Catholic dogma, between the Polish Roman Catholic Church and the Apostolic See, a bond which dictates the loyalty and submission of the first to the second and the need for a single policy and for united positions for the two, it would be incorrect to regard the Polish Church and the Vatican as a single entity. The difference between the two mainly concerns matters related to practical political issues and relations with 'terrestrial regimes'. This presumption of difference in positions and behavior between the two forces determines more complex formulas regarding environmental inputs to policy formation.

The Second World War increased the 'technical' distance between the church in Poland and its center in Rome by cutting off connections between the two. The annulment of the concordat by the Polish regime immediately after the war actually increased the independence of the Polish hierarchy from the Vatican. Despite the ambivalent implications of the annulment, the Polish episcopate resisted the regime's attempts to create a split between the two centers. However, this resistance was modified in the course of time, and the Polish Church accepted the new situation along with other facts of life determined by the new regime. Even so, the Polish bishops remained concerned over the deterioration of relations between the Vatican and the Polish government. They responded quite angrily to the intense propaganda campaign against the Vatican and the pope, although, at the time, this was not aimed directly at them.

Furthermore, in 1946 the Polish episcopate was involved in an attempt at mediation between the new regime and the Vatican. It was Cardinal Hlond who was in contact with President Bierut about the resumption of diplomatic relations between the Vatican and the Polish government. However, these efforts were unproductive and the talks were terminated. It should be mentioned that the policy of Pope Pius XII towards Poland, and especially with regard to the liberated territories, and the appointment of a permanent Polish ecclesiastical administration there—a question critical for the Poles—was of little help to the Polish episcopate. The episcopate attempted to explain to Rome the Polish priesthood's position regarding the negative (propaganda) implications of Vatican policy. Even so, the hierarchy, which sought to avoid confrontation with the Vatican, came out in defense of the pope and tried to neutralize the campaign against him.[32] However, when the Vatican toughened its position on the issue in the March 1948 letter to the Catholic hierarchy and the Catholics in Germany, the Polish Church could not avoid adopting its own unequivocal position. Cardinal Hlond issued a public statement, which included a series of arguments justifying the inclusion of the liberated territories in Poland. These arguments and justifications also appeared in the *New York Times*, 27 May 1948. One of the editorials in *Tygodnik Powszechny* (6 June 1948) asks cynically (in response to the above-mentioned letter by the pope): "Is the Holy See better informed regarding the problems of Germany than those of Poland?"! In the pastoral letter, dated 23 September 1948 and composed in Wrocław, the Polish hierarchy came out in support of the Oder–Neisse borders. (However, even here the bishops tried to minimize the discrepancy between their position and that of the pope, and to shield him.)[33] This step resulted in a greater degree of independence for the church in Poland in its relations with the Vatican—though this was not its intention—and firmly anchored it among the Polish masses as a fortress of loyalty and identification.

1.1.2 THE POPULATION

1.1.2.1 Demographic Characteristics

The Polish population, as the bulwark of the power of the Catholic Church, is a highly influential environmental factor in our discussion. At the very same time, the regime, which also hoped to mobilize the population, was particularly sensitive towards it.

The distinctive characteristics of the population and the demographic changes after the Second World War determined its role as a decisive environmental parameter influencing policy makers. The changes in the composition of the population stemmed, first and foremost, from the major transformation in Poland's demographic makeup whereby Poland, previously a mosaic of religions and minorities, became a country exceptionally uniform in its Catholic coloration and Polish national ethnicity.

In demographic terms, the Roman Catholic Church headed the list of different faiths during the inter-war period. However, in that period, which saw only marginal changes in the religious composition of the population, there were sizable numbers of Greek Catholics, Greek Orthodox, and Jews. Table 1.1 illustrates this.

Table 1.1 The Religious Composition of the Polish Population,
1921–1935 (percentages)

Year	Roman Catholics	Greek Catholics	Greek Orthodox	Protestants	Jews	Other
1921*	63.8	11.2	10.5	3.7	10.5	0.3
1929	64.0	10.9	12.3	2.8	9.8	0.2
1935	64.8	10.4	11.8	2.6	9.8	0.6

*These data conform to the results of the 1921 census, according to which the population distribution was as follows: 17,368,352 Roman Catholics; 3,032,636 Greek Catholics and Armenian Christians; 2,849,020 Jews; 2,846,508 Greek Orthodox; 1,014,577 Protestants; and 73,743 members of other faiths, such as the National Catholic Church and the Ancient Catholic Church. (See CBS, *Concise Statistical Yearbook of Poland*, 1930, p. 9; *Markert*, 1959, p. 37; *Dinka*, 1963, p. 16.)
Sources: *Świątkowski*, 1960, p. 30: *Markert*, 1959, p. 39; *Dinka*, 1963, p. 17.

A sharp change in the population composition occurred after the war as a result of the new borders. In the east, Poland lost most of its Greek Catholic and Greek Orthodox population when those territories were transferred to the Soviet Union. Some 500,000 members of the Orthodox Church with Polish, Ukrainian, and Byelorussian citizenship lived in four dioceses in the new Polish territory.[34]

In the west, the number of Protestants fell due to the flight and mass deportation of millions. Most of the Jews had been annihilated by the Nazis, and many of the survivors fled Poland. The Jewish population was reduced to between 30,000 and 70,000.[35] Under the new circumstances, the non-Roman Catholic religious denominations were of negligible significance. Poland became more Catholic than ever, with 98 percent of its population formal members of the Catholic Church, 95 percent of whom were Roman Catholics. Thus Poland not only became the most Catholic country in the socialist camp but, furthermore, nearly half of the Latin Church's believers in all of Eastern Europe were included in its borders.[36]

These demographic developments not only brought about changes in the religious composition of the population, but also far-reaching changes in the ethnic composition. Ethnic minorities in Poland between the two world wars formed approximately 30 percent of the population,[37] but after the war comprised less than 2 percent.[38]

Thus post-war Poland became a national state, smaller in population and territory than before the war but with a highly homogeneous population where membership of the Roman Catholic Church was almost identical with the country's national, ethnic composition. This was an unprecedented situation in Polish history.

1.1.2.2 Religious Participation

The new character of Poland following the demographic changes was reinforced by the population's intensified religious activism and participation in the rites of the church. Data show that the population responded eagerly to church initiatives aimed at reviving worship. This expressed itself in the population's active participation in both customary rites and pilgrimages. "Only few do not baptize their children or marry in a church ceremony. This is also true regarding members of the PPR. The only exceptions are high-ranking officials in the Communist government, and even these never officially left the church."[39]

According to church data, over four million pilgrims set off for the holy sites in 1946 compared with 230,000 in 1945 (information gathered at 62 pilgrimage destinations). Thus approximately 20 percent of the entire population participated in pilgrimages during that year, with some 10 percent of the population (2,100,000 people) making the trip to the main pilgrimage site of Jasna Góra. The previously mentioned national-religious demonstration organized by the Polish episcopate at Częstochowa on the holy day of the Virgin (8 September 1946) turned into a show of force with special reverberations. Despite the obstacles created by the police and other technical difficulties, according to the local authorities approximately 550,000 people participated in the demonstration.[40] A year later, on 8 September 1947, over one million pilgrims gathered at the site.[41] The significance of the data provided here is most impressive in light of the post-war difficulties and the population shifts and uninterrupted emigration between 1945 and 1947. In other words, precisely because of the natural tendency in such circumstances to strive for the day-to-day normalization of life, the population's readiness to make efforts to participate in a non-routine religious rite such as a pilgrimage, which required even more mobility, was even more striking. Participation in the religious rites and other church-organized activities reflected the deep religious sentiment of the population as well as its traditional patriotic emotions. As early as the period under discussion, these activities also provided the population with the means of responding to the new circumstances in Poland. This was expressed, for example, in the reception for Cardinal Griffin in June 1947.

1.1.2.3 Devoutness According to Social Group

The almost absolute religious homogeneity of the population and the large-scale participation in traditional rites certainly hinder any attempt to identify the church with a certain class or classes (in contrast to the situation in Czechoslovakia and Hungary). Even so, there are some clear, if minor, differences in the degree of religious activity and the intensity of links to the church among the different social groupings. The main social division here is that between the peasants, who constituted the most devout section of the population, and the urban population, headed by the intelligentsia. Nevertheless, it would be wrong to underestimate the church's influence over the non-rural sections of the population. There was not too great a difference in the proportion of practicing Catholics in the rural and urban sectors: almost the entire rural population was devotedly Catholic, while practicing Catholics also formed the majority of the urban population. This was the case, as it was after the Second World War, when the rural population was more or less the same size as the urban population. Barnett speaks of the influence of the priesthood mainly in the Polish village, but mentions other spheres as well. Szczepański, on the other hand, stresses the deterioration in social status of the priests in Poland after the war and argues that the main church's enduring influence was limited to the less educated sectors of the population.[42] To some degree, this argument contradicts the growing strength of the Catholic intellectual movement in the first post-war years, both among the priesthood and among 'lay' Catholics. These developments include the establishment of the Institute for Advanced Religious Culture (Instytut Wyższej Kultury Religijnej) near Gdańsk, designed for the lay public, as well as the theologians' conference in Lublin in September 1948, the first of its kind after the war. (In this context it is worth noting that most Catholic intellectuals had distanced themselves from political matters during the early post-war years.

This is confirmed by examining *Tygodnik Powszechny* of the same period). The social cleavages whereby the lower strata are more devout and the higher strata are less so, are recognized in many countries, not only in Western democracies[43] but in developing countries as well.[44] Throughout, there is a link between religious affiliation and political activity, always accompanied by a degree of deviation, such as a strong religious orientation within the elite.

1.1.3 PAX AND THE PATRIOTIC PRIESTS[45]

Despite a religious uniformity characterized by loyalty and firm adherence to the church, new Catholic groups, whose organizational *raison d'être* was to limit and reduce the influence of the Polish Church, appeared after the war and shed themselves of subordination to the hierarchy. The most prominent of these was the Lay Movement of Progressive Catholics (*Postępowi katolicy*)—Pax.

The story of Pax is important to our account precisely because of the marginal role that it and its leader, Bolesław Piasecki, occupied in the Polish cultural-political scene after the Second World War. From its inception on 1 November 1945[46] it worked only on the periphery of Polish society and its spiritual innovations met with most limited success, despite the encouragement and rewards it received from the Communist regime. This weakness as a parametric environmental factor seeking to pose as competition for the church, only served to emphasize the power of the Catholic Church in Poland. Pax's marginality is sufficient evidence for inferring the feebleness of other, even weaker, groups of its kind. Pax is of particular interest also due to the special character that it imparted to the Polish system compared to other systems in Eastern Europe. While it is true that, in some ways, the case of Pacem in Terris in Czechoslovakia, for example, resembles the case of Pax in Poland, the Czechoslovakian case was not identical with that of Poland (since the story of Pax has unique ingredients). In any event, the unique nature of the Polish case has less to do with Pax itself and more to do with the exceptional strength of the Polish Church.

Until the mid-1950s the circumstances attending the establishment of Pax were hidden by a cloud of suspicion and rumor. The suspicions were later partially confirmed and specified. Swiatło's revelations dealt,

among other things, with Piasecki and the path he traversed from being
a leader of fascist Falangists before the war to becoming a collaborator
and servant of Stalin in Poland. The revelations recount Piasecki's arrest
by the NKVD after Poland's liberation and the deal he made with his
captors, chiefly with Serov (who was closely associated with Beria and in
charge of NKVD operations in the conquered territories), and how Piasecki, in order to save his skin and to receive special immunity, agreed
to assist Soviet designs to bring Catholic Poland under Moscow's domination.[47] After being released by the Soviets, Piasecki, surrounding
himself with a narrow circle of Catholic intellectuals and priests, established an organization that enjoyed encouragement and special privileges from the government.[48] Witold Bieńkowski and Dominik Horodyński were among his closest collaborators. Piasecki and his organization enjoyed this special status by virtue of their role as faithful, almost
utterly devoted, servants of the Soviet Union. Occasionally bypassing
the local leadership, they maintained direct contact with the Soviet Union through a highly special arrangement for the Polish system, unparalleled in Eastern Europe. Even so, it would be a mistake to consider Pax
and Piasecki as mere hirelings of Moscow. Even less should they be seen
as servants of the local Communist government. In addition to their
original mission, the organization and its leader had independent doctrines, goals, and ideological foundations that went beyond their designated role and which did not always conform to the expectations of the
Communist regime or those of the Soviet Union. However, these independent tendencies were still not manifested in the first years after the
war, before the young organization had firmly established itself. Since
the organization hoped to enlist public support, and because of its new-
ness, it refrained from presenting a clear, crystallized ideological program in its early years. As we shall see, in this way it acted in a similar
way to the Communist Party itself. Pax's ideological program was com-
pleted only three or four years after the establishment of the organization.[49] Downs (1957) discusses the general phenomenon of avoiding
programmatic and ideological commitments as a means of mobilizing
public support. His conclusions are valid for our discussion despite the
totally different environment with which he deals. It appears that during
the first period of Gomułka's rule, especially the first two years, the different environmental factors refrained from presenting crystallized
ideological positions, and the entire system was characterized by a lack

of clarity, as we shall see below. In conformity with its cautious approach, Pax promoted the idea that Polish Latin Catholicism must be seen as an unalterable fact, an idea that dovetailed with Soviet strategy and the approach taken by the Polish regime at the time.

One of the important aspects of Pax's policy of 'covering its tracks' lay in its attitude to the Polish episcopate. During the early post-war years, Pax and Piasecki were exceedingly careful that their ideological announcements did not appear as an attack on the church hierarchy. The first signs of change in this policy appeared in the spring of 1947 and matured in 1948. Such signs are clearly present in the daily, *Słowo Powszechne*, that Piasecki began to publish.[50] Once more, this change in approach paralleled that of the Communists towards the church. Only then did Piasecki begin to publicize the ideological goals and values of his organization, presenting it as a preferable alternative to the church, more suitable in the way it integrated Catholicism and Communism in keeping with the time. It is necessary to state that, before the war, Piasecki never devoted much attention to the spiritual values of Christianity in general, or to those of the Roman Catholic Church in particular.[51]

A different group that cooperated with the regime was the 'Movement of Patriotic Priests'. Many of its members were mobilized from among the priests who had accompanied the armies of Rola Żymierski. This movement also based its creed on the need for Catholics in Poland to adapt to new times and the new social order. They argued for a 'grand moral revolution', or what they called 'deep Catholicism'.[52] These ideas, whether expressed by Piasecki and his people, or whether originating from other sources, remained, as we have seen, the province of a tiny group of people. This movement found a certain foothold among the intellectuals and the lower clergy, but did not succeed in breaking the unity of the church. In most cases not only did these groups fail to draw support from the population; more often than not their activities had the opposite effect.

1.1.4 THE VATICAN

1.1.4.1 Pius XII

The Holy See is one of the central environmental factors due to its un-derstandable influence on the values, positions, and tactics of the Polish episcopate. It is a key factor also for its role as a source of strength for the episcopate and church, and as a consequence of its relationship with the Polish government regarding the policy of the latter towards the church and other matters.

In the years 1945 to 1948 there was constant tension between the Vatican and the Polish regime. This is attributable, in no small measure, to the personality and actions of Pope Pius XII. (The role of the Com-munist government in creating this tension will be clarified in the dis-cussion of its policies.) In contrast to Benedictus XV and his heir, Pius XI, who identified with the cause of Polish independence and actively supported the church's administrative organization in the restored Po-land (as early as 1917 Pope Benedictus XV called for the restoration of Polish independence and in 1918 he sent Ratti, who was later to become Pope Pius XI, to Poland), Pius XII's position and actions, during and after the war, supplied ample evidence to support the claims of those who considered him pro-German. Pius XII's concessions to the Axis powers during the war met with fierce criticism and protest, not only from the Polish Communists who thoroughly exploited his actions for their own propaganda purposes, but from many other sectors among the Poles, foremost of these being the Polish government-in-exile. Pius XII also had many critics among Poland's priests. The affair of the appoint-ment of the German priest, Hilarius Breitinger, in 1942, as the apostolic administrator for German Catholics in the Gniezno–Poznań archbish-opric was a glaring example of Pius XII's policy. As early as 1940, Pius entrusted the administration of the Chełmno diocese to the bishop of Gdańsk, the German Karl Maria Splett. In addition to the changes in the Gniezno-Poznań archbishopric he also appointed German bishops to Polish bishoprics in parallel with the incumbent Polish bishops. This, in conformity with the demands made by the Nazi regime that only German bishops would deal with the spiritual needs of their people.[53] The appointment of Breitinger was not only the provisional Polish gov-ernment's pretext for annulling the concordat (12 September 1945); it had also previously met with sharp protest from the government-in-exile in London. The protest, published on 12 November 1942, stated that "Pius XII's decision is tantamount to the acceptance of illegal German demands and comprises an unfriendly act towards the Polish people."[54] After the war, the pope refused to extend *de jure* recognition to the provisional government, and consequently, Kazimierz Papée continued to represent the émigré government as ambassador in Rome. In September 1945, immediately after the annulment of the concordat, the Vatican claimed that it was not the Apostolic See's custom to extend recognition before it had formally been requested to do so.[55] In an official Vatican radio broadcast on 14 July 1946, the Vatican spokesman issued a detailed and matter-of-fact exposition of the pope's position on the issue. However, the spokesman explained that the Vatican had acted according to tradition [i.e. it adhered to the original position—H.D.] by adopting a noncommittal position and postponing recognition and the establishment of diplomatic ties pending final territorial settlement. Notwithstanding, the spokesman explained that the Apostolic See considered the government in Warsaw the *de facto* government.[56]

1.1.4.2 The Vatican Response to the Annulment of the Concordat

The annulment of the concordat polarized positions on both sides. Nevertheless, the attacks and the allegations accompanying the annulment failed to provoke counter accusations from the Vatican. The latter, however, did respond immediately, with an announcement claiming that the annulment had 'no juridical effect'[57] but without relating to the reasons for the annulment. It is to be supposed that the advantages in the cancellation of the agreement, in the matter of church appointments, were known to Pius—especially later. The Vatican journal, *L'Osservatore Romano*, which nevertheless did respond to the Polish government's accusations, presented basically defensive arguments, vindicating the pope and Rome. It justified the transfer of the Chełmno diocese in 1940, speaking in terms of 'absolute necessity,' and 'for the sake of souls,' and listing technical reasons for the action. The journal rejected accusations relating to the appointment of Father Breitinger, and explained the appointment as a temporary reaction to the German occupation. The response to the accusations by the Vatican press appeared in the *New York*

Times, 26 September 1945. It should be stated that the organ of the Jesuit Order, *La Civilta Cattolica*, affiliated with the Vatican secretary of state, published an article on 7 April 1962 defending Pius XII and emphasizing that 'special circumstances' had forced the pope to appoint German administrators to the Polish dioceses during the war.[58]

Pius' own response was limited to a single letter to the Polish bishops (17 January 1946). Here, the pope discharged himself from any need for a substantial rebuttal of the accusations and sought to absolve himself of any responsibility for the annulment by labeling the accusations absurd. These were his words: "The agreement was annulled on the basis of the allegation that the church did not fulfill its obligations. The accusation is unjustified. We do not intend to attempt to disprove it since it is so patently false and ridiculous..."[59]

1.1.4.3 The New Boundaries

A major substantive issue which increased tension between the Polish leadership and the Vatican focused on the policy of the Apostolic See towards the former German territories, a policy which was reflected in the organization of the ecclesiastical administration there. Faithful to its traditional policy, the Vatican withheld its recognition of the new territories as an integral part of Poland until the signing of a peace treaty. It refused, accordingly, to consider the Potsdam agreement as a basis for appointing a permanent Polish administration in these areas. The temporary nature of the office held by the heads of the dioceses in the liberated territories is expressed in their official title: Titular Apostolic Administrators and not ordinary (permanent) bishops. This tendency is extended in the *Annuario Pontificio*, which contains the list of Catholic dioceses throughout the world. In all yearbooks up to 1954, the administrative units of the church in western and northern Poland appear under the heading 'Germany'.

Pius XII's letter to the German hierarchy and German Catholics in March 1948 signified a serious deterioration in the Vatican's position towards Poland. The pope expressed dissatisfaction over the injustice involving the deportation of millions of Germans from the western territories, and called on the world to try to forgive the Germans for their war crimes and to make every effort to achieve peace and reconciliation.[60] The letter further stated that "facts that have been established/created (concerning the new territorial reality in Poland—H.D.) must be re-examined and (*territorial*—H.D.) withdrawal should be conducted wherever possible". The letter also defined Wrocław as a "Catholic environment in the German East".[61]

It appears, therefore, that in this period the Apostolic See, contrary to the Polish episcopate, refused to entertain formulations which might reduce tension in its relations with the Polish regime, and even intensified this policy towards the end of the period. This rigid stance conforms to its overall policy towards the new regimes in Eastern Europe. Tension in relations with the Vatican prevented, *a priori*, any attempt by the Polish government to bypass the Polish hierarchy in its contacts with the Vatican. Such initiatives by the Polish government after the 1947 elections were rejected by the Vatican, whose avowed position declared that the Apostolic See was unable to discuss a new concordat before the Polish government was able to settle its major differences with the church, and as long as the accusations against the church and the pope were maintained.[62] The pope, for his part, extended full support to the Polish episcopate and linked any overtures to regularize relations with the Vatican to an agreement of normalization of state–church relations within Poland.

1.1.5 THE SOVIET UNION

1.1.5.1 Analytical Framework[63]

After 1945 the environmental impact of the Soviet Union on policy towards the church in Poland and other areas should be examined within three main contextual settings, all dynamic in character. (a) Soviet *power struggles*, on their various levels, and the interaction between Soviet *ideological goals and basic values* and these struggles. (b) The calculation of the relative importance of the practical Soviet goals and interests which stem from (a). Here we are concerned mainly with the distinction between *major* goals and interests considered 'vital and non-negotiable' according to Soviet perceptions, and *peripheral* goals and interests, regarding which concessions are feasible. All the above must be evaluated in relation to a sober perception of reality which takes obstacles and parametric restraints into account when ranking goals. (c) The nature of Soviet influence seen, on the one hand, as a restrictive parametric environment dictating to, or seeking to impose its position on, the Polish leadership is discussed in terms of Soviet ability to impose its position, its motivation and the degree to which its wishes are realized. On the other hand, Soviet influence is recognized as a supportive and favorable environmental factor, backing the position and the policy of the Polish leadership, either explicitly or implicitly. We shall also address factors related to Poland's technical-economic, political and military dependence, which can account for Soviet influence, above and beyond ideological affinities.

1.1.5.2 The Soviet Union and Poland: 1945–1948

Soviet power struggles, which, at this particular stage, were focused on the domination of Eastern Europe, operated on two main levels (from the Polish perspective): inside Poland and on the global level. (This deals with relations with the West. Obviously, with regard to the church, the specific significance of relations with the Vatican and the Catholic world should be emphasized). The struggle met with difficulties that shaped Soviet priorities and led, at this stage, to the 'Polish Path to Socialism' and the Gomułka line being not merely tolerated but even supported and encouraged by the Soviets.

In close congruence with PPR interests and tactics[64] the Soviet Union opted for political pragmatism in its drive to create the conditions considered vital for a Communist takeover in Poland. In Poland, its immediate priority was to defeat the PSL, while globally it needed to prevent intervention by the West and deprive it of any influence in Eastern Europe. It was, therefore, in the direct and vital interests of both the Soviet Union and Poland to establish Poland's Oder–Neisse boundary in the west as an irreversible *fait accompli*. To a great extent this goal determined the Soviet Union's position regarding the Polish settlement project in the liberated territories—with its important agricultural implications—and its support and identification with the Polish leadership's opposition to the appointment of an interim church administration in the western territories. In light of the main objectives which Stalin considered critical, and in the face of the difficulties of which he was highly aware, the Soviet Union adopted, as part of its (stage-by-stage) tactics, *a policy of postponing and disguising its ideological objectives, which had exceptional significance in terms of agriculture as well as religion and the church in Poland.* The main complications recognized by the Soviet Union were: the strength of Polish Catholicism and of the church[65]; the scope of Polish patriotism; the hostility and suspicion of the general population and peasants towards the Soviet Union and Communism, and their deep hatred of forced collectivization that had gone on in the Soviet Union; Poland's peasant character, the social power of the peasants and their intense Catholicism; the fact that the Polish government had to take its first steps in a system that had suffered tremendously during the war; and the interest that the West displayed toward Poland. An extensive discussion of these difficulties may be found in the sections dealing with the aforementioned environmental spheres. An explanation of Soviet flexibility regarding religion and the church in Poland during the war and in the immediate post-war period, with emphasis on the Western consideration (i.e., to prevent the conversion of the church into a political instrument in the hands of the West) arises from the testimony of Chęciński, a member of the Polish security services between 1947 and 1959.[66] It should be noted that Soviet approval for a separate path to socialism had its roots in the war period when the Soviet Union supported this conception to broaden the basis of the fight against the Germans by supplementing non-Communist forces.[67]

1.1.5.3 The Soviet Union and the Church

The Soviet Union's postponement of a power struggle and direct confrontation with the church in Poland was remarkable if we consider the deep doctrinal and practical antagonism between the sides, Soviet experience during and after the Bolshevik revolution, and the Soviet tendency, at the time, to convert the church in Eastern Europe to a national institution administratively subservient to state authority. The Soviets avoided confrontation with the church in Poland at this stage due to the latter's tremendous influence and the Soviet hopes of harnessing the church's support, or, at the least, limiting its opposition during the first stages in the battle for power.

This special approach to the Roman Catholic Church in Poland seems striking when we compare it to Soviet policies towards the Greek Orthodox and Armenian churches in the eastern territories gained by the Soviet

Union from Poland after the borders were changed (it dismantled the organization of those churches).[68] The same held true in Poland itself with
regard to the subjugation of the Orthodox Church, swallowed by its Russian counterpart between 1945 and 1951, and the Uniates.[69]

However, if we compare the standing of the Roman Catholic Church
with that of other religions, we may conclude that the concessions and
special status afforded to the church were simply a variation of the
'policy of stages'. Thus as far back as 1945 the establishment of Piasecki's movement and the Soviet initiative that it represented may be
seen as part of a plan to solve the religious question in Poland, the
planting of a seed that would be nurtured and developed in order to undermine the strength of the Roman Catholic Church. Soviet attempts to
drive a wedge between the Vatican and the Polish hierarchy may be regarded as part of this same objective.

To sum up, the Soviet Union's environmental influence on policy
towards the church between 1945 and 1948 took the form of maximum
support for the position of the PPR and Gomułka, in contrast to the
eventual crises that occurred between the Soviet Union and the Polish
leadership in the area of agricultural policy.

1.2 POLICY

1.2.1 LEGAL BACKGROUND[70]

We find a reliable reflection of Soviet policy trends, Communist tactics,
and their shifts, in the decisions that determined the legal status of the
Roman Catholic Church. It can be said that the general trend expressed
in the formal framework testifies to a preservation of the *status quo* ensuring the supremacy of the Catholic Church over other religious denominations in the country, with slight efforts being made to reduce the
gap. However, there is a tendency to qualify the special status of the
church in statements and allusions to the temporary nature of the arrangements. The main points that shaped the legal framework appeared
in the 'July Manifesto', the 12 September 1945 decision to annul the
concordat, and the 'Little Constitution' of March 1947.

The July Manifesto, which was published by the PKWN (Polski
Komitet Wyzwolenia Narodowego, the Polish Committee for National

Liberation) on 22 July 1944, set out the programmatic guidelines for the new regime and named the constitution of 1921 as the only constitution in force. (This, in contrast to the 1935 constitution which does not receive legal recognition and is denounced as fascist. In the religious context, the significance is limited to the symbolic level, since the 1935 constitution ratified, without change, the 1921 constitution's articles dealing with religion.) *The 1921 Constitution guaranteed freedom of religion and conscience and recognized the equality of all religious denominations. Even so, it left no doubts regarding the privileged status of the Roman Catholic Church.* (The main articles dealing with religion in the 1921 constitution are 95, 96, 110–116, 120.) Accordingly, article 114 of the constitution determined that: "Since the Roman Catholic religion is the faith of the majority, it is first among equal religions in the country. The Catholic Church is administered according to its own norms. Relations between church and state are to be determined on the basis of an agreement with the Holy See subject to ratification by the Sejm." The special status granted to the Roman Catholic Church by the state, at least as *prima inter pares*, was also expressed in an exceptionally broad *de facto* interpretation of its internal juridical authority, state funding, and its position within official state institutions. (The constitution also promised financial allocations to other religious denominations recognized by the government, but in fact the Roman Catholic Church also enjoyed special privileges in this area.) Article 120 of the constitution dealing with the critical area of religious education also served to reinforce the dominant influence of the Roman Catholic Church. The article indeed mentioned all of Poland's state-recognized religions when making religious instruction mandatory in all public schools for children under 18. The main beneficiary of this arrangement is not, however, hard to identify. (Practical supervision of the implementation of this regulation was entrusted to the religious denomination concerned, while guaranteeing, however, the supreme status of the government educational authorities.)

As already noted, the July Manifesto perpetuated the rights of the Roman Catholic Church in post-war Poland. The manifesto did, however, point to the possibility of future modifications: "The basic principles of the 17 March 1921 constitution will remain in force until the convocation of a legislative Sejm..."[71] Restrictions on the exclusive rights of the church found more practical expression in a tendency, prevalent after the war, to acknowledge hitherto unrecognized religious denominations.[72] Among others, the Methodist Church was indeed recognized in the 16 October 1945 decree, along with the Evangelical Reformed Church, the Order of the Mariavites, and the Ancient Catholic Church, which gained such recognition in 1947. However, even these formal acts failed to prevent *de facto* restrictions on the religious denominations in question. For one, they were forbidden to maintain free contact with church organizations abroad, the result being the perpetuation of their inferiority to the Roman Catholic Church. On the other hand, we witness futile attempts by the government to use these denominations, and especially the National Catholic Church, as parameters restricting the power of the church. At any rate, the most radical change in the status of the Roman Catholic Church was linked with the decision to annul the concordat taken on 12 September 1945.[73]

In article 114, the 1921 constitution had already provided for an agreement (concordat) to be signed with the Vatican which would shape relations between the Catholic Church in Poland and the restored state. The agreement, signed only on 10 February 1925, granted the church many rights.[74] Moreover, it is worth mentioning that the papal bull, *Vix-dum Poloniae Unitas*, dated 28 August 1925, granted official approval to the concordat.[75] The concordat guaranteed the church full freedom in exercising its authority and ecclesiastical jurisdiction in internal affairs in accordance with canon law. According to the agreement, the Catholic clergy would not be subject to secular court jurisdiction in civil matters, and the state guaranteed to supply information on any measures taken against the priesthood and to allow Catholic priests to serve out their sentences in monasteries. Article 13 obliges the state to guarantee religious instruction in all elementary schools, high schools, and even universities. An executive order, dated 9 December 1926, extended the scope of this privilege.[76] There was also a rule whereby church property would not be subject to the proposed land reform, and the church would be indemnified for any loss of property during the period prior to the re-establishment of Poland. The church received guarantees ensuring free contact with the Vatican, and a special article dealt with the establishment of diplomatic relations with the Apostolic See. It was also resolved that the Holy See would consult with the president of the Republic on the appointment of archbishops and bishops... (An important article in the concordat, exploited for its annulment, stipulated that Polish Catholics would be under the exclusive administrative authority of bishops domiciled within Poland's borders.) Of course, the Polish hierarchy lost this solid foundation with the annulment of the concordat in September 1945, and suffered the imposition of restrictions on the work of the Apostolic See in Poland as a result of the annulment. However, this was insufficient to undermine completely the formal basis of the church's existence, since, as pointed out earlier, the church maintained its rights under the 1921 constitution. It appears, therefore, that Dinka's claim (1963, p. 57) that the church operated in a legal vacuum during the first years after the war, is inaccurate.

The spirit of legal continuity, on the one hand, and the provisional basis for the special status of the church on the other, were also maintained in the 'Little Constitution' adopted by the Polish Sejm on 19 February 1947.[76] The relevance of this legislative act regarding religion and the church lies in the section that states that, until the adoption of a new constitution, the Polish Sejm, as the supreme authority in the country, would be guided by the basic directives of the 1921 constitution and the principles of the PKWN manifesto of 22 July 1944.

Despite the lack of clarity with regard to the church's status, due to the lack of specific legal arrangements and legal lacunae in post-war legislation, which indeed left room for different interpretations and manipulation, we should not disregard the degree of judicial continuity made possible by the above documents.[78] The declaration on rights and freedoms of 22 February 1947, which recognized freedom of conscience and religion, including the right to conduct religious rites, firmly supports this conclusion.[79] This policy of continuity, guided by the new leadership's deep desire for the legitimization of their control, conformed to the general policy that characterized this period. Thus the leadership took the position of the church, the Catholic population, and the West into consideration and sought to anticipate their responses.

1.2.2 IDEOLOGICAL BACKGROUND

It is well known that the doctrinal antagonism between the Catholic faith and Communist ideology is due, from the latter's point of view, to its character as a materialist, atheistic, and explicitly anticlerical doctrine and its demand for undivided loyalty and absolute control. Moreover, Communist doctrine makes no efforts to hide its long-range goals regarding religion and the church. However, despite this ideological in-flexibility and its expressions in various spheres, and notwithstanding its weakness in the period between the two world wars, the KPP chose to abstain from emphasizing the struggle against religion. In contrast to the KPP, it was the Polish Socialist Party (PPS) which regularly raised the standard against the church, issuing slogans calling for the secularization of public life. In the years prior to the seizure of power and following the re-establishment of the Communist Party of Poland (PPR in January 1942; ZPP in March 1943), Communist tactics were aimed at attracting the Polish population's support for the party under the banner of the national struggle against the Germans. It was clear to the PPR leader-ship that the national front policy stood no hope of success if it repudi-ated the religious sentiments of the population.[80] Not only did Com-munist propaganda in the underground media exercise extreme care to disguise its ideological positions on the religious issue, on occasion it went as far as to call for the defense of the Cross and the Catholic Church against the German invader. Communist interest in genuine cooperation with the clergy and the Catholic population can be illus-trated by the story of Franciszek Kubsz, a priest who found a place in the ZPP leadership in June 1943 and also served as a priest in Berling's army. The very same approach can also be seen reflected in the forged publication by the PPR, in the spring of 1944, of a pastoral letter, os-tensibly by Archbishop Sapieha, calling on the population to remain calm in the face of the Soviet army's advance.[81] We see that despite "the basic conflict between Christianity and the Revolution", to quote Czesław Miłosz (1953, p. 206), the Communists refrained from pursuing this conflict and even tried—against the background of the war, the party's weakness and lack of popularity, and its consciousness of the in-tensity of Polish Catholicism in the general population—to gain the support of their ideological opponents.

Similar tendencies were dominant during the early years of Com-munist rule. The status of the PPR was radically transformed, but many of its previous weaknesses, and mainly its lack of popularity, persisted. It now assumed the challenge of heavy responsibilities for ensuring its control and finding solutions to the country's problems.[82] Furthermore, the PPR's ideological stance, which had clearly departed from dogma-tism, was reflected partly in non-selective procedures for the mobiliza-tion of new party members. Moreover, the broad, day-by-day, intensive confrontation with powerful Catholic realities, which had, also in the past, nurtured a difference of views between the Polish Communists and their Soviet colleagues, once more exerted its influence. Now, the significance of this meeting grew even more decisive in the face of the difficult challenges before the party.

1.2.3 GENERAL POLICY CHARACTERISTICS

1.2.3.1 Environmental Factors—Perception and Impact on Policy

Factors deeply rooted in Poland's social-political and economic soil, and which influenced policy and the behavior of the political elite, need to be examined further, with focus on the ruling elite's perception of environmental factors. The elite's relatively moderate and restrained policies may be explained only by the leadership's sensitivity toward the environment and by its realistic approach.

One of the most impressive factors to affect the system was the PPR's wartime experience. On the one hand, there was continuity in the sense that the party leadership acted according to various norms developed during the war, while on the other, there was the impact of urgent requirements dictated to the elite by the aftermath of the war. The call for a national-democratic front, which the PPR had advanced both in word and deed under the German occupation, was kept up after the end of the occupation, and paved the way for the national unity government formed in July 1945 and for the coalition built around the ruling party. The consequences of the war on the system were evident in the need to repair the devastation (to agriculture, the economy, and in other areas) and in the additional need to channel immense resources into the development and settlement of the liberated territories so that they could be irrevocably integrated into Poland. The leadership's awareness of its relative weakness was another decisive factor that dictated the general nature of its policy. This weakness stemmed mainly from a lack of popularity and experience and from the factional composition of the party. It also arose from the relative strength of competing political and social forces and from the position of the West on issues involving Poland's political and economic sovereignty. We have already discussed these factors and they will require further study.

This weakness forced the government to adopt a series of tactics designed to compartmentalize the struggle against its opponents into different stages in order to deal with each separately. In practical terms, this program emphasized the following: achieving the initial objectives in the socialization of social and economic life (agrarian reform, 1944; nationalization of industry, 1946); the reconstruction of the country after the wartime devastation, with special momentum in the western territories; conducting a fierce struggle against Mikołajczyk and the PSL, which climaxed in the January 1947 elections and ended with Mikołajczyk's flight in October the same year; and attempts towards unification with the PPS, which bore fruit in December 1948 with the establishment of the PZPR.

In the face of their awareness of the church's strength, the environmental factor under consideration and their main political goals, the Communist leaders chose to postpone any showdown with the church.[83] Fully conscious of the danger from the church were it to become a part of the opposition,[84] the leaders weighed their policy towards it carefully and opted for a policy of caution, restraint, and camouflage. They avoided all direct confrontation with the church as an institution and conflict on important, sensitive issues. Only on occasion did the leadership exploit opportunities that came its way for sporadic attacks, such as that against Cardinal Hlond in connection with the events in Kielce in 1946. In other words, the elite avoided ideological confrontation and abstained from making clear programmatic declarations in order to postpone aggravating its conflict with the church. As a consequence, many questions remained unresolved. It should be said that during the years 1945 to 1948, the Catholic Church was not attacked as an institution even in Hungary and Czechoslovakia—countries where the church had far less political power. Moreover, the Communist leaders' relatively liberal and tolerant attitude was evidenced in conciliatory measures designed to avoid provoking the church, and in their abstention from open intervention in church affairs. This went as far as providing proof of respect for the religion of the people, for example by their attendance of church ceremonies. Until 1948 this policy became part of the official PPR line towards the church, which supported the *modus vivendi*.

Despite the above policies it would be a mistake to analyze the regime's policy towards the church in unambiguous terms. Even in the period under discussion one can discern, parallel to the tolerant approach, restrictive practices, which, despite their secondary, marginal and vague nature, were designed to undermine the balance of power between the government and the church, or at least to sow the seeds and prepare the tools that would enable more intensive and overt activity in the future.

Jan Nowak (1951) supports the thesis that a plan to fight the church was elaborated and designed years before the serious campaign began against the church in Poland. The thesis is presented in a similar way in French government documents, which argue that there was a Communist plan to take over the church in all people's democracy countries, although the plan was not to be implemented at a uniform rate (Secrétariat Général du Gouvernement, 1959, p. 27). Halecki (1957, p. 225) also emphasized that "the program that the Communist government had, in relation to the Catholic Church in Poland, was drawn-out and complex." A similar view regarding a predetermined program arises from arguments offered by Beneš and Pounds (1970). Even so, it appears that despite the existence of a more or less crystallized plan it is wrong to ignore the dimension in the policy of the Communist government that arose as a direct response to *ad hoc* positions taken by the church and to actual problems in general, and the chain of responses and counter responses by the sides. Halecki, for example, neglects this dimension.

In this context, and taking the relative weights of rewards and restrictions as a key to the nature of policy, we can divide the period into two sub-periods, separated by the January 1947 elections. The elections, which ensured a massive majority in the Sejm for the PPR-led democratic bloc, marked the beginnings of a shift towards increased restrictions compared to the earlier period, and towards an increased hardening in policy which reached its climax at the end of the period, during the second half of 1948.

1.2.3.2 Objectives, Modes of Struggle, and Demands

The regime's objectives, in principle and in practice, and correspondingly in the long and short term, determined the nature of the rewards-restrictions mix. On the one hand, the rewards for the church—sometimes surprisingly lavish—were of an instrumental nature, designed to prevent hindrance from the church or even to mobilize it in helping the regime to achieve its most urgent and critical objectives. On the other hand, the ultimate policy goals towards the church remained unaltered on a long-term, ideological level. This found expression in a policy of restrictions designed to narrow the church's institutional influence as the regime's most powerful ideological and political competition.

Despite the general tendency to grant concessions, the regime continued to make a concentrated effort, from the earliest stages, to undermine the church's independence and to impair its internal organization and unity. There were attempts by the regime to realize its goals by creating a number of rifts: between the Catholic lay leadership and the church hierarchy; between priests who were 'reactionaries and foreign agents' and the rest of the priesthood[85]; between the lower clergy and the hierarchy; and between the hierarchy and the Vatican. If the attempt to forge a rift between the Polish hierarchy and the Vatican was unsuccessful,[86] the tactics designed to drive a wedge between the hierarchy and the lower clergy was only slightly more so.[87] The latter efforts included the introduction of 'class struggle' and the creation of solidarity between the lower clergy and the masses by ideological, political, and economic means. The attempt to sunder the lay leadership and the hierarchy also failed to achieve the desired results. The Communist regime even tried, usually without success, to tarnish the church's image in the population's eyes and to cause cracks in its unchallengeable support. Dinka (1963, p. 7) mentions another tactic used, namely to train new priests, faithful to the regime, and to plant them in the church administration. The regime failed in its, albeit limited, attempts to bolster other religious denominations and provide at least a symbolic counterweight to the church. This chiefly took the guise of an effort to promote and encourage the 'National Polish Catholic Church' during the early post-war years.[88]

As we can see, the regime did not refrain from using propaganda, restrictive legislation, legal persecution, administrative measures, and terror, although these measures were more characteristic of the period after the elections and the establishment of the Cyrankiewicz government at the beginning of February 1947, and especially during the period from the end of 1947, when the ruling group was busy eliminating the remnants of the legal opposition. Even so, such measures were not as systematic or as comprehensive as they became in the Stalinist period.

The demands made on the church, as a result of the aforementioned objectives, are by nature dichotomous. *Thus, from the minute they took power, the Polish Communists pressured for a non-political church while simul-taneously calling for the political involvement of the church*[89] *in response to their call that "the Church support the efforts of the party to build a new Poland".*[90] This ambivalence was expressed strikingly on the eve of the January 1947 elections[91] as well as in the preconditions for an agreement with the church, defined by General Wiktor Grosz, head of the Ministry of Foreign Affairs press division and Minister Władysław Wolski. General Grosz stressed that even though the regime did not consider the church a political partner, it would cooperate with it on condition that it ceased interfering in politics and recognized the principle of separation between church and state. Minister Wolski said that the regime was deeply concerned about the church's negative attitude to the country's reconstruction and suggested that the church call upon the people to join in the national effort. He warned that should the church refuse to do so, it would, in the end, lose this battle with the regime.[92]

We should clarify two points with regard to the threat which accompanied Wolski's demands: a) While the government employed a policy of rewards it had no compunction over using threats, especially when it failed to achieve the desired results. These threats were more overt and direct in the period after the elections and more disguised and indirect prior to the elections[93]; b) the demands, the negative statements, and the more persistent and obstinate threats were *not made in the name of the PPR.* They were issued in the name of the government and its ministers, with parties such as the PPS and the SD voicing them within the government coalition. Thus Bierut, among others, emphasizes his activity regarding religion in his capacity as a supposedly non-partisan president.

It is worth noting here that, consistent with the trends that became prevalent in the period between the two world wars, it was the PPS which continued to promote, during the early post-war years, a more open, militant struggle than the PPR against the influence of religion and the church. It is interesting that the amalgamation of the PPR and the PPS in December 1948 coincided with a hardening in policy towards the church. It was Prime Minister Osóbka-Morawski, who had raised the subject of the abuse of church sermons for political purposes before the National Council in January 1946. He demanded the repression of anti-democratic activities by the clergy, threatening severe punishment in response to such activity against the regime.[94] And again, later, it was Prime Minister Cyrankiewicz who replied to the church's accusations of a camouflaged struggle against God and the church in Poland, in his Sejm speech of 29 October 1947. In his counter-attack he said: "These activities, doomed to failure, are an attempt to involve the church in political conflict..."[95] Cyrankiewicz accused the hierarchy of an attempt "to hinder and disturb the process towards political unity" and to harm the efforts to stabilize Poland's new democracy.[96] According to this tendency, it was the Central Committee of the Democratic Party (SD) which, after the 1947 elections, claimed that "after the political bankruptcy of the émigré centers and the PSL leadership, the leaders of the Catholic Church assumed the role of opposition to the people's regime".[97] However, the methods used against the church could not be similar to those against the PSL. Hence Gomułka's words before the plenum of the Central Committee of the PPR on 10 February 1946: "The goal of our policy concerning the church is not different from that concerning an organization such as the PSL. Nevertheless, the means cannot be the same. We cannot initiate a split within the church, in the same way as in the case of the PSL. The church must be neutralized but should not be subject to a frontal offensive."[98]

1.2.4 SPECIFIC POLICIES

1.2.4.1 General

The analytical framework mentioned above, which outlined the *general* policy components—especially the use of the pattern of concessions and restrictions—will guide us in our examination of more specific policy components. Therefore, we will now proceed by distinguishing between the concessions made during this period and the restrictions. However, before doing so we will concentrate on three matters worthy of individual consideration: a) the issue of the January 1947 elections which provide an indicative example of the regime's demands of the church; b) the annulment of the concordat and policy towards the Vatican; and c) the policy towards Pax. The first matter dealt directly with policy towards the church, while the other two involved an additional set of inputs.

1.2.4.2 Policy in Relation to the 1947 Elections

Before the elections, with the fight against the PSL at a critical stage, the Communist Party, fully aware of the church's influence on the voters, made strenuous efforts to win its neutrality. It is worth noting that the habit of turning to the church in order to influence the outcome of elections had a firm place in Polish reality even before the Communist rise to power. Thus, for example, after Piłsudski's military *coup d'état* priests received orders to call on believers to vote for the government in the general elections.[99]

To achieve this, the ruling elite stressed the benefits that the church had received from the existing regime, going so far as to express good will and hint at government willingness to offer even greater rewards. The regime also increased its use of national formulations as the basis for normalization and cooperation. On the other hand, it resorted, as we have seen, to threats and pressure. *Trybuna Wolności*, the organ of the Central Committee of the PPR, expressed the conciliatory line when it wrote on 1 March 1946: "...the Catholic Church is an inseparable part of authentic Polish reality...in Poland, there is no need for the Catholic camp to harbor doubts regarding its very existence...there are realistic preconditions for democratic cooperation between the state and the Catholic Church." A similar (and complementary) opinion, to the effect that the church would probably adopt a policy of non-interference in the political game connected to the elections, after it had apparently digested the fact that it would be unable to oppose the social transformations which were taking place in Poland, was expressed by *Dziennik Zachodni* on 23 April 1946.[100]

Bierut stood out in his efforts in this direction. In a famous interview with K. Pruszyński, Bierut lists the benefits and the privileges granted to the church in Poland, referring to their conditional character, and even proposes additional benefits such as the relaxation of censorship of the Catholic press, Catholic representation in the future Sejm, and allusions to the renewal of the concordat and the possibility of an agreement.[101] All this on condition that the church recognize the new reality in Poland, and that the clergy change its passive attitude to the regime and abandon its support and sympathy for enemies of the state. As the elections approached the regime also pledged to include "special recognition for the rights of the Catholic Church" in the new constitution to be drawn up after the elections, in addition to the freedom of conscience and religion promised earlier.[102] In the above-mentioned interview Bierut added: "The church in Poland relates to it [state policy towards the church] with suspicion, as a momentary maneuver on our part. This is a mistake. We relate to our attempts at reaching understanding with the church earnestly and with long-range vision..." Verbally, Bierut also responded positively to the episcopate's demands for a representative Catholic party, explaining that Catholics have the same rights as all other Polish citizens. Moreover, he did not negate the possibility of the Catholics joining the government coalition. However, in practice the regime did everything in its power to prevent the establishment of an independent Catholic party, fearing greatly that the Catholic party would join the PSL in the opposition. The actual policy preventing the establishment of a Catholic party can be seen from the experience and fate of Stronnictwo Pracy (the Labor Party), with its Christian hue. Before the war this party represented the Christian Movement, which was based on the papal encyclical *Rerum Novarum*. Initially, the legal activity of the party was sanctioned by decisions reached at the Moscow conference of June 1945. However, this permission was conditional on the party's agreement to allow the participation of the 'Zryw' group, headed by Widi-Wirski, who was known for his pre-war anti-Catholic positions. In the summer of 1946 this group used violence in a party takeover, helped by the government and the *bezpieka* (the secret police).

As we have noted, the democratic bloc did not hesitate to use intimidation and threats in its efforts to influence the church position on the elections. In an atmosphere of growing intimidation and threats against the PSL and its leaders, on the eve of the elections, similar measures were used against the church, albeit on a much smaller scale. Threats were made against priests lest they speak out against the regime from the pulpit. The first trials of priests took place in November and December 1946. These concluded with death sentences for two of the priests, Jurkiewicz and Konczala, who were accused of subversive activities against the state.[103]

In the days before the elections the regime managed to achieve an artificial, fictitious, largely verbal and formal neutrality.[104] Presumably, both the Catholic population and the policy makers were aware that the church's 'camouflaged' positions obscured its true and natural links to the opposition. Nevertheless, after the elections the regime did not hesitate to claim that it had enjoyed the support of the vast majority of the Catholic population. In fact, it was no secret that the so-called democratic bloc, headed by the Communist Party, won this election (official results: 80.1 percent compared to the PSL with 10.3 percent) by employing fraud, falsification, and terror. Persecution and terror also continued in the period following the elections, forcing Mikołajczyk to flee Poland.

1.2.4.3 The Annulment of the Concordat and Policy towards the Vatican

From its rise to power the new regime in Warsaw adopted a hostile, hard-line policy towards the pope and the Vatican. Communist propaganda, which usually abstained from direct attacks on the clergy or the Polish episcopate, was directed against the Holy See, largely as indirect ammunition against Catholicism, while exploiting the fertile soil of the Vatican's role during the war and at its end.[105] The declaration by the provisional Polish government, dated 12 September 1945, to the effect that: "The concordat between the Polish Republic and the Apostolic See has been invalidated as a result of unilateral violation by the Holy See stemming from illegal conduct repudiating its principles during the occupation", must be viewed against the background of the regime's position and its designs against Catholicism.[106] The media, which announced the annulment of the concordat, faithful to the decision by the Council of Ministers, made every effort to stress that the Vatican had taken many steps during the war in violation of the concordat and against the best interests of Poland.[107] The Council of Ministers issued a detailed justification of the decision, in sections 1 and 2 of its announcement: "The Holy See…substantially violated article 9 of the concordat, which states that 'no part of the Polish Republic will be under the jurisdiction of any bishop domiciled outside the borders of the Polish state'. In violation of the article, the Apostolic See granted jurisdiction over the Chełmno diocese to the German Karol Maria Splett, the bishop of Gdańsk. [On 2 February 1946 it was learned that Bishop Splett had been sentenced by a special tribunal in Gdańsk to eight years in prison, denial of civil rights for five years, and to confiscation of property]. Moreover, during the war the Vatican appointed the German bishop, Hilarius O. Breitinger, as the apostolic administrator for the Gniezno–Poznań diocese, granting

him jurisdiction over the German residents in these territories—in contradiction to the interests of the Polish people and state."[108] The Council
of Ministers, which held the Vatican responsible for the crisis due to the
latter's pro-German policies, went on to cite the refusal of the Holy See
to extend recognition to the provisional government and to establish
diplomatic relations with it. This fact, in and of itself, contravened the
concordat's *raison d'être.*[109]

Thus we find the possible explanations for the annulment, or at least
the key elements for understanding this move, present in the text, along
with the propaganda elements of the declaration. In fact, the reasons
offered for the unilateral annulment are linked *to the operative aims of that
phase* towards both the Vatican and the church in Poland. This step can
be seen as a maneuver designed to put pressure on the Vatican to change
its hostile attitude to the new regime, *to force it to recognize the provisional
government*, established in Moscow on 28 June 1945, *and the new territorial reality in Poland*. Among other things, this was done by changing the
temporary and indefinite makeup of the ecclesiastical jurisdiction in the
former German territories established a month earlier (16 August 1945),
and by showing concern for its Polish character. These aims, which
characterized the regime's relations with the Vatican, and the later attempts to reach a new agreement, confirm this. Nevertheless, we need to
evaluate the annulment on the basis of its immediate and direct results,
even though not all had been envisaged by the regime in advance.

It is reasonable to believe that, through the annulment of the concordat, the regime sought *to limit the privileges of the Catholic Church, which
certainly diverged from the principles of a socialist state.*[110] An identical argument appears in the following quotation: "Even had the Vatican not
acted against Polish national interests during the occupation, and even
had it not violated the concordat's principles, the concordat could not
have remained in force in People's Poland. The concordat, with its special privileges for the Catholic Church (to the point that these impinge
on national sovereignty) was unacceptable in a socialist state, which
promised fully to realize the principles of freedom of conscience and religion."[111] The precisely phrased announcement of the annulment clearly
distinguishes between the pro-German Vatican and the Polish Catholic
Church, with which the regime hoped peacefully to coexist, and makes it
very clear that the regime's act was only "a step to clarify the international relationship between the new Polish state and the Vatican, a step

not directed against the church, *per se.*"[112] Thus, with this formulation, which *was a seemingly indirect action*, the regime succeeded in eliminating the church's privileged juridical status and thus avoided a head-on collision with the church. The Polish government's drastic step of annulling the concordat was also linked to its desire to rid itself of all the limitations associated with the Polish Catholic Church's relations with the Vatican. As we have already stated, this desire is reflected in the regime's efforts to transform the Catholic Church into a 'national' church and to isolate it from all outside control. The annulment was also designed to drive a wedge between the Catholic population and the Vatican, the means employed being the accusation of the Holy See of pro-German tendencies and the manipulation of popular anti-German sentiment. We should emphasize that the annulment was unique in Communist policy in Eastern Europe. Not only did the concordat agreements with Czechoslovakia, Hungary, and Romania remain in force, but, at a later stage, they even served as a weapon against the church because they gave the regime the power of veto over the appointment of bishops. (Of the 39 members of the episcopate at the start of the 1950s, 20 had been appointed by the pope after 1945). In Poland, on the other hand, the annulment granted the pope—though this had, of course, not been the intention—a free hand in the appointment of bishops. In this sense the state lost the legal basis for intervention in church matters, creating a *de facto* separation between church and state.

At that very early date the annulment of the concordat was the most drastic of the measures taken by the regime against the Apostolic See and provided a starting point for future policy. In the years 1945 to 1948, and later, the Polish regime was involved in futile attempts to solve problems caused by the annulment and in unofficial and unsuccessful efforts to reach a new agreement. Meanwhile, the Communist propaganda apparatus was working feverishly against the pope and the Vatican. The regime-sponsored media attacked them both severely for their pro-German tendencies and their connections with US imperialism[113] while exploiting the population's patriotic feelings and its unswerving bond to the liberated territories as an integral part of Poland. Despite the line of demarcation that the regime drew between its relations with the episcopate and the church (on the one hand) and between the Vatican (on the other hand), its attacks on the Holy See could be seen as indirect attacks on the episcopate. Damaging the episcopate by indirect measures conformed to the

rules of the game imposed by the regime in this phase, and this is the way
the episcopate saw it. The propaganda continued even during the regime's
contact with Rome. It is worth noting that the government's contacts, designed to renew diplomatic relations with the Holy See, were characterized, up to the elections, by attempts at mediation by the Polish episcopate, which linked an agreement between the church and the Polish state
to the resumption of diplomatic relations with the Holy See. It is against
this background that one must see Hlond's visit to Rome at the end of
1946—a mission that failed, at least partly due to the interview granted by
Bierut to Pruszyński.[114] In this interview Bierut denounced the Vatican's
pro-German policies as the main obstacle to harmony between church and
state in Poland. After the elections the government once again initiated
direct, but unofficial, contacts with the Vatican, striving to bypass the
Polish hierarchy. It tried to pave the way to a separate agreement with the
Apostolic See for the resumption of diplomatic relations which would not
necessarily be linked to an agreement regarding church-state relations in
Poland. In order to prove the great importance that it attached to the negotiations, the government included Professor Grabski, one of the concordat negotiators in 1925, in the delegation to Rome. Grabski was recalled after refusing to discuss the possibility of a new concordat, and the
responsibility was entrusted to Pruszyński.[115] Pruszyński's mission, which
involved two visits to Rome, six weeks apart, floundered, and thus it was
that *the attempt to bypass the Polish hierarchy failed.*[116] With these developments the government stepped up its attacks against the church, the hierarchy, and mainly the Vatican. The pope's epistle to the German Catholics in March 1948 met, as was to be expected, with the sharpest of responses from the government. In addition to its propaganda value, the
Communist government saw the missive as an act encouraging German
revisionism and revanchism, as well as proof that the Vatican was still a
long way from recognizing Poland's western boundaries.

Towards the end of the period it became clear that the problem of
relations with the Vatican had not only remained unresolved, but had
actually deteriorated. The positions on both sides polarized and served
as an introduction to the battle and the recurrent, bitter attacks during
the next stage.

1.2.4.4 Pax as an Instrument of the Government

In the context of the general policy and the tactics adopted by the Communists *vis-à-vis* the Catholic Church in Poland during the early post-war period, the importance of Pax and its leader, Piasecki, stood out as an instrument used to weaken the church by 'boring from within' and splitting the clergy. Lucjan Blit, basing himself on Światło's report, recounts Piasecki's special relationships with the Fifth Department in the Ministry for Public Security, which was also involved in the war against the Catholic Church.[117] The government created Pax to carry out its own work and gave the organization its full support during those years.[118] This support was expressed in the freedom of action and privileged status in the cultural and political field given to the organization from its inception, and especially in the economic privileges which placed the organization on a strong financial footing. The government allowed the 'progressive Catholics' to publish their own weekly, *Dziś i Jutro*, in 1946, and early in 1947 granted them an exclusive license to publish a Catholic daily, *Słowo Powszechne*. The movement also received assistance in its activities as a profitable book publisher.

The government also enabled Piasecki and his movement to engage in energetic political activity.[119] Thus the doors of the Sejm were open to three 'progressive Catholics', namely *Dziś i Jutro* activists who established the Social-Catholic Club after the 1947 elections. The three were Jan Frankowski, Aleksander Bochenski, and Witold Bieńkowski. Piasecki himself was a member of the Council of State. Pax established many small industrial projects, usually devoted to the production of religious articles as well as commercial projects. All these were exempt from taxation and some were even exempted from the tax on state enterprises. Despite the serious shortage of foreign currency in post-war Poland, Pax was permitted to hold Western currency received by projects it controlled.[120] As we have already mentioned,[121] all these benefits and privileges failed to help Pax achieve the goals set for it by the government.

1.2.4.5 The Policy of Rewards and Concessions

*1.2.4.5.1 Gestures by Government Leaders and the Status of Religion
in Official Institutions*

From the time it took power, the elite made efforts to dispel the fear of
the church and to soften government positions by issuing declarations
and formulations, designed to guarantee the status of the churches as
traditional, spiritual institutions, and by recognizing the principle of
freedom of religion and faith, with special emphasis on the Roman
Catholic Church. When Bierut came to Warsaw in January 1945, he
issued, in his capacity as acting president of the KRN, guarantees for
"normal relations between the church and the state" and for "full religious freedom for Roman Catholics and other religious denominations".[122] Henryk Świątkowski, the minister of justice and responsible for
relations with the church, also declared that "the government is of the
opinion that, first of all, full religious rights must be extended to the
Roman Catholic Church..."[123] The soothing announcements by the government included moderate positions on social and political issues such
as, for example, denoting the importance of private enterprise in post-
war Poland.

The Communist leaders did not confine themselves to tolerant
phrases and formulations testifying to the government's good will, but
considered it appropriate to supply striking, public proof of their cordial
attitude while appealing to the national, patriotic, and even clerical
feelings of the population. Conspicuous among these gestures was the
active participation by public officials, including President Bierut, in
church events and ceremonies.[124] The participation of the army in religious parades, and the fact that Communist heroes received resplendent
Catholic funerals, is also worth noting. Church baptism and a Catholic
education for children of Communist Party members, including senior
party members, had already exceeded these gestures and bore witness to
the extraordinary influence of the Polish Church.

In addition, the special consideration which the church received from
the government was expressed in the formal, ceremonial bonds between
the state and its institutions and the Catholic religion. Thus the religious nature of the presidential oath was maintained on the basis of the
"Constitutional Law, dated 4 February 1947, regarding the election of

the president of the Polish Republic". Article 11 of this law determines that the oath by the president-elect on the assumption of office would include the phrase "So help me God." Article 10 of the law states: "If the president-elect refuses to accept the position, or if, when called on—by the chairman of the Sejm—to take the oath, he abstains from taking the oath specified in this Law—a new president must be elected immediately."[125] A similar religious formulation was also preserved in the army oath, but only up to July 1947. The formulation was included in an ordinance dated 21 August 1944.[126] The influence of religion in the army was not confined to the oath and also found expression in the status of the priests who continued to function in the army and in the recently established militia.

1.2.4.5.2 Material Rewards

Another kind of concession, often employed by the government, was the granting of material rewards to the Catholic Church.[127] These were granted in order to demonstrate the government's friendly attitude toward the church, and stemmed from the ruling elite's genuine interest in obtaining the church's assistance in rebuilding devastated Poland,[128] especially its contribution to establishing the church organization in the liberated territories. These rewards were particularly striking if we consider Poland's economic difficulties at the time. In this manner, the government assisted in the restoration of churches and other church buildings damaged during the war. In practice, expenses were divided between the church and the government, with the latter carrying the main burden.[129]

The Ministry of Reconstruction appropriated $40,000 for this purpose in 1946.[130] Financial support was not confined to the reconstruction of church buildings but also extended to improving the income and living conditions of the clergy and other employees in religious institutions. One indicative example was the decision by the minister of public administration to raise the salaries of all instructors of religion in public schools.[131] Also relevant here was the distributing of food rations to the clergy. *But the most far-reaching concession was the exemption of the church lands, including monasteries, from the agrarian reform which the PKWN declared in September 1944.* The reform, which applied to all real estate owned by private individuals and legal bodies, whose size exceeded a certain limit, also exempted the other religious denominations. It is important to note that Wanda Wasilewska testified in her memoirs (1939–1944) that the decision not to include church land in the agrarian reform was taken by Stalin himself.[132] The temporary exemption of these lands was stipulated in article 2, sub-section 1, of the reform decree, dated 6 September 1944, which stated that their final status would be determined by the Sejm, when constituted. The perpetuation of this status was maintained, practically, in later legislation on the subject. Moreover, the government transferred to the Polish Catholic Church—as well as to other religious denominations—the ownership of many churches which had previously belonged to German Protestants in the western territories, including church property, land, and other real estate holdings.[133]

It is worth noting that the termination of different grants resulting from the annulment of the concordat had only a marginal practical impact due to the exemption from the agrarian reform and the continuation of other grants, such as payment for war damages.[134] Thus the church continued, with government assent, to possess the wherewithal to make independent activity possible.

1.2.4.5.3 Charitable Activity and Freedom of Organization

Another kind of concession, that of channeling material aid, not to the church or its functionaries but through the church to the population, was expressed in the activities allowed to the Catholic charity organization Caritas. This organization, whose work was interrupted by the war, was reorganized at its conclusion. The organization's importance increased, since it became the main channel through which material and financial aid flowed to Poland from abroad. This aid was made possible thanks to private initiative, mainly by Catholic organizations and Polish immigrants in the United States. It is superfluous to cite the influence and the power that this charitable activity granted to the church. The government did not consent to register Caritas legally, however, but the organization continued to operate while the government turned a blind eye.

Another organization, which existed more or less up to the end of 1948, was the Catholic Society for Young Men (Katolickiego Stowarzyszenia Młodzieży Męskiej). There was also intensive activity during this period on the part of organizations whose exclusive field of endeavor was devoted to religious rites, such as *Sodalicja Mariańska*. The government also tolerated the fact that the monasteries ran private hospitals, schools, and boarding schools for children and youth.[135]

1.2.4.5.4 Freedom of the Press and Publication

Important concessions related to permission for Catholic newspapers and publications.

About a month after the Russians entered Kraków, the Metropolitan Curia of Kraków obtained a license to publish a social-cultural periodical. On 24 March 1945 the first issue of *Tygodnik Powszechny* appeared. Later, a whole range of Catholic periodicals sprang up. Six outstanding periodicals were aimed at the Catholic intelligentsia. At the same time, other Catholic periodicals were aimed at the entire religious population.[136]

The policy that made freedom of the press possible also permitted the operation, as in the past, of six major Catholic printing plants, though these were, in theory, subject to nationalization according to the Council of Ministers' decision of 11 April 1947.

In this context, the importance of the special privilege given to pastoral letters "as the only form of public criticism voiced in Poland after 1944"[136] should be mentioned.

1.2.4.5.5 Concessions in the Area of Education

The government revealed extreme caution in the sensitive area of 'shaping the nation's soul' through education and religious instruction in public schools. Thus religious studies continued, as before, to form part of the educational curriculum between 1945 and 1948. The legal basis for this arrangement can be found in the Ministry of Education circular, dated 13 September 1945, which revalidated article 120 of the 1921 constitution.[138] A further legal basis for the arrangement was the president's 1948 letter to the Polish bishops.[139] The presence of religion in the schools was appropriately symbolized by the crosses which were left

hanging in the classrooms. Seminars for the priesthood were in operation at the time, a matter of great importance due to the shortage of
priests. The government also permitted the reopening of the Catholic
University of Lublin almost immediately after the Germans left the city.
The Catholic University of Lublin (KUL) was established as a result of
private initiative in 1919 and modeled after the Milano example. The
university continued to operate its two ecclesiastical departments, of
theology and canon law, and its three secular departments, of law, social
economics and humanities. Independently, the government allowed the
operation of theology departments at the Jagiellonian University in
Kraków and the University of Warsaw.[140]

The picture derived from an overall view of the concessions and
privileges granted to the church explains its recovery and reinvigoration,
and the revival and flourishing of religious life during this period. However, in order to gain an accurate picture we also need to examine the
countervailing trends that appeared in various areas of policy.

1.2.4.6 The Policy of Restrictions

1.2.4.6.1 Steps towards the Secularization of Society

Alongside its policy of concessions, the government took, as we have
said, slow, deliberate steps to limit the church's domain and reduce its
influence. One of the first steps was the introduction of new legislation
on marriage and divorce, which established standard procedures for civil
marriage and divorce throughout Poland.[141] The Marriage Law adopted
on 25 September 1945, which came into force on 1 January 1946, invalidated the legal force of religious marriages (article 37). In practice, the
government considered the new law a temporary measure and began,
already in this period, preparing for a general reform of the entire codex
of matrimonial laws.

The Public Health Service Law of 28 October 1948 should be seen in
a similar context. The law authorized the minister of health to relate to
health institutions maintained by communities, organizations, or religious denominations as if they were public institutions belonging to the
health service. Moreover, the law authorized the Council of Ministers to
nationalize medical institutions without indemnification and to transfer

them under government administration.[142] This, in fact, provided the basis for transferring church hospitals into state hands. The same legislative framework transferred registration of births and deaths from church authority to the state through the civil courts. Only the cemeteries remained under the direct supervision of the churches. An earlier step towards secularization had been taken in 1947, with the cancellation of the requirement that citizens report any change in their religion. The registration of religion in official documents was subsequently eliminated in 1948.[143]

The secularization campaign also affected the oath customary in the state's institutions and its different bodies. As early as December 1944 the religious oath required for swearing in judges and public officials was replaced with a secular oath.[144] On the other hand, the military oath was only secularized after the elections, under a law dated 3 July 1947.[145]

The annulment of the concordat also brought about a significant incursion on the status of the church in the army. One consequence was that the Vatican could no longer appoint the military chaplains (*ordynariusz*) and the Communist government intervened directly in these appointments. Despite its reservations and lack of confidence regarding the military priests appointed by the government, the church resigned itself to the situation so as not to deny soldiers religious service. In July 1948 the bishops and apostolic administrators published a church decree providing strict guidelines for army chaplaincy activities.

1.2.4.6.2 Tendencies Contradicting Moderate Formulations and Gestures of Friendship

Despite their tolerant statements and conciliatory gestures toward the church, government leaders and representatives began resorting to methods which contravened the promised religious and civil rights. While this phenomenon was in evidence before the 1947 elections, it became even more pronounced afterwards and found expression in statements that threatened the church indirectly, and through practical efforts to disrupt religious rites, for example by organizing political conferences and meetings especially for this purpose. Bierut's comment in his interview with Pruszyński about maintaining the material privileges that had been awarded to the church must be seen against this background.[146] Bierut declared: "This state of affairs...depends only on whether the clergy in Poland clearly and unequivocally shows that it stands on the realistic ground...that grants it all this." A more severe tone appeared in Cyrankiewicz's speech, dated 30 October 1947, in which he denounces the "attacks by the clergy against the people's democracy" and berates "those members of the church who abandoned their people during the occupation" (alluding to Cardinal Hlond) for being "troublemakers".[147]

The government, which found itself quite helpless in the face of the pastoral letters and the church's capacity to influence the population's behavior, accused the church of abusing the freedom given to it and of inciting the faithful against the state and the democratic bloc. This was done in response to the Częstochowa's pastoral letter, dated 8 September 1947, which was read out in churches throughout Poland on 28 September 1947. The letter testifies, indirectly, to the pressure exerted on the Catholic population, especially during the second half of 1947, to join the democratic bloc parties, sometimes under threat of being fired.[148]

The increasingly hostile atmosphere was clearly evident from the government press. *Głos Ludu*, PPR's chief organ, came out against the church hierarchy's position, stating that "it proves that the path to harmony between the church and the government will not be easy".[149] Bitter anti-Catholic articles appeared in the atheistic and materialistic literature which the government began publishing, with the assistance of such associations as the Society for Free Thinking.[150]

The government also revealed its arbitrary position through the nature of its contacts with the church, which were conducted in a manner dictated by the government and unacceptable to the episcopate. Despite the episcopate's demands for the establishment of a committee for this purpose, the contacts were in fact conducted through a representative from each side. The initial talks took place between the government representative, Wolski, and the episcopate's secretary, Bishop Choromański, as early as October 1946, and continued with breaks until the middle of 1948. At that point, Choromański issued a demand to establish a commission which Wolski, in a discussion that took place on 25 November 1948, responded to as follows: "If the episcopate is interested in a commission, let it establish one. The government has no need for a commission. I am its representative and that is enough."[151]

However, the most drastic indications of the hard-line position to-wards the church were manifested in the legal persecution and police surveillance of certain priests. This intensified at the end of 1947 and the beginning of 1948 and was marked by an increase in state-terror methods employed by the government and which could be discerned in the media publications of the day. The political trials came as a response to immediate government needs, but they should also be seen as the early stages in the gathering of legal and propaganda material for use against the church at a future date.[152] On 24 July 1948 an official com-muniqué was issued by Radkiewicz, the minister in charge of the security services, concerning the arrest of 21 priests accused of subversive activ-ity. Among those arrested were Leon Pawlik, head of the Warsaw branch of Caritas, and the priest Grzechnik, who was in charge of the Holy Mother parish in Warsaw. Pawlik's trial opened on 5 August 1947, at the same time as the trial of Augustyński, the former editor of the PSL organ. The two were charged with gathering secret military infor-mation and conveying it to organizations hostile to the regime, both at home and abroad. Augustyński was sentenced to 15 years and Father Pawlik to 10. Among the unfriendly steps taken by the government, we should also refer to the recognition of other religious denominations (see section 1.2.2 above) although there is no reason to exaggerate its importance as it had little practical influence. We should also mention the propaganda campaign against the Vatican and the episcopate in 1948, in relation to the pope's message to the German bishops.

1.2.4.6.3 Censorship and Publication Restrictions

From the end of the war, the scope of the Catholic press was limited and subjected to preventive censorship and paper rationing. Censorship was not particularly onerous at this stage, however, and wide press circula-tion was permitted. From the outset, preventive censorship was also im-posed on pastoral letters and papal encyclicals. Immediately after the war, at any rate, the government still refrained from obstructing the reading of pastoral letters from the pulpit.

The policy of restricting periodicals and Catholic publications changed from time to time and corresponded to general political devel-opments in the country. As part of government efforts to increase its own power and weaken the focal points of opposition, mainly during the election campaign, a central bureau for the supervision of the press, publications, and films was established in the first half of 1946. In that same year there was an intensification of censorship that affected, *inter alia*, the Catholic press. Many copies of publications were confiscated, causing financial damage, and circulation was restricted by cutting paper supplies. After the January 1947 elections censorship of Catholic publications was many times more oppressive. The episcopate bears witness to this in its pastoral letter, dated 8 September 1947: "...among the most degrading restrictions...censorship of the press. This censorship does not exclude those with the most lofty moral authority...prevents the publication of papal encyclicals, pastoral letters, Catholic books..."[153] The restrictions included the sporadic nationalization of Catholic printing plants and the refusal to allow the publication of a Catholic daily. This was in contrast to the license granted to "worthy" Catholics.[154] Moreover, the Catholic Press Agency that had existed before the war was not permitted to renew its operations, an action that was indicative of a more general tendency to limit freedom of association. The government also made it difficult for various Catholic organizations to resume their activities and prevented their reconstitution. Among these were Akcja Katolicka, which, before the war, had had branches all over Poland, and Inventus Christiana.

Despite this, there were periods of relaxation and attempts by the government to prevent an escalation in the confrontation towards a *Kulturkampf*.

1.2.4.6.4 Restrictions in the Area of Education

Although an unambiguous policy in education was only to be expected, the restrictions were imposed slowly. To start with, the government concentrated on the schools administered and supported by the church. The church was not granted the licenses necessary to reopen many of the schools which had existed prior to the war. Moreover, many of the schools that were reopened after the war were re-closed.[155] Thus in 1946 only about a quarter of the country's private schools were in the hands of the church.[156] Concurrently, propaganda was disseminated against "the evil influence of these [church] schools on the youth, for instilling values that do not conform to the spirit of any democratic regime".[157] This contrasted with the encouragement and support for the establishment of secular schools given by the Association of Friends of the Children. This association inherited the place of the Socialist Workers' Association of Friends of the Children, which had operated secular schools prior to the war. A great number of state schools were transferred to the association. The government took pains to praise the public benefit of the association's educational work and curriculum in those of its schools where religious instruction had been canceled. After the elections, pressure increased on parents to register their children for these schools.[158]

Religious education in state schools was also subject to great obstacles and severe restrictions. As far back as 1945 it had been decided that only priests could teach religion. This, in practice, decreased available staff and narrowed opportunities for teaching.[159] Later during this period, political qualifications were required from priests wishing to teach, and many were dismissed from teaching on false pretexts.[160] A Ministry of Education circular from 1945, allowing parents to decide whether their children should receive religious instruction, had little practical effect since almost all parents wished their children to attend religious classes. In 1947, as part of the secularization policy, the number of hours devoted to religious instruction in vocational schools was reduced from two hours to one and completely eliminated from adult education. In the academic world, the trend was reflected in the fact that the many requests by the clergy to re-establish the theology department at the University of Wrocław, in place of the departments that existed before the war in Lvov (Lwów) and Vilna (Wilno), went unheeded.

The Communist-organized Teachers' Congress of 1948 accurately exemplifies the growing tendency to drive the church from the educational arena. The congress demanded that clerical influence in the schools be torn up by the roots and that the curriculum be based on Marxist principles. A similar tendency was expressed, for example, in attempts at an exclusive and massive mobilization of youth into a government youth organization, following the PPR's decision to unite all youth organizations under a single umbrella. This formed part of an effort to remove Polish youth from the church's sphere of influence. An overview of the chronological development of the state policy of restrictions shows that the 1948/1949 academic year marked a turning point and signaled the beginning of the elimination of religion from schools.

1.2.5 SUMMARY OF GOVERNMENT POLICY

The balance sheet of government policy towards the church in the years 1945 to 1948 was positive for the church. Undoubtedly, the church had been severely curtailed relative to its situation before the war. However, when we weigh the restrictions imposed on the church against the benefits it received, and compare this with that of the other social, political, and ideological non-Communist institutions—especially considering the processes that had overtaken Poland and the state of affairs in other East European countries—then we see that the Polish Roman Catholic Church was in an exceptionally good situation.

1.2.6 PERSONAL POLICY

1.2.6.1 Basic Positions and Values

Exposed as Gomułka was to the ideas of the left, from his earliest youth through both his father and his own activities in socialist organizations, he had also internalized the ideological principles regarding religion and the church. However, within the scope of his revolutionary activities in the ranks of the KPP in Poland between the two world wars, Gomułka had been able to see at first hand the discrepancies between ideological dogma and practical politics present also in everything that related to the Polish Catholic Church.[161] His pragmatic approach and firm grasp of realities were reinforced during the Second World War. As the secretary of the small, weak PPR, whose main efforts were directed to waging an underground struggle against the Germans, Gomułka's was the loudest voice of those in his camp calling for a united national effort, which would bring together the most far-flung parts of the nation. His experience of cooperation with non-Communist elements during the war included religious individuals and church figures. Chava A., who was accepted into the underground by him and who worked with him during those years, has also spoken (to the author) about this cooperation.[162] Gomułka and his comrades found this experience highly useful to their struggle.[163] On the other hand, his practical approach to the church and religion was influenced by another aspect of his ideological make-up: Gomułka's devotion to socialism was extremely straightforward and did not involve any deep, complex, theoretical examination of socialist doctrine. This was the source of his firm and open atheism, which was a creed and way of life, leaving no room for lenience toward religious beliefs and convictions and even causing him to scorn them. Emma Mazur, who was in close contact with the Gomułka family, tells of the unambiguous contempt that Gomułka showed toward the church and the clergy on many occasions.[164] Gomułka's tendency to focus on practical politics engendered, therefore, an apparently contradictory approach to religion. His close contact with religion did not moderate his position: it had, in fact, just the opposite effect. Like other Polish Communists, Gomułka was influenced by the fact that Catholicism was a day-to-day reality, which cast its influence in all directions. It was a challenge he needed to face in his immediate surroundings, in his own family. He certainly did not approve of his mother's or his sister Ludwika's devoutness. However, according to different testimony (e.g. Emma Mazur) his main anger was directed against the religious development of his son, who, during the war, was educated by his mother and absorbed her religious views and habits. Gomułka did not rest until his son's 're-education' was complete. It is worth citing, in this context, his wife Zophia's Jewish origins. Additional vital factors, necessary to explain his personal attitude and his policies toward the church during the first years after the war, stemmed from the formal functions and capacity in which he operated during the period,[165] his place in the new regime, and the system of power relations.

1.2.6.2 Characteristics of Personal Policy

An examination of Gomułka's actions and his statements regarding religion and the church in this period reveals three outstanding characteristics, which conform to the direction of the general systemic policy: a) superficially, Gomułka's activity appears to have been restricted, veiled, and undistinguished, especially in the national sphere; b) of the priorities that Gomułka attaches to different policy areas, little importance is granted to the church; and c) an analysis of Gomułka's sparse statements and actions related to the church shows a favorable position towards the church on the tactical level.

In compliance with the general line of the PPR, which refrained from presenting the position towards the church as the position of the party[166] the first secretary also abstained from any public activity on the issue (i.e. from outwardly representing that policy). He acted with similar restraint in his other capacities as deputy prime minister and minister for the liberated territories. This approach was all the more striking given the role played in this matter by other non-PPR members of the government, starting with Prime Minister Osóbka-Morawski, followed by Cyrankiewicz,[167] and ending with the transport minister, Jan Rabanowski. Impressive corroboration of this can be found in the differing responses by the prime minister and the first secretary to the Kielce pogrom of 5 July 1946. In contrast to Osóbka-Morawski, who on 8 July 1946 explicitly denounced the Roman Catholic Church in Poland as being equally responsible with the supporters of Mikołajczyk's Peasant Party for the pogrom, Gomułka did not mention the church at all in his response and pointed an accusing finger towards members of the PSL and people from Armia Krajowa (the Organization for Military Resistance, which operated between 1942 and 1945 under the control of the Polish government-in-exile), blaming them for the blood bath. Indeed, Gomułka's relative inactivity is even more conspicuous when compared with Bierut's intense involvement and activity where the church was concerned. Gomułka was not partner to Bierut's public gestures towards the church,[168] or to his open contacts with Hlond and other members of the hierarchy (such as, for example, the talks he held with Hlond in 1946 concerning the resumption of diplomatic relations with the Vatican), or even to the demands and warnings that Bierut sent their way. An examination of Gomułka's speeches before the 30 June 1946 referendum and the January 1947 elections reveals an abundance of national and patriotic slogans. However, they do not include a direct approach to the church on this matter. This is striking if we compare the appeals by Bierut and Osóbka-Morawski during the same period.[169]

The policy of deferring confrontation with the church to a later stage was conspicuously evident in Gomułka's case. We see this from the relatively scant attention that he paid to the subject, and by the slow and cautious way he chose to deal with the problem. The goals that the PPR set out to achieve through its policy of stages therefore formed the focus of Gomułka's efforts. His positive stance towards the church was part and parcel of a strategy to delay confrontation with it.

The main evidence of Gomułka's personal policy can be seen in his activities as minister for the liberated territories. In this capacity, in which he played a key role in mobilizing new settlers for the territories, Gomułka in fact granted material incentives and benefits to religious elements and church staff, while promising that religion would have a place in the new Poland (including the allocation of funds for building new churches and rebuilding existing ones). A Western diplomatic source, stationed in Warsaw in 1945, reported that Gomułka paid personal visits to several bishops to exhort them to concern themselves with bringing priests to the liberated territories while promising his assistance. According to the source, this was his response to the widespread reluctance to settle in the western territories if the government failed to organize religious services for newcomers.[170] The constraints, which go a long way toward explaining Gomułka's seemingly radical moves in this matter, were presented in a highly dramatic way in a report submitted by Father Nowicki, the apostolic administrator of Gorzów. In a paper published in 1947 for the fourth session of the Scientific Council for the Liberated Territories, Nowicki describes how "...the populace desperately searched for a Polish priest everywhere...and when they did not receive help from the government, they began to help themselves in a most unusual way—they began searching for priests on the trains which carried repatriates and begged them to remain. And if the effort, which was not always a success, indeed failed, they took the priest's baggage and forced him in this way to discontinue his trip. In other locations settlers abandoned their places and wandered tens of kilometers searching for a community that already had a Polish priest."[171] Such facts explain the absence of confrontations in Gomułka's personal relations with the church hierarchy during this period. Gomułka, who desperately needed the assistance of the church in order to fulfill the mission of the party and the nation, took pains to 'stay clean of incriminating evidence' in his relations with the church and its leadership. This also explains his relations with Hlond, which were free from any special tension. The same diplomatic source reported his positive relations with Wyszyński, the future primate of Poland. According to this source, the first contacts between Gomułka and Wyszyński took place in 1945 on the issue of mobilizing priests for the liberated territories.[172]

Gomułka's speeches and articles during these years mirrored these tendencies faithfully. The three characteristics noted above are clearly evident from these documents. We are struck by the minimal amount of space devoted to religion and the church in Gomułka's articles and speeches.

From one of Gomułka's rare statements on these issues[173] one can learn of the important role of religion in defining Polish nationalism and of the significant contribution made by Catholic activists and other Christian elements to the cause of Polish nationalism in the liberated territories. On the occasion in question, Gomułka mentions five principles adopted by the Association of Poles in the German Republic for their program to define Polish nationalism. He points out that the second principle, which determined that "the religion of our forefathers is the religion of our children", has, for him, eternal validity. He continues: "...we recall that the defenders of Polish nationalism, the defenders of the Polish people in the liberated territories, were, in the past, Catholic social activists as well as Protestants...who strove to maintain the Polish language and fought against the Germanization of the Polish people".[174] In order to maintain a balance, and so as not to overstate his praise for the Catholic Church, Gomułka is careful to mention the Protestant contribution along with the Catholic contribution. Similarly, he refers to both factors when detailing the religious rights and benefits granted by People's Poland, conforming to the general policy of stressing the equality of religions. "People's Poland does not impose on any citizen religious beliefs alien to him. The Catholic and the Evangelical churches can develop in total freedom and enjoy the state's protection."[175] Reference to the positive policy of the new government regarding religion and the church in the same breath as the contribution of religion to the cause of Polish nationalism was, it appears, designed to diminish the weight of that contribution. It is no coincidence that the rare occasions on which Gomułka expressed himself publicly and positively on the religious issue involved the liberated territories, which demanded almost all his attention at the time, and where religion, as we have seen, was a crucial factor. The abundance of articles and speeches referring to the liberated territories provides stark evidence of the central role that the subject fulfills in his public, and his behind-the-scenes, activity. Moreover, in his speeches and articles on other subjects, the issue of the territories is repeatedly mentioned.

Thus we find him stating that, "the autochthonous Polish population in the liberated territories will not encounter even the slightest of hindrances by the government in maintaining the religion of their forefathers and in the education of their children in accordance with this religion. The democratic principle of freedom of conscience, and hence also the freedom of faith for all citizens, will be fully guaranteed."[176]

1.2.6.3 Restrictions

Gomułka's caution and his overtures of peace toward the church did not prevent his indirect, veiled activity in the opposite direction. Even if this activity was narrow in scope it involved, as one would expect, very substantive decisions and steps. Thus Gomułka was actively involved in promoting Piasecki's political career. His positive attitude towards Pax, and his personal contact with it, were conspicuously evident in his meeting with Piasecki in September 1945, when the latter was released from prison. Gomułka then expressed his personal approval of the main points in the action program advanced by the Progressive Catholic Movement.[177]

Gomułka also participated in the criticism and attacks against the Vatican—once again on a limited scale and by particularly indirect means. On the rare occasions that the Holy See was mentioned in his speeches and articles we find that Gomułka was more sharply critical of the Apostolic See than his colleagues in the government, outside the context of Polish politics.[178] Moreover, his criticism of the Vatican and the church in Italy in fact included references to demands and principles which Gomułka demanded should be fulfilled in church-state relations and which, as we have seen, he avoided doing in the Polish context: "...the results of the Italian elections were also affected by the unprecedented intervention of the Vatican and the church in politics. The church, that is supposed to be the house of God for all believers, became, in Italy, a clubhouse for De Gasperi's party. The clergy, that was supposed to spread the Christian teachings of peace and love, became, in Italy, the seed of fanatic hatred for democrats and the main support for the ambitions of US imperialism. Pope Leo XIII, who understood the danger to the church from intervention in politics, once said that 'help by the church for one party against its opponent amounts to a crime against religion'. Despite this, the church in Italy joined the election campaign against the democratic front...the Italian bishops...exploited religion and their hold on the believers in order to influence the outcome of the elections...such methods do not strengthen the status of the church and will not increase its prestige among its supporters."[179]

1.2.6.4 The Church as a Component in Gomułka's Conception of the Polish Path to Socialism

Bowing to the dictates of Polish realities (Gomułka stresses again and again in his speeches the importance of the real links between theory and practice), which raised severe parametric obstacles at this stage, and without forfeiting long-range programmatic goals, Gomułka postponed direct confrontation with the church to a vague future date.[180] He was not the originator of the conception of the distinct Polish path to socialism in regard to the church (and also agriculture). As early as the 1920s there had been supporters for this conception in the Polish Communist camp. In subsequent years it was Lampe who preceded Gomułka in the formulation of a step-by-step plan which took into account the power of Polish Catholicism (and the difficulties in introducing collectivization into agriculture). The conceptual influence of Bieńkowski, who was among Gomułka's own circle of associates, is no secret.[181] The former's strategic conception, which sought to weaken the hold of the church and religion by spreading apathy towards the whole issue, while avoiding any direct struggle was discernible in Gomułka's behavior and formulations. It is reasonable to assume that this was one of the considerations determining the limited treatment of the subject in Gomułka's speeches and in the party's theoretical organs. All this, together with the dominant Soviet conception and PPR's systemic policy, does not detract from the fact that, due to his personality and status, Gomułka, more than anyone else during this period, represented both the practical and theoretical sides of policy towards the church, a policy which formed a vital component of the Polish path toward socialism. His ousting from the leadership did indeed mark the end of an era and the beginning of a fundamental turn for the worse in policy towards the church.

2. The Stalinist Era

2.1 POLICY ENVIRONMENTS

2.1.1 The Roman Catholic Church

2.1.1.1 The Balance of Power during the Period

It is customary to consider 1949 as the year which marked the beginning of a serious deterioration in the position of the church in Poland. This was part of the general shift in Communist policy in Eastern Europe at the time. The shift, as is known, was characterized by intensive terror and the increased use of administrative measures in all walks of life. However, despite the repressive tendencies and the contraction in the base of its power resources—to a point which created serious doubts about the future existence of the church in Poland—we can say, in retrospect, that *the church's hold on the Poles did not weaken, but, on the whole, in fact found itself further strengthened. As in the past, the period of suffering and pressure carved the church's martyrological image even deeper and became a latent source of power, mainly for the coming periods.* The church's perseverance in the fulfillment of its traditional national role and its refusal to surrender brought under its roof not only devout Catholics but many others who wished to protest, in this way, against the regime and its policy.[1]

2.1.1.2 Organizational Consolidation

During the period under review, church organization in fact moved towards stabilization. The reconstruction of the church organization throughout Poland, which began, as noted, immediately after the war, was concluded, more or less, at the beginning of the period under discussion.[2] The remarkable expansion experienced by the church in the liberated territories was not blunted nor did it lose its effectiveness as a result of the new political trends. In an interview that Wyszyński granted to the editor-in-chief of the weekly *Tygodnik Powszechny*, J. Turowicz, in February 1951 after his return from visiting the Vatican, Wyszyński stressed the vigorous activity of the church in the western territories during recent years and the rapid development of the church organization there: "More than seven million Catholics live in these territories today…in the Gorzów diocese alone there are more than a thousand churches and chapels, where, before the war, there were less than a hundred."[3] The dismissal of the apostolic administrators in the liberated territories[4] also contributed, paradoxically, to the stability of the church organization in these territories by creating a more permanent structure.

A highly significant and remarkable source of stamina, at the time when the government was raising many difficulties for the church, revealed itself in the figure of Archbishop Stefan Wyszyński. The death of Cardinal August Hlond towards the end of the previous period (22 October 1948) did not leave the primate's office empty for long. Approximately three weeks after Hlond's death, on 16 November 1948, the pope appointed the bishop of Lublin, Father Wyszyński, to be the archbishop of Gniezno-Warsaw. (This appointment was published at the beginning of January 1949. The exact date appears in Wyszyński's first pastoral letter, which was read from the pulpits on 6 February 1949). Wyszyński was well known in Poland for his activities with the Christian trade unions and for his publications on labor issues. During the pre-war years he was one of the outstanding figures among those Catholic circles which supported social progress and held that the church should adapt itself to modern conditions[5] without relinquishing the influence of Catholic spirituality on state and society. In 1948, due to his relatively young age (47 years old), which was a marked contrast to the age of his predecessor, and owing to his special qualifications and qualities, Wyszyński succeeded in breathing new hope into the Polish Catholic Church.[6] The death of Cardinal Sapieha in Kraków on 23 July 1951 underscored even further a changing of the guards between the different generations in the church leadership and directed the spotlight toward Wyszyński. The special stature enjoyed by Sapieha in the church (his courage and devotion[7] had been the cause of his broad influence among the masses in the previous period) continued until his death and was manifested towards the end of his life in his defense of the church against government attacks. Wyszyński's appointment as cardinal and fellow of the Sacred Collegium in November 1952[8] came as the formal endorsement by the Apostolic See of his unchallenged stature as the Polish primate and preeminent figure in the Catholic world.

2.1.1.3 Value System and Positions on Current Issues

The church's steadfastness in this difficult period stemmed largely from the principles, rules of conduct, and forms of action that it adopted. Its adaptability was enhanced by the cumulative lessons of its activities under pressure between 1945 and 1948, in wartime and even earlier. Once again, these principles and methods dictated a spirit of militancy, which was grounded in a striking political realism. In other words, the church had the ability to adapt to the new situation—on the one hand by firm adherence to fundamentals, which were, for it, a question of life or death (*non possumus*), and on the other hand, by demonstrating political flexibility and making calculated concessions to the government, designed to avert any reason or justification for employing drastic measures against it. This sophisticated policy, which represented a combination of restrained militancy and concessions that did not amount to surrender, was designed to preserve those rights that the church still enjoyed and to dissipate tensions in its relations with the state. The church also sought to act in conformity with the principle of *raison d'état*, both in theory and practice, and to avoid the imposition of severe trials on the faithful.

The church's uncompromising stance on crucial issues was also impressive at those times when its leaders were tending more toward concession and compromise. One example of this can be found in the way the church modeled its public response after signing the April 1950 agreement. An article by Stanisław Stomma and Jerzy Turowicz, which appeared in *Tygodnik Powszechny* on 10 December 1950[9] and reflected, as became clear, the views of the episcopate, explained that

> Catholics can make concessions—and in Polish reality they do indeed abstain from struggling over the political goals of the state, and from the struggle to establish a social order in accordance with their ideals. This is done in conformity to life under a different regime. *As against this, they will never, in any circumstances, refrain from the struggle for Christian culture and Christian life content. They cannot give up the struggle for tomorrow's Christian culture.*
>
> ...the duty to fight for the Christian ideal of life binds all Catholics...however, when speaking about the establishment of a new culture, Catholicism in Poland has a dangerous competitor, Marxism...with its different ideal of culture...this [materialist] ideal is opposed to the Catholic ideal...two great dynamic camps, each with its own intensive ideological convictions, are now engaged in an attempt to realize their cultural ideal in Poland. Therefore, conflict is inevitable...it is fundamental and laden with pathos. We are talking about the ideological future of the coming generations in Poland. (Emphases added.)

In a later article,[10] which explicitly addressed the 1950 agreement, the same writers presented the position of the hierarchy again, explaining: "The agreement is a practical compromise for coexistence between the church in Poland and the Marxist camp which rules the country...it is a non-ideological compromise for coexistence...*which does not abolish the ideological struggle.* The agreement...comes to achieve social peace in Poland, to facilitate cooperation between Catholics and Marxists *on behalf of the national cause.*" (Emphases added.)

Moreover, when heavy-handed repressive action increased, the episcopate came out with appeals—necessarily political in nature—against atheism and materialism[11] and directly attacking Marxist ideology: "The responsibility...falls on the Marxist ideology [of the doctrine]...it is incredible how an ideology which claims to base itself on science and facts can make *a priori* assertions regarding religion without any evidence..."[12] The church's unwavering position on the preservation of its status and role according to the dictates of the faith can be found earlier in *Pro Memoria*, which was transmitted to the priests by the episcopate in May 1951[13]; this position was also prominent in the episcopate's memorandum concerning the 1952 draft constitution[14] and in *Tygodnik Powszechny*'s article regarding article 70 in the above draft.[15]

2.1.1.4 Response to Government Attack and Restriction

Despite increasing repression and coercion, and precisely as a consequence of such acts, the episcopate frequently responded to government moves. The church proclaimed its reactions and its protestations in pastoral letters; through the albeit censored press; in memoranda, missives, and telegrams addressed to the government leadership; and in sermons from church pulpits, which proved most effective. In this way it also fortified the strength of the believers. The following are examples of the church's responses.

As early as 13 April 1949 a pastoral letter from the episcopate replied to a series of attacks by the government following the PZPR unification congress. The letter, which was completely censored, was nevertheless read out in the churches on 24 April 1949. The takeover of Caritas did not occur without resistance. The next day Cardinal Sapieha, chairman of Caritas National Headquarters, sent a telegram of protest to Bierut.[16] A pastoral letter to the Polish clergy, read out in the churches on 30 January 1950, was yet another form of protest. (With the exception of those which were disturbed by the secret police). In this letter the bishops denied the government's allegations, which had appeared during the takeover, and sharply protested the Caritas takeover.[17] There was also a protest proclamation signed by all archbishops and ordinary bishops. Both the secretary of the episcopate, Bishop Choromański, in a letter to the minister of public administration, Wolski, dated 4 February 1950, and Cardinal Sapieha, in a letter dated 16 February 1950 and sent to President Bierut in the name of the entire episcopate, repeatedly emphasized the church's protest.[18]

The church leadership repeatedly complained against government actions which contradicted explicit commitments, such as those included in the 1950 agreement, the decree concerning freedom of conscience and faith, and in the 1952 constitution. Thus, in a message addressed to President Bierut and drawn up in Częstochowa in September 1950, the bishops complained about the violations of the 1950 agreement. They also remonstrated that "the last five years in the history of the Catholic Church in Poland have witnessed unprecedented damage and abuse".[19] At the same time a letter, written in the same vein, was sent by the Polish primate and by Archbishop Sapieha to the Polish president complaining against the anti-church positions which contradicted the government's statements.[20]

The government's dismissal of the apostolic administrators in the liberated territories met with an immediate response from the episcopate, which saw the step as a blow to autonomous church administration.[21] In addition to the written appeal by Sapieha and Wyszyński to President Bierut (which went unanswered), Wyszyński met with Bierut personally. The contents of the talks and their results are not known. An extremely sharp response to state intervention in internal church affairs was also issued some time after the 9 February 1953 decree on ecclesiastical appointments was published. *In a memorandum from the episcopate to Bierut, dated 8 May 1953, the bishops enumerate the links in the chain of coercive measures and persecutions suffered by the church since the signing of the 1950 agreement.* Among other things, the episcopate memorandum emphasized its reservations regarding activities designed to force the clergy into political involvement. One example of this was participation in the 'Peace Operation', which required priests to sign the Stockholm Peace Declaration. Another was the pressure placed on priests to participate in demonstrations against German revisionism. A third example of interference in internal church affairs appears in the memorandum relating to the closure of *Tygodnik Powszechny* by the authorities pending replacement of its editorial board. The bishops stated bluntly that they were unable to obey a decree which contravened the constitution and harmed the laws of the church. "We do not have the right to render up to Caesar that which belongs to God."

The episcopate presented its memorandum as "testimony before God and history", thereby implying that there was no longer any basis for talks with the government, and referred to the damage resulting from the blows against religion and God inflicted by Marxism on the Polish people.[22] The government's exacerbation of the conflict evoked fierce responses by church figures. This was the setting for Cardinal Wyszyński's complaints against the wave of arrests and show trials of high-ranking members of the clergy, the outstanding case being that of Bishop Kaczmarek, which led to the primate's arrest. Wyszyński's speech at the 1953 Corpus Christi celebrations must be seen in the same light: "The Polish episcopate will defend its faith even at the cost of bloodshed."[23]

Whenever it could, the church did not stop at protestations and complaints and took more direct steps to frustrate government restrictions. Thus, for example, it refused to allow the registration of religious orders, thereby undermining the Decree Concerning Changes in the Provisions of the Law of Associations, dated 5 August 1949, which the government wished to employ in order to tighten its control of these orders.[24] It is also worth noting that during this period the church hierarchy preferred to attack Pax and the Patriotic Priests directly, in contrast to the previous period when they were satisfied with more moderate and indirect measures such as deleting Pax publications from the lists of Polish Catholic publications that appeared in *Tygodnik Powszechny* on 13 July 1947.

Wyszyński's arrest[25] did not radically affect the church's mode of operation in this period, and its protests and opposition continued.

2.1.1.5 Church Concessions and the Desire to Maintain the National Formula

Hand in hand with its unswerving spirit of militancy, the church nevertheless showed restraint, even in the face of the severest attacks and restrictions by the government. It took pains to clarify the rules governing its restraint, making it clear that these were dictated by the interests of the nation and the guidelines of Catholic doctrine. It is evident, however, that tactical considerations also contributed significantly to this approach.[26] This way, the church restricted its activities and statements mainly to church affairs. Only in mid-1955 were the pastoral letters dealing with national and social questions published.

The policy of concessions expressed itself in the *de facto* recognition extended by the church to the Communist regime, a recognition, which received indirect, formal approval in the 1950 agreement. This approach was also reflected in the good faith and positive attitude that the church expressed towards the goals and plans for national construction and development put forward by the regime. In their jointly authored article published in *Tygodnik Powszechny* on 10 December 1950,[27] Stanisław Stomma and Jerzy Turowicz wrote: "Socialism is a fact for us. We recognize the victory of the Communist camp and respect the faith, struggle, and sacrifices that this camp has made more than once for building the new regime. The Catholics who live within the framework of the socialist state are loyal to the regime...and we declare a readiness, on our part, to keep the struggle within the sphere of ideological, and definitely non-political, contradictions. We take upon ourselves restraints in this matter for two reasons: because of our future in the common homeland and because of the commandments of Christian ethics." The authors called for cooperation "wherever required". They expressed support for the six-year industrialization plan, which would, in their words, lift Poland out of its cultural backwardness, though the plan was motivated by a socialist ideal. Conforming to the same approach, in his pastoral letter of May 1951 Primate Wyszyński praised the "national economic effort", calling on the clergy "to abstain from interfering in political matters".[28] In addition, the church allowed further concessions, to the point that it guaranteed its neutrality regarding collectivization in agriculture. Moreover, church leaders chose not to protest the nationalization of church lands, wishing to avoid supplying the government propaganda machine with ammunition by creating the impression that their objection stemmed from the blow to the church's material base.[29] On the eve of the 1952 elections, the bishops called on the population to vote. This was similar to their position on the eve of the January 1947 elections and was in accord with government demands.

Within the framework of the national formula, the church repeatedly demonstrated full solidarity with the Communists regarding the liberated territories and Poland's boundaries.[30] In the 1950 agreement, the church undertook to convince the Vatican to recognize permanent Polish administration in the liberated territories. The episcopate even decided to agree to the appointment of capitular vicars in these territories as per the 26 January 1951 decree, despite the fact that it viewed the action as an open violation of the 1950 agreement[31] and saw the dismissal of the apostolic administrators as a miscarriage of justice against individuals.[32] Accordingly, on 18 February 1951 *Tygodnik Powszechny* published the primate's proclamation recognizing the authority of the capitular vicars and calling on believers to obey them and assist them in their work. Wyszyński initiated practical cooperation regarding these appointments in August 1951.[33] In December 1951 the same weekly published an interview with Primate Wyszyński on the subject of the church in the western territories. In this interview, the primate maintained that the episcopate's relationship to the territories had been consistent and clear from the moment of their restoration to Poland. Wyszyński also stressed that the entire population, the episcopate, and the government were of the same view with regard to the territories.[34]

Thus the church consistently maintained this position in order to frustrate government propaganda on this decisive issue and maintain its patriotic image in the eyes of the population.

The church's desire to reach a *modus vivendi* with the government in this period found expression in its position regarding two, decisive formal documents: the 1950 agreement and the 1952 constitution. Even before the 1950 agreement the church had indicated its desire for an understanding with the government during sessions of the joint commission on church–state issues. The accelerating campaign of repression strengthened its resolve even further because of its eagerness to protect and defend its status against future wrongdoing and repression. According to the agreement the church undertook to call on the priests to instruct the faithful to respect the law and the state authorities (articles 1 and 2); to endeavor to persuade the Apostolic See to change the interim ecclesiastical administration in the western territories into a permanent administration; to oppose by all means anti-Polish and revisionist activity by the German clergy (articles 3 and 4); to instruct the priests to desist from opposing collectivization in the countryside; to refrain from exploiting religious feelings for anti-state purposes (articles 6 and 7); to punish, under canon law, priests who took part, in any way, in subversive actions against the state; and to support all efforts for peace and against warmongering (article 9). In an attached protocol a concession regarding Caritas was also included.[35] According to an article by Father S. Wawryn that appeared in *Przegląd Powszechny*, No. 5, in May 1950 (under the title "The Logic Behind the Agreement Between the State and the Church"), the episcopate found itself in dire straits and was forced to make concessions: "...representatives of the episcopate came to the conclusion that concessions were necessary in order to guarantee the church freedom for religious and spiritual activity...[the church] agreed to concessions that it would not have accepted in other circumstances". In an episcopate communiqué, issued in Gniezno on 22 April 1950,[36] the bishops stressed that the national cause and public interest had motivated the church to sign the agreement. At a later date, in conjunction with their protests against the violation of the agreement and persecution, the bishops similarly explained their motives: "We wanted to supply decisive evidence of our good will and earnestness for peaceful coexistence...The church in Poland does not neglect or overlook anything that can advance peace, agreement, and conciliation, even if this de-

mands greater and greater sacrifices on its part...”[37] The extreme concessions made by the church in the 1950 agreement were especially
striking in light of the papal boycott—even though the church stressed
that the agreement was not equivalent to a concordat and that the Vatican had no part in it—and in the face of bitterness and complaints from
significant numbers of the faithful who protested and depicted it as a
compromise which would harm the church's image and its popularity
among the masses. The great importance that the church attached to the
agreement was demonstrated a month after the signing, when it realized
that it was unable to avoid signing the Stockholm Peace Declaration,
despite its understandable reservations.

On the eve of the adoption of the new 1952 constitution there were
deep anxieties among church circles that the new constitution would
damage the advantages achieved in the 1950 agreement. These concerns
led them to present a unified position to the effect that the April 1950
agreement must be considered the juridical basis for church–state relations. This position was presented straightforwardly in *Tygodnik
Powszechny* on 16 March 1952. It also emerged from the interview with
Wyszyński, which appeared in the same weekly two years after the
agreement was signed (27 April 1952) and in which he described the
agreement as a positive step in Polish life.

The fidelity to the 1952 constitution was expressed in an article in
Tygodnik Powszechny in August 1952, nearly two weeks after its confirmation on 22 July 1952. There, the constitution was presented as the
"foundation of national life". The writer calls on all Poles "to exhibit
genuine responsibility and creative endeavor in order to increase the
homeland's strength, within the framework of the social and political
reality defined by the constitution".[38]

2.1.1.6 Attitude towards the Vatican

Contact with the Vatican during the Stalinist era continued to provide a
vital source of strength for the Polish Church, and to a great extent dictated government action. At the beginning of the period, this contact,
which included updates and the coordination of positions, was maintained through visits to the Vatican by members of the episcopate. For
example, in December 1949 a delegation of the episcopate visited the

Vatican to clarify the situation regarding the church in Poland. Later, with the imposition of restrictions on these contacts by the Communist government (as we know, Wyszyński did not travel to Rome in order to receive the cardinal's red hat after his appointment as cardinal, for fear that he might not be permitted to return to Poland), the hierarchy found secret channels to maintain the connection. Griffith, a former United States' ambassador to Poland, testified in his memoirs: "From time to time I served as a secret emissary, delivering letters to the Holy See from high officials in the church."[39]

The protests by the church against the government's attacks and persecution included uninterrupted efforts to counter the venomous propaganda directed against the Holy See by the government press and radio, and to present the position of the Vatican on the western territories in a more positive light. In an interview that Wyszyński granted to the editor of *Tygodnik Powszechny* after visiting Rome, Wyszyński made an effort to emphasize the pope's good intentions and the amount of time he devoted to him in an effort to solve the problem of ecclesiastical administration in the western territories.[40] Approximately two weeks later, in an interview devoted to the question of the church in the western territories,[41] the primate found it necessary to stress the pope's more sympathetic position to Polish interests in the liberated territories, citing as evidence the "permission he granted for the establishment of church institutions in the western territories and his agreement with the decisions of the Polish episcopate".[42] Unqualified loyalty to the decrees and sanctions imposed by the Apostolic See in everything concerning the church's internal affairs was expressed in an interview given by Wyszyński to mark the second anniversary of the 1950 agreement[43]: "The Apostolic See and the Holy Father constitute for the Polish Church the unquestionable authority in questions of religion, morality, and judgment. Therefore, the internal organization of the church and internal discipline cannot be undermined." Despite the general nature of the wording, it is difficult to avoid seeing the statement in the context of the Vatican's 30 June 1950 decree of excommunication issued against schismatic priests in Eastern Europe, and which, in Poland, was directed at the Patriotic Priests and their like. It is also possible to interpret the statement by the primate in the context of the papal boycott of 28 June 1949, which received the force of a decree on 13 July 1949. On the other hand, the church considered it a duty to obey the decree concerning the

"defense of freedom of conscience and faith", from 5 August 1949, issued by the government as a measure against the papal boycott.

2.1.2 THE POPULATION

The loyalty and support of the Polish population, as became clear, did
not diminish as a result of the secularization measures and their accompanying pressure and terror. The government's initiative in this direction met with only limited success. The church even increased its hold
among the opponents of the regime, who, as we have seen, gave their
massive support to the church for understandable political reasons. Religion continued to develop its roots among the population and the
population continued to attend religious rites and ceremonies at the
churches *en masse*, despite the prevailing hardships. The people continued to exert social pressure on those who refrained from participating in
religious ceremonies, often as a result of direct pressure from the
priests.[44] Popular religious devotion at this time is perhaps encapsulated
best of all by the famous case of the Lublin Miracle. In July 1949 there
were rumors that the Madonna of Lublin Cathedral had shed tears of
blood. In the wake of the rumors, masses of believers streamed to Lublin
to witness the 'miracle'. Despite denials by the church about the existence of a miracle, believers did not lose their enthusiasm.[45]

     The large, enthusiastic crowds which greeted the primate and other
church leaders on their visits throughout Poland revealed sympathy and
support for Primate Wyszyński and the church. (A phenomenon that
stands in marked contrast to the limited number of people attending
party meetings). Such a mass reception greeted Wyszyński on his visit to
the western territories in late 1951. Special significance lay in this particular demonstration of sympathy. After this success, the government
prohibited *Tygodnik Powszechny* journalists from covering the primate's
visit to the western territories.[46] Moreover, the episcopate's moves and
its response to the ever-increasing restrictive measures introduced by
the Communist government were warmly welcomed by the masses. The
assault on the church leadership evoked still greater identification with it
and with the organization it represented. It is not difficult to gauge the
sentiments of the Catholic masses at the sight of the primate's vacant
seat following his arrest in 1953.

2.1.3 PAX AND THE PATRIOTIC PRIESTS

For Pax and the Patriotic Priests the years of repression in Poland were the signal for more direct and undisguised activity which expressed itself in both organizational-structural and functional ways.

The structural consolidation of the government-sponsored Catholics was characterized, at first, by activity in separate groups and, towards the end of the period, in 1955, by organization under more united auspices. On 1 September 1949 the unification conference of the Association of Fighters for Freedom and Democracy (ZBoWiD, Związek Bojowników o Wolności i Demokracji) took place in Warsaw and included a group of the Patriotic Priests. Later, a decision was adopted to organize a priests' section in the ZBoWiD framework. The Priests' Commission associated with the ZBoWiD was created in this manner.[47] Later on, subsequent to the unification of the Polish Committee of Fighters for Peace in November 1950, the Commission of Catholic Intellectuals (Komisja Intelektualistów i Działaczy Katolickich Przy Polskim Komitecie Obrońców Pokoju) was established. Mainly Catholic priests were mobilized into the commission.[48] On 12 July 1955 these two groups and their branches united with Pax and established the Progressive Catholic Movement. At the end of 1955 the movement numbered 5,000 priests and 2,500 militant Catholics. Additional members were mobilized at the beginning of 1956.[49]

At this time, in contrast to the earlier period, we witness the final crystallization of Pax's ideological program and its open dissemination, paralleling similar processes inside the Communist Party. Thus Bolesław Piasecki published an article called "Two Paths of Catholicism", in which he called for determined cooperation between believers and Communists,[50] and the book *Vital Issues*. In addition to the readily understood conflict with the church hierarchy, which sharpened as a result of these developments, it became clear that Piasecki's political vision, which definitely exceeded the role assigned to Pax by the government, also created some tension with the latter. Lucjan Blit goes so far as to describe Pax as a movement which, while collaborating with the ruling Communist Party, did not simply serve it, but saw itself as a competitor and even an alternative to it.[51] In this phase, the Patriotic Priests—whose structural and organizational consolidation was accompanied by ideological declarations and moralistic slogans calling for 'purges' and 'reforms' in the church—were also characterized by the open proclamation of their ideas and their consequent acclaim.

Pax and the Patriotic Priests supported the government's steps with evident enthusiasm. This support was expressed first of all in extensive and systematic propaganda in their specially privileged press (the weekly *Dziś i Jutro*; the daily *Słowo Powszechne*; and *Głos Kapłana* representing the commissions of priests associated with ZBoWiD). Their activity on behalf of the government, in addition to their active support for its policies towards the church, included the dissemination of propaganda and assistance in implementing collectivization in agriculture and the fulfillment of other government set assignments. Stehle points out that, up to 1950, Pax was to a large degree a mediating force between the state and the church. He stresses Piasecki's contribution to reaching the agreement in April 1950.[52] There is no other evidence for this finding, which does not seem likely in the light of the episcopate's reservations.[53] These circles played an increasingly growing part in the mounting acts of repression against the church[54] through their active participation in all the government's propaganda campaigns and even through their own initiative. In their protest, dated 8 May 1953, the bishops complained that "in all of the disputes between the church and the government they always took sides with the government, praising it noisily and supporting its every step against the church."[55] The empirical evidence in fact confirms the bishops' claim. In the campaign waged by Pax and the Patriotic Priests against the church establishment, these elements came out with attacks against the "reactionary" hierarchy, its members,[56] and even the Vatican. Despite their continued acknowledgment of the supreme authority of the last, they condemned its support for "reactionary" policies. Their efforts to reach an agreement with the Vatican, as it turned out, were a total failure.[57]

During these years Pax continued to enjoy, and even to consolidate and expand, the privileges awarded to it in the past. The 'patronized' priests received special personal, material compensation, either through increased income or by reductions in, and exemption from, taxes. The doors to the Sejm, however, remained closed to them.[58] Despite the relatively broad opportunities and power resources open to Pax and the Patriotic Priests, their practical influence in society and among the clergy remained marginal.

2.1.4 THE VATICAN

Between 1949 and 1956 the Apostolic See maintained its firm, negative position regarding the new situation in Eastern Europe, including Poland, while stubbornly refusing to establish diplomatic relations or to recognize the Oder-Neisse boundary. Moreover, the Vatican intensified the struggle against the regimes in Eastern Europe in response to their increasing repression of the church. Thus in June/July 1949, the Holy See took a drastic step, mainly in response to unprecedented efforts to destroy the unity of the church in Czechoslovakia. On 28 June 1949 the plenum of the Holy Synod adopted a decision which stated that Catholics who supported or belonged to the Communist Party consciously and willingly and who read and disseminated Communist propaganda were considered, *ipso facto*, as having deviated from the Catholic faith and therefore sentenced to ostracism and ex-communication by the Apostolic See and denied the Holy Sacraments. This decision was ratified by the pope and published as a papal edict in *Acta Apostolicae Sedis* on 13 July 1949. The Vatican organ, *L'Osservatore Romano*, referring to the above edict in its issue of 27 July 1949, did clarify that those Catholics who were lured by the promises of Communist leaders, or whose positive attitude to Communism was motivated by aspirations of social reform, *but who did not adopt its basic doctrine*, would not be ostracized.[59] (Emphases added.) In any event the church encountered serious difficulties in enforcing the edict in the Eastern European countries. A later, supplementary step in the Vatican's efforts to preserve the church's unity found expression in a decree, dated 30 June 1950, which ostracized schismatic priests in Eastern Europe.[60] The Vatican revealed its official position towards Pax openly, and towards Piasecki personally, only on 8 June 1955, when it denounced the theories represented by *Dziś i Jutro* and forbade believers either to read or assist in the distribution of this weekly. Lucjan Blit ascribes the late date of the denunciation to the Vatican's efforts to deny the Stalinist regime in Poland any pretext for a campaign of persecution against the church.[61]

In the face of the repression and persecution the Holy See sent missives to the episcopate denouncing the government's restrictions and encouraging the bishops, the clergy, and the Catholic population to stand firm. For example, the pope's missive to the archbishop of Kraków, Sapieha, sent in September 1949, marking ten years since the

German aggression, reviewed the actions by the Communist government against the church. The Holy Father stressed that the "hour of trial is not yet over", and that "Poland has not yet achieved full independence".[62] In his letter to the Polish episcopate, dated 1 September 1951,[63] the pope urges the Polish clergy not to despair in the face of repression and persecution.[64] (The missive must be seen in the context of the beginning of the new school year.) Following Wyszyński's arrest and suspension the Vatican published a decree on 1 October 1953 excommunicating everyone involved. (The decree is identical in content to decrees published in previous years in connection with the arrest or arbitrary suspension of church leaders in other Eastern European countries such as Hungary and Czechoslovakia).

2.1.5 THE SOVIET UNION

As is known, the years of repression in Poland (1949–1955/56), as in other Eastern European countries under Soviet domination, were characterized by gross intervention in internal and external affairs. One of the main aspects of this intervention was the intensified Sovietization of all spheres of life, in imitation of existing Soviet models. Ideological entrenchment took place under conditions of increased Polish dependence on the Soviet Union and was linked to developments on the international level, mainly a polarization between the blocs, reflected in the Cold War and the Korean War. There was a clear deterioration in relations between all countries in the Eastern bloc and the Apostolic See. Hence, in the years under review, steps were taken to accelerate, as far as possible, the closure of the gap between the situation in Poland and the Soviet model regarding religion and the church. The role of religion in the Soviet regime was defined in article 114 of the Soviet Constitution: "In order to guarantee freedom of conscience to the citizens, the church in the Soviet Union is separated from the state, and schools from the church. All citizens enjoy freedom of religious ritual and freedom to conduct anti-religious propaganda."[65] As known, the right to religious freedom and even the right to conduct rites in Soviet reality was, in practice, violated. Despite the joint program for all the Peoples' Democracies, which received a special boost in this period and which encouraged the Polish Communists to attack the church and the clergy and curtail their activity,[66] the policy makers in Moscow restrained themselves, even then, from implementing this policy in Poland's case. Stalin did not completely disavow the existence of "special conditions for building socialism" in Poland and was ready to grant the Polish regime approval to make concessions, mainly where the church was concerned. This, despite the fact that after the defeat of the legal opposition the church was the strongest remaining organized enemy in Poland, and apparently for this very reason. The existence of a special section in the Soviet embassy in Warsaw, which monitored party policy on church issues, was impressive evidence of Soviet involvement in this area.[67]

2.2 POLICY

2.2.1 LEGAL BACKGROUND

During the Stalinist era the legal basis for the existence of the church in Poland became relatively fixed, clear, and defined as the trends alluded to in the earlier period crystallized. The trend towards repression and coercion did not exclude formal decisions—especially those authorizing restrictive practices and those taken to preempt offensive action by the church or church efforts against non-believers. However, as strange as it seems, the church continued to preserve quite extensive rights under the new conditions.

The main formal basis for the church's existence in this period is found in the agreement of 14 April 1950 and the 1952 constitution. Having said that, two decrees, which were published simultaneously at an earlier date (5 August 1949) are worth reviewing[68]: a) the Decree on Freedom of Religion and Conscience (*O Ochronie Wolności Sumienia i Wyznania*); and b) the decree dealing with several revisions in the Law on Associations ("*O Zmianie Niektórych Przepisów o Stowarzyszeniach*").[69] The first, and more important, decree came as a direct response to the boycott by the pope and mainly sought to guarantee a defense for Catholics at risk of sanctions by the church leadership. Despite the fact that the decree was designed—in response to the conditions which provoked it—to defend non-believers and 'free thinkers', it extended its defense, also, to believers. Article 2 of the decree provides for the imprisonment of anyone restricting the rights of any citizen on the grounds of religious affiliation, religious belief, or lack of the same. The decree prohibits the coercion of others, by any means, to participate in religious rites (article 3), and raises its voice against the misuse of religious freedom by denying religious services to people because of their political, social, or scientific activities or views (article 4) and the abuse of religious freedom for ends hostile to the regime and the Polish Republic (article 8). The decree also threatens imprisonment for whosoever exploits human gullibility for personal or financial gain or for any other purpose by disseminating false rumors (article 9), and for anyone accessory to these offenses. The decree also prohibits incitement against people because of their religious affiliation, and defines sanctions to be leveled against anyone guilty of offending religious sensibility by publicly deriding religious objects. In essence, the decree must be seen as an act which sought to threaten the church and limit its steps by interfering in matters of internal church jurisdiction and by imposing obligations which contradicted the papal boycott. However, government attempts, which undoubtedly stemmed from recognition of the church's power, to counteract and moderate this trend by calling into play articles in the defense of believers and their worship, should not be ignored. The second decree, which amends certain provisions of the Law on Associations, in effect attacked the church by mandating the supervision of religious orders and by creating a legal framework for unofficial associations (which had not existed in the past), thus canceling the advantages enjoyed by accredited religious associations until then.

The agreement, signed unexpectedly on 14 April 1950, between the Polish government and the Polish episcopate[70] contained substantial and far-reaching concessions by the Communist government. There is, therefore, nothing surprising about the fact that the Polish episcopate clung to the sections of the agreement in the years that followed.[71] In the agreement the government guaranteed to allow religious instruction in public schools—both elementary and secondary—as in the past, and decided that the curriculum would be drawn up jointly by the school authorities and representatives of the episcopate. The agreement guaranteed religious instructors equal status to that of other teachers, and stated that the appointment of religious instructors would be subject to approval by the church authorities. Pupils whose schools did not offer religious instruction would be allowed to transfer to schools that did if their parents so wished. Moreover, pupils were promised freedom of worship without any restrictions. The agreement gave equal status to Catholic and public schools. It was further decided that the Catholic University of Lublin would continue its work without any changes in the scope of its activities. *It is worth noting that a state guarantee of religious instruction, from elementary school level through to university, is unheard of even in the most liberal democracies, let alone in authoritarian Communist states!*

In the agreement the government acknowledged the principle that the pope was the supreme authority in the church in religious matters, morality, and ecclesiastical jurisdiction. The right of the church to maintain religious orders and associations, subject to the decree on associations (from 5 August 1949), was recognized. The document also recognized the right of the church to conduct charitable activity, to maintain its own press and publications, and to organize pilgrimages and processions. The government promised to regulate army chaplaincy activities and to permit religious services in hospitals and prisons. In a protocol attached to the agreement the authorities committed themselves to granting financial appropriations to the bishop's bureaus from the 'Church Fund' which was to be established upon the implementation of the decree for nationalizing church lands—an act that would strengthen the higher echelons of the church and that represented a departure from what the regime initially had in mind.[72] The government also guaranteed permission for priests to be active in Caritas (even though the organization did not revert to the direct control of the church), and granted deferrals from military service until the conclusion of their studies for students studying for the priesthood in religious seminars. It also exempted priests and monks from the burden of military service.

The new constitution of 1952, which was supposed to provide a less ambiguous and more permanent basis for the status of the church than in the past, did indeed take a step forward in this matter—by distancing itself from the transitory patterns of the first period, which had their origins in Poland's non-Communist past. However, it was still a long way from presenting the authentic Communist objectives on the question of church and state. The presence of ambivalent trends in the constitution stemmed from the fact that it was based, at one and the same time, on both the rigid model of the 1936 Stalinist constitution and on Poland's constitutional past. (The new constitution did not include an article concerning the freedom of anti-religious propaganda as appears in the 1936 Soviet constitution). Article 70 of the 1952 constitution is devoted to questions of the church.[73] Clause 1 of article 70 guaranteed citizens "freedom of conscience and faith" and permitted the church and other religious denominations to fulfill their religious functions freely. (Recognition for the special status of the Catholic Church relative to other religious denominations is implied here.) According to the article it was both forbidden to prevent citizens forcibly from participating in a religious rite and equally forbidden to force participation in such a rite. This, in contrast to the 1949 Decree on Freedom of Conscience and Religion which is explicit only regarding the last prohibition. Clause 2 stipulates separation of church and state, a principle recognized for the first time as a norm of constitutional consequence. In the spirit of the above mentioned 1949 decree, clause 3 stipulates that "the abuse of freedom of conscience and faith for purposes harmful to the interests of the Polish People's Republic is punishable by law."

2.2.2 GENERAL POLICY CHARACTERISTICS

With the consolidation of their political strength, a process which culminated in the Unification Congress in December 1948 and the establishment of the PZPR, the Communists had more freedom to concentrate greater efforts and attention on the church. In line with the prevailing tendency toward repression and coercion at this stage throughout the Eastern bloc,[74] Poland also experienced a tendency toward decisive operational decisions and an inflexibility in the pursuit of ideological objectives and the ruling group's goals. However, the policy makers' sense of their own gathering strength did not eliminate their perception of the special influence of religion and the church. Elements of political realism continued to characterize the leadership and to limit the means of struggle, though these were clearly intensified. As noted earlier,[75] the status of the church had deteriorated on the formal, legal level. However, in effect a gap was revealed which showed the church in a more grim light and which was emphasized by the reoccurring violation of official commitments. The characteristic policy line of this period was to narrow the church's living space, to limit its activity to the mere conduct of rites, and to replace it with pro-government clergy. Moreover, efforts to exploit the church and its influence with the populace in order to legitimize the regime and enlist support for its actions took the form more of coercion and threats and less of concessions and benefits than in the past.

As in the previous stage, the government demanded from the church not only loyalty to the regime and operation within the law, but also cooperation and assistance in achieving the government's goals. Once again the emphasis was on mobilizing the church for activity in the liberated territories, and, in economic terms, the guarantee of its support for the six-year plan promulgated by the Fifth Plenum of the Central Committee on 15 July 1950. The demand addressed to the church, to maintain a separation between religion and the state, did not apply to those areas that were of interest to the government and was, in light of governmental interference in church matters, a rather one-sided affair. In the period following the government's consolidation of power, the demands were made more overtly in the name of their actual source, that is, the PZPR. This tendency can be seen in Zawadski's declaration at the Unification Congress in December 1948.[76]

This stage of developments is characterized more by direct and open strategies for engagement and less by apprehension over the response of the church and its Polish and foreign supporters. As in the past, the government sought to drive a wedge between the hierarchy and the Vatican, to sow discord in the church, and to win over individual priests. However, now, as we have seen, even more brutal and extreme methods, supplemented by unremitting propaganda and open attacks, were brought into play.[77] *The intensity of the struggle did not wane on Stalin's death (in March 1953), but only increased,* and the harsh trend continued, in fact, until Gomułka's return to power in October 1956.

There are those who seize on the ethnic element, that is, the high percentage of Jews in the Communist leadership in general, and in the Stalinist leadership in particular, to explain the harsh policy toward the church and the injustices of the Stalinist era. Such arguments are spurious. It would be a mistake to highlight the antagonism between Catholicism and Judaism as representative of the clash between the political leadership and the Catholic Church in the People's Republic of Poland. Indeed, the matter of the Jewish background of the Stalinists in the leadership had less impact on policy than their dedication to Communism.

It is important to recall that the harm caused by these people to their 'brethren', the Jews living inside and outside Poland, was no less fierce than their attack on the members of any other religion. All in the name of Communist doctrine. Hence the issue of the role of the Jewish members within the political leadership is both a complex one of historical significance, as well as being emotionally loaded. This subject, however, lies outside the scope of this book.

2.2.3 SPECIFIC POLICY

2.2.3.1 The 1952 Elections

The period that preceded the elections to the Sejm (in 26 October 1952) once again proved how much the regime continued to respect and value the crucial role of the church in mobilizing the population and gaining its support. As in the previous period, government attempts to harness church cooperation in the approaching elections were characterized by a combination of concessions and threats. This time, however, the scope of concessions was narrowed, while the threats to eliminate or curtail the grounds for rewards grew more explicit and menacing. By stressing its patriotic approach, the government by this time was able to justify itself and prove its contribution (to the national cause) by citing concessions to the church in the 1950 agreement and in the 1952 constitution. The church's positive stand on the agreement and the new constitution reinforced the basis for cooperation. By emphasizing the very same common patriotic formula, the government tried to prove that it made no distinction between believers and non-believers.[78] Thus, during the three months prior to the elections, there was relative calm in the struggle against the church.[79] According to Zawadski,[80] the government agreed, during this period of calm, to the episcopate's demand that the Patriotic Priests not be allowed representation in the new Sejm—a demand which seemed to serve the interests of the government itself. However, as early as the beginning of November, immediately after the elections, a new period of persecution set in.

2.2.3.2 Policy towards the Vatican

Antagonism between the Polish government and the Apostolic See intensified between 1949 and 1955/56 as a result of the Communist government's campaign against the church and its overall policy of repression. This antagonism was due also to the Vatican's increased hostility to the Eastern European regimes, and the polarization between the two blocs (East and West). This trend was mirrored in the constant barrage of intensive propaganda, both initiatory and responsive, on the part of the Polish regime. Not only did hostile statements regarding the Holy See become increasingly direct and severe, and responses to moves and declarations made by the Vatican become immediate and vigorous, but any incident or confrontation involving the church as an institution, or even individual priests, was always accompanied by attacks and propaganda against the Apostolic See.[80] As was to be expected, the papal excommunication was a warning signal for the government. In an immediate rejoinder, released on 26 July 1949, the government declared that the papal decree could neither be published nor implemented since it contradicted the norms of Polish positive law. Moreover, the authorities declared that the papal decree should be defined as "an offensive action against the Polish state".[81] Ten days later, on 5 August 1949, the government emerged with a more concrete reaction, by publishing the two restrictive decrees applied to the church and other religious denominations.[82]

Conflict with the Vatican continued, almost incessantly, throughout the period. Even the contacts that preceded the signing of the 1950 agreement between government and episcopate representatives failed to put an end to the government media campaign against the Holy See. In fact, even though the agreement had recognized the pope's supreme authority in matters of internal ecclesiastical jurisdiction, it can also be seen as a further attempt to deepen the rift between the Polish hierarchy and the Holy See, as in the past. This, should be seen against the background of the papal excommunication and the Vatican's policy towards the regimes of Eastern Europe. This tone of the relationship also continued after the signing of the agreement. Thus, for example, the government's response to the pope's message to the Polish bishops, dated 9 September 1951, was to accuse the Vatican of trying to spread moral and religious terror in the country. Anti-Vatican propaganda resumed immediately after the October 1952 elections, at the same time as the renewal of the struggle against the Polish episcopate. Throughout November the pro-government press came out with fierce, systematic attacks against the Apostolic See, at which it leveled three main charges: a) the embezzlement of funds (*Sztandar Młodych*, 14 November 1952; *Trybuna Ludu*, 10 and 14 November 1952); b) support for neo-Hitlerism (*Trybuna Ludu*, 16, 25, and 30 November 1952; *Głos Pracy*, 16/17 November 1952); and c) collaboration with the United States' anti-Polish policy (*Trybuna Ludu*, 26 and 28 November 1952; *Życie Warszawy*, 19 November 1952).[83] The state press and radio portrayed the Vatican as a fortress of capitalism, and the pope as "someone who continues to entertain false hopes concerning the former influence of the Vatican in Poland". In this spirit, *Trybuna Ludu* quotes Makarenko's article (mentioned above), published in *Pravda* on 17 July 1952 under the title "The Enemies of Polish Democracy". It is easy to understand, therefore, that the various attempts by the regime to deny the personal nature of its attacks against the pope proved unsuccessful. Even Politburo member Ochab, one of the three government representatives on the Joint Commission and the permanent representative to the talks with the episcopate, attacked the Vatican in his speech before the Seventh Plenum of the Central Committee of the PZPR in June 1952: "...we must remove the costume disguising the Vatican's policy [which actually serves] as a tool of the class enemy, a tool of imperialism, a tool of Poland's enemies."[84] The media campaign intensified with the elevation of Wyszyński, the Polish primate, to the status of cardinal by Pius XII. The PZPR reacted negatively to the appointment, describing it as a maneuver designed to serve foreign interests.[85]

The propaganda campaign against the Apostolic See in fact accompanied all the restrictive measures implemented by the government against the church in Poland itself. The attacks that accompanied government moves regarding the ecclesiastical administration in the liberated territories were especially fierce. These intensified in the face of Pius XII's persistent refusal to revise his position regarding recognition of the Polish regime and of the new boundaries, and as a result of the failure of the regime's initiatives, with episcopate mediation, to achieve this recognition. The legal and police persecution of the clergy was accompanied by powerful propaganda and harsh accusations against the Vatican throughout the media, in a campaign which climaxed with Wyszyński's arrest.

2.2.3.3 Pax as a Government Tool[86]

The intensification of the struggle against the church was marked by the mounting, concentrated, and systematic activation of Pax and the Patriotic Priests. While efforts to impair church unity by splitting the clergy met with extremely limited success, undermining the church through Pax and the government-patronized clergy was understandably more effective, since the government transferred control of organizations and institutions previously held by the church into their hands. Moreover, Lucjan Blit emphasizes the efforts by the Bezpieka (the secret police) to transform Piasecki into the only legitimate Catholic leader in Stalinist Poland.[87] Nothing can be learned from this regarding *the level of popularity enjoyed by Pax and the Patriotic Priests, which remained low*. The transfer of funds to competing organizations and support for other denominations designed to weaken the church are also mentioned in the bishops' protest of 8 May 1953. The bishops denounced the support and the encouragement granted to "the artificial creation that goes by the name 'the Polish Catholic Church', known for its collaboration with the German conqueror in the recent war".[88] We should also note the exploitation of Pax and its emissaries for propaganda in the West, especially that aimed at Catholic public opinion. The government did not, however, approve of Piasecki's ambitions and independent declarations, due to the growing gap between the basic task it had assigned to Pax and Pax's own political and ideological ambitions which became clear once its own program had crystallized.[89] Similar reservations regarding the Patriotic Priests prompted the government to adopt a negative stance regarding their participation in the new Sejm following the 1952 elections.[90]

2.2.3.4 The Policy of Restrictions

2.2.3.4.1 Hostile Statements in Party Forums

The hardening of policy towards the church during the Stalinist period was highly perceptible in explicit statements made by Communist leaders in party forums. As early as the Unification Congress of the PZPR (15–23 December 1948), Aleksander Zawadski formulated the program for the struggle against the church: "The PZPR holds...the position which does not allow for the church's intervention in state policy...the reactionary section of the Polish clergy exploits the religious sensitivity of the believers to attack the people's state...the PZPR stands for the separation of the church from the state, based on the secularization of the schools and all state institutions."[91] In March 1949 the minister of public administration, Wolski, attacked the church with the unprecedented accusation that it had collaborated with the Nazis, declaring that many priests were "agents of Anglo-American imperialism".[92] In a parallel action, the government organized demonstrations and meetings to protest against activity by the Polish clergy.[93] In his speech at the Central Committee plenum on 20 April 1949, Bierut presented the choice before the church in unequivocal terms: either to be loyal or to be "an ally of the enemies of the people and the regime".[94] At the Seventh Plenum of the Central Committee (14–15 June 1952), Edward Ochab drew up the battle lines against the church with even greater bellicosity: "The party organizations must step up the fight against the enemies among the reactionary clergy...the main organized force that stands behind [the kulaks] is the reactionary section of the clergy."[95] Again, at the PZPR's Second Congress (10 March 1954), Bierut, in his new capacity as prime minister, warned that the misuse of religious office for political purposes hostile to Poland would be met with a fierce response. All these formulations were strongly echoed in the Sejm and on other political platforms serving the government.

2.2.3.4.2 Steps towards Secularization and Restrictions in the Sphere of Religious Rites

The secularization policy, which had already been crowned with considerable success in the earlier period when it had expunged religion from official institutions, was designed, in the present phase, to achieve a foothold in those spheres which had previously avoided government control.

The new family codex, issued on 27 June 1950[96] was one of the most impressive efforts in this direction. *Inter alia*, this legislation failed to mention the possibility of a religious ceremony being incorporated in the civil marriage, and determined a more general and quite liberal list of reasons for divorce, in contrast to the more conservative formulations listed in the decree of 25 September 1945.

Contrary to declarations and promises, efforts at secularization also found expression in attempts to disrupt religious observance. This was done either through the cancellation of religious holidays and the imposition of other, direct restrictions, or by subtle, indirect means such as showing movies at reduced prices on Sunday mornings during the hours of worship and the dissemination of atheistic literature. As a rule, these measures failed to meet with any success.[97]

2.2.3.4.3 Propaganda in the Media

The intensification of Communist propaganda against the church, which was directed chiefly against the Apostolic See, did not overlook the Polish Church. It took aim against the church as an institution and the episcopate as a group, singling out specific members of the lower-ranking clergy for attack. Later, it ended its restraint with respect to personal attacks against the hierarchy.

During the entire period, the campaign in the press and on the radio against the church and religion continued almost unabated, with the exception of several weeks prior to the signing of the 1950 agreement and the months before the 1952 elections. The propaganda attacks peaked as incidents and disputes between the church and the state intensified. This campaign included not only the exploitation of opportunities for wide-scale offensives, such as the Lublin Cathedral incident ('the Lublin miracle'), but also the initiation of such opportunities, which appeared to be the case in the affair of the Stockholm Peace Declaration. The media repeatedly accused the episcopate of violating the 1950 agreement and of showing disloyalty to the regime, while, at the same time, the government violated the agreement in a scenario reminiscent of the accusations heard during the annulment of the concordat. Thus, for example, an article under the title "What the Primate Forgot" ("O Czym Ks. Prymas Zapomniał"), published in *Trybuna Ludu* on 7 May 1952, accused the episcopate of tolerating hostile propaganda from a section of the clergy and of uttering "words of hatred for the people's state from many platforms". The writer also complained of the episcopate's lack of a sincere wish to fulfill the agreement, and described the primate's promises regarding the loyalty of the church authorities to the state as "verbal promises without any basis".[98]

Particularly bitter attacks and accusations accompanied the legal and police persecution of the church leadership. Such was the case, for example, during Bishop Kaczmarek's trial and at the time of Wyszyński's arrest.[99, 100] In the second case, the media came out with accusations against the primate before the arrest and after it, and linked the two events together.[101]

2.2.3.4.4 Police and Judicial Persecution

We have noted[102] how earlier, between 1945 and 1948, priests were arrested—albeit on a small scale—either for collaboration with what was termed "reaction" or on moral charges. (All this in order to defame the church and sow mistrust against its officials among believers.) During 1949 the number of arrests on the grounds of collaboration with "reactionary underground movements" was constantly on the rise. At first, the arrests were restricted to members of the lower-ranking clergy, but step by step they overtook even the church leadership. These actions paved the way for the coming blows. The drastic developments in the international arena, and Poland's place within this context, supplied the reasons and excuses to step up the persecution of the clergy. Mass arrests of clergy had already been carried out subsequent to the papal decree of 28 June 1949; however, the damage to the church leadership was still to come later. The escalation of the Cold War and events connected to the war in Korea, as well as intense industrialization and the associated economic difficulties, provided the grounds for accusations of espionage and anti-state activity. In addition, several priests were put on trial for violating currency regulations and carrying out illegal transactions.[103]

Against this background Bishop Kaczmarek of Kielce was arrested during the second half of 1952, on the charge of espionage. In November the same year the bishop of Katowice, Adamski, and his assistants were suspended for actions defined as "political sabotage," but in fact after a petition by their community relating to religious instruction in the schools. That month, members of the Kraków curia were arrested for espionage and subversion against the People's Republic of Poland, followed closely by the arrest of Baziak, archbishop of Lubaczów for economic offenses. Among the trials that took place in the wake of the arrests, the trial of the bishop of Kielce, who was sentenced in September

1953 to 12 years' imprisonment, was particularly striking. The arrest of Cardinal Wyszyński, announced by the government on 28 September 1953, came on the heels of the aforementioned verdict and brought additional arrests in its wake. At the beginning of 1954 there were nine bishops and several hundred priests in Polish prisons.[104]

2.2.3.4.5 Interference in Internal Church Affairs

The government's repeated violations of the 1950 agreement, of its declarations and promises regarding freedom of religion and conscience, and also of the articles in the 1952 constitution which dealt with the separation of church and state, were particularly conspicuous with regard to the fundamental and practical issue of church appointments. This phenomenon expressed itself in all its severity in the matter of ecclesiastical appointments to the western territories.

On 26 January 1951 the government published a decree establishing a permanent ecclesiastical administration in the liberated territories.[105] The background to the decree should be seen in the treaty, signed on 6 June 1950, between Poland and East Germany, in which the latter recognized the liberated territories as an integral part of Poland. The decree suspended the apostolic administrators appointed by Hlond, and the councils of the dioceses elected five capitular vicars in their place.[106] It is worth noting that the government took pains to stress that the changes were implemented in accordance with canon law.

A later step which, from the church's point of view, made the situation intolerable, was taken on 9 February 1953 with the publication of the decree concerning appointment to church offices by the Council of State.[107] This decree made all church appointments and changes in appointment procedures subject to governmental approval and set out criteria that every candidate for a church post would have to meet. Consequently, priests appointed in accordance with the decree were required to pledge an oath of allegiance to the "People's Republic of Poland"—a step that served to widen the chasm between the Patriotic Priests and the clergy faithful to the church authorities. The decree, which came to grant stronger official status to practices and measures that had already, in practice, been launched against the church, served as the basis for further measures. These continued, as noted, even after the primate's suspension and arrest, and were reflected, *inter alia*, in the pledge of allegiance imposed, in word and practice, on the church and the entire clergy in December 1953.[108]

2.2.3.4.6 Material Restrictions

The Bierut period was characterized by a serious contraction in the base of the church's economic resources. These restrictions must be seen in the context of the Communist program of stages, which then reached the point[109] of sweeping and decisive decisions, with the reduction of the church's political strength constituting a serious, open objective. These restrictions must also be viewed as part of the pressure on the church to submit to the government's demands and conditions.

The first salient step designed to erode the church's economic strength was a decree by the minister of the treasury, published on 5 July 1949, which obliged priests to keep financial records.[110] Eight months later *a much more serious and far-reaching step was taken with the nationalization of church property and lands without compensation*. This was done under the law concerning the "transfer of property of the deceased to the state [the matter related to properties bequeathed to the church and where there was generally included a stipulation that the lands were not to be sold], the guarantee of ownership of agricultural holding to parish priests, and the establishment of a church fund".[111] This law, which came, theoretically, to supplement agrarian reform and its legislation dated 6 September 1944, was designed, in fact, to impair the church's economic independence and create rifts between the episcopate and the lower clergy by granting parish priests preferential status and by freeing them from material dependence on the church authorities (section 4, sub-section 2). The law itself contains formulations which can be interpreted as a threat (section 12) or as pressure and temptation (section 8). Paradoxically, the application of the agrarian reform law to its lands was, to some degree, useful to the church, as it freed it from government charges of feudal exploitation designed to damage church prestige among the populace. Jan Szczelecki also admitted this in a symposium, notes from which were published in *Nowa Kultura* in 1957.[112]

A different kind of blow was dealt to the church when the charity organization, Caritas, was taken out of its hands on 23 January 1950 and transferred to the Patriotic Priests.[113] The transfer, which was executed under the pretext that the organization's funds were being exploited for anti-state political purposes, deprived the church of an important instrument for garnering support and influence in the populace, in addition to the immediate material implications of the act. Even before then, on 21 September 1949, the Council of Ministers had issued a decree ordering the nationalization of church-owned hospitals, which in fact was already taking place prior to the decree being issued.[114]

2.2.3.4.7 Censorship and Restrictions on Publication

The years under discussion were marked by increasing, systematic deterioration in all that concerned the dissemination of periodicals, books, and other Catholic publications. This was a characteristic element of the intensive political, ideological, and cultural campaign against the church. The restrictions included intensified censorship, paper rationing, limitations on the scope of activity of publishers and printers—closures and confiscations (of publishing houses and printing plants)—and, at the same time, the prevention of the circulation of newspapers and various Catholic publications. Thus the monthly *Znak* was shut down as early as 1949, and the government's announcement concerning the confiscation of Catholic printing plants was published on 20 June 1949. The severity of these restrictions is all the more striking in light of the preferential treatment given to publications hostile to the church and Christianity— mostly periodicals belonging to Pax and the Patriotic Priests. The climax of the campaign to curtail and destroy the Catholic press was the takeover of the Catholic weekly, *Tygodnik Powszechny*, and its transfer to Pax control. The last independent issue came out in Kraków on 8 March 1953.[115]

2.2.3.4.8 Restrictions in the Area of Education

The penetration of Soviet ideological patterns into the Polish educational system was naturally linked to the elimination of religion from the schools and attempts to destroy its influence. Moreover, the pivotal nature of the subject transformed the issue of the education of the young and the struggle against religion in the schools into a critical arena of direct conflict between the state and the church. This state of affairs was accurately reflected in "The Program for Struggle against Religion in the Schools", presented by the minister of education, S. Skrzeszewski, at the Unification Congress in December 1948.[116]

Thus the battle that had started some months before the 1948/1949 academic year took the form of a systematic and gradual campaign to expel instructors of religion from public elementary schools and high schools. Thus religious instruction was actually expunged from the curriculum of the vast majority of Polish schools, as these were subsumed by the Association of Friends of the Children network (TPD). In 1952 religious instruction was found in only about 20 percent of schools, and by January 1955 religious courses had almost completely been eliminated,[117] although, by law, religion continued to be a compulsory subject throughout this entire period. In those few public schools which still offered courses in religion, the efforts at secularization mainly consisted in cutting the number of hours, issuing selective permits to only specific priests to serve as teachers, eliminating crosses and other ritual articles from the classroom, and by the prohibition of religious rituals and ceremonies in the schools. This last restriction was imposed in the 1950/1951 academic year. Distinctions between believers and non-believers were introduced as a criterion for admission to higher education and professional work. All this, of course, in addition to the promulgation of atheistic, ideological views in the schools.

At the same time, the government adopted harsh measures to close down seminars and other institutions administered by the clergy. The discharging of priests, monks, and nuns from offices and positions did not bypass other social institutions, and included their dismissal from the army (mainly from 1951 onwards) and a prohibition against their employment in hospitals and sanitariums. Monks and nuns suffered especially harsh treatment. A massive expulsion of monks and nuns from monasteries and nunneries in the western territories took place during the winter of 1954. From 1950 onward, following the nationalization of church property, we see a harsher policy towards the Catholic University of Lublin, including budgetary discrimination and the closure of different faculties or their reduction in size. The same policy of repression continued during 1954 to 1956. In these years, the government closed the two faculties of theology at Kraków University and Warsaw

University. An academy of Catholic theology was in fact established in their place in Warsaw in November 1954. However, this was run by the 'progressive Catholic' leadership and operated under stringent political supervision.[118] The secularization drive and the efforts to sever the young from religion even included the elimination of religious youth movements, the re-organization of existing youth movements along Soviet lines, and the promulgation of anti-religious propaganda in nursery schools, schools, and youth recreation camps.

2.2.3.5 Benefits and Concessions in Policy

2.2.3.5.1 General

Notwithstanding the measures described above, the deterioration in government policy towards the church stopped short of the unbridled use of all possible measures and failed to produce an absolute, irreversible split between the two sides. The government continued to be sensitive to public opinion and chose not to ignore, even then, the actual and the potential power of the church. The still harsher measures were not introduced with excessive speed, but gradually, over a period. It is worth noting that the restrictive measures were felt mainly in the large cities, and to a much lesser degree in the towns and villages. Even during the period of rising repression the leadership was careful to leave itself options for reducing friction and for solving problems *vis-à-vis* the church by the use of verbal or practical concessions. The tactic of allowing the church breathing space, the possibility of existence, and the ability to function—though under increasingly cramped conditions—enabled the government actually to neutralize the church's capacity for resistance by reducing the effectiveness of church action and increasing the dangers it entailed. Support for this argument may be found, perhaps, in the sharp protest issued by the episcopate on 8 May 1953 (see above), which is explained almost explicitly by the fact that the church was pushed to the limit and therefore did not have any breathing space left.

Despite the serious discrepancy between the legal foundation for the existence of the church in this period and the realities of its condition, the concessions and relative advantages which the church enjoyed by law cannot be ignored. The government regarded the concessions under the

1950 agreement to be a far-reaching step that was unavoidable as a means of achieving "rehabilitation in the eyes of Catholics in Poland and abroad".[119] The episcopate, for its part, was aware of these considerations, and of the fact that the concessions were indeed far-reaching from the government's point of view.[120] The indications of non-acceptance and dissatisfaction among government circles over the agreement after its signing emphasized ten times over the significance of the concessions made. Among the indications of this feeling, one can count, according to Nowak,[121] Wolski's dismissal from his position. As we know, Wolski served as the party's liaison with the church for a number of years. He lost his position as the minister of public administration shortly after the agreement was signed, and dropped out of the political arena several months later. He was sharply criticized at the meeting of the Central Committee plenum in May 1950. That same year the Ministry of Public Administration was dismantled, and governmental responsibility for relations with the church passed mainly into the hands of the Bureau for Religious Affairs (Urząd do Spraw Wyznania).[122]

2.2.3.5.2 Formulations and Statements

The concessions policy was reflected in the formulations and statements made by the leaders of the regime. They often referred to the formal benefits that the government had granted the church, remarking that the commitments would continue to be honored, expressing the desire for normalization in the relationship, albeit on their terms, and including moderate formulations along with accusations. Thus we find that Zawadski's declaration at the Unification Congress of the PZPR in December 1948[123] begins with the words: "Our party, the PZPR, knows very well that the majority of the Polish people are devout Catholics...the PZPR does not fight against religion. Moreover, the PZPR stands for the defense of freedom of conscience and freedom of religious faith and worship...the party has no intention of interfering in the internal affairs of the church..."[124] Only later in his speech did Zawadski slip into allegations, threats, and warnings against the church. Thus, in a declaration dealing with church-state relations made in March 1949, the minister of public administration, Wolski, guaranteed the preservation of freedom of worship in Poland while at the same time attacking the church.[125] Evidence of the same tendency can be found in Bierut's speech at the Second PZPR Congress of 10 March 1954.[126]

2.2.3.5.3 Contacts

Despite their many failures, efforts to resolve the serious obstacles affecting church-state relations found expression in the numerous meetings that took place between the two sides. Following these meetings the Joint Commission was set up on 26 July 1949 and its efforts bore fruit, after lengthy contacts, with the signing of the agreement in April 1950.[127] (Immediately following the publication of the papal boycott decree, Wolski called Choromański and agreed to establish the commission. Its sessions began on 5 August 1949.) Contacts between the sides also continued afterwards.

2.2.3.5.4 Ideology and Worship

Despite increased ideological rigidity that was reflected in all areas of life, *Tygodnik Powszechny* wrote on 10 December 1950: "There is no inclination on the part of the Marxist camp to impose on us any ideological conceptions, or even political conceptions that stem from theoretical assumptions that are foreign to us." The authors of the article, Stomma and Turowicz, did not intend, of course, to shower words of praise, *per se*, on the government. On the whole, the ceremonial aspects of freedom of worship were maintained. Administrative measures to break the link between the population and the church were not used, except in several isolated cases. The churches remained open and were filled regularly by throngs of worshippers. The government did not even prevent public ceremonies and holiday pilgrimages, which continued to attract great crowds. Moreover, in contrast to rumors about closing churches in Poland, the government actually *continued to assist in the construction of churches and religious buildings*, although there were exceptional cases to the contrary. There is convincing evidence to this effect in the acknowledgment by the bishops, particularly in their protest dated 8 May 1953.[128] *As absurd as this seems, the government, at the height of the Stalinist era, assisted in organizing the country's mass pilgrimages by providing special trains for pilgrims and preparing the holy sites to absorb the pilgrims during religious holidays.*[129] Such gestures were carried out, of course, unobtrusively and with tacit church approval. It is also worth noting that the government did not prevent religious wedding ceremonies and funeral processions, and these continued to be the rule.

2.2.3.5.5 Material Concessions

The nationalization of church lands and other property did not completely deprive it of its material means of existence, but meant rather the erosion of its basis and an increase in its political and economic dependence on the state.[130] As is known, the lands in question were not redistributed among the peasants. The Nationalization Law, dated 20 March 1950,[131] stipulated the establishment of a church fund explicitly devoted to the needs of the church and for charitable purposes (article 8). The law also guaranteed a clerical representation in the fund's bodies (article 10), and also allowed for certain properties to remain in the hands of the religious denominations (article 7). As we have pointed out,[132] the parish priests especially benefited from reservations in the law that left large holdings in their hands to ensure their livelihood (article 4, sub-section 2). Thus, even after the nationalization of its lands, the church continued to control approximately 64,000 hectares—held mainly by parish priests and religious orders.[133]

The tax reductions granted to the priests of the western territories should be noted among the material concessions.[134] Moreover, access to Caritas was not denied for very long to members of the clergy faithful to the hierarchy. Indeed, the 1950 agreement included a stipulation whereby Caritas would be reconstituted as a Catholic company, and although its administration was not restored to the episcopate, faithful clergy were allowed to be active in its ranks.

2.2.3.5.6 Restraint in Legal Persecution

Although the term 'restraint' is far from appropriate for the state measures used during the period in question, the government did show some degree of constraint in its legal moves and relations with the media. This is particularly striking if we compare it to events in other countries in the bloc. One illustration of this are Wyszyński's conditions of imprisonment and the fact that he was never subjected to a trial. This contrasted, for example, with the trial of Cardinal Mindszenty, the Hungarian primate, which opened as early as 3 February 1949 in Budapest.[135, 136] (Heyman, for example, presents the situation in a similar way.) There was also the fate of Archbishop Grösz, who had signed the Hungarian state–church agreement on behalf of the church on 30 August 1950 (according to the example of the April 1950 agreement in Poland). Grösz was arrested, tried, and sentenced to 15 years in prison in June 1951.[137] We should also note the atmosphere of terror accompanying the 1950 agreement in Hungary, compared to the relatively relaxed atmosphere surrounding the agreement signing in Poland.

2.2.3.5.7 Other Spheres

Other relative concessions emerge, indirectly, from the discussion of the government's restrictions.[138] The educational field is a salient example, since, as we have noted, *religious instruction according to the law persisted in the schools albeit in a highly diminished form.* This is also reflected in Bierut's announcement to the episcopate on 1 September 1948. Religious education continued in the seminaries and other educational institutions administered by the clergy, despite persecution and the closure of most of these establishments. Despite the restrictions imposed on religious instruction in the universities, *the Catholic University of Lublin continued to operate—as a unique institution in the entire Eastern bloc.*

2.2.4 SUMMARY OF GOVERNMENT POLICY

Though one should not exaggerate the government's concessions to the church in this period, their significance in the years 1949 to 1956 is especially impressive when comparing the situation in Poland with that in other East European countries, and in comparison with other non-Communist groupings in Poland. (The official Vatican survey on the status of the Roman Catholic Church in the countries under Communist rule, published on 4 February 1952, also supported this claim). The campaign against the church in Poland developed along more gradual and moderate lines. This difference stemmed from the Communist rulers' consciousness of the "special Polish conditions", despite their tendency towards ideological rigidity. In this context, the government's inability to destroy the roots of the church's power, at a price the former was willing to pay, can clearly be seen. Maintaining a struggle against the Catholic clergy in a devout country such as Poland was incomparably more difficult than subduing a Protestant or even an Orthodox clergy. (As we know, the Orthodox Church had been subject to the authority of the secular government since the period of Peter the Great). Polish leaders learned through hard experience the limitations of their capacity to break the church's unity in their country by using other religious denominations and other groups under the regime's patronage. Time and again the government met with failure in its efforts to isolate the church from the Vatican and to alienate it from the populace. *The sophisticated tactics adopted by the episcopate, and by Wyszyński at its head, constituted a major contribution to the church's capacity for resistance and to the fact that it emerged from this period without breaking.*

The transformation in policy and in state-church power relations during the Stalinist era was not simply a function of the absence of Gomułka's imprint and his personal influence on the system, as we shall see in the next chapter.

3. THE SECOND PERIOD OF GOMUŁKA'S RULE

3.1 POLICY AREA ENVIRONMENTS

3.1.1 THE ROMAN CATHOLIC CHURCH

3.1.1.1 The Balance of Power during the Period

The ability to function and the wide range of opportunities made possible by the events that open our new period, namely the 'Polish October' and Gomułka's return to power, cannot obscure the negative and positive impact of the Stalinist period on the church's power base. The church's tremendous powers of endurance and its success in producing the maximum achievements under the most dire circumstances proved to be a source of strength for the church. This was not only due to the impact that these qualities had on the church's powerful bond with the Polish people and the broad public support that it enjoyed in Poland, but also to their impact on the church's perception of itself and its power. A morale-boosting pastoral letter, dated 15 September 1955, amply illustrates this source of strength, which had become integral to the church's self-image as a result of its endurance under adversity: "Through all the storms of history and its woes…the church always came out victorious and stronger…the church in Poland does not merely survive, but is characterized by a vitality as strong as ever; its foundations are submerged in deep bedrock that no human force will ever be able to move…"[1] It is superfluous to point out the positive reinforcement that this approach received when the years of oppression were over.

Another important source of power, rooted in the past, is enshrined in the common historical destiny shared by the church and the Polish nation, and came to the fore once again in the years 1949 to 1955/56. This common destiny determined, to a large degree, the firm integration of religion and the church in the Polish October and the events that preceded it. The call for the release of Cardinal Wyszyński, together with the other demands raised by the masses during the June 1956 events in Poznań,[2] must be viewed in this context. It should be added that the Catholic clergy showed initiative in the matter, for example in the letter from the Gorzów diocese clergy, dated 7 July 1956, which was delivered to Prime Minister Cyrankiewicz.[3] This is also true regarding the mounting demands for the release of the cardinal from prison during the demonstrations on 20[4] and 22[5] October, and their submission to the party leadership by numerous delegations in the days following the Eighth Plenum.[6] Moreover, the policy towards the church, as an integral element of the October program, further strengthened the cohesion between church and society in Poland.

The Polish October clearly signified an increase in church power and a religious revival in Poland following the years of repression. The gains achieved by the church in the 1956 agreement and the actual room it had to maneuver following that October[7] signified the church's unprecedented status in People's Poland. The church took the offensive in an effort to win victories and gain real advantages, determined to make the most out of the 1956 agreement and the opportunities created for it as a consequence of the country's post-October mood and the party's weakness. This was a striking departure from the church's demeanor between 1945 and 1948; not only did it signify the church's power, it was a source of that power. The lack of consolidation within the political system and Communist government during the earlier period of Gomułka's rule had dictated a cautious policy by the church, characterized mainly by anxiety regarding the future. As we have seen, despite the outcome of the war the church's resources and its actual ability to function before their erosion between 1949 and 1955 was what brought about the adoption of a policy designed to maintain the *status quo* in Poland. Although it no longer enjoyed the same gestures and broad privileges from the state that characterized the early post-war period, the church's power during the second period of Gomułka's rule was not, in fact, weakened. In fact it even increased in many ways, since at that point the church represented the only organized force in Poland in competition with the Communist government. Its hold on the Polish population did not diminish and it was perceived by many as the force which best represented the interests of the Polish people. The church organization, its leadership, and the alignment of the forces in the Catholic camp during these years, all point to the same trend. Even the retreat from the policy of October could not significantly change this situation.

3.1.1.2 Church Organization

3.1.1.2.1 General

The damage to the church organization during the years of repression cannot be compared with the damage of the Second World War. There was therefore no need to devote excessive time and effort to repairing the church organization. The resumption of activity by the church leadership under Wyszyński, who was released on 28 October 1956 and returned immediately to his post as primate, was speedy and without any special difficulties. Restoring the church organization to a solid footing therefore did not require the same level of mobilization as seen in the years following the Second World War. The main efforts were concentrated on discharging government-backed priests appointed following the decree on ecclesiastical appointments of 8 May 1953.

The church organization at this time was characterized by an increase in the number of clergy and a similar increase in the number of churches compared with the pre-war period and the two post-war periods. In an article dated 29 March 1959, *Sunday Times* correspondent Anthony Terry reported the existence of more than 10,000 churches and chapels in Poland. According to Roos there were 10,881 churches in 1962 compared with only 7,251 before the war.[8] At the end of the period under discussion the church was structured as 5 metropolitan districts, 7 archbishopric capitals, and 18 bishoprics, according to a report on the organizational state of the church published in January 1959.[9] According to the same source, there was 1 cardinal, 3 archbishops, and 49 bishops serving in the church. According to another source (mentioned above), the church's desire to enlarge the clergy and arrive at a ratio of one priest to every 1,000 persons led to the appointment of 800 new priests annually.[10] While in 1958 Poland had 12,713 diocesan priests, by 1971 the number had increased to 14,122.[11]

3.1.1.2.2 Stefan Wyszyński

There is no doubt that the character of Cardinal Wyszyński was a very important source of church power. Events in his early life undoubtedly influenced the way he led the church. His childhood in a Polish village heightened his awareness of the problems experienced by the peasantry. The manner in which his academic career and his formal training were integrated with his ecclesiastical career shaped his sensitivity to the interests of the Polish workers and the country's social problems. Stefan Wyszyński was born on 3 August 1901 in the village of Zuzela in northeast Poland, half-way between Warsaw and Białystok. His father was a nobleman who had lost his property and who taught in the village school. Wyszyński acquired his higher education at the Włocławek Seminary on the Wisła (1920–1924), and it was there that he first became acquainted with Poland's social problems; these left a permanent imprint on his personality. He received the degree of Doctor of Jurisprudence in 1929 from the Catholic University of Lublin. The subject of his dissertation was "The Right of the Family, the Church and the State to Education". He later wrote several books and in fact began his ecclesiastical career as a journalist. Between 1931 and 1939 he served as a professor of sociology and social economics at the Włocławek Theological Seminary and published many pamphlets and studies on social issues and education. Wyszyński adopted Pope Leo XIII's slogan: "Go to the workers", and considered it an important foundation in the clergy's efforts to establish links between the church and the believers. On 12 May 1946 he was appointed resident bishop of Lublin, from where it was a short step to the lofty ecclesiastical appointment of primate of Poland, following the death of Primate Hlond.[12] Wyszyński's presence in the country during the Second World War, and his service in the resistance movement against the Nazis in Warsaw and Lublin, were of great significance—in contrast to Cardinal Hlond, who spent the war years abroad.[13] His personality, which was characterized by a patriotic spirit, steadfastness to principle, organizational ability, courage, and wisdom, enhanced both his ability to lead the church and his prestige among the populace. Despite the authority and respect enjoyed by Cardinal Hlond, it appears that Wyszyński's personal influence on the population was far greater. Cardinal Hlond did indeed represent, for many Polish Catholics, the *pays réel* as opposed to the *pays légal*—an image that was strengthened by the fact that he had headed the Catholic Church before the Second World War. However, Wyszyński, whose ecclesiastical career was bound up with the history of Communist Poland, became an object of admiration which infused the church and the people with new spirit, while serving as a symbol and a guiding light to those around him. Through his personal behavior he demonstrated how the church and its followers should meet the challenges and protect themselves under the new circumstances they faced, with precisely the sense that their position was not inferior. Thus Wyszyński continued to serve as the "living conscience of the nation".[14]

The strength of his leadership was conspicuous against a backdrop of the deployment of forces and the power centers in the Polish Church at the time. In contrast to Hlond's leadership, which confronted another power base in the person of Sapieha of Kraków, Wyszyński's leadership in the period in question was not obscured by any other factor. The first three years of Wyszyński's ecclesiastical leadership during the preceding period also saw, as is known, activity on the part of Sapieha. However, the difference in their ages produced a totally different situation: one was about to depart the arena, and the other was newly arrived on the scene, bringing new energy and spirit to the church and building up his position within the leadership. Wyszyński continued to dominate such men as Magister Kominek and Archbishop Baraniak, and not merely because of his rank as the sole cardinal.[15] His authority was unchallenged not only in the episcopate but throughout the entire Polish Church, despite criticism from extremist elements angered by his concessions and moves toward 'cooperation' with the Communist government. Among the formal positions held by Wyszyński, he was the *ex officio* head of the High Council of the Polish Episcopate and chairman of the bishops' committees on the 'Catholic University of Lublin', 'the pastoral needs of the Polish Diaspora', and 'for the press and information'." The *appointment of Archbishop Karol Wojtyła from Kraków, who had stood out for his organizational skills, as a second cardinal in the 1960s did not essentially change the situation. Wojtyła (who later became John Paul II) and the other members of the episcopate continued to express their support and complete faith in Wyszyński's leadership.* This was done, for example, in their letter dated 4 September 1964, in which they criticized Pax, and in the millennium celebrations that commenced on 2 May 1966. The unsuccessful attempts of the government to drive a wedge between Cardinal Wyszyński and the then Bishop Karol Wojtyła can be inferred from the documents annexed to Dudek's book.[16] In fact, Wojtyła intended to strengthen clerical discipline and loyalty towards the Wyszyński leadership at all levels of the church hierarchy.

3.1.1.3 Changes in the Catholic Political Map

As a consequence of de-Stalinization and the Polish October, there was a basic change in the alignment of forces within the Polish Catholic camp. The Catholic political map became more complex, compared with that seen during the first period of Gomułka's rule. As part of a tendency towards differentiation, not only in Polish Catholicism but throughout the entire system, new groups, expressing a variety of views, appeared between the two poles represented by Pax and the church. The activity of the newly emerged Catholic groups was impressive compared with 1945 to 1948, when Catholic intellectuals not associated with Pax had steered clear of the political arena. The monopoly of Pax, the only political organization until then to offer an outlet for lay Catholics, was impaired. Among the groups that remained loyal to the Polish episcopate there was a noticeable one that mediated between it and the government. As such, it occupied a special position and suffered criticism from both sides.

In this context, the advent of the Znak group appears to be of significance. This group of intellectual Catholic writers, most of whom had become known as the editors of the Catholic newspapers *Znak* (this was the source for the name of the group) and *Tygodnik Powszechny* before they were suppressed, was encouraged by the new mood in the country. The group adopted the essentials of the program presented by Gomułka at the Eighth Plenum. It was attracted by the slogans on democratization and humanitarian socialism, and developed high expectations. Thus, on 23 October 1956, the group publicized its support for Gomułka's reforms and promised to assist in their implementation.[17] This was in the same vein as a decision published later on behalf of the primate. The snowball effect—Znak recognition by Gomułka and the advantages enjoyed by the group—are all well known and do not have to be detailed here. Even so, we should mention here the fundamental transformation in the political map that occurred following the election of nine Znak members to the Sejm in the January 1957 elections (which involved 458 representatives). The group's members, who functioned as a circle and not as a party, subscribed to the view that there cannot be an ideological bridge between Catholicism and Communism, and they directed their interests towards a pragmatic form of cooperation based on political realism, which promoted the national formulation of *raison d'état* within the framework of the existing social and political conditions.[18] In this, Znak did not actually differ from the church. However, the fact that Znak was not a completely monolithic group proved to be a source of friction with the church. Despite its small number of members, clashing opinions circulated within the group. The author Stefan Kisielewski (Kisiel), one of Znak's important representatives, succeeded in describing the group's conceptual diversity and defended it: "Since Catholic representatives represent so many millions of people with a Catholic outlook, their duty is to reflect the wide spectrum of opinion...therefore, it is positive that Catholic representatives are not of one opinion and do not make up a single 'monolithic' group (club)."[19] The fact that there were differences of opinion even about this approach can be learnt from additional statements by Kisielewski, reporting on the first session of the Sejm after the elections: "I tried to introduce a bit of variety by abstaining, but the president of our club, Stanisław Stomma, gave me a sharp and penetrating look..."[20] Differences were expressed in the way Znak members saw the role of the group. Stanisław Stomma held that: "As Catholics, we took upon ourselves to remain faithful to the church and not to betray its instructions, but we also have a duty to be concerned about the welfare of the nation. These two principles do not necessarily contradict one another. In reality it is hard to reconcile them, but it is possible and necessary to find the formulation that will achieve this. Our job is to find this formulation."[21] Jerzy Turowicz had a similar view of Znak's role, which he described in his article "Catholics, Politics, and Tolerance".[22] In contrast to these two, Stefan Kisielewski defined Znak's role as "a channel through which different social aspirations are formally conveyed to the party leadership".[23] Adam Bromke also stresses Znak's mediation role, describing it as "a barometer registering the direction of political pressures in Gomułka's Poland".[24] Within this spectrum of positions, the activists headed by Stomma and Turowicz, who were centered around the weekly *Tygodnik Powszechny*, continued to constitute the group closest to Cardinal Wyszyński and most acceptable to him. Now, however, political activity prevented them from representing the church with the same supreme loyalty as in the past, especially since the church had serious misgivings regarding the value of Znak's activity. The well-known writer and dramatist Jerzy Zawieyski, who served as *Znak*'s chief editor when the magazine resumed publication in June 1957, and also as a member of the *Tygodnik Powszechny* editorial board, enjoyed special status within the Znak group. His popularity stemmed from his membership of the Council of State and his role as mediator between Wyszyński and Gomułka. Zawieyski, who saw in this a patriotic mission, enjoyed the trust of both leaders.[25] Znak's disappointment over the retreat from October can be seen from a memorandum it sent to the government in February 1959.[26] Notwithstanding its disappointment, the group did not immediately retreat from its chosen path. They did not fall back even after the drop in number of Znak Sejm members as a result of the 1961 elections. Even so, absence of signs of democratization, which they had counted upon, left them with a permanent sense of despondency, which seemed to characterize the group's activities during the 1960s. This bitterness was expressed mainly by Stefan Kisielewski, who had proven himself in the past to be a person who did not gloss reality or hesitate to make regular use of his sharp tongue—to the frequent embarrassment of the rest of the group. As early as 1963, Kisielewski had voiced his disappointment by comparing Znak's efforts to those of Don Quixote.[27] Two years later he resigned from the Sejm. Zawieyski was different from the others in that he demonstrated great optimism and believed it wrong to talk in terms of a retreat from the essence of the Polish October. This characterized him until the later stages, when he resigned from the Council of State in May 1968.[28] The tragic end to the chapter of Zawieyski's life and activity came shortly afterwards.

Any analysis of the Catholic political map in the late 1950s and 1960s would be incomplete without a description of the group that appeared around the monthly *Więź*, which was first published in 1958. (The chief editor of the monthly was Tadeusz Mazowiecki.) The monthly saw itself as the organ of the Catholic intelligentsia clubs, and the group that backed it openly declared its links to "the model of French Catholicism".[29] On the other hand, this group, which held more radical views than Znak on social issues, maintained its loyalty to the church and therefore stood half-way along the continuum between Znak and groups not loyal to the hierarchy.

The various groupings which played a role in the Catholic political system may be aligned, therefore, along a continuum, stretching from the episcopate to the government, in the following order: Znak (which included the *Tygodnik Powszechny* group on the one hand, and Kisielewski on the other); *Więź*; the circle of priests associated with Caritas; the Frankowski group; and Pax.[30] From this we can conclude that there was a 'leftwards' shift compared with the years 1945 to 1948.

Even so, the main point is that despite the multidirectional politicization and the fragmentation that occurred in Catholic intellectual circles close to the church, the episcopate and Cardinal Wyszyński continued to enjoy the loyalty and support of these groupings. Moreover, Wyszyński himself even enjoyed the backing of those members of the episcopate whose position was more radical than his. The result was that the church could put into play its entire, unimpaired strength.

3.1.1.4 Cooperation and Concessions

3.1.1.4.1 General

Now, as in the past, the basic dualistic pattern of cooperation and concessions on the one hand, versus militancy on the other, characterized the church position towards the government and continued to constitute the foundation for the church's accumulating power. However, the concessions in the second period of Gomułka's rule were not of the same type as those found in the previous periods. The reason for this was that the Polish October, Gomułka's return to power, the dramatic release of the primate and other bishops from prison and their return to their posts (among them were bishops Baraniak, Adamski, Bednorz, and Bieniek), the work of the Joint Commission of the episcopate and the party, and the conclusion of the 1956 agreement, were all supposed to open up a new page in church-state relations in Poland.

3.1.1.4.2 The 1956 Agreement and Support for the October Policy

The understanding reached between the church and the PZPR in December 1956, and the episcopate's support for the government's policy—as well as its support for the government itself and for Gomułka
personally—are clearly reminiscent of the church's *de facto* recognition
of the government, mainly after the January 1947 elections, and its support for the government, with the introduction of the social and economic reforms during the post-war years. However, the changed conditions dictated a level of support and a type of assistance different from
those of the past. Church cooperation at this time was characterized by
the official stamp it bore. The official recognition of the existing regime
stemmed from political realism, as the hierarchy declined to be enticed
into dangerous adventurism. This quality had also characterized the
church in previous years; but this time it was clear to the church that
despite a certain lack of consolidation in the system, the foundations of
the Communist system in Poland were firm and the regime even enjoyed rather broad legitimation. The church, which always considered it
its duty to reflect the 'soul of the nation' and to guide the offspring of
the nation, thus remained loyal to its task. This was reflected in the formal recognition extended to the government. The consolidation of Soviet rule in Eastern Europe at the beginning of a period of peaceful coexistence, and the Communists' immediate interest in loosening the
reins on the church, served as the background, the basis, and a catalyst
for this process. The 1956 agreement symbolized the change.

In contrast to the first period, whose beginning was marked by the
annulment of the concordat—an act which hinted at future restrictions—the second period opened with an agreement between the sides.
The agreement was not equivalent, of course, to a concordat, but constituted a real-life compromise which provided proof of a basic improvement in church–state relations. (The episcopate took pains to emphasize
that the 1956 agreement was not a concordat. This was similar to its
position regarding the April 1950 agreement.)[31] Contacts between the
church and the state in the first period never gave birth to any agreement. Even so, the 1956 agreement was not reached in a vacuum but
against the backdrop of the 1950 agreement, which was signed precisely
during the years of coercion and persecution. The church did present
the agreement as a "continuation of the 1950 agreement", pointing out,

however, that it indeed included "radical changes in certain questions concerning church-state relations".[32] Though well known, it is worth emphasizing the differing backgrounds to the two agreements. The 1950 agreement was signed under difficult conditions of constraint and was mainly a preventive measure linked to the preservation of the church's ability to function. The 1956 agreement, on the other hand, was signed in a much more relaxed and positive atmosphere, which reflected the hopes and expectations of the church, aroused by the Polish October. From this, one cannot conclude that the 1956 agreement was free from constraint. This time, however, unlike in the past, the emphasis was on forces basically linked to the external system: the threat of Soviet intervention and the fear of seeing Hungary's fate repeated in Poland, which undoubtedly guided the deliberations and the moves made by Wyszyński and his people. The writer of an article in *Tygodnik Powszechny* (13 January 1957) was apparently referring to a different kind of restraint, one that was internal and linked to the years of persecution in Poland, when he wrote the following: "The current agreement was not concluded under pressure...we believe that it is our duty to accept it faithfully and with understanding of the general situation and to do everything in our power to ensure that it will be implemented in the spirit that accompanied its signing." In contrast to the past, this agreement, and the level of cooperation it reflected, assumed a personal note in the understanding reached by the two leaders, Gomułka and Wyszyński, and was a demonstration of the outstanding nature of their leadership. It is superfluous to point out that in comparison with the past, the contents of the October program facilitated the church's supportive position vis-à-vis the state. *The above factors all contributed to shaping church support for the government—support that was more positive, direct, and forceful than ever before. This support was bestowed with the 'national formula' adopted by the church reaching its fullest dimension.* This was well mirrored in the first sermon delivered by Wyszyński after his release: "We are witness to a difficult and extraordinary period in our national life, a period in which our duty commands us to speak less of our rights and more about our obligations. We turn to the heart of our nation, so well known for its preparedness to sacrifice for the homeland. But today, the willingness to toil for the homeland is even more important than the readiness to make supreme sacrifices. The Poles know how to die courageously, but they must learn how to work courageously..."[33] This sermon was delivered on

4 November 1956, at the Church of the Holy Cross in Warsaw. Wyszyński granted his full support to Gomułka and his policies, against the factional forces opposed to him within and outside the party. On the other hand, he stressed, as in the past, the church's apolitical character. In a communiqué on behalf of the joint government-episcopate commission, established in November 1956, the episcopate's representatives, its secretary, Bishop Choromański, and the bishop of Łódź, Klepacz, pledged: "...to assist the government's efforts to introduce and consolidate legality, justice, and peaceful coexistence; to improve public morality; to redress injustices...; to strengthen and develop People's Poland. Furthermore, to unite the efforts of all the citizens to labor together for the good of the country; for the conscientious preservation of the laws of People's Poland, and for the fulfillment of the citizens obligations to the state."[34] All Wyszyński's declarations in the months immediately following the signing of the agreement were similarly patriotic in nature and reflected a similar desire to establish peace between believers and non-believers.[35]

3.1.1.4.3 The Call to Reduce Tensions

One of the main means by which the primate and the church assisted Gomułka and the government leadership found expression in the influential calls to the populace to preserve order, to refrain from rioting, and to act with moderation and tolerance. Such calls, which assisted in reducing tensions at times of crisis or when faced with fears of an impending catastrophe, were a recurrent theme throughout the Communist era.[36] However, given the atmosphere of October, and with the highly concrete danger of Soviet intervention imminent, these calls assumed special significance and infinitely greater importance. Thus Cardinal Wyszyński turned to the Polish people immediately upon his release, calling on them to remain calm and united in order to prevent a holocaust and bloodshed.[37] Wyszyński's calls were read from the pulpits in all Polish churches. Similar expressions were voiced by other church leaders. Bishop Klepacz, for example, stated: "Even though our hearts are beating more rapidly, we must control ourselves in order to guarantee our future in the best manner."[38] In the face of the Soviet invasion of Hungary, Wyszyński cooperated with Gomułka's efforts to staunch the outburst of anti-Soviet feelings, and called on the Poles to show restraint and self-discipline. The primate's New Year greeting to Poland for 1957 included "blessings for patience".[39] The same sense of responsibility and political realism persisted when relations between the church and the state took a turn for the worse. Even as the danger of Soviet intervention receded, as Gomułka drew closer to the Soviet Union and his strength in the party was consolidated, and when incidents and recriminations between the church and the government increased, Cardinal Wyszyński and the other members of the hierarchy continued calling for an abatement in the enraged passions of the highly involved Catholic populace. Wyszyński's reaction to the police raid at Jasna Góra in the summer of 1958 was a sterling example of this approach. He went to the Jasna Góra monastery in order to restore calm and soothe the agitated Catholics' response to the incident.

Similarly, the bishop of Częstochowa, Goliński, turned to his angry congregation in a missive read out in all the churches of the diocese in which Jasna Góra is located, asking them "to maintain calm and to behave like Catholics".[40] Once again, faced with increasing tension between the sides in the summer of 1959, the primate was heard calling for moderation at the Conference of Bishops (September 1959).

3.1.1.4.4 The Position Regarding Elections

One of the most significant expressions of the church's support for the state immediately following the signing of the 1956 agreement was its position regarding the January 1957 elections, a position which had a decisive influence on the outcome and on Gomułka's victory.[41] As in previous periods the church came out again, this time with a call to the populace to participate fully in the elections, describing it as a moral obligation. However, unlike the elections of January 1947, when the episcopate did everything to hint at its true position—namely opposition to a party whose principles were in conflict with its own—while taking care to maintain formal neutrality, this time, in January 1957, the church worked with dedication, of its own free will, and with a special sense of emergency, to stimulate full participation by the population. It did not hide its sympathy for Gomułka, and in fact instructed the population to vote according to his wishes,[42] although it refrained from issuing any formal declaration in this direction and its support remained unofficial. The episcopate's communiqué contained the following formulation: "Catholic citizens will fulfill their conscientious duty by voting. The Catholic clergy must organize worship and religious services in a manner which will enable all the believers to fulfill both their religious duty and their electoral duty without any obstacles."[43] Furthermore, various reports tell us that, in certain areas, parish priests led their congregations to the polling station and urged them to vote for the candidates of the National Unity Front.[44]

Even so, it is worth noting that, in contrast to Cardinal Hlond's active role during the first period of Gomułka's rule in formulating public statements on the eve of the elections, Cardinal Wyszyński refrained from special announcements of this type on the eve of these elections. Such announcements were delivered by figures from the second echelon in the hierarchy, such as Bishop Choromański.[45] Together with the support given to the government during the elections, Wyszyński explicitly demanded the representation of Catholics in the new Sejm. This resembled the episcopate's demand made on 10 September 1946.[46] However, even though the wording regarding the inclusion of independent Catholic candidates in the electoral list stressed that this was a minimal requirement,[47] it represented a less demanding position on the matter, in comparison with the first period. Moreover, it is worth noting that this extraordinary high point, reached in January 1957 in terms of church support for the government and Gomułka, is striking not only when compared to the past, but also when compared with the behavior of the church in future elections in the People's Republic of Poland. Thus, for example, prior to the Sejm election in April 1961, after relations between the church and the state had deteriorated, the church leadership no longer issued clear instructions to believers regarding their votes.[48] In contrast, Znak, headed by Stomma, called on all Catholics to vote and not to behave like "internal emigrants". According to Frank Dinka,[49] Wyszyński called on the faithful not to vote. This assertion seems doubtful when compared with everything known about the behavior of the church and of Wyszyński in all other election campaigns, and in light of the fact that it is not confirmed by additional sources.

3.1.1.4.5 The Position Regarding the Liberated Territories

Between 1956 and 1959, church policy regarding the liberated territories faithfully continued to reflect the supreme importance of the national and patriotic component in its leadership's consciousness. This component constituted a basic moral position and a symbolic element, which determined the extent to which the church represented the Polish people. In fact, during the years 1945 to 1948, this policy found expression mainly in *practical* efforts linked to the reconstruction of the church organization. Only at the end of the period, and mainly in light of the affair of the pope's message to the German bishops in March 1948,[50] were there *declarative* attempts by Hlond and the hierarchy to eliminate doubts regarding the church's unequivocal support for the fact that the territories were an integral part of Poland, while the period in question here was characterized by *explicit* support which was unequivocal in both words and deeds. The appointment of resident bishops for the liberated territories narrowed the gap between the church's position and that of the government compared with earlier periods. On numerous occasions the church took care to stress that there was full unanimity across the entire Polish people on this vital question.[51]

This very policy regarding the territories was continued during the 1960s. At the celebrations during June to September 1965, to mark the twentieth anniversary of the establishment of the Polish Church's administration in the western territories, Poland's Catholic bishops expressed their unfailing support for the Oder—Neisse boundary as Poland's western border. The primate referred specifically to the "historical Polish character" of these lands in his speech in Olsztyn on 20 June 1965 and in Wrocław on 1 September 1965. As in the past, the episcopate was careful not to reveal vulnerable points that would facilitate propaganda against it on such a sensitive issue. The cracks revealed in its position following the missive to the German bishops against the background of the millennium celebrations in 1966—an affair largely analogous to that of the pope's message to the German Catholic bishops in March 1948[52]—did not exist for long. During 1969 the secretary of the episcopate, Dąbrowski, worked on a memorandum from the Polish episcopate to Pope Paul VI, the contents of which dealt with the further stabilization of the church's organization in the western and northern territories of Poland. This document was signed by all the Polish bishops on 1 October 1969 and was handed by Wyszyński to the pope on 5 December 1969. It contained a call for full normalization of the Polish Church's jurisdiction in the liberated territories and a demand that the administration in these territories should cease to be treated as temporary. This goal was achieved in 1970 when the Polish Church hierarchy did gain jurisdiction over these territories.[53]

The government responded with little enthusiasm to the church's own efforts to gain recognition for the incorporation of these territories within Poland during 1970, at a time when this goal was in sight. Gomułka and the Communist leadership, while attributing the utmost importance to this issue, did not sympathize with the independent initiatives of the church and sought to block them.[54]

3.1.1.4.6 Restraint Regarding Clashes with the Government

The basic tenet which continued to guide the church after October dictated the avoidance of any frontal collision with the regime, or steps that might lead to an unmanageable explosion at tense focal points. This was of infinite importance because of the increase in the number of clashes in local arenas which, although limited, were relatively high in intensity mainly towards the end of the 1950s and subsequently. The concessions made by the church, along with its militant actions,[55] mainly when tensions peaked, undoubtedly contributed to reducing tension and moderating the response of the population directly involved in these conflicts. Thus the church assisted in checking the repeated clashes with the authorities while managing to present itself to the population as the force working toward "fraternal understanding", moved by patriotic sentiment and a concern for the population. The concessions by the church regarding the assistance and gifts arriving from the United States during the first half of 1958,[56] the Jasna Góra affair in the summer of the same year,[57] and the affair of Bishop Kaczmarek, for example, should all be seen in this context. (In the last affair there was, at the least, a verbal concession.) These particular concessions, which entailed a retreat from positions held by the church at earlier stages of the conflict, are essentially different from those made in the past. This corresponded to changes in the behavior of the sides during this stage of the power struggle between them[58]—a striking phenomenon in light of the fact that previously, the sides had done everything possible to eliminate such outbursts before they erupted, or in their earliest stages.

The desire to maintain the *modus vivendi* was expressed in the consistent refusal by the primate to support the demands of the radical faction within the episcopate. As in previous years, the conciliatory approach toward the government was striking, wherever issues were concerned that the cardinal did not consider to be vital or a question of principle. This approach applied mainly to spheres in which government propaganda against the church's conservatism, and its description of the church's 'personality' as one which denied modern reality, threatened to become more and more convincing. Accordingly, for example, the primate refused to join a declaration by Polish priests stating that civil marriages "are immoral and illegal" unless performed in church.[59] Two additional facts demonstrate the conciliatory nature of the church's policy in this period: a) The church waived the promulgation of a pastoral letter issued in September 1960, similar to the one issued in the previous period, listing the government's restrictions one by one.[60] Similarly, in the summer of 1970—just before Gomułka was ousted—the church refrained from reading the 'anti-Soviet' pastoral letter.[61] b) During the entire period, until the end of Gomułka's rule, the church's representatives continued to be active in the joint government-church commission, and this, when the government representatives hindered the work of the commission.

3.1.1.5 Militancy and Methods of Struggle

3.1.1.5.1 Ideological Offensive

The rapprochement in relations between the government and the church at the beginning of the period did not, of course, include ideological concessions. As in previous periods, the ideological confrontation was not even disguised. Moreover, the church actually embarked on an unprecedented ideological offensive in the face of the advantageous conditions and new prospects which developed as a result of changes in the government and the new agreement of December 1956. There is evidence of the scope of this offensive in the complaints of other religious denominations (not Roman Catholics) regarding the church's intolerance.[62] This offensive was marked, for example, by explicit measures opposing Pax and its actions[63] and also an explicit reservation regarding the Frankowski group, which the church did not consider to be a force capable of representing Catholic doctrine, although the group did show some positive signs.[64] The church tried to maximize its advantages from the *modus vivendi* and from the prevailing weakness of the PZPR and Gomułka. In this battle the church drew immense strength from its powers of endurance in the previous period. This factor, combined with the slackening of pressure and the considerable gains achieved in this period, encouraged it to adopt forms of struggle more daring, open, and extreme than those employed during the previous two periods. The circumstances, which involved relatively less danger, explain the apparent deviation by the church from the rules of caution that had guided it in the past.

Through their formulations and actions, and more now than ever before, Wyszyński and the hierarchy reveal the supreme importance they ascribed to the future of Christianity in Poland. This trend found striking expression in the preparations and clerical campaign surrounding the Polish millennium, which began in the summer of 1958. In conformity with this trend Wyszyński declared that "despite the important role of the past in the millennium celebrations, the future is even more important—the future of Polish Christianity."[65] The church likewise announced that it would celebrate the millennium "separately" [from the state] and declared the 'Magna Novena'—nine years of celebration, devotion and steadfastness, from 1958 to 1966.[66] The practical purpose of these measures was to revive the Catholic spirit among the Poles, to strengthen their bonds to the church, and to enhance the church's role as the representative of the nation in its competition with the government. In a similar vein, Wyszyński's sermon in Warsaw Cathedral on 7 February 1974 emphasized that the bond between the church and the people is stronger than the bond between the nation and the state, and highlighted the church's contribution to the very survival of the Polish nation. Consequently, he concluded, it is the church that in fact represents the Polish nation.[67] This initiative by the church also reflected its efforts to overcome problems of indifference to religion in a developing industrial society.

In the framework of this ideological offensive, especially during the deterioration in relations between the church and the state in the middle of 1958—and faced with increasing clashes, which included, *inter alia*, an intensification of the atheism campaign—the episcopate, headed by Wyszyński, came out with counterattacks and accusations in which they repeatedly emphasized the contradiction between Catholic and socialist morality, and described the Communist camp as having aggressive and totalitarian aspirations. This form of struggle, namely emphasis on ideological antagonism, had been adopted in the past, as we have pointed out, during the years 1945 to 1948—also in the context of a deterioration in church-state relations (as, for example, immediately after the 1947 elections, with the publication of the pastoral letter of 23 April 1947, but also in the period preceding the elections)—as well as in the Stalinist period.[68] However, at the end of the 1950s and particularly afterwards, along with the frequent use of this form of struggle, more detailed and explicit charges were leveled, with sharp attacks on atheism. Even so, the emphasis on ideological antagonism was never linked to direct opposition to the Communist regime. This, for example, was the background to the episcopate's missive of 15 March 1962,[69] which denounced atheism and described it as one of the greatest sins, and to Wyszyński's fierce attack against atheism at the shrine of the Black Madonna in Częstochowa (26 August 1962).[70] This was not enough, however, and the primate washed his hands of Gomułka's policy after the retreat from the October program. We find an example of this in the agricultural sphere, where Wyszyński refused to lend his support to the 'agricultural circles'.[71] This was a striking move, given the church's support for the agricultural reform during the first period of Gomułka's rule, its commitment to neutrality and non-interference regarding collectivization in the 1950 agreement, and in light of its obvious support for the de-collectivization policy set out in the October program.

3.1.1.5.2 Intensification and Diversification in the Forms of Struggle

The church's militancy at the end of the 1950s and during the 1960s was characterized by the frequent use of diversified measures—direct and indirect, initiatory and reactive. These measures included increased and more extreme use of pastoral letters, petitions, and protest letters to representative government bodies.

Cardinal Wyszyński's statements on abortion provide a clear illustration of his direct and daring expressions of protest. At the beginning of

1959 the primate denounced abortion in a pastoral letter. During an exchange of allegations with the government in the same context, he declared in January 1960 that, were land in Poland to be utilized properly, it would be able to supply food not only to "30, but even to 50, 60, 80 million Poles".[72] In March 1964 he severely criticized the government's birth-control policy, comparing it to the genocide perpetrated by the Germans.[73] A similar attitude can be seen with respect to the Jasna Góra affair (summer 1958) when the church authorities, while calling for calm and an avoidance of rioting, vigorously rejected the government's accusations[74] and made every effort to present events in a way which proved they had acted within the law.[75] At the same time as publishing a pastoral letter expressing sorrow over the incident,[76] Goliński, the bishop of Częstochowa, together with Ludwik Nowak, head of the Pauline Order in Jasna Góra, and Father Bronisław Dąbrowski, in the name of the episcopate secretary, Bishop Choromański, sent a petition of protest to the public prosecutor. Cardinal Wyszyński also dispatched a letter to the public prosecutor on this subject.[77] The use of protest measures by the church was demonstrated once again in the affair of Bishop Kaczmarek, when Cardinal Wyszyński bitterly complained against intervention in the church's internal affairs.[78] The complaint came in his letters of the end of June and beginning of July, in response to a letter from the head of the Bureau for Religious Affairs, Sztachelski, and concerned Bishop Kaczmarek's suspension and violation of canon law. The secretary of the episcopate even issued a formal complaint to the Council of State on 10 July 1959, accusing the government of trampling formal decisions and obligatory norms.[79] In his efforts to prevent state interference in ecclesiastical appointments, and with regard to other restrictions, Wyszyński was not satisfied with making even the sharpest protests. He also took practical steps to stymie the intervention, mainly where penetration by the Patriotic Priests was concerned.[80] Similarly, in a letter (not published) to the government, dated 15 April 1959, the episcopate came out with a series of complaints concerning obstacles to building churches, tax regulations, and other matters. This was its response to Gomułka's declarations at the Third Congress in March 1959.[81] The church went even further in its reaction to the Poznań incident of November 1961.[82] Cardinal Wyszyński's letter to the chairman of the Sejm, Czesław Wycech (30 November 1961), sent in the name of the episcopate, enumerated the government's violations of formal undertakings in six specific areas. The letter also refers to violations of the Polish constitution, the 1956 agreement, and the United Nations Declaration of Human Rights.[83] Furthermore, the hierarchy then turned to the Sejm, demanding the establishment of a commission of inquiry to examine the above allegations. Wyszyński's protest letter was read out in the Poznań churches on 17 December 1961.[84] The demand for a commission of inquiry was raised by Cardinal Wyszyński once again on 29 March 1962.[85] Sharp protest by the primate could be heard once more in relation to the draft legislation regarding the right of assembly.[86]

3.1.1.5.3 Dissemination to the Faithful of Information on Restrictions and Protests

The hierarchy attached great importance to disseminating information concerning the restrictions and hostile measures taken by the regime. This was done not only as a means of exerting pressure for a change in government policy, but also, and to no less a degree, in order to boost the church's influence on the populace, chiefly among the Polish youth. This was the background to Cardinal Wyszyński's edicts on 11 August 1958 which determined three special months of prayer throughout the country in protest at the government's attacks on the church and commemorating the incident in Jasna Góra. On this occasion the primate did not hesitate to use the same weapon as that used by the government itself in the struggle against the church, namely exploitation of the population's anti-German feelings. He compared the government's measures to those used by the Germans during the war, and pointed out that even the Germans "did not launch attacks on Jasna Góra".[87]

The primate used the weapon of exposure in his speech at the Corpus Christi celebrations held on 4 June 1958, when he told believers of the government's refusal to grant permits for the construction of new churches.[88] Similarly, in a sermon marking the same celebrations on 28 May the following year, the primate spoke of religious persecution, of manifestations of violence and force, and of the government's public insult towards religious feelings.[89]

3.1.1.5.4 The Struggle in the Educational Arena and for the Souls of the Young

The educational sphere and influence over the young continued to be a key arena in the fight to attain the church's goals. However, in the face of changes in the ideological battle and the intensification of the methods used in the struggle, the nature of the battle surrounding this central area was, of course, also transformed. The battle in the educational field, which was linked to the trend of the general struggle, was conducted in two main stages: the first began at the end of 1956, and the first signs of the second began to emerge in the second half of 1958, becoming clearly evident in the early 1960s.

The first stage saw an effort to generate maximum advantages from the concessions and the circumstances that arose, while creating a series of *faits accomplis* on the ground. All this was accomplished, to a large degree, by mobilizing and activating the religious population and by calling on parents to assume responsibility for their children's education. Indeed, such a call had already been issued between 1945 and 1948 and was contained in the pastoral letters issued by Hlond and the episcopate during that period.[90] This time, however, its formulation was more specific and explicit and had the nature of a practical directive. The emphasis on parental responsibility was specially important now, in the face of the new opportunities that had arisen and because of the article in the agreement requiring parents to express their wish for their children to receive religious instruction. Accordingly, Cardinal Wyszyński took the trouble, in his sermon on 9 December 1956, to make it plain to parents that they must take responsibility for the religious instruction of their children.[91] This call was repeated in a letter from the primate and the bishops, dated 19 June 1957.[92] In a pastoral letter dated 18 August 1957, which was read out in all the churches in Poland, the primate instructed parents to demand religious education for their children, even before the new school year opened. Several days later the bishops came out with a joint pastoral letter, in which they reminded parents of their obligation to send their children only to such schools which guaranteed religious instruction for their children.[93] The primate even turned to the young and to the pupils themselves, appealing to them to take action on this subject and calling on them to become more involved in the life of the Catholic Church.[94] At the same time, the church took pains to address the teaching community and to mobilize it on behalf of the cause by organizing pilgrimages and conferences for teachers at holy sites.[95] Among these practical efforts, energetic steps were taken to train members of the clergy and others as religious instructors.

During the second stage, as government restrictions and attempts to thwart and limit the church's influence developed,[96] the tactics employed in the struggle became increasingly intensified and extreme. The hierarchy continued to appeal to parents and to apply the measures used in the preceding period. Now, however, the measures became more varied and severe, and included accusations and instructions to disregard the government's restrictive regulations. This can be seen, for example, from the pastoral letter read out in Polish churches on 2 September 1962.[97]

The episcopate's most bitter response, which came in the face of the prohibition preventing members of monastic orders from serving as religious instructors (towards the beginning of the 1959/1960 academic year), was characterized by this militant spirit. In response to the directive of the Minister of Education, dated 4 August 1958, and a Ministry of Education circular on the same matter dated 6 August 1958, on 9 August 1958 the secretary of the episcopate sent a note of protest to Sztachelski, the government representative for relations with the church. The note claimed that the directive was illegal, and argued that the government's action constituted discrimination against monks and violated the 1956 agreement by preventing *via facti* religious instruction.[98] The same worsening in the government's policy was evident from the beginning of the new school year in the prohibition on morning prayers— which, since October 1956, had become the custom in many schools— and served as the basis for Wyszyński's statement in his sermon commemorating the fortieth anniversary of Lublin University. Here he talks about the struggle between "God's empire" and "the devil's empire".[99] In the face of growing efforts on the government's part to interfere in the selection of religion instructors, at the start of the 1960s, and their attempt once more to eliminate religious instruction in the public schools, and in the face of the increasing tendency to reduce the church's influence, the hierarchy mobilized its maximum resources to fight back. Accordingly, it called for a refusal to comply with the new restrictive regulations relating to the approval of teachers appointed by the clergy[100]; it published more and more pastoral letters of an unyielding and accusatory nature as well as personal letters to the clergy in which it prohibited priests serving as religious instructors from signing new contracts with the Ministry of Education. The hierarchy presented its complaints to representative government bodies again and again, repeating its accusations that the government had violated agreements and norms with legislative standing. In his sermon given at Częstochowa on 26 August 1961, the primate attacked the new education law of 15 July 1961, which finally removed religious instruction from the schools.[101]

Neither the legislated expulsion of the church from the public schools, nor the obstacles placed by the government in the path of the church's plans for teaching religion within its own framework, stymied its vision and aspirations for Poland's youth. Adapting itself to the new situation, the church once more attempted to maximize the potency of the tools still remaining at its disposal. Accordingly, there was increased emphasis on indirect measures, which were linked to its activity as the force that granted behind-the-scenes, and even open, support to the voices of protest on social and public issues. Moreover, the church acted, as in the past, to 'milk' propaganda from the very fact of its persecution.

3.1.1.5.5 The Position with Respect to the Vatican

As is known, the Polish October made it easier for the primate and members of the episcopate to travel to Rome. This 'relaxation' was indeed exploited by the bishops and was marked by frequent contacts between the Polish hierarchy and the Apostolic See—usually through broad participation in ecumenical congresses and other events held in the Vatican. The trip by Wyszyński, and the bishops who accompanied him, to Rome shortly after the signing of the 1956 agreement symbolized a new page in the relations between the state and the church and epitomized the dramatic changes that had taken place in the whole system. The symbolism of the visit to Rome was accentuated by the fact that the occasion enabled Wyszyński finally to receive the cardinal's hat. A different significance was ascribed to the trip by those who interpreted it chiefly as an attempt to justify the agreement and the Polish hierarchy's cooperation with the Communists at the Vatican. This is highly probable, since the Polish delegation's agenda included reporting, clarification, and justification concerning the new developments in church-state relations—and it was considered necessary to receive the pope's approval for Wyszyński's policy. The importance of such approval was many times more vital due to the existence of circles within the Vatican that continued to oppose cooperation with Communist regimes, as in the past when the 1950 agreement was signed. This opposition persisted despite the fact that both agreements stressed, as we have noted, that their terms did not constitute a concordat, such a pact being the exclusive prerogative of the Holy See. Upon his return from Rome the primate, who had obtained Pope Pius XII's approval for his policy in Poland,[102] stressed the Polish people's bond with the Vatican and Western culture, describing this as a link maintained through the church and through the church's consistent loyalty to the teachings of Christ.[103]

After the death of Pope Pius XII and the coronation of John XXIII, Cardinal Wyszyński and the Polish Church did everything in their power to bolster the new pope's standing in Poland and to stress his exceptional good will and loving intentions toward Poland. These efforts were facilitated by the new pope himself, who, in an extraordinary manner, emphasized "the love for the Poles that we feel deep in our heart".[104] Thus the primate, who generally abstained from talking of his personal experiences, reported, in an interview to the Polish Catholic press, that during the coronation of the new pope, John XXIII had endeavored "in a manner for all to see, to keep him in his presence for as long as possible, so as to express, in this way, his affection for Poland".[105]

As during the post-war years, the Polish Church once again assumed the role of mediator between the Polish government and the Vatican. However, this time its efforts met with greater, if not total, success. As in the past, the focus was first and foremost on the issue of recognition for the Polish Church's jurisdiction in the liberated territories, and on the diplomatic recognition of the Polish regime. In both these matters there was a shift in the position of the Holy See—mainly after the ascension of John XXIII—narrowing the gap in the understanding with the Polish government, with the primate and the Polish Church playing no small role in the change. The part played by Wyszyński[106] in John XXIII's decision to dismiss the (London-based) Polish government-in-exile's representation at the Vatican is particularly well known. The argument that Wyszyński presented to the pope before the decision was taken—namely that the existing situation created difficulties for the Polish hierarchy in Poland[107]—had been raised on numerous occasions in the past. However, this time, due to the new set of circumstances in both the Vatican and Poland, the words fell on sympathetic ears. The new attitude emanating from the Vatican that appeared with the coronation of John XXIII and which started with demonstrable fraternity between the Holy See and the Polish episcopate, also saw retreats during the 1960s. The primate was not completely satisfied with the peace initiatives set in motion by John XXIII and his successor, Paul VI, and it appeared that the Polish hierarchy was willing to pay a different price for an understanding with the Communist government than that acceptable to the Vatican. Outwardly, the Polish Church faithfully upheld the Vatican's position. However, Cardinal Wyszyński did not rush to implement the decisions of the Second Vatican Council, which began on 11 October 1962. In any case he had reservations, mainly concerning government attempts to reach agreement with the Vatican by bypassing his authority. Indeed, he stood his ground even though, compared with 1945 to 1948, the chances of reaching a direct agreement between the government and the Vatican were higher, mainly because of the increasing willingness on the part of the Holy See to respond to overtures from the Polish regime.

3.1.2 THE POPULATION

3.1.2.1 General

Data on the religiosity of the population in the years following October 1956 indicate, as a rule, a tendency toward stability compared with the two earlier periods. The demographic indicators determining Roman Catholic homogeneity did not change significantly: over 90 percent of Poland's residents continued, in the 1960s as well, to be affiliated to the Roman Catholic Church.[108] The trends towards industrialization and urbanization, which began to exert their influence on the system as befits the early stages of a society in transition, had no real impact on the religiosity of the population. Despite modern atheism, which indeed had some following in Poland, the vast majority of Poles, mainly in the rural areas but also to a considerable degree in Poland's cities,[109] continued to nurture deeply religious feelings.[110]

As during the years 1945 to 1948, now, too, there was a display of religiousness *per se*, together with religiousness mixed with national sentiment. Both of these found expression in a mass public response to church initiatives, substantiating, in this way, the public's firm links to the hierarchy and the church establishment as moral authorities worthy of obedience—which were, in fact, obeyed. This provides overwhelming proof of the church's influence in Poland. Even before the Polish October the churches were filled with young and adult believers, and there was evidence of increased participation in religious ceremonies. Almost a million and a half pilgrims came to Częstochowa on 26 August 1956—prior to Wyszyński's release—for the annual Holy Maria festivities, which that year were combined with a mass protest.[111] The removal of the fetters of the previous period and the further relaxation at the beginning of the new phase were celebrated with a religious revival in which the population mobilized itself fully to exploit the new opportunities that were opening up. Accordingly, more than half a million pilgrims visited Częstochowa annually.[112] Also, when celebrations were held at Częstochowa at short intervals apart, for example on 15 August and 26 August 1958, hundreds of thousands of believers continued arriving for the second event marking the holiness of the Jasna Góra monastery.[113] Churches and assembly centers were filled with people during the holidays and other occasions. Thus, for example, several million Catholics participated in the Corpus Christi events in May 1959.[114] An incident reported by *Tygodnik Demokratyczny* (4–11 March 1959) illustrates the devoutness of the population in an original and amusing manner, despite the fact that a city with a special religious character such as Częstochowa was under discussion. The weekly reported that two swindlers had bought all of the pictures of Karl Marx in the town, painted golden halos over his head, framed them, and sold the pictures as portraits of St. Joseph. In short, the two managed to sell almost all the pictures before being apprehended. As in 1945 to 1948, many party members and officials attended church events and ceremonies, although they did so covertly. This is the subject of Gomułka's complaint in an article published in *Trybuna Ludu* on 2 November 1958, under the title "Facing a Difficult Test". The student newspaper *Po Prostu* had warned of this at an earlier date (*NYT*, 19 July 1956). Of the 459 Sejm members, of whom only 12 had been elected as Catholic representatives, no fewer than 200, according to their own declaration, were strict about their presence at weekly Sunday mass.[115]

The deep religious consciousness of the population found full expression in the issue of religious instruction in schools: on 15 January

1957 over 95 percent(!) of parents signed petitions demanding that their children be allowed religious instruction.[116] There were also displays of extremism and intolerance by the Catholic population in all that related to religion in the schools.[117] This was evident from, among other things, attitudes to pupils who did not register for religious instruction and to pupils of other religions, and in the public's response to attempts to remove crosses and other religious symbols from the walls of classrooms. The latter led to clashes between the faithful and the militia, and in many instances believers threatened the lives of the officials sent to carry out the order.[118] Under pressure, and facing growing threats to religion and the church in Poland, the Catholic population showed even greater support and affection for the church—on the whole, by increased church attendance. An illuminating demonstration of this could be seen in the packed churches and the crowded church entrances, when millions of Poles gathered there for several days on the occasion of the shift in Gomułka's policies signified by the PZPR's Third Congress.[119] We find further evidence of Polish Catholic sentiment in the Nowa Huta events of April 1960, which so vividly demonstrated the power of Roman Catholicism in Poland. As has been documented, the spontaneous religious feelings flared up in opposition to the erection of a school on a site designated for a church, resulting in a clash with the militia.[120]

3.1.2.2 Religious Consciousness and Links to the Church According to Social Status

As in previous periods, the church continued to enjoy a traditionally strong influence among the peasants. More than a few events, in different places, bore witness to the fact that the village priest's word was decisive in determining the degree of peasant support for the economic plans and goals set by the government. The church also held considerable sway among the urban workers. Among the latter was a stratum of worker-peasants who played an important role in strengthening the religious orientation of the entire urban population by maintaining constant contacts between the city and the countryside. This important role was also fulfilled by those workers who had recently abandoned the villages, as in the Nowa Huta case. Secular trends appeared chiefly among the intellectuals.

Various data clearly confirm, as noted earlier,[121] the well-known finding shared by much of the research on societies in the throes of modernization: the inverse relation between religious faith and educational level was also evident in Poland. According to Jaroszewski[122] the believers were distributed among the different strata of the population as shown in Table 3.1.

Table 3.1 Believers and Non-believers by Social Stratum, 1966 (percentages)

Social Stratum	Non-believers	Believers	Total
Intelligentsia (with higher education)	39.9	60.1	100
Intelligentsia (others)	34.0	66.0	100
Skilled workers	25.0	75.0	100
Unskilled workers	17.8	82.2	100

Source: Jaroszewski, *Kultura i Społeczenstwo*, 10/No. 1, p. 138.

It is worth noting the clear majority of 'believers' throughout all strata of the population. Similar trends appeared in an earlier survey carried out in 1959. Of the 1,000 teachers who were questioned, 38.6 percent declared themselves 'active' Roman Catholics, as opposed to 34 percent who defined themselves as non-believers.[123] Moreover, the church found a common ground with many of those who considered themselves 'non-believers', either through shared protest formulas or through social pressure which dictated maintaining outwardly traditional appearances, or else by virtue of internalized traces of traditional influence which also persisted within this group. Thus many 'non-believers' continued their participation in church ceremonies and religious events such as baptism and religious weddings. Many who did not consider themselves believers continued to be loyal to "the principles of Catholic morality".[124]

Naturally, the movement toward modernization and secularization took its toll, to no small degree, on the attitude of the young toward religion and the church. The church was aware of the fact that it was less attractive to this age group, but refused to accept this as irreversible. A study conducted in 1960 by the Institute of Sociology at Warsaw University, designed to examine attitudes toward religion among Polish youth, confirmed that religious consciousness was dwindling among the university population. While 94 percent of students' mothers and 78.3

percent of their fathers testified to being believers, only 76 percent of the female students and 64 percent of the male students belonged to this category. Even so, only 4 percent of all students defined themselves as complete atheists.[125] (Among undergraduate university students, no less than 70 percent declared themselves believers, whether passive or active, in the Roman Catholic Church.[126]) Similar trends were observed in studies performed by the Department of Sociology at Warsaw University in 1958 and 1961. The second survey pointed to a further reduction in the number of believers among the student population compared with the 1960 survey.[127] Various reports showed a certain reduction in the degree of religiousness in the general population as well.[128] However, from all this one must conclude that despite the drive toward modernization and secularization, which was accelerated during the 1960s, the decisive Roman Catholic hue of the country persisted, indicating that the Communist government in Poland would have no choice but to contend with this reality for a long time to come.

3.1.3 PAX AND THE CHRISTIAN-SOCIAL SOCIETY

3.1.3.1 Pax

In contrast to the previous period, this period saw a considerable deterioration in the standing of Pax and of Piasecki. The Polish October pushed them into a corner, since they played such an active part in the system it came to negate. This trend intensified because of the support given by Piasecki and his movement to the Natolin group during the struggle between the various forces that preceded Gomułka's resumption of power. This was the basis for the ultimately mistaken impression of many of the observers of the time that Pax was poised to vanish from the political arena. The return of many of the Patriotic Priests to the bosom of the church during the October Revolution,[129] and the split in the Progressive Movement at the end of November 1956,[130] provided additional grounds for such expectations by demonstrating the weakness of the movement. Indeed, the fall in the political participation of Piasecki and his group in the first six months following October 1956 was drastic.

However, it could be seen that Piasecki's retreat was only temporary, and that he had no intention of being satisfied merely with Pax's economic empire, which remained unimpaired for the time being and continued to enjoy the same privileges as in the past. (Jerzy Turowicz considered Piasecki's announcement before the Pax plenum on 7 May 1957 as the turning point. His speech reflects Pax's unbroken desire for continued active political involvement. Turowicz clarifies his conception in an article in *Tygodnik Powszechny*, published on 26 May 1957.[131])

Indeed, Piasecki proved his ability to survive politically despite the obstacles he faced. His political survival can be ascribed either to his covert connections with the Soviet secret police, or to the vital service he rendered, or was expected to render (as a force capable of weakening the resistance of Polish Catholicism to Communism), to the Communist government in Poland. Bromke (1967, p. 215) believed that Piasecki's attempt to make contact with Gomułka in 1956, prior to adding his support to the Natolin group, helped him considerably in preventing the collapse of Pax. With Pax's survival assured, and later even strengthened by the meeting between Gomułka and Piasecki in the summer of 1957, the members of the group and its leader stepped up their activities and attacks on such forces as *Tygodnik Powszechny* and Znak,[132] going so far as to 'preach morality' to the PZPR in their criticism of party factionalism.[133] Through their press, the Pax members conducted orthodox Communist propaganda, supporting the Soviet Union in a style that surpassed that of the Stalinist faction in the PZPR.[134] In a manner that was direct and harsh, and that was striking compared with the years 1945 to 1948, Piasecki presented his conception of the role of the church and its obligations toward Communist Poland.[135] The 1961 elections returned members of Pax to the Sejm once again, but not in the numbers that they had hoped for.[136] The same year saw, for the first time, a narrowing of Pax's economic base and the cancellation of certain important economic privileges that the organization had hitherto enjoyed. However, as the rest of the 1960s proved, this was not the harbinger of a policy designed to eliminate Pax's economic base, and ups and downs were still evident in this regard.[137]

Despite Pax's attempts to launch a renewed offensive in the political arena, and despite the government backing that it continued to enjoy, Pax remained a marginal factor in Polish Catholic life. On the other hand, as long as there was no substantial change in the power of the church in Poland there was a basis and support for Pax's *raison d'être* as a unique phenomenon in Eastern Europe—if only for the trouble and limited damage that the organization nevertheless managed to inflict on the church.

3.1.3.2 The Christian-Social Society

As we have seen,[138] Pax lost its monopoly as the sole representative of the lay Catholics after October 1956—not only with the appearance of Znak and *Więź*, but also as a result of the split that occurred in the organization at the end of November 1956. This split produced a new grouping, organized formally as the 'Christian-Social Society', which was concentrated around the weekly *Za i Przeciw* (For and Against). The group was composed mainly of former Pax members, although several previously non-affiliated figures also joined. The most renowned members of the group were Jan Frankowski, Dominik Horodyński, Anna Morawska, Konstanty Łubieński, and Wojciech Kętrzyński—all former Pax members.[139] The *Za i Przeciw* group, which supported the October democratic currents, declared bitter war on Pax. The group saw itself as a non-party group, which on social issues belonged to the left-wing camp, mainly by virtue of its support for socialist economic objectives. At the same time, however, the group was interested in maintaining its special character within the Left, as a body of people with a spiritual outlook based on Christian ethics and morals.[140] However, even though the organization was more acceptable to the church than to Pax, it took pains to clarify in no uncertain terms that it could not be considered an exponent of Catholic doctrine. Basically, the group never became popular and remained, in all senses, peripheral.

3.1.4 THE VATICAN

The new winds blowing through Eastern Europe with the relaxation of the Cold War did not permit the Apostolic See to maintain the same hard line and uncompromising position it had hitherto held toward the Communist regimes in Europe. With regard to Poland, this trend was evident from the position adopted by the Holy See toward the 1956 agreement and Wyszyński's policy of reconciliation. However, various press reports presented differing, and even contradictory, versions regarding the reception given to Wyszyński and the Polish bishops during their visit to Rome in 1957. Different sources describe conflicting responses by the Vatican and the pope regarding the 1956 agreement. Several reported that Cardinal Wyszyński, and to a greater extent Bishops Klepacz and Choromański, were received coolly due to the Polish hierarchy's concessions to the state, which the Vatican, as with the 1950 agreement, regarded as excessively far-reaching. The same sources added that the Holy See instructed the primate to demand further concessions from the government—first and foremost the return of Caritas to the church; the re-establishment of theological faculties in Polish universities; a permit to publish a Catholic daily; and the right to distribute grants and donations from abroad.[141] According to Krahn, who claimed to have received his information from progressive Catholic circles, during his visit Wyszyński received orders opposing loyal cooperation with the state.[142] According to other sources, however, the Polish hierarchy was received warmly, and the pope even expressed admiration for the Polish people, the Polish clergy, and the episcopate. According to this version, the Holy Father approved Wyszyński's policies in Poland while stressing that they could not serve as a model for other countries.[143] It is reasonable to assume that certain sources tended, whether intentionally or not, to ascribe to the pope positions and opinions expressed by other Vatican figures who belonged to the most extremist circles. Markiewicz's claim that "during the reign of Pope Pius XII, Polish–Vatican relations were tense and there was no sign of their improvement"[144] serves to support the first version.

At any rate, it appears that even if there was some shift in Pope Pius XII's position, it was relatively marginal. No doubt the pope remained suspicious of the Eastern European regimes and of the strategy that the 1956 agreement concealed. In December 1956 the pope warned of "the illusion of counterfeit coexistence". Even so, one cannot ignore the change in the Vatican position captured in the statement by Pope Pius XII's counselor as early as September 1956: "The church will seek out...every opportunity to guarantee minimal religious services wherever these do not exist. It will search all the ways to achieve this...it will exploit every opportunity for a *modus vivendi*."[145]

Consistent with his policy in previous periods, Pius XII did not extend the Apostolic See's recognition to Poland's western boundaries. This was not merely a question of extending *de jure* recognition, which would have been listed in the *Annuario Pontificio*—it was also a question of the practical approach to the problem. Even though the pope refrained in this period from making embarrassing statements concerning "the bitter fate of the Germans who were victims of the deportations in the liberated territories"[146], no agreement was reached during his reign concerning the permanent Polish ecclesiastical administration in these territories. It is superfluous to point out that, under Pius XII, the Vatican continued to support and encourage the episcopate and the believers in Poland who found themselves faced with renewed restrictions toward the end of 1958 (close to the time of his death). This was also true for the Jasna Góra affair and the issue of religious instruction in schools.[147] Similarly, the pope continued to denounce Pax and the Patriotic Priests and to issue orders to boycott their enterprises.[148] Thus, on 29 June 1955, a decree was issued denouncing Piasecki's book *Essential Problems*, which had appeared in 1954.

A new mood was felt in the Vatican with the coronation of John XXIII, who was elected on 28 October 1958. The new pope was not associated with the position of his predecessor towards the Eastern European regimes. Already at his coronation ceremony he greeted the bishops, led by the primate, with gestures towards Poland and expressions of sympathy and understanding for its special circumstances.[149] The pope was inclined to be more convinced than his predecessor of the problems generated by non-acknowledgment of Poland's demand for sovereignty over the western territories, which supplied the government with the ideal grounds for anti-church propaganda. John XXIII evinced immediate proof of his open-mindedness on this matter by withdrawing accreditation from the diplomatic representative of the Polish government-in-exile in London, the position held by Kasimir (Kazimierz) Papée until 26 December 1958, when his name was removed from the list of heads of delegations to the Vatican.[150] Even so, there was no official change in the papal position on the Oder-Neisse question at that time.[151] That change was to take place in June 1972, with the decision of the Apostolic See regarding the final settlement of the church's organization in the western and northern territories following the Bundestag's ratification earlier that month of the 1970 agreement between the Federal Republic of Germany and Poland.[152]

As part of his well-known peace initiatives during the 1960s, John XXIII tended towards reaching an agreement with the Polish regime. This was also true for his successor Paul VI. The attempts were largely unproductive, as we have said, due to Wyszyński's position.[153] Pope Paul VI's attempt to visit Poland in 1966 failed, despite his keen interest to do so. The Polish government, while creating obstacles, explained that they had refused to allow the visit due to difficulties caused by Wyszyński himself.[154]

3.1.5 THE SOVIET UNION

As in the first period, during the second period of Gomułka's rule the Soviet Union granted clandestine support to the Polish regime's policy regarding the Catholic Church. Khrushchev's latent agreement regarding 'the Polish path to socialism' and the economic, political, and military dependence on the Soviet Union, during the second period constituted the foundation for supportive and restrictive Soviet influence with regard to the church and agriculture. Compared with the first period, we now witness a greater sensitivity and deeper understanding of Polish reality and its difficulties. Soviet support for the Polish government—during both periods—regarding policy towards the church was more far-reaching and firmer than its support for agricultural policy.[155] One supposes that the reason for this difference stemmed not only from the institutional power of the church and its limiting parametric influence, but also from the fact that, in this area, there was no room for serious doubt regarding the authenticity of the tactics and the pragmatism of the Polish Communists. This was so precisely because of the depth and clarity of the ideological antagonism, and particularly because of Gomułka's clear, forthright position. These factors determined the secondary nature of the issue as a basis for accusations of ideological deviation against the Polish regime within the framework of internal Communist power struggles. It is probable that the Soviets were mindful of the danger that a sharp debate on the issue of religion might strengthen, rather than damage, the status of the Polish Church. The Soviets therefore never came out publicly against the Polish leadership's policy regarding the Catholic Church. (This, in contrast to the agricultural issue.) Nonetheless, one should suppose that behind the scenes there were questions, criticism, and pressure relating to the concessions made to the church.[156] According to Erwin Weit's formulations,[157] it appears that the Soviet Union, among the other countries in the bloc, did not abstain from expressing reservations and criticisms regarding the freedoms granted to the church after October—even though Weit does not testify to this explicitly. Bromke's claim (1967, p. 134), that "the Soviets never came out against the policy of the Polish Communist regime in regard to the church", should therefore be amended to: "...never came out publicly...", and would, probably, be a more accurate formulation.

This Soviet position was linked to developments and Soviet power struggles following Stalin's death. Moderation and resignation toward the position of the new October leadership should be explained against the background of the thaw, de-Stalinization, and the relaxation of Soviet practice itself where religion was concerned. This trend found important expression in Khrushchev's announcement of a more moderate line towards religion at the meeting of the Central Committee of the CPSU in November 1954, and, as known, at the Twentieth Congress. Regarding the impact of the changes in the nature of the power struggle, it is clear that, with respect to the internal Polish arena, Moscow attached primary importance to restoring party control and to the restoration of order in the country. Soviet recognition of the ongoing, and even increasingly serious, power of the Polish Catholic Church, and the need for its backing for these efforts, undoubtedly influenced Soviet support for Gomułka's line and his concessions to the church. The factional struggle within the CPSU (and the connection between this and the struggle taking place in the PZPR) explains the pressures and the criticism that nevertheless existed in this arena.[158] To a large degree the minor nature of these pressures, and the less hesitant Soviet backing for the regime where the church was concerned, stem, as we have said, from the secondary character of the church issue, compared with the question of agriculture, as an arena of factional and intra-Communist struggle.

On the level of relations with the West, the moderating influence of the policy of 'peaceful coexistence' on the Soviet position was felt. Thus, for example, the change in position affected the way the Soviets observed the rules of international law and their efforts to prove that those linked to religious faith were in fact honored. Cracks in the attitude of forces in the Vatican hostile to the Soviet Union and the Communist world, even before the death of Pius XII (but especially afterwards) and the change in atmosphere that accompanied the accession of John XXIII to the papal throne, stirred up Soviet hopes of a possible agreement with the Vatican which would finally result in recognition for the new order in Eastern Europe. These factors all contributed to producing steps and decisions designed to appease the Vatican—especially during the 1960s. In the Polish arena during the 1950s this tendency was expressed by approval for Gomułka's line. However, with the aggravation of policy towards the Church in 1959 and during the 1960s, the above-mentioned Soviet line had *a moderating effect and inspired attempts on different occa-*

sions to check Gomułka and prod him towards an understanding and concilia-tion with the Polish Church and Wyszyński.[159] The same sort of influence can be ascribed to the Communist Party of Italy and to the importance that Moscow attached to its positions.[160]

The increased weight of the other countries in the Communist bloc, aside from the Soviet Union, and the pressure they exerted on the Gomułka leadership with regard to the policy of October and the Polish path to socialism, were felt more in the sphere of agriculture. Nonethe-less, we shall cite certain evidence based mainly on the testimony of Erwin Weit, who served as Gomułka's personal interpreter during his second period of rule.[161] According to Weit, not a single Communist delegation that came to Warsaw failed to express reservations regarding the concessions toward the church made by the Polish leadership during and after October.[162] Weit relates that the East German leadership launched repeated attacks against the new policy line in the months fol-lowing October, and even tried to intervene, both with regard to the agricultural policy and with regard to policy towards the church.[163] Moreover, the joint decision by East Germany and Poland in 1958 not to publicize the differences of opinion between them was not honored by the former. The East German leadership did indeed refrain from any direct attack on Gomułka or the PZPR leadership, but came out instead with accusations against the "clerical pressure and the violation of the 1956 agreement by the clergy". The accusations intensified in the wake of the Jasna Góra affair.[164] There is no doubt that, despite the apparent support for the PZPR's position, indirect pressure was brought to bear in an attempt to force a harder line against the church. A far more deci-sive trend is evident from Weit's testimony on the abusive language used by Ulbricht in Warsaw at the end of 1958; this included his allegation that Poland's policy towards the church made a mockery of "the con-struction of socialism" and constituted "an unforgivable compromise". According to Weit, Ulbricht went on to claim that, if this line contin-ued, it should be seen as a clear contradiction of the principles of Marx-ism–Leninism.[165]

3.2 POLICY

3.2.1 PRELIMINARY COMMENT

A highly significant ramification, in terms of content and structure, which stemmed from the inter-periodic changes in the environment and the parameters for determining policy, was linked to the open, prominent role fulfilled by Gomułka in representing the PZPR's 'systemic policy' towards the church during his second period of rule. This fact leaves less room—in comparison to the first period—for distinguishing between Gomułka's 'systemic' and 'personal' line during the second period. We shall therefore concentrate on the policy of the ruling elite, stressing Gomułka's role. For the same reason there will be a narrower account—compared with the first period—of those more relevant personal aspects that distinguished Gomułka from other members of this elite.[166]

3.2.2 LEGAL BACKGROUND

3.2.2.1 The Role of the Stalinist Period

The formal status of the church in this period was based chiefly on the church–state agreement of December 1956 and the 1952 constitution.[167] The continuity maintained through reliance on the 1952 constitution, as well as the link between the 1956 and the 1950 agreements—despite the amendments included in the first—in fact bear witness to the trend of continuity and to the roots that the legal situation in this period had in the preceding period. This continuity was maintained despite the fact that the 1956 agreement was characterized by the elimination of the restrictions identified with the period of repression and pressure. Moreover, elements of continuity in the formal foundation were preserved even in the 1945 to 1948 period—usually by preservative, positive norms, which had been determined in the intermediate period and incorporated into different sections of the 1950 agreement and the 1952 constitution. However, the changes in the second period of Gomułka's rule, in contrast to the first, also carry the legal imprint of the intermediate period.

From all this there is no reason to conclude, of course, that there was strict conformity to the formal decisions adopted between 1949 and 1956. However, despite the unprecedented atmosphere of conciliation in church-state relations at the beginning of this period, the new decisions showed that, from the beginning, *the government did not entirely relinquish the advantages it had gained in the previous period with respect to advancing Communist goals on the issue of the church and religion.* Only at first glance did the government position seem unclear, while the extreme restrictions during the period of repression undoubtedly helped to underline the advantages of the new period from the church's point of view.

3.2.2.2 A Comparison between the First and the Second Period of Gomułka's Rule

The 1956 agreement canceled the 9 February 1953 decree,[168] which granted the state exclusive supervision of appointments to ecclesiastical positions, and cited a new legal act according to which appointments would be subject to approval by a joint committee (principle 1 of the agreement). Such a new decree dealing with appointments to ecclesiastical positions was indeed published on 31 December 1956.[169] It determined that various senior appointments would require the approval of both the church and the state. The effect was that, whereas during the first period of Gomułka's rule the state's intervention in ecclesiastical appointments was not anchored in formal decisions—a direct outcome of the annulment of the concordat[170]—in this period such intervention was explicitly included in the agreement and mandated by the above decree. Moreover, it was decided that appointment to a church office would involve taking an oath of allegiance to the state. This was not the harsh wording of the oath used in the intermediate period (from 1953), but was still in contrast to the first period when no oath was required at all. (The text of the new oath published in the 31 December 1956 decree concerning ecclesiastical appointments states: "I swear allegiance to People's Poland, to observe its laws, and to refrain from any act which might threaten its interests.") Regarding appointments in the liberated territories, the 1956 agreement stipulated government approval for the appointment of five new bishops (now with the status of resident bishops) in the western dioceses of Poland and Gdańsk—despite their being only apostolic vicars and not permanent bishops (principle 6 in the agreement). This decision did indeed cancel the arbitrary appointment of capitular vicars, which had been introduced under government pressure back in 1951. However, as we know, during the first period of Gomułka's rule the apostolic bishops in these territories were appointed without government interference. Similar to the explicit stipulation contained in the concordat, all church appointees at this time had to be Polish citizens.[171] It seems, therefore, that at this point the government's aim was to neutralize the damage that it had suffered in the first period by the annulment of the concordat.

Similar to the situation between 1945 and 1948, and in keeping with the 1921 constitution, it was resolved that religious instruction would be offered in all elementary and high schools, but now only as an optional subject, to be taught either before or after the regular study hours. It was further decided that religious instruction would be given to all those pupils whose parents demanded it. (The extent of the studies was one hour per week in the first grade of elementary school; two hours per week from grades 2 to 7; and in high school one hour per week for all grades.) In accordance with the agreement, religious instructors were appointed by the educational authorities, subject to church approval (according to the names of lay people or clergy recommended by the church who were certified to teach religion)—similarly to the 1950 agreement—and received their salary from the Ministry of Education. Thus it appears that, despite the restoration of religious instruction to the schools, the government remained determined to impose formal, strict supervision in this important area. This was in contrast to the first period of Gomułka's rule, in which the right of supervision anchored in the 1921 constitution was formulated in general and non-explicit terms. Another difference between the two periods was that the religious instructors were materially dependent on the government—as stipulated in the education section (principle 2) in the 1956 agreement—a dependence not found in the first period. Unlike the first period, in which the government refrained from intervention in the religious study curriculum, during the second period the program of studies in religion required approval by the church and the educational authorities—as in the 1950 agreement. It was also resolved that pupils could fulfill religious obligations outside the schools, in contrast to the first period in which this had also been allowed in the schools. Already on 8 December 1956, the day the agreement was published, the minister of education issued a regulation concerning school religious instruction.[172]

The 1956 agreement, like the 1950 agreement, determined that religious services would be provided for the hospitalized (principle 3) and for prisoners (principle 4). In these matters there was continuity with the first period. On the other hand, the 1956 agreement did not mention the problem of the military priests, an issue requiring solution in the 1950 agreement. It was also resolved that the parish monks and priests expelled from Opole, Wrocław, and Katowice in 1953 should be allowed to return to their positions.

Like the 1921 constitution and the Declaration on Rights and Freedoms of 22 February 1947, the 1956 agreement and the 1952 constitution contained clauses relating to freedom of conscience and religion. However, in contrast to the more general formulation in the 1921 constitution, according to which this freedom was subordinate to state law, the 1952 constitution contained an explicit prohibition, with accompanying sanctions, regarding "the exploitation of religion against People's Poland". As already noted, the 1956 agreement included a commitment from the episcopate on this matter. A further difference stems from the fact that religious tolerance, which was guaranteed unilaterally in the formal decisions of the first period of Gomułka's rule, and which therefore appeared to be a privilege granted to the church, was presented as a two-way affair in the 1952 constitution and the 1956 agreement. This approach stressed that tolerance was also demanded from the church. Earlier, this side of the two-way demand had been underscored in the Decree Concerning the Freedom of Conscience and Religion of 5 August 1949.

The separation of church and state, which had lacked formal approval during the first period, became explicit in the 1952 constitution. As we know, this worsened the status of the church in the second period, since the distinct separation was chiefly intended as a check on its activity. The first place that the Roman Catholic Church occupied among other 'equal' religions under the 1921 constitution failed to receive any formal sanction in this period, since the acceptable formulation during this period was "the equality of all religious denominations". This was stated in various legislative acts, such as the clarifying act put forward by the Ministry of Education on 9 April 1957 concerning religious instruction in schools.[173] However, it should be recalled that in practice the govern-

ment also pursued a policy of equality during the first period of
Gomułka's rule, in order to undermine the Roman Catholic establishment.

3.2.2.3 Conclusions

During the second period of Gomułka's rule we find a stable legal foundation that is relatively clear-cut and specific and designed for concrete,
practical implementation. This contrasts with the legal base in the years
1945 to 1948, which was characterized, as we have said—against the
background of vagueness and uncertainty of the first period—by its
transitoriness and more general formulations. Now we see a clear shift
in favor of a reduction and withdrawal of the many benefits enjoyed by
the church in the first period. This deterioration was expressed in increased supervision of church activity through direct and indirect means,
as well as by intensified trends towards secularization and more exacting
demands from the church. The government, for its part, did not refrain
from using the threat of sanctions. Added to this was the fact that the
losses and damage, on various levels, incurred by the church during the
Bierut period, were perpetuated during the second period (as in the nationalization of church lands; the removal of Caritas from church
authority; the re-endorsement of the decree of 5 August 1949 relating to
the supervision of religious denominations, etc.).

3.2.3 IDEOLOGY VERSUS PRAGMATISM

In the period under review, as in 1945 to 1948, the ruling group continued its faithful adherence to the guiding principle which, on the one
hand, opposed concessions or compromise on the ideological level (this
also appeared in the 1956 agreement), while, on the other hand, supporting gradualism and the attainment of ideological goals through practical
policies grounded in a realistic evaluation of environmental factors. The
differences between the periods are embedded in this very principle, in
that the second period of Gomułka's rule represents a more advanced
stage in the realization of the Communist program, both in terms of religion and overall, relative to the first period—this against the back-

ground of the changes in the power of the ruling party, the power of the environmental factors, and their perception by Gomułka and the political leadership. Thus the second period was striking for the open display of ideological objectives, in contrast to their camouflage in the first period, and for the attempts to advance these objectives by undermining the church's ability to compete with the regime. In this sense, therefore, the first year after the agreement resembles the events of the first period more closely than the subsequent years of the second period. This resemblance, which arose from an intense consciousness of the state of emergency in the country, of the weakness of the party, and of the church's immense power, was reflected in gestures towards the church which included, *inter alia*, formulas for national cooperation and peaceful coexistence along with de-emphasis of ideological tensions. Despite this, in the very same year, at the Ninth Plenum of the PZPR Central Committee on 15 May 1957, Gomułka declared: "It is superfluous to point out that the party's doctrine is based on the scientific conception of dialectical materialism, and that idealist views are foreign to us...the agreement with the church has created a situation in Poland that has no parallel in any other socialist country or even in capitalist countries such as France and the United States...It is understood that this state of affairs does not conform to the views of our party."[174] Indeed, on continuing his speech Gomułka did not refrain from stating explicitly that reality could not possibly be ignored. This style of address, in an official forum, was totally uncharacteristic of Gomułka in the first period of his rule, and, as we have shown, of his comrades in the leadership. In a similar vein, but in a sharper, harsher manner, Tadeusz Mrowczyński stated in a contemporaneous article published in *Nowe Drogi* in May 1957 ("Comments on the Subject of Religion"): "...Communism cannot remain indifferent to religion...moreover, Communism is principally an ideological movement which aims at the transformation of social reality and must, therefore, clash with religion...one should not reach any conclusions about the ideological program of the party on the basis of its current policy—these are two separate areas..."[175] The severity of Mrowczyński's words, which, on the one hand, accentuates the differences between the two periods, conforms, on the other hand, to a similar trend witnessed in the first period when, typically, the most bitter attacks on the church were launched by forces which did not belong officially to the party leadership. The differences between the two periods

tended to sharpen with the passage of time following the 1956 agreement, in the context of what is customarily referred to as the 'retreat
from October', and as the consolidation of Gomułka's control over the
party progressed. The church's cooperation came to be seen as less vital
to the survival of Gomułka's control. Together with acts of conciliation,
there was an increase in formulations based on dogmatic arguments
positing that there was no room for appeasement between socialism and
religion, and stressing the scientific world-view and its objectives. However, as we know, verbal and practical restraint was nevertheless maintained. Thus Gomułka, responding to claims regarding the absurdity of
religious instruction in schools, countered with the following comment
at a national conference of party activists in the educational field on 24
September 1958: "Comrades, let us not forget something very fundamental: We are living in a period of transition—in a period of revolutionary changes and accelerated economic development, and, together
with this, slow changes in the consciousness of the people. We cannot
say that we live in a period that allows us to realize all the imperatives of
our ideology."[176]

The growing offensive to check the church's influence was transformed into a clear policy in Gomułka's formulations at the Third
PZPR Congress held in March 1959, which also served as a policy basis
throughout the 1960s. In this context, Gomułka attached great importance to purging the party itself of "religious prejudice".[177] Even though
the ideological offensive by Gomułka's regime in the second period
never matched the scope, intensity, or characteristic trends of the years
of repression during the intermediate period, and despite the fact that
the principle of making gradual progress and of "educating the people"
through persuasion was not abandoned, the overall picture relative to
the first period shows a considerable decline in the need and willingness
to show patience and toleration on the ideological issue. This inter-
period change was even more marked in Gomułka himself, in so far as
he was the one who openly represented the party's policy throughout
the second period. The affair of the Polish millennium celebrations was
the climax of both the ideological and the power struggle[178] in which the
personal confrontation between Gomułka and Cardinal Wyszyński
played an important role.[179]

3.2.4 GENERAL POLICY ATTRIBUTES

3.2.4.1 The Perception of Environmental Conditions and Their Impact on Policy

The beginning of the second period of Gomułka's rule was to a great degree reminiscent of the environmental conditions present during the Communist government's activity in the area of religion and the church, as in other areas, between 1945 and 1948. This was a system introduced following a period of pressure and repression, with a new regime and under conditions of emergency, uncertainty, and instability. The overall atmosphere was one of anxiety and insecurity, since the ruling Communist Party showed serious signs of weakness as it struggled to consolidate and stabilize its rule. The introduction of grand economic plans was the order of the day, and popular support a vital element in their realization. Furthermore, in both periods the political system demonstrated sensitivity to Western public opinion and its sanctions. It is these similarities that explain the benefits, restraint, and the "gradual path" chosen with regard to government policy concerning the church and religion in both periods. However, closer examination of these similarities does reveal differences between the two periods. The prism of the ruling group's positions, which continued to be characterized by political realism, was responsible for determining these differences and the consequent policy lines.

The turning point in Poland's history that occurred in the year 1945 was more significant than that in 1956. The birth pangs experienced during the first period of Gomułka's rule were far more painful. The first period was basically characterized, many times over, by uncertainty and instability regarding the future of Communism in Poland. The deformities of the Stalinist system, the efforts at de-Stalinization, and the reforms in the economic, social, and political system were minor compared to the demand for reconstruction and building in the wake of the devastation left by the war. This was all the more true in light of the fact that the government had to begin shaping itself as a Communist regime from scratch. Thus the first period called for a policy of restraint and caution and the postponement of a trial of strength with the church. The second period, however, was to witness such a trial of strength, albeit limited: the gestures towards the church were not as far-reaching as in the first period, while the demands, now presented in the name of the party, were more forceful and bore the threat of sanctions. These policy attributes stem, to a great extent, from the difference in the standing of the Polish Communist Party in the two periods. Throughout the second period, the PZPR operated as a formally united party which had accumulated experience and learned the lessons of a ruling power, while achieving legitimacy, albeit partial, at home and abroad. This, despite the stormy events of the Polish October which threatened its continued rule, and in contrast to the party's lack of legitimacy, lack of popularity, and absence of governing experience during the first period. In this context it is important to recall what had occurred in the liberated territories. There, facts had already been created on the ground, while the fears relating to their incorporation in the Polish state were greatly minimized relative to the first period. Also, with regard to the territories, the role of the church had been far more crucial during the first period.[180] Other pertinent, essential differences in the standing and character of the Communist Party, as well as in the overall political picture, were linked to factionalism, which was accentuated in the wake of de-Stalinization and the Polish October, and which sowed discord and oppositionist tendencies—dogmatism on the one hand, and revisionism on the other—in the party. All this contrasts with the first period of Gomułka's rule, when the internal factional structure was far less pronounced and left less of a mark on the system, and when tendencies opposed to the government policy were concentrated outside the party in the form of a legal political opposition (until 1947). The effort to consolidate his personal rule was more manifest in Gomułka's drive, during the second period of his rule, to strengthen the party's unity—by the defeat of the "revisionists" as well as the hard-line "dogmatists". This contrasts with the first period, during which the main struggle was against forces outside the party. It appears that the political picture during the first period was less complex and more polarized, both in regard to the regime's supporters and its opponents. In the second period, this was magnified by the presence of groups willing to meet the government half-way.

Correspondingly, the policy of the ruling group during the first period was characterized by more monolithic features, while the map of the forces pressuring Gomułka and his colleagues in policy making during the second period was more complex, more limiting, and less manageable, since it shaped a wavering line of alternating, aggravating, and moderating trends. (This was in contrast to the opinion that local leaders had greater freedom to maneuver after Stalin's death: (a) This opinion is not valid in the case of Gomułka when we compare the two periods of his rule; (b) due to the fact that, although direct pressure from the Soviet leadership was certainly less marked than during the Stalinist period, in the second period pressures of a different kind emerged). This was the source of the arguments used by opponents of Gomułka's policy during the 1960s—Bieńkowski on the one side, and the neo-Stalinists on the other side—concerning the "lack of consistency" and the absence of "rational criteria" in policy towards religion and the church.[181] The mosaic of pressures was many times more onerous due to increased, provocative pressure exerted by the church, by means of the population which supported it, and through attempts by the church establishment to reap maximum advantage from the 1956 agreement and the new situation that followed it.

The factional struggle within the PZPR had conflicting implications for Gomułka's policy towards the church. On the one hand, there was support for concessions due to the church's increased importance as a 'strong political partner', despite the declared opposing positions of the government regarding the politicization of the church. This trend, which backed the policy of Gomułka's 'centrist' faction as a counterweight to the dogmatists and the neo-Stalinists, reached its peak with the 1956 agreement. It grew weaker the more Gomułka consolidated his rule in the party. However, during the 1960s it became increasingly important whenever factional pressures and threats on Gomułka were felt and as his position weakened. An example of this was the meeting between Gomułka and Wyszyński in 1968 and their decision not to attack each other while Gomułka was under threat from Moczar. On the other hand, an opposite tendency became more conspicuous as the retreat from October continued, and as efforts to unify the party were more successful. It was reflected in a hardening of the policy towards the church, and was accompanied by concessions to the dogmatists. All this, against a background of a relative decline in the importance of the alliance with the church, but also as a result of the exploitation of the war against the church as a means of unifying the party and undermining the strength of the radical dogmatists. During the Ninth Plenum, the members of the Natolin group, and Mijał in the main, fiercely attacked

Gomułka's policy towards the church, on agriculture, and with regard to the workers' councils. The Zambrowski group was also dissatisfied with the policy of reaching an accord with the church and was willing to tolerate the church only as a temporary measure. Its approach was similar with regard to agriculture.[182]

In addition to the perpetual factional pressure from the party's central organs during the second period, great pressure was also exerted on Gomułka and the party leadership by the local conservative apparatuses, encouraged by the security bodies. This pressure, which had, according to Bieńkowski (1971, pp. 41,42) played a decisive role in the "retreat from October", did not exist in the first period, when local party elements were less organized and cohesive. Moreover, these forces, which refused to accept the concessions granted to the church under the 1956 agreement and which opposed the October program, repeatedly refused to obey orders from the center and operated arbitrarily.

The new forces pressuring Gomułka to "fulfill the ideological imperatives" were, as mentioned earlier,[183] the leaders of the East European bloc, chiefly Ulbricht, and the Communist leaders of other countries, led by the People's Republic of China. It is clear that Gomułka's desire for recognition and support from the forces which disapproved of the 1956 agreement and which emphasized the achievements of the other socialist countries in achieving programmatic goals, also contributed to the retreat from October. The ideological robes in which Gomułka wrapped himself, chiefly towards the end of the 1950s and during the 1960s, stemmed also, to a large degree, from past guilt with regard to the "right-wing nationalist deviation" of which he had been suspected. This conformed to the growing importance he attached (also, a. o., as a result of his advanced age and failing health) to his image in the Communist world and on the pages of world history.[184]

Heavy pressure on the part of the Soviet Union in October 1956, and the threat of armed intervention, which was one of the main motivations for the unprecedented alliance with the church in December 1956 (especially in an attempt to gain popular support and to prove that Communism still governed Poland), were gradually supplanted by the famous friendship between Khrushchev and Gomułka and their backing for one another.[185] It can be assumed that the close relations and understanding between the two leaders had equivocal implications where policy towards the church was concerned. On the one hand, Gomułka was left with greater freedom, but on the other, he became even more de-termined to please his Kremlin ally. But when all is said, the difference between the two periods in terms of Soviet pressure on Gomułka is not so considerable, given the dominant tactical considerations of Soviet policy in the first period, and the prevailing tendency in those days to 'disguise objectives'. We should also mention[186] that *towards the end of the 1950s, and even more during the 1960s, we witness Soviet demands to reduce pressure on the church as part of the effort to establish relations with the Vatican.* It should be stressed that the change in policy towards the church in 1959 cannot be ascribed to direct Soviet pressure since there is no evidence for this. On the other hand, there is no shortage of proof of factional pressures and pressure by the other countries in the bloc.

The role of the West must be counted among the environmental factors influencing policy in this area. In this period, trade agreements and material benefits from the West, as part of the policy of peaceful coexistence, fulfilled an important function. It is clear that in this context the PZPR leadership sought to impress Western public opinion and Western policy makers with the spirit of religious tolerance in Poland. Weit, for example, tells of such efforts by the Polish authorities during the visit of an Austrian parliamentary delegation to Poland.[187] The same tendency was also present in the earlier period, but then it was motivated more by a desire to consolidate and gain recognition for the regime. In contrast, the attitude during the first period towards Western economic aid was steeped in suspicion and guided by considerations of principle designed to prevent political interference through financial assistance. Hence, for example, the famous rejection of the Marshall Plan.

Thus, the policy makers' overall perception of the area and general environmental factors shaped, as in the first period, a simultaneous policy of restrictions and rewards. Except, perhaps, for a very short period after the 1956 agreement, the overall trend was towards a less favorable policy *vis-à-vis* the church. The restrictions were relatively severe, while the benefits were often reduced and subjected to constant erosion, in practice even more than legally. This tendency intensified during the 1960s.

3.2.4.2 The Psychological Environment

As in the first period, political realism, which continued to characterize Gomułka and the PZPR leadership during the second period, served to narrow the potential gap between reality and its problems and its perception in the eyes of the policy makers. In other words, in both periods policy did not stem from such a potential gap, but was influenced to a large degree by an authentic picture of reality. Through their behavior and formulations, Gomułka and the governing elite showed a heightened awareness of the environmental transformations discussed above, and of the parametric foundations that remained unchanged. Among these, the perception of the power and the sway held by religion and the church in Poland was prominent, and continued, undoubtedly, to constitute a major factor in the formation of policy. In Weit's words: "Despite its materialist world outlook, the leadership of the party had to admit, grinding its teeth, that the people were loyal to the church."[188] Moreover, in the second period the Communists went so far as to admit publicly that Poland could not have made its way into the modern civilized world without Christianity.[189] This was indeed consistent with Marxist thinking, which saw Christianity as having been a progressive phenomenon—in its own day.

In the famous interview granted by Gomułka to *Le Monde* in 1961, he stated: "Religion has deep roots among most of the [Polish] population, it would be illogical if we attempted to impose a transformation of mentality and beliefs through administrative methods...it is hard to say for how long religious faith will persist in Poland—certainly tens of years and maybe even more..."[190] At an earlier date, during a meeting with Fidel Castro (27 September 1960), Gomułka had warned his colleague against scorning the power of the Roman Catholic Church.[191] Ironically, Castro finally accepted this advice many years later, when the Polish pope visited Cuba after the fall of Communism. The same tone was present in a conversation with Ulbricht in 1963, in which Ulbricht explained how the church was handled in East Germany using scare tactics, recommending the same methods to Gomułka, who responded with skepticism: "Here, things are not so simple."[192] Tadeusz Mrowczyński, in an article already quoted here, stated: "Religious fanaticism is very powerful in the country. Many religious people even refuse to debate the subject as the very idea is taboo for them...and the only words that they have for those who do not share their beliefs are curses."[193] These problems, then, which had by now penetrated deep into the consciousness of the Polish policy makers, were also very much felt in the economic area. The government did not ignore "the influence of the church on the peasants, on whose cooperation in increasing agricultural production the entire five-year economic plan stood or fell".[194] The leadership was also aware that "in many districts in the country, the word of the priest is the decisive factor in the peasant's refusal to join cooperative farms".[195]

However, not only the general difficulties, but also the changes in the map of the Catholic forces in Poland, were fully grasped by Gomułka and his government comrades, and influenced their policy. This awareness affected government attempts to reach an understanding with the church and saw the exploitation of the new groupings for mediation. It also had an impact on efforts to restrict the church by trying to bring about confrontation between the new groups and the church hierarchy. The belief in the advantages that time (i.e. industrialization and modernization) would bring to the Communist regime in its struggle with the church was also founded on the fact that some Catholic groups had, from the beginning of the period, begun to display more positive attitudes towards the Communist regime despite their loyalty to the episcopate. This also applied to the attitude displayed by other groups within the population toward the government and the church. Thus Gomułka stated, in explaining the party's principles in relation to religion and the church: "A similar position is being adopted in Poland by different and more enlightened circles among the Catholics, who are trying to march towards progress and are searching for their place in a society building socialism. Several of these groups openly declare their support for socialism."[196]

3.2.4.3 Goals and Demands

It is superfluous to state that the government's basic objectives regarding religion and the church did not change. The differences between the periods were linked, first and foremost, to the strategy of dissimulation used in the first period, as against the relative exposure in the second. This was also the source of the different nature of the demands derived from these basic goals and of the means of struggle used to achieve them in the second period. In contrast to the first period, the demands made on the church by the government in the second period were more far-reaching, affected wider areas, and were much more forceful. These demands, which were explicit in the second period, were presented directly, in the name of the PZPR and its leadership, and accompanied, more than once, by threats and sanctions. Nevertheless there were elements of consistency and continuity, and more than a few demands and claims were reminiscent of tendencies and elements that existed during the first period.

Once again, the ambivalence in policy was striking as, on the one hand, the government demanded from the church—in accordance with the principle of separation between the church and the state, then explicit in the 1952 Polish constitution—to stay out of politics and public life, and to abstain from exploiting religious feelings for political objectives that had nothing to do with religion. In short, it was to concentrate its activity within the narrow confines of religious worship. At the same time, the government presented demands to the church to demonstrate active loyalty to the regime and to its policies—in the economic sphere and other areas—which clearly constituted political support. This tendency towards the politicization of church-state relations came to a climax in the events surrounding the 1956 agreement. Thus Gomułka himself appeared at a session of the Polish bishops in Warsaw on 2 November 1956 and called on the clergy to assist him in restoring peace and order.[197] Again, in his speech at the Ninth Plenum on 15 May 1957, Gomułka stated: "…the church must recognize the fact that Poland has changed its social system and that it is building socialism. We wish that in matters which concern the vital interests of People's Poland and the nation that the church will come along with us on the Polish path."[198] It should be added that in both periods the future of the relations between the church and the state were conditional on the positions and the line of action that the church chose, and the degree to which it responded to government demands. Thus, for example, there is a similarity in this respect between Gomułka's address to the Ninth Plenum[199] and statements made by Bierut in his famous interview of 20 November 1946 (mentioned on several occasions above), which included a threat regarding the removal of the basis for church concessions and benefits. In contrast to demands for church support for the government, which were emphasized at the beginning of the period and which smacked of politicization, the greater the distance from the Polish October the more forceful the demands presented to the church became. Thus the church was pressured fully to observe the laws of the state, to show religious tolerance in relations with non-believers and other religious denominations, and to desist from intervention in political affairs. These demands reached a climax at the Third Congress, where they were heavily stressed in comparison to similar demands made during the first period. As early as 9 January 1957, at an election meeting in Warsaw—against a background of social pressure on the children of non-believers in the schools—Gomułka warned that any discrimination on a religious basis comprised a serious infraction of discipline and would be met with punishment.[200] On the occasion of the events at Jasna Góra, Jerzy Sztachelski, the head of the Bureau of Religious Affairs, declared that even though the government was not interested in conflicts with the church "it cannot permit, and it will not permit, violation of the law. Similarly, the government vigorously opposes the exploitation of religious feelings for purposes that have nothing to do with these feelings."[201] At the Third Congress of the PZPR, Gomułka issued a stern, and even threatening, call:

> ...the church is separate from the state and is free to act only on the basis of the recognition of the social regime existing in Poland and on the basis of behavior appropriate to the *raison d'état* of People's Poland...the work of the church cannot, in any circumstances, be exploited for political purposes, to set believers against non-believers, for an attack against the policy of our party and against the rule of the people...we will not agree to any reactionary activity by the church...in social issues, in matters connected to the interests of the state and its policy. The church and the clergy must behave according to the laws of the state. This means that they must act with absolute loyalty towards the People's government. We warn the church hierarchy against the violation of state laws and decrees—which it has done again and again. We advise them to abstain from provocation against the People's government, since this will not be to the church's advantage...the church must remain only a church, it must restrict itself to its own area and concern itself only with matters of faith.[202]

In any case, the government continued to expect and demand loyalty to the regime and the support of the church on different societal and state issues until the end of the period. Thus, in a conversation between Bishop Bronisław Dąbrowski, secretary of the episcopate, and A. Skarżyński on 10 December 1970, a few days before Gomułka was ousted, the latter said: "...on many moral issues the church can help...in spite of everything..."[203]

3.2.4.4 The Means of Struggle

3.2.4.4.1 General

The year that followed the 1956 agreement was characterized by a freeze in the use of both direct and indirect means of struggle, both on the practical level and verbally. The basic contrast between this year and the years of repression which it ended—with Gomułka acting as the architect of this policy—created an exaggerated sense of continuity with Gomułka's 1945 to 1948 policy.[204] As in the first period, and in the spirit of the *modus vivendi* that had been achieved, the government did not interfere in the internal affairs of the church immediately after October, and refrained from attempts to damage its independence or its internal organization. In everything connected to the church organization the government behaved in a manner more far-reaching than in the first period, abstaining from even indirect measures, designed in the past to sow discord in the church; it also abandoned its previous attempts to exploit Pax and the Patriotic Priests for this purpose. However, the freeze in the use of these means of struggle could not, by the very nature of things, continue for long. The ideological dichotomy, and the competition for advantages and the accumulation of power—once again, strikingly, in the area of education and the schools—grew even sharper than in the past, due to developments in environmental conditions as previously discussed.

In 1958 signs of an open struggle began to appear. These can be explained, from the viewpoint of the government, by the 'unnatural' restraint of the previous year, by factional and bloc pressures on Gomułka, and by the offensive initiated by the church.[205] As in the first period, the changes did not, of course, acquire the character of a frontal attack. However, there were open clashes that prompted the repeated appearance of a mechanism that involved 'throwing the ball from one side to the other' until a crisis was reached, whereupon both sides searched for a compromise formula. The use of this particular confrontation mechanism was a faithful indicator that the tension of the first period, which had emanated from a sense of 'a future clouded in mist', had disappeared, and attested to a relaxation of tension in the Polish and Eastern European systems following de-Stalinization. In the current phase, and even more so during the 1960s, the means of struggle and conflict between the sides were marked by aggravation and intensification, in contrast to the first period and the situation in 1957. However, as we have said, these were not as far-reaching as they had been during the Stalinist period. Gomułka did not return to the Stalinist system of persecution,[206] but after the retreat from October pursued a path characterized by a diversity of both direct and indirect methods and measures, including sophisticated tricks and 'administrative harassment'.[207]

3.2.4.4.2 Bieńkowski's Approach

As long as the alliance with the church was a critical and fundamental element of Gomułka's policy there was room for tolerance and the application of formulations authored by the minister of education, Bieńkowski[208]: "Only by creating indifference can we pave the way to a narrowing of the church's influence"[209]; "...religion never died because of persecution"[210]; "A blow to the prestige of religion can never be achieved by battle with it, but by the problem burning itself out."[211] Although the predominant tendency in statements by Gomułka and other members of the leadership during the second period was to negate the measures of the past as Bieńkowski had argued, it was doubtful whether they were ever prepared to pursue the logic of these statements to the end. At any rate, it was clear that Gomułka could not sustain Bieńkowski's line for long, in the face of the environmental policy inputs already presented above, just as it was clear that he could not be completely loyal to the 1956 agreement. Government policy in 1958 clearly attested to the fact that Bieńkowski's principles were not being upheld. Differences of opinion between Gomułka and Bieńkowski regarding the school crisis that year, and the intensifying internal party debate over Bieńkowski's theses[212] pushed him into a position of isolation. His dismissal in 1959 signified the deathblow to his conceptions, in terms of their impact on party policy.

3.2.4.4.3 Administrative Measures

The policy of the second period was based, to a great degree, on the negation of Stalinist methods of repression, including the arrest and suspension of senior clergy. These methods, which were for the hierarchy a matter of *non possumus*, had strengthened the church in the past and created public sentiment hostile to the regime of which the government was aware. This was indeed the dominant theme in Gomułka's speeches at the Eighth and Ninth Plenums,[213] which also found expression in the party press.[214] The same theme is reflected in the words of Jerzy Sztachelski, who represented the government's policy towards the church: "The tactics used before October 1956 were a mistake. The measures taken against the hierarchy and the religious orders...caused an intensification of religious feelings."[215] This position on administrative and police measures was what determined the similarity and the continuity between the first and second periods. However, the tone of things changed during 1958. That year witnessed a shift away from an unequivocal rejection of administrative measures in favor of an affirmation, albeit with reservations, of such measures, both in word and deed. On the practical level, the change was emphatically expressed by the search conducted at Jasna Góra on 21 July 1958. In a speech given at the national conference of party activists in the educational field, which was published on 24 September 1958, Gomułka stated: "We do not reject administrative methods. The socialist state is a powerful administrative instrument...But administrative methods should be used only when we know that political consciousness is high."[216] In his speech before the Plenum of the Central Committee in October 1958, in response to heavy pressure from the dogmatists to reintroduce administrative methods, Gomułka explained that the state was indeed "an apparatus for the use of force against hostile anti-socialist elements", but described these methods as an auxiliary factor, better avoided. He also added: "Let us not go down the same [Stalinist] path again, that cannot bring victory...only a path that calls for a firm connection with the masses is good enough to lead us to victory."[217] The speeches by Gomułka and Cyrankiewicz before the Third Congress made it clear that the party would not refrain from using administrative methods combined with "the formation of social consciousness", even though it continued to regard them as emergency measures, to be employed when no other alternative was left. This position was put into practice, in real life, during the clashes and incidents which increased from the second half of 1958 and through the 1960s. At any rate, the government was unwilling publicly to admit to the use of police tactics against the masses, just as it was unwilling to stress the existence of a massive opposition. It tended, therefore, in the propaganda war that it waged around these events, to represent those elements against which it employed police methods as deviant social forces, not representative of the general population. This explains the frequent use of such phrases as "hooligans incited by clericalism", as, for example, during the denunciation of the demonstrators at Nowa Huta on 14 May 1960.[218] On the same occasion the demonstrators were presented as parasitic elements who did not represent the local workers. The method was also adopted by the Gierek regime, for example during the affair of the Radom and Ursus riots.[219] In contrast, during the first period the use of the militia was restricted mainly to those elements among the clergy, who were indeed also represented as deviants and "hooligans", which collaborated with the opposition and "the subversive gangs". This was a more limited phenomenon and was not accompanied by verbal declarations.

3.2.4.4.4 Threats to Church Independence and Internal Organization

Evidence of the retreat from October in the area of religion and the church was also to be found in the ever-increasing attempts to undermine the church's independence and its internal organization. These efforts differed from similar efforts in the first period. Now, along with indirect methods, the authorities did not hesitate to employ measures far more direct and severe. This found expression in a resumption of interference in ecclesiastical appointments in 1958. Until then, the government had not exercised its right of veto under the terms of the 1956 agreement. In addition to the pressure to cancel the appointment of Bishop Klepacz, while the hierarchy, on its part, delayed its response to the government's demands, Wyszyński testified that on several occasions during the 1960s he had changed the list of candidates for ecclesiastical positions following state interference.[220] There was also a gradual aggravation in the use of fiscal methods, such as the imposition of different kinds of taxes. As already noted, such methods were not common in the

first period. The second period, however, saw increased attempts to sow
discord and division within the church, including efforts to isolate the
hierarchy from the rest of the clergy, the population, and the Vatican.
All this, with the emphasis that the struggle was not against religion and
all believers but against the activity of some of the clergy.[221] It was
against this background that Wyszyński reprimanded the priest
Stanisław Owczarek, on 21 August 1962, for cooperating with the
Communist government. Wyszyński's words were: "The Communists
destroy the church...under these circumstances, how can you drink
vodka with them on the occasion of the 22 July reception?"[222] The presentation of such measures as part of the 'class struggle' lost much of its
earlier impact due to the confiscation of church lands and property during the Stalinist period. Nevertheless, the government did not refrain
from pointing an accusing finger at members of the clergy, who were
described as possessing feudal tendencies and plotting to restore lands
that had been confiscated legally and justly. As early as 1958 the
authorities accused "certain clericalist circles" of seeking to create a rift
between the church and the state, by involving themselves in different
types of educational and social activities unrelated to the functions of the
church.[223] This tactic of distinguishing between 'positive' and 'negative'
elements, which also appears in Gomułka's speeches of that year (1958),
is reminiscent of the technique used in the first period. For the first time
since 1956, Cyrankiewicz referred once again at the Third Congress to
"anti-socialist political activity by a section of the clergy", and blamed
the hierarchy for "resolute activity to eliminate all the priests whose attitude to the people's state is that of good citizens".[224] Moreover, in contrast to the first period, and even to the Stalinist period, the divisive efforts were now—and chiefly during the 1960s—connected to efforts to
stir up antagonism among different bishops, and even between the bishops and Wyszyński himself. *There were attempts to slander and isolate
Wyszyński, to create alternative power centers to that of the primate, and to try
and influence the appointment of an additional cardinal, Wojtyła.*[225] Another
unique feature at the end of the 1950s and during the 1960s, was the effort at manipulation on the part of Gomułka and the party, aimed at exploiting the various Catholic groups and setting them against the
Catholic hierarchy.[226]

As in the first period, there were attempts in the 1960s to bypass
Wyszyński and the Polish hierarchy with respect to establishing rela-

tions with the Vatican. This time, however, the government, in its attempt to drive a wedge between the hierarchy and the Apostolic See, sought to exploit the special position of John XXIII and his 'Pacem in Terris' policy in order to show that some of the Polish bishops had deviated from the path chartered by the pope. The government also tried to stress that Wyszyński's 'reactionary' views diverged from the spirit of the new outlook in the Vatican. As policy towards the church hardened, and in order to discredit the hierarchy and Cardinal Wyszyński in the eyes of the population, the government once more attacked their positions regarding the liberated territories. This trend reached a climax in the affair of the letter to the German bishops against the background of the millennium celebrations. As in the first period, the government also used the tactic of accusing priests of economic offenses (such as the accusations against Jesuit priests for illegal trading reported in *Głos Pracy*, 21 April 1959).

We need to add a number of subjects to the methods used in the government's struggle (see later) which will provide illustrations of the general policy. These include media propaganda; press censorship; pressurizing various groups within the population, such as factory workers, to denounce "disgraceful maneuvers" by the clergy[227]; bureaucratic harassment and technical restrictions (for example, the prohibition of the use of loudspeakers by churches outside churches buildings)[228]; refusal to grant permits to travel abroad to leaders of the clergy; and withholding licenses for the construction of new churches. None of these measures, even those applied in a limited manner, were in any case characteristic of the first period.

Thus Gomułka did not abandon the idea of allowing the Catholic Church in Poland special treatment, and continued to adhere to the principles of his 'Polish path'. Nevertheless, he succeeded in restricting, to a large extent, the political, social, and economic living space of the church in comparison to the years 1945 to 1948.

3.2.5 SPECIFIC POLICY

3.2.5.1 The January 1957 Elections

The atmosphere surrounding the January 1957 elections was totally different to that of the elections in January 1947. The sense of distrust and
anxiety clouding the earlier elections was replaced, in this period, by a
spirit of cooperation, unprecedented in the history of Communist Poland. The proximity of the elections to October and to the December
1956 agreement enveloped them with a sense of *modus vivendi* that could
be seen in positions adopted by both sides. In contrast to the 1947 elections, both the state and the church profited from this cooperation. The
government, which this time around demanded genuine support, which
it desperately needed, was not to be appeased with the church's neutrality and non-intervention as it had been in the past. This time, it did not
have to work hard to achieve this support. As we have seen, the church
itself was interested in offering this support, and consequently there was
no call for the government to resort to threats, as it had in the first period. The hierarchy, and Wyszyński himself,[229] realizing that there was
no chance of the government agreeing to an independent Catholic
party, demanded that independent Catholic candidates be included in
the electoral list and was met with a positive response from Gomułka.
The support from lay Catholic intellectuals in the run-up to the elections undoubtedly facilitated the granting of this request. Thus the Znak
group enjoyed an unprecedented representation of five Sejm members as
well as the status of a faction (the Znak circle of representatives) in the
Sejm, although they were formally included as individuals in the National Unity Front lists. In addition, another four 'independent' Catholics joined their 'club' in the Sejm. However, Gomułka's stand against
the establishment of a Catholic party remained inflexible and final. This
position was to continue as a permanent element in the policy of the
Communist government throughout all the periods. Thus, once again,
when speaking about the electoral system at the Central Committee
meeting in 1965, Gomułka commented: "There is no place for representatives of the believers of the Catholic Church as such."[230] Similarly,
Gomułka displayed consistent opposition to the revival of the Christian
Democratic Party.[231] The spirit of cooperation and understanding
manifested during the elections did not disappear once they were over.

This time around the government recognized the importance of the church's influence on the election results and continued to see its alliance with the church as providing an important basis of support. A letter from the Politburo to all levels of the party and its organizations, dated February 1957, stressed that the position of the church must be listed among the factors responsible for the election victory.[232] In contrast to the January 1947 elections, which had marked a change in government policy towards the church and which were followed by a period characterized by attacks and restrictions, government policy in the period following the 1957 elections continued to provide for benefits in the spirit of the pre-election promises. This difference between the two periods stemmed from the difference in the post-election power of the party and the Communist government in the two periods. In the first period, the defeat of Mikołajczyk's legal opposition actually removed the main obstacle hindering the consolidation of the party's power, whereas Gomułka's victory in the 1957 elections failed to overcome the problem of factionalism in the party which continued to prevent the consolidation of the regime. Thus after the 1957 elections the church preserved its status as a vital source of support—a status whose importance increased even further due to the fact that relations of trust and support between the new government and the leadership of the Soviet Union had yet to be consolidated.

3.2.5.2 Policy towards the Vatican

In this period the government distanced itself from the previous pattern of bitter antagonism toward the Apostolic See, according to which the Vatican had been perceived as "the fortress of imperialism supporting the revisionist and revanchist tendencies of Western Germany". The change came, as we have already mentioned, to a large degree as a result of the new winds blowing through the Vatican, which found expression in new Vatican positions and policies. These changes in the attitude of the government, which were already felt during the rule of Pius XII, became more pronounced during the reign of Pope John XXIII. The Polish government was progressively encouraged by the new pope's policies of coexistence *vis-à-vis* the non-Catholic world, and by his more conciliatory position towards the Communist world and Poland. The sense of satisfaction, with some degree of anxiety, which characterized the position of the Polish government at the start of the new pope's reign, was later supplanted by relatively high expectations for the solution of the outstanding problems that posed obstacles to relations between the sides. Gomułka and the government leadership responded more and more positively to gestures by John XXIII, whom they regarded in a much more positive light than Pope Pius XII, who had been seen as "the Cold-War pope".[233] Thus the incumbency of John was considered to be a sign of the dawn of a new era. The moderately positive response in Warsaw[234] to the pope's step with regard to K. Papée's diplomatic status in the Vatican,[235] gave way to a tendency towards greater enthusiasm at the beginning of the 1960s. This took the form of compliments from Gomułka himself and from other comrades in the leadership, quotations from the pope's words,[236] and energetic initiatives to reach an agreement, and even to renew the concordat.[237] Victor Vinde, the chief editor of *Stockholms Tidningen*, explained, with regard to an interview that Gomułka had granted him: "I understood that Gomułka considered Pope John XXIII a much more modern Catholic than the cardinal in Warsaw."[238] Although it appeared that Gomułka was guided by Poland's interest, in fact his changed attitude toward the Apostolic See formed part of Moscow's policy of rapprochement with the Vatican. This policy even involved, as we have said, the exertion of pressure from Moscow brought to bear on Gomułka and on the PZPR.

Despite the general trend, the amelioration in relations was not marked by smoothness or continuity. Thus, in April 1959, the government press forsook the conciliatory line towards the Apostolic See, which it had adopted since the coronation of John XXIII, and launched an attack, reminiscent of the past, against "pro-German circles in the Vatican, who take pleasure in their increased activity and the revival of their influence". It also reported "the pope's surrender to pressures by [these] pro-German circles".[239] For the first time in several months, *Trybuna Ludu*, for example, initiated attacks against the Vatican in April 1959. An article which appeared in May in *Życie Warszawy* (12 May 1959), criticized the unchanging face of the new pope's policy with regard to the liberated territories, Poland's western borders, and other matters. As in the past, this shift must indeed be seen in the context of a hardening of the policy towards the Polish Church. This took place against the background of the Third Congress, which met in March, and attacks against the church were once more evident in the heightened propaganda attack on the Vatican. It does seem, however, that the severity of the problems facing the two sides in fact forced the gap in the two sides' positions and frustrated the movement toward improved relations. This basic gap proved to be the source of recurrent disappointments. Thus the elevation of the Berlin bishop, Döpfner, to the rank of cardinal, which came at the same time as a refusal to approve Polish government demands for the appointment of an additional Polish cardinal,[240] constituted the reason for a regression in the policy towards the Vatican. The government did not refrain from exerting pressure on the Vatican regarding the Oder–Neisse borders, among other things, by organizing demonstrations by priests. Such demonstrations, which received wide press coverage, were held ostensibly in the name of the church. These methods recall the government's policy in the Stalinist period and its demands that the episcopate participate in protesting German revisionism.[241] A similar regressive tendency during the 1960s was seen to emerge after attempts to reach an agreement with the Vatican failed.

Despite all this it is possible to conclude that in contrast to the first period, in which many attacks on the Vatican served as an indirect means of attacking the Polish episcopate, and in contrast to the Stalinist period, which was marked by the expansion of attacks against both the Vatican and the episcopate, the retreat from October, chiefly during the 1960s, was marked mainly by attacks and propaganda efforts aimed, first and foremost, against the Polish Church itself, and to a much lesser degree against 'certain circles' in the Vatican.

The attempts to circumvent the Polish primate and the hierarchy in relations with the Vatican, witnessed in the first period, were more far-reaching in the 1960s, when the government was acting with the intention of bringing about Wyszyński's resignation or, at least, his transfer to the Curia in Rome.[242] These attempts at bypassing the church, which were reminiscent of the mediation efforts by different lay Catholics during the first period, included the exploitation of mediation services by Znak members such as Jerzy Zawieyski,[243] which turned out to be unsuccessful.[244] When the government failed, both in its maneuvers against Cardinal Wyszyński and in the previously mentioned bypass attempts, to reach an agreement with the Vatican, it turned again, as in the previous two periods and in parallel with the resumption of visits by the church leadership to Rome in May 1957, to the hierarchy, in an effort to appease it in order to avail itself again of its mediation services.[245]

3.2.5.3 Pax as an Instrument of the Government

Gomułka's second period in power was characterized by a lessening in the importance of Pax and the Patriotic Priests as a government tool to be used in the battle with the church. This was so relative to the first period, and even more so in contrast with the period between 1949 and 1956. Gomułka's return to power signified a low point in the status and activity of Pax and the Patriotic Priests. This created room for speculation over the elimination of the organization and the end of Piasecki's career. Such conjecture was based on the fact that these forces had been an integral instrument of the now denounced previous system, and because the *raison d'être* for Pax no longer existed due to the new circumstances on the ground. The changes in scenario now prompted Gomułka to take an interest in cooperation with genuine Catholic leaders in order to strengthen the popular base of his newly restored rule. Piasecki's personal animosity toward Gomułka was no less important a consideration when evaluating the chances of the organization and its leader for survival. Piasecki's hostility was displayed when Gomułka and his wife were arrested in 1951[246] and Piasecki expressed his support for this step; and, once again, when he revealed his opposition to Gomułka's return to power.[247] However, despite the prevailing lack of sympathy for Piasecki and other members of Pax—an attitude which contrasted starkly with Gomułka's positive attitude toward the movement in the first period[248]— and despite Gomułka's approval, encouragement, and support for the Frankowski group's split from Pax, Gomułka made no move to eliminate the group and put an end to Piasecki's political and public activity, and even refrained from publicly denouncing them. Pax continued to enjoy the stable economic privileges it had accumulated in the past and to administer an extensive complex of projects, with enormous funds at its disposal. It still owned the only Catholic daily. Even its political activity, though diminished, did not cease completely; in the 1957 Sejm elections it gained one seat, as did the Frankowski group. This was in contrast to the three seats it had in the Sejm that had convened after the 1947 elections. While the government refused to allow what were referred to as

"Catholic intelligentsia clubs" to be set up, Pax was able to establish a wide network of its own clubs and local organizations. While the party refused to sanction authentic Catholic representation in the local councils, it recognized Pax candidates in 300 districts and cities.[249]

As in the past, public thinking ascribed the survival of Piasecki and his organization to his special relations with the Soviet secret police. However, it seems that in the late 1950s and during the 1960s, Gomułka himself did not forgo the services that Pax performed for him. This, despite the organization's failure to strike roots among the Polish Catholics, to gain the confidence of the Vatican, and to isolate the hierarchy, and despite its constant support for the dogmatists on the one hand, and, on the other hand, Piasecki's 'brazen' declarations that "Pax is unwilling to continue to serve as a vassal of the party forever."[250] Gomułka continued to view Pax as a tool for splitting the Catholic forces, since a multiplicity of groups on the lay Catholic political map, at this stage and during the 1960s, gave him an advantage of power in his relations with each of them and increased the possibilities for setting them against Wyszyński and the episcopate when policy towards the church took a downturn.

The increasingly tense relations between the church and the state, and the retreat from October, marked a new expansion in the scope of Pax activity. In his address to the Third Party Congress in March 1959, Gomułka spoke favorably about "Catholics who clearly declare themselves supporters of socialism".[251] This tendency became more pronounced in a meeting between Piasecki and Gomułka, which took place at the latter's initiative in the summer of 1959[252] and at their meeting in November 1959.[253] At both meetings Gomułka made it clear that Pax was free to expand its activities and that the PZPR would support them. However, the 1960s prove that this was not a new impetus for Pax's reestablishment. The fluctuations in the government's attitude toward Pax that characterized these years contrasted with the government's attitude in the first period, and were expressed in a policy which alternately combined the bestowal of benefits and the imposition of sanctions. These were determined mainly by the extent of Pax's success in fulfilling the government's goals, by the differences between Pax's formulations and the positions held by Gomułka and his political allies, and by the degree to which Pax tried, or was able, to accumulate power by exploiting the factional struggle within the PZPR. These factors played a role in the economic and political blow dealt to Pax following the meeting between Gomułka and Piasecki on 25 January 1961. At the same meeting Gomułka called on Pax to cease disseminating its ideological position on a "plurality of world-outlooks" and to halt its self-adopted initiative to spread Communist propaganda. The ideological-political program was detailed in Piasecki's book *Polish Patriotism*, and in *The Ideological Guide*, published in 1958. According to one source, at the above meeting Gomułka demanded that Piasecki cease Pax activity with regard to collectivization.[254] He described their demands for partnership in the leadership and for the status of an equal partner in building the Communist system as "irritating and impudent", especially in light of their poor track records.[255] According to one source, on which an RFE interview report was based, the return of Roman Zambrowski and Jerzy Albrecht to the government served to undermine Pax's position.[256] Gomułka persisted in his opposition to a political party sponsored by Pax, just as he opposed the idea of a political party for other lay Catholic groups, although he did find the Christian Social Society (the Frankowski group) more amenable to him and his party.[257] Pax's accomplishments once again influenced a change in policy—this time in a positive direction—with Piasecki's return from Rome at the beginning of 1963, when Gomułka agreed to increase Pax's yearly income along with other benefits.[258] On the other hand, Pax's support for Moczar during the second half of the 1960s led to increased taxation on Pax enterprises and Piasecki's personal income.[259]

Gomułka's repeated complaints to Piasecki during the 1960s, regarding the negligible success in the recruitment of priests and the very low level of activity undertaken by Pax,[260] clearly demonstrated Gomułka's increasingly ambivalent attitude to Pax and its leader. Although he did not abandon the organization, his disappointment deepened and his expectations decreased—a striking tendency in comparison to the first period.

3.2.5.4 The Policy of Benefits and Concessions

3.2.5.4.1 The Polish October

Gomułka's return to power in October 1956 brought with it far-reaching concessions and gestures towards the church. This well-known fact has already been described in a different context. The opening in this direction, which appeared as early as September 1956, and which was reflected in the release of prelates who were in prison or under house arrest and their return to their dioceses, was impressive. Bishop Kaczmarek was the first to be released. He was followed by the three Silesian bishops, Adamski, Bednorz, and Bieniek (27 September 1956). Archbishop Baziak was set free in October, and Baraniak and Bernacki were released on 5 November 1956. At the end of October (28 October 1956) the political process reached a climax with Cardinal Wyszyński's release from isolation at the Komancza monastery by two distinguished figures from among Gomułka's colleagues—Zenon Kliszko, the recently appointed deputy minister of justice, and Władysław Bieńkowski, who was still director of the National Library in Warsaw.[261] The government's readiness to reach a far-reaching settlement that would settle the disputes was reflected in the joint communiqué, dated 8 December 1956, which declared the government's willingness "to remove all the obstacles preventing the realization of the principle of full freedom for religious life"[262] and, of course, in the practical concessions offered in the December 1956 agreement.[263] According to testimony given by Makarczyk, a Znak representative in the Sejm, on 12 July 1957, Gomułka and the PZPR made far-reaching promises in this regard during the winter of 1956/1957, which went beyond those of the 1956 agreement and which went especially far where education and material benefits were concerned.[264] Gomułka's gestures and concessions may be seen to a large degree as steps intended to correct the injustices of the previous Stalinist period—a policy also stressed in Gomułka's address to the Eighth Plenum. These measures helped to improve the church's situation by restoring many of the benefits that had been withdrawn during the Stalinist period. However, the conditions of the first period were not fully restored, as was evident in all matters concerning the status of religion in state institutions, the contraction of the church's material basis, and the absence of exceptional overtures by the leaders of

the regime towards religion and the church—which had been made
more than once during the 1945 to 1948 period. However, even in the
spheres of education and ecclesiastical appointments, which were considered to be areas in which the church had scored impressive achievements within the framework of the December 1956 agreement, there
was a retreat in comparison to Gomułka's first period of rule. In a number of areas, however, there was a return to the *status quo ante*, as exemplified by the permission to publish the two important periodicals *Tygodnik Powszechny* and *Znak*. Moreover, in certain other spheres the
benefits were even more far-reaching than in the first period. This phenomenon was particularly impressive in the issues linked to the representation of lay Catholics in the Sejm. It could be seen in the opportunity created to introduce five members of the Znak group into the Sejm
in the 1957 elections, and the establishment of the Znak circle in the
Sejm with the participation of four Catholic representatives who had
participated as independents in the list of the National Unity Front.[265]

3.2.5.4.2 Freedom of Worship and the Construction of Church Buildings

Gomułka's policy towards the church remained consistent throughout
both periods with regard to basic rights allowing religious observance. It
also refrained from any sharp attacks on the concept of divinity or religious dogma. In the middle of 1957 the Ministry of the Interior canceled
a circular that had been issued on 23 November 1949[266] by the minister
of public administration, thereby creating serious obstacles to carrying
out demonstrations, pilgrimages, and religious ceremonies.[267] Likewise,
after the retreat from October the government made no moves to close
churches or prevent believers from attending religious services or receiving the sacraments. Nor did it try to stigmatize the church faithful,
whose support was still considered to be vital. Moreover, although such
anti-clerical activities had not been employed even during the years of
repression, in the period of the retreat from October the government
continued to respond to initiatives by the primate and hierarchy, and
even continued to appropriate resources to reconstruct church buildings
and build new churches—though indeed to a lesser degree than in the
first period. It was this approach, in fact, which provoked the critical re-
marks by the correspondent of the Yugoslav *Borba*, Duško Jovanovič (in

an article on the conflict between the state and the church in Poland), who complained about the increase in new churches, claiming that (7 September 1958): "About seven hundred new churches and chapels have been built in Poland since the Second World War. Two hundred and eighty are still under construction..."[268] In response to church complaints on the subject, lower numbers were cited by the government. In an announcement issued in November 1960, it was pointed out that 151 churches had been reconstructed since the war, 373 new churches and chapels built, and approximately 250 additional church buildings "were still in the process of construction".[269] Radio Tirana came out at a later date and sharply accused "Gomułka's clique" of "assistance in the reconstruction of 500 churches and the construction of 600 new ones".[270] Despite the fact that the numbers were influenced by the various agendas of the spokesmen, the scope of the assistance can be learnt from all these sources.

Alongside the technical restrictions that came to impede the work of the priests, such as the 1958 prohibition on the use of loudspeakers outside church walls,[271] the government, in an apparently surprising move, continued to provide technical assistance for the religious population, for example by arranging transportation during pilgrimages and other religious events. However, there was far less willingness to extend this kind of assistance than in the first period.

3.2.5.4.3 Conciliatory Formulations by the Leaders of the Regime

The extraordinary attempts by Bierut and other government representatives during the first period to demonstrate an 'exaggeratedly' friendly attitude to the church and the religious population were not repeated in the second period. However, verbal gestures did persist, along with practical benefits and standard formulations regarding freedom of conscience and worship.[272] These demonstrations of good will were designed to build bridges between the two sides and bring about cooperation between them, even during deterioration in the relations between the church and the state and at times when threats by the Communist leaders were being voiced. The government always left the window slightly open for conciliation around focal points of tension, incidents, and clashes, and there were always moderating assertions. This was because the government could not, under any circumstances, relinquish the support of the believers and their enlistment for national objectives. A Polish Communist presented the matter in the following way: "The need for agreed cooperation between believers and non-believers in the construction of People's Poland, in the formation of a modern socialist society, and in the strengthening of the Polish people and state among the nations, was and is consistently emphasized in all programs of our internal policy."[273] In his speech to the Ninth Plenum (May 1957), when the main points in the agreement were still being observed, Gomułka called for peaceful coexistence and travel along a common path toward building up socialist Poland: "Our party proceeds on the assumption that the idealist world-outlook will continue to exist for a long time, alongside the materialist world-outlook. Thus, believers and non-believers, the church and socialism, the people's rule and the church hierarchy will dwell alongside one another...we have reached the conclusions about inevitable coexistence...we do not interfere when, in matters of faith, the church pursues its Roman doctrine (though it must recognize the change in Poland's regime)."[274] In another speech Gomułka stated: "We have created an appropriate atmosphere for normalization in the relations between the state and the church and we have demonstrated good will, as far as possible, in this matter. We have created conditions for public and organizational activity for various Catholic trends and groups, on the basis of consensual cooperation between believers and non-believers in the development of People's Poland."[275] Again, during his speech at the Third Congress, Gomułka continued to emphasize that: "Our party aspires to combine all the forces of the people. In no circumstances, does it draw a dividing line in society according to the position towards religion. It judges the behavior of the citizens according to their practical attitude to socialism. The basic value of the citizen is evaluated on the basis of his work for the country—his real role in the construction of socialism."[276] Later in his address, after voicing warnings to the church hierarchy, Gomułka found it appropriate to add: "We repeat, once again, we do not want war with the church."[277] Also, at the national conference of PZPR activists in the educational field, held in September 1958, Gomułka said: "We are not looking for wars with the church, we have given many proofs of this..."[278] Peaceful declarations, such as these by representatives of the regime, remained a permanent fixture, despite increasing confrontations between the church and the state. Thus, against the background of the events at Jasna Góra in July 1958, Jerzy Sztachelski, the government representative for church affairs, declared that: "The government is always interested in reaching an understanding with the church and is not looking for conflict or for a stalemate..."[279]

3.2.5.4.4 Conciliation Contacts

The tendency to overcome the stalemate and to settle conflicts, the intensification of which was considered a source of great danger by Gomułka and the members of the elite during the second period, found practical expression in the increased number of mixed episcopate-government commissions at the end of the 1950s and during the 1960s. This tendency was commensurate with the fact that the conflict and struggle were all the more explicit during the second period. Relative to the years 1945 to 1948, the commissions now fulfilled a more important role in coordinating relations, despite the fact that, once again, many obstacles were raised in their path and their efforts were met with repeated failure. The relative success of the commissions during the second period should largely be seen in the light of the different character of the tasks they undertook. In the first period, it was generally a matter of searching for an overall solution—which usually led to a dead end—while in the second period the tendency was to identify solutions to pressing, concrete problems, and to find some way to avoid real confrontation. In addition, the commissions' mode of operation was more acceptable to the church in the second period relative to the difficulties that had arisen due to the authoritarian attitude and dictates of Minister Wolski in the first period.[280]

The period in question opened with the work of the Joint Commission, which was composed of Politburo member Jerzy Morawski; the government representative for church affairs, Jerzy Sztachelski; the bishop of Łódź, Michał Klepacz; and the episcopate secretary, Bishop Zygmunt Choromański.[281] This commission, established at the beginning of November, succeeded in bringing about the signing of the December 1956 agreement. The Joint Commission, which convened on 31 July 1958, in which the government was again represented by Jerzy Sztachelski and also by Zenon Kliszko, while the episcopate was again

represented by bishops Klepacz and Choromański, contributed to the
solution of the Jasna Góra affair. In the same year the Joint Commission
took an active role in achieving a compromise solution to the famous
conflict on the distribution of foreign grants to the Catholic Church.[282]

The meetings between Gomułka and Cardinal Wyszyński also involved attempts to pave the way to a solution and end the church-state
stalemate.[283] General questions, though not specific problems, were often discussed at these meetings. The more general discussions were designed to prepare the psychological foundations for contacts on the operational level, rather than to achieve any real solutions. Members of
Znak, such as Jerzy Zawieyski[284] and Stefan Kisielewski[285] were another
channel that Gomułka tried to mobilize to assist him in solving outstanding problems with the church. Of course, contacts through this
channel existed only during the second period.

3.2.5.4.5 Material Benefits

The extraordinary economic concessions won by the church in the first
period were not duplicated in the second period. The non-cancellation
of the law imposing agrarian reform on the church, and the fact that
Caritas was not reinstated, were, as said before, highly conspicuous.
Nevertheless, the Polish October restored to the church a number of
economic privileges lost during the Bierut period. Even though the concessions did not fulfill all the promises—including those specified in the
communiqué dated 8 December 1956—they helped the church to revive
from past pressure and to renew its activity. From the beginning of 1957
the Ministry of Justice issued instructions designed to regulate the financial status of church personnel. This included full or partial exemption from taxes, which had been levied on funds designated for religious
needs, education, charity, and social services.[286] A reduction in tax was
also granted to parish priests, by deducting the amount they received as
housing grants. Agricultural property owned by priests was deemed
subject to taxation within the framework of the general regulations
dealing with peasants' private property. However, a promise was made
to consult the bishop before raising taxes.[287] Church functionaries were
also exempted from submitting reports on expenses and income as they
had been forced to do in the years of repression, until this requirement

was reintroduced in 1959.[288] The restoration of certain real estate to the church must be added to the list of material benefits appearing on the asset side of the balance sheet,[289] together with, of course, the sums allocated by the state for the reconstruction, repair, and construction of churches and chapels.[290]

To a great extent the retreat from October eliminated or restricted these material benefits, thus reducing material benefits relative to the 1945 to 1948 period.

3.2.5.4.6 Freedom of the Press and Publication

The renewed permission to publish the lay Catholic press, whose positions were close to the episcopate, conformed to the interests of the Polish Church. In fact, this step by the government was one of the most important rewards given by the government to the church in exchange for its support. However, this was first and foremost a direct payment to the lay Catholic forces for their direct support of Gomułka and his program. The significance of this act of singling out a group of lay Catholics for reward, which had never taken place in the first period, becomes even sharper with the increase in tension in church-state relations, when differences appeared between the positions of the hierarchy and the Znak group (and certainly in the relations between the hierarchy and the *Więź* circle). We must bear in mind that the unity of the Catholic groups in the first period had not been disrupted, and *Tygodnik Powszechny* had continued faithfully to represent the Polish episcopate's positions. This phenomenon turned the freedom of the press into a more complex and ambivalent matter in terms of the hierarchy's interests and rewards. It appears that the change, which constituted an important element in Gomułka's relations with Znak and the other lay Catholic groups[291] explained, to a great extent, the toleration of larger numbers of lay Catholic publishers and periodicals in the second period of Gomułka's rule than during the first period (37 periodicals, 14 publishing houses[292]). It also explained the political representation of these circles in the Sejm, in keeping with the above trends and in contrast to the first period.

It is also worth noting in this context that, as in the first period, pastoral letters continued to serve as an effective, direct instrument in the hands of church leaders, while government censorship was impotent to obstruct them.

3.2.5.4.7 Concessions in the Area of Education

The convincing concessions made by Gomułka and the PZPR in the important and sensitive area of education dramatically highlight their strained and difficult position at the beginning of Gomułka's second period of rule. Moreover, according to Bieńkowski, the steps taken in the area of education should not be considered concessions, but should be evaluated within the context of the constraints and circumstances imposed on Gomułka. "The repeated claim that the Gomułka leadership, which was responsible for implementing coordination with the church, introduced religion into the schools, is mistaken. In fact, the new government faced circumstances that forced it to accept this fact, as it lacked the appropriate forces necessary to repel the strong social pressure."[293] *The church–state December 1956 agreement in effect brought about the reintroduction of religious instruction* to 23,197 of Poland's 23,223 elementary schools.[294] Religious instruction was also renewed in the high schools. High schools run by religious orders and seminaries for young priests were also re-established. In all these cases the government demonstrated a liberal attitude in all matters relating to the supervision over religious instruction. The Society of Friends of the Children, which had worked for the secularization of the schools, lost its influence in those days. It was reported that during 1957/1958 school year, religious instruction was still absent from the curriculum of only 60 of 28,000 schools in the countryside.[295] Even the University of Lublin, though it did not regain all the prerogatives it had enjoyed in the first period, gained increased autonomy in its activity and continued to be an extraordinary phenomenon on the political and cultural East European scene. In fact, as we have noted, the extensive freedom of activity that the church enjoyed in the period after October was reflected in an accentuated form in the church's *instinct for conquest*, which at this time found an intensive outlet in the field of education. This was in contrast to the first period, when the dominant behavior displayed by the church could be described as *a conquest of its instinct*—out of its fear of losing what it had. Thus, in contradiction to the government's basic position and the decision regarding the new secular character of the schools, which was also contained in the agreement, crosses and other religious symbols continued to adorn school walls. This retreat from the party's secularization goals to a large extent turned back the clock and established a similarity—if not an identity—with the church's earlier prerogatives in the field of education. Even later, as its campaign to secularize schools and restrict the impact of religion on the young intensified, the government did not take any immediate, drastic steps, but made a concerted effort to prove that the changes were by no means designed to harm the religious population. In his speech at the national conference of party activists in the educational field, published in September 1958, Gomułka stated: "The party does not intend to retreat from the agreement with the church. Religious lessons, as electives, will continue in the schools"[296]; and "The elimination of religious instruction will not be resolved administratively."[297] The suspension of the benefits gained in the Polish October was, therefore, a gradual and vacillating matter. Legal authorization lagged after facts 'on the ground', and on the whole instructions from the center suggested refraining from the forced imposition of confining legal norms. Thus, as with the government's instructions to the municipalities not to be over-zealous in implementing the order against the presence of crosses and images of the saints in schools,[298] similar instructions were issued after religious instruction was deleted from the curriculum in July 1961. In fact, no supervision was imposed on church pedagogical centers, 'catechism sites', and theological seminaries, contrary to instructions requiring such supervision. Up to 1964 only 82 out of more than 15,000 pedagogical centers had registered with the authorities of their own free will(!).[299] There is no doubt that this bears witness to government efforts to abstain from the use of administrative or police measures—a policy observed by local factors on the operative level, despite known violations of orders from the center.

The continuation of religious teaching by the church,[300] the Catholic University of Lublin, the Theological Institute, and at 40 seminaries,[301] coupled with the aforementioned restraint exercised by the authorities regarding problems in the educational field (which also went on through the 1960s), all clearly demonstrate the wide room for maneuver that was unique to Poland among all the other Communist bloc countries. This was so despite increased restrictions compared to the first period and the days that followed the Polish October.

3.2.5.5 The Policy of Restrictions

3.2.5.5.1 Propaganda in the Media

In contrast to the first period, the differences in the nature and methods of media propaganda used during the second period were particularly marked in 1958, when church-state relations took a turn for the worse. The link between the changes in the nature of the propaganda and shifts in general policy characteristics does not require any proof. Direct and open attacks, and an increase in their frequency and strength, characterized government propaganda during the second period.

In contrast to the first period, the active and open participation of the PZPR leadership in media propaganda was striking. Yet even now Gomułka was among the last of the party leaders to join in the campaign of attacks and was, relatively, one of the moderates. The party press, under the direction of the PZPR, showed less hesitation and anxiety in the formulations it used to denounce the church. *Życie Warszawy* stood out among the newspapers, while *Trybuna Ludu* was relatively moderate and usually published anti-church material later than the other newspapers. In this way, the relative importance of the parties aligned with the PZPR and their organs in the dissemination of anti-clerical propaganda was reduced. In the second period, the organs of the other parties in the National Unity Front (FJN) were more in the nature of an auxiliary force supporting the attacks launched by the party itself. It is in this light that one should see, for example, the editorial which appeared in *Dziennik Ludowy* (the organ of the ZSL) on 30 July 1958, criticizing the church and "a small group of people among the clergy" for their behavior in the Jasna Góra affair.[302]

For similar reasons, there was a reduction in the use of attacks on the Vatican as an indirect tool for propaganda against the Polish Church. When attacks against the Vatican appeared, they were usually combined with direct accusations against the Polish hierarchy, as, for example, during the period after the Third Congress.[303] Moreover, the hopes aroused in the leading circles of the regime in Warsaw by the election of John XXIII, regarding the establishment of diplomatic relations with the Vatican, not only reduced media accusations against the Vatican itself to a minimum but also caused a reduction in attacks against the church in Poland—a tendency that was apparent in the period between October

1958 and February 1959.[304] The very same tendency continued to characterize propaganda during the 1960s whenever there were contacts regarding this subject or environmental changes pointing towards improved relations between Poland and the Vatican.

The personal attacks against Cardinal Wyszyński and certain bishops in the hierarchy, such as, for example, the bishop of Wrocław, Kominek,[305] constituted a new departure in comparison to the first period. The attacks were aimed at vilifying them personally and defaming them publicly. Accordingly, the Defense Ministry weekly, *Żołnierz Wolności*, published an attack against Cardinal Wyszyński on 2 June 1958—the first since his release in 1956—accusing the cardinal of violating the 1956 agreement and refusing to denounce the "wild fanaticism of the clergy". The personal propaganda against Wyszyński was so far-reaching that it became a subject of discussion in the West. Thus, for example, the *Washington Post* of 13 August 1958 dealt with the subject in an editorial. Similar subjects were discussed in an article by Halperin which appeared in the *Münchner Merkur* on 8 August 1958, a translation of which appeared in the *Daily Telegraph* on 11 August 1958.[306] A similar set of bitter personal attacks against Wyszyński had appeared in the Communist press at the beginning of August. In addition to *Życie Warszawy*, the weekly *Polityka* and the bi-weekly of the Federation of Jurists, *Życie i Prawo*, also took part in the onslaught. Without mentioning Wyszyński by name, at the end of August *Trybuna Ludu* also came out against statements made by the cardinal at a conference of students where he argued that the destruction of private property as a basis for society was the source of all of the symptoms of moral decay and that only the church could guarantee moral health.[307] At the beginning of August, *Życie Warszawy* attacked Wyszyński openly and directly on this subject.[308]

Government propaganda in the media during the second period reached new heights during clashes between the church and the government, and when the authorities implemented restrictive policy measures. In such instances the propaganda was usually directed toward justifying government actions in the eyes of the population, trying to convince the public how much the government was interested in its welfare but all the while pointing an accusing finger at the episcopate, the clergy, and Cardinal Wyszyński. The church and its people were charged with a variety of accusations, chiefly the violation of laws and/or commitments stipulated in the agreement. Further accusations constituted, to one degree or another, details of this primary accusation, and included: activity against the regime; reactionary policies and behavior; reporting false information; expressions of fanaticism and intolerance towards non-believers—something that was fundamentally opposed to the constitution; economic crimes (as in the past, economic offenses attributed to the clergy were designed to sully its image and bring it into disrepute—thus the clergy was also charged with "feudal behavior"); and use of illegal corporal punishment in education, including sexual offenses. Most of these categories of accusations against the church were fully exploited in the Jasna Góra affair[309] as well as during the events in Nowa Huta and Zielona Góra. Moreover, *Trybuna Ludu* and *Życie Warszawy* published an official communiqué from the public prosecutor on 30 July 1958, blaming the church for violating the law and disseminating false information concerning the incidents that accompanied the searches at the Jasna Góra monastery. Radio Warsaw attacked the episcopate on 2 August 1958, repeating the same accusations—as did *Życie i Prawo* on 10 August 1958. In July 1958 *Nowe Drogi* published a long and biting article (in two installments) against the church's reactionary political objectives and accusing the priests of exploiting their pulpits for these goals.[310] Accusations against the church and Cardinal Wyszyński, denouncing the political objectives behind their religious activity, their violation of the 1956 agreement, their ambitions to establish a "state within a state", and their activity against socialism and the regime, appeared in an article in *Życie Warszawy*.[311] Even before this, at the beginning of August, Korotyński, the chief editor of the same newspaper, published a set of two articles in which he accused the church of violating the 1956 agreement and of radically changing its attitude towards the state for the worse since Wyszyński's visit to Rome in May 1957.[312] These complaints appeared again and again in government propaganda. On 16 August 1958, *Trybuna Ludu* published an article in which a supreme court justice accused the clergy of encouraging violations of the law.[313] As early as 16 May 1958, *Życie Warszawy* described the lack of tolerance that the Roman Catholic Church revealed towards other religious denominations. The government media, including *Trybuna Ludu*, attacked the church with special force for intolerance towards non-believers in all that concerned the educational system and participation in religion classes.[314] On 16 November 1958 *Trybuna Ludu*[315] published the resolutions of the Central Committee of the Association of Polish

Lawyers, passed a day earlier, in which the lawyers and the chairman of their organization, Jerzy Jodłowski, accused the clergy of intolerance towards non-believers, of attempting to disrupt public order, and of violating laws. In December 1959 the press attacked the church for its opposition to government action on the issue of birth control—*inter alia*, by pressuring Catholic doctors on this issue.[316] The church was also blamed for justifying economic crimes.

Against the background of tensions surrounding the millennium celebrations, *Trybuna Ludu* came out on 16 October 1958 (in its article "On Tolerance versus the Campaign of Religious Fanaticism") against the massive campaign organized by the church to exploit the occasion. (An intensification of media attacks on the church and its leadership, which even included allegations of collaboration with the Nazis, occurred with the approach of the millennium celebrations in the mid-1960s. The main attack was on the letter to the German bishops.[317]) In the same spirit, in an article published in *Trybuna Ludu* on 23 October 1958, Jerzy Licki, of the Ministry of Labor, attacked the episcopate's position on consignments from abroad and its attempts to exploit this issue to launch a clerical offensive. In another article the church was accused of imparting a clericalist hue to cultural and political life.[318]

Along with the general measures and the material restrictions imposed on the religious orders, articles appeared in *Trybuna Ludu* (21 April 1959) accusing the voivodeship (provincial) curia of the Jesuit order in Warsaw of serious tax violations.

On 14 November 1958 the Warsaw youth newspaper *Sztandar Młodych* published a report of the trial of Father Zieliński, who had been accused of using corporal punishment on pupils in his religion classes. This kind of propaganda and slanted information was, as we have said, also known during the first period. The special nature of this case stemmed from the fact that, despite the dismissal of the charge for lack of evidence, the newspaper persisted in its allegations and even criticized the court's verdict.

Along with other accusations, the tactic of portraying the clergy as a feudal group exploiting the peasants, well known in the Stalinist period, was retained. Publications of this sort appeared, for example, in *Trybuna Ludu* of 12 August 1958, blaming several priests of confiscating property that the church had lost in the agrarian reform; and also in *Dziennik Ludowy*.[319]

3.2.5.5.2 Accusatory Formulations by the Leadership

As we have already pointed out,[320] the second period, in contrast to the first and in contrast to the behavior of the PPR and its leaders between 1945 and 1948, was marked, especially towards the end of the 1950s and during the 1960s, by the direct participation of the PZPR leaders in the government's propaganda and in attacks on the church. The contrast between the two periods is mainly evident in everything linked to Gomułka's policy and behavior as the secretary-general (first secretary) of the party. The form and content of the media propaganda were common to statements made by Gomułka and other government representatives. In fact, the intensification in the accusations by the party leaders served as the basis for encouraging the media's attacks. Even so, as we have pointed out, Gomułka's public statements although sharper in comparison to the previous period, still lagged behind those of other members of the political leadership. The aggravation in propaganda against the church, which began in the middle of 1958, was nourished, therefore, not only by a latent change in policy, but also by an explicit change in the statements made by the leaders—hence the famous statement by Politburo member Jerzy Morawski, published on 23 May 1958, in which he called for an intensified struggle against "clerical pressure in Poland". When speaking at the national conference of the Society for Secular Schools (Towarzystwo Szkół Świeckich), Morawski also called for an intensification of secular propaganda and a demonstration of the superiority of secular education over religious education. Morawski blamed "certain religious circles" for erecting a barrier between believers and non-believers.[321] On 30 July, against the backdrop of the tension caused by the Jasna Góra affair, the minister Jerzy Sztachelski, head of the Bureau for Religious Affairs, blamed Cardinal Wyszyński for intentionally inflaming relations between the church and the state. The minister claimed that since Wyszyński's visit to Rome in May 1957, the latter had abandoned his previous positive attitude towards the regime.[322]

In September 1958 Gomułka joined the anti-church campaign for the first time since his rise to power in 1945. In his speech on 24 September 1958 to the national conference of party activists in education, as already mentioned, Gomułka accused the clergy of conducting both open and secret activity against the existing order and of abusing the 1956 agreement.[323] Even so, on this occasion his statement was still quite moderate. At the

Third Congress, when stressing that "the party does not want war with the church", Gomułka warned the clergy "to cease activity against Communist rule".[324] On the same occasion the prime minister, Cyrankiewicz, launched a more bitter attack against "addiction to anti-socialist activity by certain elements in the clergy—especially in the higher ranks".[325]

As we have already pointed out,[326] Gomułka's formulations regarding the church took a striking turn for the worse in the period after the Third Congress. In an election speech on 18 March 1961, he accused the church of being "an agent of foreign forces hostile to Poland, taking orders from the Vatican", stating that: "The leaders of the church are bodily present in our country, but in their spirit they belong—according to the canon laws of the church—to the Vatican."[327] Gomułka's bitter attack on the episcopate, in an interview he gave in 1961 to Hubert Beuve-Mery, editor-in-chief of *Le Monde*, should be seen against a similar background.[328]

3.2.5.5.3 Steps towards the Secularization of Social Life

When Gomułka returned to power in 1956 it was apparent that, despite the concessions to the church, he was determined not to retreat from achievements in the secularization of social life, and that he even wished to move forward along the same path. For the time being, and for understandable reasons, Gomułka did not exert pressure to advance these goals. However, from the second half of 1958 we witness an offensive along several fronts, designed to institute sweeping changes—by law—in the spirit of the regime's goals. In addition to steps 'in the spirit of the times', taken by the government with respect to birth control and the legalization of abortion (1958), the government initiated steps to reform the marriage law. The new law determined that civil marriage must *precede* the religious ceremony, that is, that the religious ceremony could only be held after receipt of certification that the civil marriage had taken place.[329] There were many violations of the law, mainly in the villages. A law adopted by the Sejm at the beginning of 1959 was designed to solve controversial problems concerning burial; the law transferred supervision over burial to the local authorities, and determined that joint, secular cemeteries would be established next to the special cemeteries for members of different religions.[330]

The secularization trends were also clearly reflected in the government's increased support for the Society of Atheists and Freethinkers. With the resumption of its activities this society, which had existed before the Second World War (it was then called the Society of Freethinkers), held its first congress in Warsaw on 9 November 1957. Its declared goal was to disseminate "atheist propaganda and rationalist views and to struggle against clericalism and for the secularization of social life".[331] This was achieved mainly through the monthly *Argumenty*.[332] Through these and other channels, government propaganda disseminated ideas about the gradual disappearance of religion.[333]

3.2.5.5.4 Legal Persecution

Despite the fact that Gomułka clearly abstained from returning to the path of political trials against the clergy—trials that were especially characteristic of the period that preceded his return to power (as well as of the end of the first period)—the government decided to put several priests on trial. This was done both to vilify the clergy by striking specific, limited blows in order to justify the regime's restrictions,[334] and as a measure for imposing the law and issuing warnings against its violation—in other words, as a means of signaling 'we mean business'. Already at an early stage in the second period Gomułka insisted that every priest who had lost his civil rights as a result of a legal procedure must be dismissed from his church office.[335] This caused deep dissatisfaction within church and Catholic circles. For example, the Catholic priest Józef Czaranecki was brought to trial on 16 February 1958, for incitement and organizing riots in order to prevent the burial of Stanisław Nikieł, chairman of the Żuromin council. However, when the district court in Warsaw issued a verdict of 18 months' probation, it was clear to everyone that he had been let off with a light sentence.[336] At the Third Party Congress Władysław Wicha, minister of the interior and member of the Central Committee of the PZPR, reported that, in the second half of 1958, the administrative courts had examined the cases of approximately 600 priests charged with various administrative offenses such as violation of building regulations, currency offenses, bribery of government officials, violation of the law of assembly, and illegal collection of contributions.[337] The number of trials and legal sanctions increased relatively and grew more severe,[338] against a background of incidents and tensions in church–state relations, and preceded the introduction of restrictions. Yet the trials and the sanctions were never systematic or widely prevalent in the second period, since the government fully understood the implications of such steps.

3.2.5.5.5 Material Restrictions

The turn for the worse in government policy, from the point of view of the church, in the second period in comparison to the first period, was particularly striking on the material front. This stemmed, first and foremost, from the continuing validity (and enforcement) of the law that included the church's lands and properties within the scope of nationalization. Indeed, even in this area the step by step approach, and the use of 'brinkmanship' and 'half-way' measures, characterized Gomułka's policy, which always left the bishops and the clergy in a situation where they had something to lose. The episcopate devoted special attention to these circumstances and saw these tactics, in a similar way to Nowak's view of the tactics used by the government in the first period,[339] as part of the government's original intentions.[340] In fact, these events, which created real advantages for the government, could be seen as a consequence of Gomułka's response to difficulties and constraints and not necessarily as a result of sophisticated pre-planning by the government designed to exert pressure on the church. The clarity of the gap between the two periods, on the one hand, and the use of 'half-way' measures and 'brinkmanship' on the other hand, are well exemplified by both governmental supervision and interference in everything concerning charity and the distribution of material resources, and also by the government-instigated campaign at the beginning of 1958, designed to weaken the economic position of the church.

Immediately upon returning to power Gomułka adopted a relatively unyielding position in all matters concerning the economic tools that had allowed the church to accumulate political capital and prestige. As we have seen, the expectations of the episcopate and its demand for the return of Caritas to its control were disappointed, and Catholic charitable activity was greatly restricted compared with the first period. Even so, the clergy's activity within Caritas was, as noted earlier, permitted once again.[341] The same principle guided Gomułka in the matter of charitable grants and gifts sent to the church by Catholic circles in the United States for charitable purposes. Eventually a compromise was achieved in this affair: it was decided that the distribution would be carried out also in the name of the state, thus giving it some of the prestige involved in this activity.[342]

The economic campaign initiated by Gomułka in 1958 to reduce the material resources of the church had, of course, far-reaching political implications, and increased the dependence of the church on the state. The main expression of this policy was an unprecedented, though not devastating, tax war. On 25 February 1959 the Ministry of Finance issued a circular canceling the tax exemptions and tax reductions awarded to the church in a previous ministry circular, dated 5 June 1957. The new stipulations were as follows: the tax exemptions only related to income whose source was in funds used for maintaining church organizations and buying religious articles; there was to be a graduated income tax, up to 60 percent on parish funds in the dioceses and on funds devoted to social welfare, charity, and construction; the church was prohibited from collecting money outside church premises, while a tax of 60 percent was imposed on funds collected within the churches; there was a sharp increase in the taxation levels levied on the clergy's income and on buildings held by the various religious orders; rent was imposed on the church for the use of property in the liberated territories.[343] The monastic orders were the main victims of the new tax regulations, and the Jesuit order was the first upon which the regulations were imposed. Retroactive taxation from 1950 onwards, which seriously damaged its budget, was also imposed on the University of Lublin.[344]

According to an order by the minister of finance, J. Trendola, of 24 March 1959, the church, its institutions and its members, were required to submit income and expenses reports—an obligation from which the church had been released two years earlier.[345] An additional blow was dealt to the church when all its community institutions, the dioceses, and the seminaries, were declared to be 'private companies' and required to pay a 65 percent tax on all their funds.[346] About six months earlier a similar tax had been imposed on religious denominations and companies.[347] An additional aggravation stemmed from the sanctions imposed for failure to pay taxes regularly. Indeed, these sanctions were not implemented systematically, but they sometimes involved confiscation of property and even the closure of institutions convicted of being in arrears on outstanding debts. Against this background two church seminaries were closed in July 1960.[348] A law adopted in the Sejm on 14 July 1961, regarding the ownership of property that had once belonged to the German Evangelical Church in the western territories, should be added to the list of material restrictions.[349] According to this law, all this property was transferred to the state, while before, as is known, a great part of it had passed into the hands of the Roman Catholic Church.

3.2.5.5.6 Censorship and Restrictions on Publication

As in the first period, the Catholic press was subjected to restrictions and preventive censorship in the second period. It appears that censorship was even more heavy-handed now, both because of the environmental changes that we have already cited, but also, to a great extent, due to the politicization of the Catholic press itself. Thus Makarczyk, the Znak representative in the Sejm, complained about the ongoing struggles that the Catholic weekly, *Tygodnik Powszechny*, had to wage with the office of press supervision. In his words: "Almost every issue published is subject to painful experience in the censor's office."[350] Nowak points out, on the basis of information from other sources, that on average 15 percent of every issue was banned by the censor[351] and, furthermore, in 1959 some 17 out of 30 subjects in the publication plan of *Tygodnik Powszechny* were proscribed by the government for various reasons.

The extension of the scope of censorship and of other restrictions on publication in the second period, whether imposed by law or simply imposed in practice, was mainly evident in all that concerned internal publications, such as those of the Catholic University in Lublin or other internal publications issued by church and episcopate bodies. Hence Makarczyk claimed, in a speech to the Sejm in July 1957, that 20 of the 48 publications planned by the Catholic University in Lublin had been rejected by the censor.[352] In contrast with the first period, matters were brought to a head as a result of the methods used in dealing with publications by the Primate's Institute in Jasna Góra, when, as known, the government sent in the police to confiscate material the publication of which was forbidden.[353] As in the first period, once again the publication of a Catholic daily was not permitted. There was also a prohibition on the publication of various declarations by the cardinal and the bishops: the censor prevented the publication of a communiqué by Wyszyński in which he expounded the church's negative position regarding Pax organs and publications, and in which he forbade believers to publish through the Pax press.[354] As in the first period, difficulties were created for the establishment and running of printing plants and publishing houses. Even the agreement by the government, at the end of 1958, to the opening of a publishing house by the Znak (*Tygodnik Powszechny*) group, was not quickly translated into action. Six months after approval was granted the printing house was still unable to begin work, since no decision had been reached regarding its legal status—that is, whether it was considered a public or private company.[355] As part of the increased efforts towards secularization, government censorship restricted the possibility of producing religious propaganda, and prevented and restricted the presentation of church opinions on issues under dispute, for example state supervision of birth control, and civil marriages and divorces.

With Gomułka's retreat from October, and due to the fact that the point of departure for Znak's position remained the 1956/1957 reforms which, *inter alia*, allowed the publication of the monthly *Więź* in 1958, Znak publications became subject to even greater censorship. The moderating influence of Gomułka's position, which had been based on his hopes regarding the Znak group, was now greatly weakened. The circulation of *Tygodnik Powszechny* was reduced significantly only in 1961, and once again in 1964.[356] In September 1963 the Polish customs authorities confiscated 60,000 copies of a collection of Cardinal Wyszyński's sermons.[357] These were published by Catholic sources in Paris.

3.2.5.5.7 Restrictions on Freedom of Organization

As in the first period, the government obstructed the establishment of organizations for Catholic youth and intelligentsia, especially when these organizations had political implications. The recognition of Znak, and the political and other privileges granted to the group, had their roots in the very same new reality created in the wake of the Polish October. On the other hand, as already noted,[358] the government prevented Znak from setting up a national organizational network by denying recognition to most of the clubs for Catholic intelligentsia (with five exceptions) and by preventing their participation in local government. Thus the government refused to recognize other religious organizations, such as the Organization of Catholic Students at Poznań University. Tensions and restrictions regarding freedom of organization and freedom of assembly increased at the beginning of the 1960s. This tension was reflected, for example, in an incident at Poznań, when a meeting of Catholic youth in the city's Dominican church was dispersed by the militia.[359] The new law on public meetings, adopted in the Sejm on 30 March 1962, also indicated a similar trend. According to this law, public assemblies had to receive prior approval by the authorities. The law imposed additional restrictions on pilgrimages, on traditional parades, and on other religious assemblies.[360] As far as the church was concerned, these restrictions also were a blessing, because they increased the identification of different groups of the population—mainly the young and intellectuals—with the church's struggle against the evils of the authorities.

3.2.5.5.8 Restrictions in the Area of Education

Gomułka's policy of restrictions in the area of education accurately exemplified the influence of the complex map of forces exerting pressure on him with respect to decisions affecting the church and religion in the second period, in contrast to the first period. Despite Gomułka's repeated attempts to defend the October policy against attacks by the dogmatic forces in the party and from criticism in the Communist world, it appears that the offensive launched by the church—which was especially striking in the area of education—already caused him concern at an early stage, as it pushed the gap between ideological imperatives and current pragmatic policy beyond the limit of tolerance. When the pragmatic agreement of December 1956 was reached under pressure, Gomułka was unable to see the consequences, nor did he have sufficient time for maneuver and for evaluating the sum of results that would stem from loosening the reins by returning religion to the public schools. The government certainly did not intend to grant the church advantages and opportunities that were sometimes more advantageous for the dissemination of its views than those granted to the materialist doctrine itself.

The point of departure in the agreement was already *secular schools* and the option for *supervision and intervention* by the state. Gomułka did not hurry to express his disappointment and to point an accusing finger before conditions had ripened. However, there were already voices in the party—and not only those of the Natolin group and conservative elements—which grew clamorous at an early stage.[361] This conforms, once again, with his behavior during 1945 to 1948, when there had been other forces which had protested and leveled accusations against the church. Only when the increase in his strength and his hold on the party had approached their highest point—when he felt himself strong enough and more free to do battle with the church, and due to the high price he had paid in order to reach this goal—did Gomułka end his restraint and his silence and come out with measures to curtail the church's influence. This is the background to a directive by the minister of education and to the circulars that he issued at the beginning of August 1958. The directive concerning religion instructors, issued by the minister of education on 4 August 1958, stipulated that people who belonged to religious orders could not serve as religious instructors in public schools.[362] Nor was the pill sweetened by a new Ministry of Education circular, dated 6 August 1958. Article 2 of the circular actually created a path for some sort of retreat, that is, an opening for employing members of religious orders as teachers of religion in extraordinary circumstances and subject to prior approval by the Ministry of Education.[363] A much more severe blow was dealt to the church in a Ministry of Education circular dated 4 August 1958, which dealt with the "Preservation of Secularist Principles in the Schools".[364] This circular prohibited the introduction of religious symbols into the classrooms and banned prayer before or after mandatory study. It also prohibited the activity of teachers and educators in organizing the participation of pupils in religious ceremonies and pilgrimages. The circular also stipulated that religious lessons would be offered only before or after compulsory studies. These directives significantly contributed, *via facti*, to eliminating religion from the public schools. As a result of the shortage of religious instruction staff, created when 2,300 monks and nuns had their teaching permits withdrawn, and due to the restrictions in the hours of instruction, thousands of schools were actually left without religious teaching. At the end of the school year in the spring of 1958, there were 14,400 religious studies teachers, lay people and clergy. Each taught, on average, at two schools.[365] In 1960 about 3,000 Polish schools remained without religious instruction.[366] In contrast to Rosenthal (above), who, as already noted, reported that 2,300 monks and nuns had been prohibited from teaching by the new orders, other sources fix the number at only 2,000.[367]

Although these measures did not directly prohibit the teaching of religion, they are nevertheless reminiscent of the indirect methods used by the authorities in the first period, and even during the Stalinist period, as a means of eliminating religion in schools without actually taking any unequivocal legal action. Thus, in order to produce the same practical difficulties caused by reducing the number of teaching staff available, the government, in the first period, had limited the number of teaching permits issued to the clergy, aware of the fact that there was a considerable shortage of priests during that period. During the Stalinist period, on the other hand, restrictions had in fact been more direct and had eliminated the teaching of religion in most of the country's schools. Bieńkowski's writings express his sorrow that Gomułka's leadership had rejected a legal solution directly expunging religion from the schools, while still providing other ways of satisfying the country's religious needs. In his words, the leadership had chosen the path of "political influence", whereby religion would gradually be pushed out of the schools to the extent that society was ripe for this step.[368] An important consideration in this regard was the desire to maintain governmental control over religion classes. It appears that a similar consideration had guided the government leadership, in the first period as well, when it concentrated on restricting the activities of private church schools by not re-opening many of the schools that had existed before the war, and through the systematic closure of other private schools.[369] In this way the government prevented the development of centers of religious instruction far from its control. Along with the practical restrictions mentioned above, Gomułka blamed the church for deviating from the 1956 agreement and for violating the principle of separating religion from the state. He began by threatening opposition elements in the church and those interested in frustrating the implementation of the new directives. Thus, in his speech at the national conference of party activists in the area of education, on 24 September 1958, Gomułka stated: "The schools belong to the state and not to the church...and only the state has the right to issue instructions concerning the schools...only the state has the right to determine which symbols can be hung on the walls of the schools."[370] In the same context, *Głos Nauczycielski* (1 June 1958) presents accusations of overly aggressive behavior by the church during the reintroduction of religious instruction in the schools and in its activities with regard to youth movements. *Nowe Drogi*, in its July 1958 issue, also accuses the clergy of exaggerated activity in mobilizing parents and children to hang crosses and religious symbols in the classrooms and to hold prayers, not only during religious lessons, but also before and after classes. Only at this point did Gomułka choose to stand on legalities: "In the agreement between the church and the state of December 1956, and in all other agreements, there is not even a hint about hanging religious symbols in the schools or about an end to the prohibition of prayers or religious ceremonies in the framework of studies..."[371] Later in his speech Gomułka accused the church, saying "what the church did not succeed in achieving legally, it tried to achieve in other ways", and he called upon the government "to take severe measures"—but not administrative measures—"to prevent sabotage of the work in the schools".

During 1959 there were increased allegations of intolerance, discrimination, and fanaticism on the part of the church in the school system.[372] At the same time, there was a growing trend towards the secularization of the public schools, mainly in the cities and to a much lesser extent in the villages. *Sztandar Młodych* of 23 March 1959 (the writer's initials "A.R." appear) reports that at the beginning of 1959 there were 210 schools in Poland at which religious instruction was not offered, which represents a threefold increase compared with June 1958. In contrast to 198 urban *schools* without religious instruction, the periodical gives a figure of over 80,000 *pupils* in village schools not receiving religious instruction.[373] Once again there was an increase in the influence of the Society for Secular Schools (Towarzystwo Szkół Świeckich), which, during the second period, occupied the place of the Society of Friends of the Children, whose influence had waned, as we have said, with the Polish October. Bieńkowski was replaced in 1959, after the shift in policy, by W. Tułodziecki, who had been active in the Society of Atheists and Freethinkers. According to the former, the Society for Secular Schools was established only ten days after the Eight Plenum by elements who opposed October, and its organizers were almost all employees of the security services and party apparatus who had been dismissed by the 'October revolution'. Only later did large numbers of teachers and educators join the society. This society gradually became, in Bieńkowski's words, "the party's second Ministry of Education", and was supported by the local committees against the school authorities.[374] On 19 March 1959 the party congress decided to reinstate the compulsory study of Marxism in schools.[375] The secularization trend grew stronger and stronger after 1959, and with it the assertive argument put forward by the government that education was the exclusive task of the state, especially in a socialist state.[376]

Finally, in January 1961 an unprecedented decision was adopted at the plenum of the Central Committee. It determined that all traces of religious instruction in all public schools were to be totally eliminated.[377] Subsequent to this decision, on 14 July 1961 the Sejm passed an educational reform law, withdrawing religious teaching from public schools.[378] As with the restrictions introduced in August 1958, the passing of the reform law was, once again, followed by government directives which modified the reform law and created possibilities for lenient interpretation. Thus the directive of 19 August 1961 stipulated that religious teaching in schools would come under the jurisdiction of local school committees; it reduced the time devoted to religious instruction; and ordered that only teachers certified by the state would be permitted to teach religion, and then only as salaried state employees.[379] A new directive, dated 12 September 1961,[380] also affirmed the directive of August 1961 referred to above. It appears that in the second period complex, overt, and indirect pressures on Gomułka, coupled with personal difficulties and hesitancy in reaching decisions,[381] hindered the implementation of decisions and created, on the basis of the feedback from these decisions, a vagueness, ambiguity, and inconsistency in policy which were basically different from the kind of uncertainty known in the first period. This was so because this time the real goals were not camouflaged as they had been in the earlier period, nor was the strategy of postponing problem resolution employed to the same extent as before. The government also made a more concerted effort—and this was even more true once religious instruction had been erased from the public schools—to impose government supervision and restrictions on 'private' religious instruction in church educational centers. These attempts were also characterized by a lack of consistency and by countless indirect tactics. We should also note the matter of the curtailment of the rights of Catholic higher education institutions early on in the second period, through measures negating the rights of the Catholic University in Lublin and of theological seminaries to function as institutions of higher learning. The exemption of theology students from military service was discontinued in 1960, though few were actually inducted. The constraints applied to these institutions were exemplified by the refusal to grant the Catholic University in Lublin permission to reopen the faculty of law, social science and economics, and by the refusal to allow the faculties of theology at the Jagiellonian University and the University of Warsaw to reopen. Nevertheless, these restrictions were all less severe than those imposed in other Eastern European countries.

All in all, freedom of religion in education was curtailed in such a tortuous, complex manner, that in the end the church gained clear relative advantages.

3.2.6 A SUMMARY OF GOVERNMENT POLICY

The curtailment of the rights of the church in the second period (relative to the first) was manifested in the imposition of further restrictions, over and above those in the spheres discussed above.[382] These included: the refusal, in certain cases, of permits for new churches; indirect technical disruption of worship; making it difficult for bishops and other clergy to obtain foreign travel permits; refusal to grant permits to foreigners invited to participate in events sponsored by the church and different Catholic groups[383]; the dismissal of nuns from hospitals despite a shortage of nursing and medical staff, and disrupting the work of priests in the army, prisons, and hospitals.

However, despite the reduction of the positive balance in government policy towards the church in the second period, the church continued to maintain its relative advantage thanks to the 'Polish path' and Gomułka's leadership.

3.2.7 PERSONAL POLICY

3.2.7.1 General

Even though there was less of a discrepancy between Gomułka's 'systemic' and 'personal' policies in the second period—at a time when Gomułka was focusing on his role as first secretary and in the absence of competitors for his high position[384]—we nevertheless need to stop and examine the personal aspects of his policy, for the following reasons: (a) to gain a focused evaluation of the continuity and change in the various leaders' personal background variables and the impact these had on policy variances; (b) due to the great significance, in the second period, of the personal relations between Gomułka and Cardinal Wyszyński; and (c) in order to illuminate, to a degree, certain informal aspects of Gomułka's policy making *vis-à-vis* the church, while examining Gomułka's interactions with his personal advisors and factional opponents within the party.

3.2.7.2 Value Infrastructure

During the second period there was no change in Gomułka's basic position towards religion and the church, and he continued to reveal the same ambivalent attitude, which combined atheism and mockery with a deep political realism and pragmatism. At this juncture, however, in addition to the systemic pressure he was under,[385] Gomułka was carrying the heavy burden of a personal desire to expedite the fulfillment of ideological goals. It may well be that Gomułka was feeling the pressure of his advanced age and failing health, and this made him appear in a hurry to attain his goals and desirous of leaving his imprint on history. This pressure was considerably exacerbated by the aggressive behavior of the clergy, with Cardinal Wyszyński at their head. We see evidence of this, for example, in Gomułka's address to a national conference of party activists held on 22 December 1958,[386] in which he called for countermeasures that would repel the "invading clergy" (the frame of reference here was the organization of Polish youth). Gomułka here explicitly described the church as a competing and antagonistic body: "Wherever we are not operating, there our opponents are operating." Additional confirmation of the impact of vigorous efforts by the church to gain advantages, and of the hardening of Gomułka's position, can be found in testimony that records his utter fury on receiving statistical data concerning the construction of churches in Poland after 1945. This anger was provoked even further by Wyszyński's initiative regarding the building of 15 churches in Warsaw.[387]

3.2.7.3 Attributes of Personal Policy

After 1956 a genuine transformation occurred in all three of the factors related to Gomułka's personal policy, as discussed in the earlier section on Gomułka's personal policy during the first period. This change meant that in addition to his invisible, behind the scenes activities, in the second period Gomułka fulfilled a straightforward role as the representative of PZPR policy; this was highly conspicuous, for example, in the context of the 1956 agreement and at the fundamentally different Third Congress. During the 1960s his involvement reached unprecedented heights, mainly against the background of the millennium celebrations. At the same time, as noted earlier, he continued to display certain elements characteristic of his behavior in the first period. During the 1950s he had, in the main, lagged behind other forces in the party in terms of timing, as well as in terms of the severity of his formulations (and not only on a factional basis) wherever open attacks and accusations against the church arose. The change also meant that, of the policy issues addressed by Gomułka, the church received far more attention in the second period; and that, in contrast to the positive approach implied by Gomułka's words and actions in the first period, in the second period his position appears more complex and hesitant. His formulations and actions are not unequivocal and exhibit a mixture of positive and negative elements. The only time the change was not felt was in the short period immediately following Gomułka's return to power, in which, more than it ever would be again, the similarity to his behavior towards the church in the first period was sustained. Gomułka's personal appearance, for example, on 2 November 1956 at the meeting of the Polish bishops in Warsaw, and his appeal to the clergy to assist him in restoring peace and order, can testify to this short-lived continuity.[388] Undoubtedly, this step is reminiscent of his personal initiatives in his contacts with the bishops and the clergy in the 1945 to 1948 period.

3.2.7.4 The Reflection of Policy Features in Gomułka's Speeches

We have looked at examples of Gomułka's speeches in our discussion of systemic policy, and there is no further need to bring them as evidence of the changes in the above policy features. Even so, we must qualify our conclusions and point out that, despite his tendency to deal more and more openly with church issues, his speeches address this subject conspicuously less than other subjects, such as relations with the Soviet Union or agriculture. Again, a similar tendency characterized the approach to the subject in *Nowe Drogi*, where more articles appeared on the subject of religion and the church than during the early post-war period, although in terms of frequency and scope, the extent of this coverage was less than that of other subjects. It is assumed that, as in Gomułka's first term in office, his wish for his policies and programs in the various spheres to be seen in a positive light was in fact influential in terms of policy making and led, to a certain extent, to abstention from altercations with the church which would in fact have served the church more than the government itself.[389]

3.2.7.5 Changes in Position

One highly significant change stemmed from the simple fact that, in the second period, Gomułka did not serve as the minister for the liberated territories—this ministry had, in the meantime, been abolished[390]—and his practical activities as head of the system were formally (and firmly) backed by his position as the first secretary of the PZPR and as a member of the Council of State. It appears that this change—in addition to the *fait accompli* in the liberated territories once the basic objectives regarding their integration into Poland had been achieved—actually diminished the importance of Gomułka's positions regarding the territories in terms of their impact on policy towards the church.[391]

3.2.7.6 The Relationship between Gomułka and Cardinal Wyszyński

Despite the turn for the better that characterized relations between Gomułka and Wyszyński at the start of Gomułka's second period in power, and despite the positive associations (linking past and present) which accompanied the release of the primate, the late 1950s actually witnessed the onset of intense personal antagonism between the two men. The new pattern of relations contrasted not only with Gomułka's relations with the previous primate during the first period, but also with the relatively good relations that Gomułka had at that time with Archbishop Wyszyński himself.[392] Thus, in the second period, we are witness to the impact of the rising sense of rivalry between the two, which greatly aggravated the climate of competition between the church and the state. During the 1960s this rivalry, which, in Gomułka's case, was highly emotional in character, assumed rather serious dimensions. This not only affected relations between the PZPR and the episcopate but also the party's internal power relations, and went so far as to threaten the future of Gomułka's rule.

A growing sense of enmity dominated Gomułka's attitude toward Cardinal Wyszyński, which, besides stemming from the growing institutional conflict, was largely due to factors related to the leaders' power and popularity. It is highly likely that the fact that the careers of these men often ran parallel to one another was a highly significant factor, and this must have involved them in competition over similar sources of power and prestige: both men were concerned, in their early years, with the fate of the workers and social issues in Poland; both had been active in the anti-German Polish underground within Poland during the war; and both were arrested and victimized during the Stalinist regime. Added to this was a rivalry related to an apparently similar public image: age similarity, strong and patriarchal personality, courage, organizational and executive ability. The primate's higher formal education, which gave him some advantage in prestige over Gomułka, if only potentially, also tended to exacerbate the friction. This was all the more true in the light of Gomułka's suspicion and resentment toward the intelligentsia and university graduates.

Obviously, all these factors were frustrating for Gomułka, while the stubbornness and adherence to doctrine of both these figures made matters even more difficult. Wyszyński's steady popularity during the 1960s, which contrasted with Gomułka's drop in standing, made matters intolerable for the latter. Gomułka, who was impotent to contend with this phenomenon, increasingly gave vent to anti-clerical feelings and expressions of personal animosity towards Wyszyński. Matters came to a head during the millennium events, when Gomułka lost control and was unable to overcome his personal rage. (Testimony to the fact that Gomułka lost his self-control whenever Wyszyński's name was mentioned can be found, for example, in RFE, Pers. File [Gom.], Item No. 784/Be-8673/k, 24 May 1966.) All this led to Gomułka's practical efforts to undermine Wyszyński's prestige and limit his freedom of activity, and his failure to achieve these and other goals only served to feed his animosity to an even greater extent.[393]

3.2.7.7 Factional Opponents and Personal Advisers

Just as Gomułka's pragmatic policies and his concessions toward the church in the years following the Polish October became the perpetual target of criticism and attacks by the Natolinists and neo-Stalinist elements in the party (among the most famous of these being Mijał's attacks), in the 1960s Moczar and the Partisans exploited Gomułka's weaknesses, his sensitivity, and his mistakes with regard to the church, in order to attack him during factional struggles within the party. This was so despite the fact that, in many cases, it was they who had encouraged him to make these mistakes. Thus the Partisans criticized Gomułka for his faulty tactics in handling the millennium events and in this way damaging the party and the effectiveness of its propaganda. This was also the background to the friction and clash with Moczar.[394] Gomułka's policy towards Wyszyński and the church met with sharp criticism from provincial (*voivodeship*) activists (thus the decision to refuse a travel permit to Wyszyński met with criticism) and also from other forces in the party, and paved the way to the reduction in his authority and influence in the party.[395]

Apart from several allusions, the sources do not disclose the identity of the personalities who exerted an informal and covert influence on Gomułka's positions and church policy. However, they tend to stress his habit of not delegating authority, his lack of sympathy for independent evaluations produced by his subordinates, and the fact that he had confidence in only a few select people.[396] Where policy towards the church was concerned, Zenon Kliszko stood out among those who enjoyed Gomułka's confidence and also fulfilled formal roles during the second period. Kliszko, who became Gomułka's chief advisor on church relations after October 1956, in addition to his role in the joint commissions, pushed Gomułka towards inflexibility and intransigence in policy towards the church, both at Kliszko's own initiative[397] and through his support, agreement, and approval for the initiatives of others in the party.[398] The sources cite, with some hesitation, a number of other individuals who influenced Gomułka's policy towards the church. Their impact was generally sporadic, and they usually rapidly lost Gomułka's support. Thus, for example, Henryk Korotyński, the editor-in-chief of *Życie Warszawy*, is noted as one of Gomułka's personal and influential advisors where church policy was concerned.[399]

Even in open societies it is difficult to evaluate the precise influence that interpersonal relationships have on policy makers. Nevertheless, as far as is possible under the circumstances, we have fulfilled the three main goals that we set for ourselves: an examination of the balance of power between the environment and the policy makers; the identification of the accumulated outcomes of policy in later periods; and an examination of the personal role of the leader within the system.

4. CONCLUSION

In the last two chapters (this concluding chapter and the epilogue) we will concern ourselves with two main objectives. First, we will try to fine tune our answers to the main questions raised in the introduction. In particular, we will be examining the differences in the inter-period balance of power that existed between environments and policy makers and will address the conclusions arising from an integrative examination of the various facets of the system. Secondly, we will conduct a brief survey of state-church relations in the post-Gomułka era—the 1970s, the 1980s, and the 1990s.

To achieve the first objective, we will continue to employ the same analytic approach used in the earlier chapters and will address ourselves to each of the systemic components separately.

4.1 POLICY AREA ENVIRONMENTS

4.1.1 THE ROMAN CATHOLIC CHURCH

There is no doubt that the church in Communist Poland was a unique phenomenon not only in Eastern Europe but, in many ways, elsewhere as well. The church enjoyed an organizational and institutional status that made it almost the only organized opposition that continued to survive in Poland. The church derived its power from its well-known institutional character and, to a decisive degree, from its manifestly national nature. Its institutional power was seen in its ability to recruit a talented leadership and to penetrate all corners of social life. Owing to

these peculiar traits of an establishment whose history had been inter-
woven with that of Poland since the very beginning of the state, and
whose role had been bolstered by the demographic changes brought
about by the Second World War, the church's position was extraordinary. Since the ordeals it faced were identified with those faced by the
Polish people, the church was not only able to represent and lead the
people through the trials of the past, but succeeded in becoming an integral part of the new Poland's national aims. In this fashion the church,
in its almost inherent capacity to reflect both the variables and constants
of Polish public opinion, not to mention its power to shape that opinion,
constituted a competitive factor *vis-à-vis* the government. The moral
authority of the church extended beyond the frontier dividing its adher-
ents from the rest of the people. Indeed, the church was a serious rival to
the government with respect to shaping the personality of the Polish
nation.

*It was indeed the regime's profound awareness of the power of the church
that resulted in the far-reaching privileges awarded to the church during
Gomułka's first period in power.*

During the Stalinist period, the church maintained its power despite
the fact that its freedom was greatly curtailed. This was formally reflected in agreements reached between the government and the church,
and was an expression of the degree to which the regime felt it expedient
to enter such agreements. The second period of Gomułka's rule did not
witness a return to the far-reaching liberties known by the church between 1945 and 1948. However, the historical developments in the later
period indicated that, for the foreseeable future, the church was quite
secure—a situation that was unprecedented even in the best days of the
first period. In addition, the church's adaptability and its role in providing a haven for protest brought it greater support and admiration, and
hence greater power, which accrued specifically from the very blows it
was dealt.

The course taken by the church could best be described as strategi-
cally planned. Its approach in all three periods was a stance of militancy
directed toward the optimum maintenance of past gains. Yet this trend
was limited by a tactical flexibility and adaptability to changing political
conditions—which held true even of Cardinal Wyszyński who, in retrospect, does not appear to have been a compromiser by nature. The
church's militancy was demonstrated not only in its high aspirations for

improving its position but, even more significantly, in its readiness to draw a 'red line', the crossing of which meant 'war'. This would explain, on the one hand, the episcopate letter of 8 May 1953, when matters had become intolerable, and, on the other, the church's aggressive, 'grab-all-you-can' behavior following the Polish October. This policy was generally successful, but in certain instances it was accompanied by negative side effects: the church offensive launched after October 1956 succeeded in arousing the anger of Poland's new-old leaders, with Gomułka at their head. In any case, it is important to note that three of the variables responsible for the church's power reached their symbolic and actual peak at the start of the second period of Gomułka's rule. These were Wyszyński's unchallenged leadership; organizational growth, including the establishment of many new churches; and the regime's need to use the church in order to regulate public feeling—especially through its calls for moderation and for participation in elections.

4.1.2 THE POPULATION

The Polish population in general constituted a nearly stable, supportive environment for the positions and activities of the church. In the long term, Poland had been marked by the typical phenomena affecting most developing societies: industrialization and modernization had brought about cultural and social changes, including a decline in religious observance and processes of urbanization. However, in spite of the acceleration in some of these processes in Poland, it seems that the church continued to enjoy large-scale support.

The unwavering support of the population can be linked, in addition to the cumulative historical impact, to Poland's post-war demographic features. As noted, the country became more Roman Catholic than it had ever been in the past. The correlation between religious faith and Polish nationalism has already been elaborated above. We have learnt, and we shall add details to this below, of the activities of the church with respect to political issues crucial to Poland, even when such stands contradicted the positions held by the Vatican. The statistical data presented above have demonstrated the impressive level of worship during religious holidays and at regular times—a phenomenon that demonstrates the religious commitment and devotion to the church of the Pol-

ish populace. We have seen that, despite the tendency of the urban and
the young, educated population to be less religious, the Polish episcopate continued to enjoy massive support among these groups. The
church consolidated its support because of its organizational character
and due to its positions towards the regime and on current issues. This
was also the result of non-religious considerations and could also be seen
among secular elements of society—as, for instance, the support enjoyed
by the church, associated with the retreat from October and during the
entire preceding Stalinist period.

4.1.3 THE SOVIET UNION

Clearly, throughout most of the period examined the USSR should be
regarded as a supportive environment for the Polish policy makers,
while possessing, at least militarily, the ability to bring the Polish system
to its knees. Our findings regarding the role of the Soviet Union may be
expressed schematically in terms of three basic factors: 1) the impact of
the power struggles; 2) the scale of interests; and 3) the courses of action
pursued as both a restrictive and a supportive environment.

Soviet policy concerning church and religion in Poland should be
perceived within the framework of its attitude towards the 'Polish path
to socialism'. The essence of this path is reflected in the agricultural
sphere on one hand, and in the sphere of religion and the church on the
other.

The Soviet Union exhibited greater involvement with regard to the
agricultural as opposed to the clerical sphere, and there were sharp
fluctuations in the degree of Soviet pressure on the Polish regime where
agriculture was concerned. This was a function of the role played by agricultural policy in the various power struggles, and gave agriculture
greater weight on the scale of Soviet interests than the church. Furthermore, the Soviet leadership appeared to regard the Polish government's
relations with the church as a question of coping with an existing set of
circumstances, whereas the agricultural policy was seen as a test of the
Polish leadership's ideological reliability.

Prior to Gomułka's overthrow in 1948, the Soviet Union had
strongly supported the Polish leadership in both the agricultural and
clerical spheres. To the Soviets, the molding of a Communist govern-

ment in Poland was the primary goal; other objectives had to be postponed, particularly in light of the difficulties Poland faced in these two areas, of which the Soviets had already been aware during the Second World War. The shift that occurred at the end of 1947 and beginning of 1948 was primarily linked to the conflict with Yugoslavia. The desire to implement collectivization, in the belief that conditions were ripe, and Gomułka's disapproval of this move, resulted, from the Soviet point of view, in the inevitable outcome. Thus was born the Stalinist period, which was characterized by a strong emphasis on collectivized agriculture. With regard to the church, however, Soviet aspirations to narrow the gap between Poland and the Soviet model were also significant. The Soviet embassy in Warsaw even maintained a special department for clerical matters. Still, it was in the agricultural sphere that the conflict within the Soviet bloc, the escalation of East-West conflict, and the circumstances concerning the change of leadership in Poland led to Soviet pressure for more radical policies. Consequently, the shift that occurred in October 1956 was quite sharp with respect to agriculture. The Soviet Union then showed tacit approval for Gomułka's actions. Indeed, the Soviets later found themselves, on different occasions, trying to restrain the Polish leader from going too far, so as to avoid domestic tension and prevent conflict with the Vatican. The reasons for the USSR's position during the second period are associated with a wide range of factors: a) the consolidation of Soviet power; b) the lessons learnt from the agricultural policy in the Soviet Union itself; c) the marginal place of intra-bloc conflicts on this issue in the second period compared with the confrontation with Yugoslavia in the first period; d) the developments in other East European countries where the Polish precedent was not as dangerous as it had been in the past; e) the changes in Gomułka's policy in the second period—when he clarified his unequivocal stance against revisionism—compared with his obstinacy in the first period; f) the ideological relaxation following de-Stalinization; g) coexistence with the West; h) the support given by Poland to the Soviet Union and its leaders on issues perceived as being the most vital; and i) the personal friendship between Khrushchev and Gomułka. During the 1960s one should add the growing importance of Polish support given the exacerbation in the Soviet-Chinese conflict, and the growing Soviet hope of reaching an understanding with the Vatican following Pope John's accession. All this did not mean that the Poles were allowed to act independently: non-systematic, limited pressures did continue, and stronger pressure was brought to bear, albeit indirectly, by other members of the Soviet bloc. Heading these states were those whose ideological accomplishments were greatest, while a personal note could be heard in the scolding of the Poles by the East German leader.

4.1.4 OTHER ENVIRONMENTS

The general conclusion emerging from our analysis of the power, influence, and positions of the additional environmental spheres—despite the differences among them—is that although they were not capable of imposing significant constraints on the actions of the policy makers, their very existence demonstrated the limited power of the Polish government.

The organized bodies within the Polish system seem to have lacked the power to alter the system of relations between the government and the primary environmental spheres. In other words, the weakness of these bodies actually demonstrated this vacuum. It is in this light that one should judge the role of Pax; other organized groups were of even less importance. Our discussion regarding these groups only serves to underscore what is lacking in light of the wretchedness of their performance.

The persistent failure of Pax, despite its extraordinary privileges and opportunities, both during the Stalinist period and the first period of Gomułka's rule, underlines the government's weakness. During the second period the picture became more complicated due to the split in the Catholic political sphere. At the beginning of the period Pax was weakened and seemed to disappear from the scene. Its own independent initiatives failed to strengthen it and of course did not help the leadership, which limited Pax's privileges. Whichever way you look at it, Pax was a marginal element. The introduction of new bodies, even Znak, presented a potential threat to the church. This was so because of the independent activities of such elements, their search for formulas of cooperation with Gomułka's regime, and the way in which they recognized the regime and accepted the government. All these included positions and moves that did not correspond with the positions held by the church and Wyszyński. Nevertheless, the basic loyalty of such elements to the church and its hierarchy proved the continuing power of the latter. The government failed to locate or create a significant weak link in the church's chain of power.

The Vatican, it transpired, was (and still is) the only other significant environment related to state-church relations, providing a source of strength to the church. Even the controversial personality of Pius XII, given his stance regarding recognition of the regime, the new boundaries, and cancellation of the concordat, also strengthened the Polish episcopate. This occurred because of the church's subsequent independence of action, which fortified its nationwide leverage, especially with respect to the crucial issue of the liberated territories. During the Bierut period the Vatican bolstered the leadership of the Polish Church. It was in fact during the post-Stalinist period—particularly when John XXIII stepped into the pontificate—that this unequivocal support for the Polish Church began to be undermined. Attempts during the 1960s at establishing direct contacts between the government and the Vatican had the potential to threaten Wyszyński's power as a mediating factor; hence his stubborn opposing stance. In a similar vein, Wyszyński's reservations concerning Vatican II can also be partially explained.

4.2 POLICY

4.2.1 IDEOLOGICAL AND LEGAL BACKGROUND

Theoretically, due to the ideological dichotomy, the policy of the regime should have been the reverse of the positions held by the church. Thus, on the ideological level, the situation might have been perceived as a zero-sum game. It is true, however, that the identification between the government and the national representation on the one hand, and between religious beliefs and Polish nationality on the other, served to lessen this dichotomy. Nevertheless, the competition over national representation magnified the contradiction once again.

In practice, during the first period the political elite postponed ideologically prescribed goals. With respect to the church this was done at times to an absurd degree, precisely because of the deep-rooted contradiction of ideologies. Yet one can discern here an attempt to build a foundation for the future advancement of the regime's basic ideological goal, namely paving the Polish path to socialism.

The legal outcome of this situation was, on the one hand, the preservation of church privileges as expressed in both the July Manifesto of 1944 and the Small Constitution of March 1947, notwithstanding the cancellation of the concordat, and, on the other hand, vague wording in documents relating to this subject, hinting at the tentative nature of the decisions.

During the Stalinist period the regime's goals concerning the church were not as camouflaged and the legal patterns became more established. Nevertheless, the church did retain substantial rights. This was reflected in the agreement of April 1950 and the constitution of 1952. Thus, despite the toughening of the juridical policy toward the church, the legal norm of freedom of belief and worship was preserved. On the other hand, prohibition of the imposition of religious worship was reiterated and defined by the government as demonstrating "tolerance toward non-believers".

The second period of Gomułka's rule may be viewed as a combination of the first period and the Bierut period, holding true in the ideological as well as the legal aspects.

This combination was characterized at the ideological level by adherence to the ultimate goal, while working towards it in a gradual fashion based on a realistic appraisal of the situation similar to that applied in the first period. The limitations of this 'realism', influenced by the ultimate aims, may be seen dramatically in the response to the church's post-October offensive. On the legal level, the heritage of the Bierut period is apparent in the continuity of the 1952 constitution. However, the agreement of 1956 opened a new page, though it certainly did relate to the agreement of 1950.

An example of this policy, which was enshrined in the legal background, was the issue of religious studies in schools. These studies were returned to the curricula but became optional rather than mandatory as had been the case during the first period. Another example was the question of senior church appointments, where state involvement decreased, yet a joint committee of church and state representatives was established for this purpose. The principle of mutual religious tolerance was emphasized, as it had been during the Stalinist era.

4.2.2 THE POLICY OF REWARDS AND CONCESSIONS

In terms of the concessions and rewards enjoyed by the church, the first period represents the pinnacle of achievement.

The regime made important overtures to the church, not only in word but in deed as well. The preservation of the religious status of state institutions was demonstrated in an unusual form by the army's participation in religious processions and the presence of the new regime's leaders at religious gatherings. The church gained many material rewards, including funding for church renovations and construction, and a significant amount of property acquisition, particularly in the liberated territories. The most far-reaching material reward was the exemption of the church from agrarian reform. The freedom granted to the church in carrying out its traditional functions was reflected in the organization of charitable activities by Caritas, and by large-scale educational activities ranging from the schools to the Catholic University in Lublin, which was reopened. Other sanctioned enterprises included convent-administered hospitals, schools, and boarding schools. Freedom of expression was manifested in Catholic periodicals, the continued activities of Catholic publishers, and in the pastoral letters, which for a long time had been the only surviving form of written criticism in Poland.

The most noteworthy characteristic of the policy of concessions and rewards during the Bierut period was that this policy did not vanish despite the years of persecution.

Even during the period's most oppressive moments, the regime maintained the means for diminishing friction. Although the church's freedom was restricted in all respects during the Bierut period, it was far from being eliminated. The regime, sensitive to the reactions of the population, left the churches open, and crowds of worshippers flocked to them. Yet the height of concessionary policy in this period was continued assistance in the form of transportation to pilgrimage centers and the construction of additional churches.

In general, the policy of concessions and rewards after 1956 was a deliberate divergence from the Stalinist period, and more closely resembled the first period of Gomułka's rule. Nevertheless, certain factors reflected an improvement in the church's status compared with the first period.

There were two aspects to the later phenomena. First, Catholic groups associated with, and loyal to, the episcopate were granted representation in the Sejm. Second, head-on conflicts between the church and the state were no longer avoided but channeled into a permanent mechanism of joint committees. These committees took the wishes of both sides into account and regulated conflict by smoothing out any points of friction. Government declarations were characterized by a relatively conciliatory tone; toughness was accompanied by moderating formulas. In various spheres—material benefits, Catholic education, the 'extraordinary' gestures by the leadership, and other areas—the clock was not turned back, but there was a clear improvement compared to the period of retreat.

4.2.3 THE POLICY OF RESTRICTIONS

The main policy fluctuations that emerge from the analysis of the demands and restrictions are essentially no different from those evident over time in the policy of concessions and benefits.

Between 1945 and 1948 the restrictions on the church were relatively moderate. The negative position of the regime was expressed in verbal attacks that were at first indirect and took the form of accusations against the Vatican; in steps towards the secularization of society, the most striking examples of which being the new marriage and divorce laws; in refusal to renew the licenses of certain religious schools that had been active before the war; in censorship of even the pastoral letters; and in police persecution. The latter, which was witnessed at the end of 1947 and in 1948, clearly marked the shift that had occurred in the period following the elections. This shift occurred simultaneously in the areas mentioned above. In this context the government tried to combat hostile elements by driving a wedge between them, as in the attempt to split the clergy.

The increasingly hard-line policy toward the church during the Stalinist period was evident in all the forms listed above, and reached its nadir in September 1953 with the arrest of Cardinal Wyszyński. Attacks on the church became more direct. Atheist literature was widely distributed and an all-out propaganda campaign was waged in the media which even targeted the episcopate as a group and finally attacked individual church leaders. The frenzy of secularization was clearly manifest in the new family code issued in June 1950. Material restrictions peaked with the cancellation of the church's exemption from agricultural reform; a huge portion of church land was nationalized without payment of compensation. In the educational sphere, the regime did not stop at eradicating religion from the schools; seminaries and other educational institutions administered by the clergy were closed down, as were the theological faculties at the universities of Kraków and Warsaw.

After the Polish October there was a conspicuous relaxation in the policy of limitations. However, after an interval, action against the church re-emerged in numerous ways. The relative increase in restrictive action taken against the church in the second period of Gomułka's rule, compared with the first period, was again evident in all the categories mentioned above, with the signs of greater deterioration evident during the second half of 1958. In September of that year, when Gomułka himself joined the anti-clerical campaign, verbal attacks were launched accusing the church of breaching the 1956 agreement. Cardinal Wy-szyński was attacked personally. On the material plane, an unprece-dented tax war was waged against the church. Limitations had already been placed on church publications earlier, but toward the end of the 1950s and during the 1960s censorship was also intensified against Znak publications. The deterioration in the educational sphere was gradual, reaching a climax with the order issued by the minister of education in September 1958, and the resolution passed in July 1961. The minister's order prohibited religious instruction by teachers from monasteries and religious orders, even though the principles of secular education, and government control over such education, had already been emphasized in the agreement of 1956. The July resolution finally outlawed religion in public schools. All in all, the attainments of the Stalinist period in terms of moving toward social secularization were substantial. New steps were also taken later on, including the legalization of abortion, an amendment of the marriage laws, and support for elements involved in promulgating atheism.

4.2.4 PERSONAL POLICY

A comprehensive analysis of the personal policy of Władysław Gomułka needs to address two questions: a) What was Gomułka's personal stand on ideological issues; what were his attitudes on *realpolitik* issues; and what was the balanced result of his personal policy given his positions on these two points? and b) What was the difference between Gomułka's positions (and especially the balance of his personal policy) and the position of the policy-making system in general?

Gomułka's personal stand regarding the church during his first period of rule clearly reflected the perplexities within the policy-making system in general. On the one hand, there can be no question of Gomułka's absolute atheism and his disdain for religion, just as one cannot doubt his ideological position on this subject. On the other hand, Gomułka demonstrated a political realism that derived from his internalization of Polish reality. Three characteristics stand out in Gomułka's behavior: 1) his lack of prominence and minimal 'external' activity; 2) the marginal significance that he accorded to religion relative to his emphasis on other policy areas; and 3) his positive stand on the tactical level—particularly demonstrated in the liberated territories, which correlated with the overall system's notion of deferring the conflict over this issue. Hence his moderate participation in imposing restrictions, including his personal role in the promotion of Piasecki's career, and his relatively rare contribution to anti-Vatican accusations.

On the agricultural issue Gomułka's behavior was idiosyncratic to the point of leading to a clash, which eventually resulted in his removal from the system. His nonconformity was compounded by the blatancy of his action in this area; indeed, he was more dogged and brazen in this sphere than in any other. As long as the party remained focused, with Stalin's blessing, on more urgent goals, the inevitable outcome of the discrepancy between Gomułka's personal policy and the system's policy remained latent. However, once the regime's urgent objectives had been met and the system stabilized, the danger of opposition disappeared, and the question of agricultural policy became increasingly acute in view of the conflict with Yugoslavia, there was no place for Gomułka, who was ousted from the policy-making elite.

During his second period of rule Gomułka's personal behavior in the clerical sphere became distinct from that of the system. Here, Gomułka's increased personal involvement—which was molded by his personal relations with Cardinal Wyszyński—tended to cloud his position as a representative of the system's policies. This personal involvement made his function in this sphere more salient, transformed his tactical stance into one of increasing ambivalence and hesitation, and made his behavior more emotional and intolerant than in the past.

Finally, we should not lose sight of the fact that Gomułka's role ultimately appears to be rather limited in relation to the historical process and the tendencies of the entire system, as evident from the following: a) Gomułka, after all, dropped out of the system when his views diverged too greatly from those of the other policy makers; b) clear elements of the 'Polish path' had been preserved even during the toughest days of the Stalinist period; and c) Gomułka did not return to his position of the first period but instead, after October, attempted to preserve the 'achievements' of the Stalinist period that appeared to be realistic and consistent with the general ideology.

4.3 THE BALANCE OF POWER BETWEEN ENVIRONMENTS AND POLICY MAKERS

The active power of the primary environment, the church, relative to that of the policy makers reached its peak in the first period of Gomułka's rule. While in the Stalinist period there was a serious regression in the active power of the church, its passive power suffered less. The level of its active power improved significantly after October, although it failed to regain its status in the first period.

During the 1945 to 1948 period policy makers were limited by a relatively low level of power. The regime was new, it was faced with an uncertain future, and had to work under difficult environmental conditions—including having to deal with the extensive influence of assorted parametric environments, which had nothing to do with policy toward the church. Two major tasks faced the new government at this juncture, the first being to establish a power base, and the second to reconstruct post-war Poland within its new borders. The episcopate benefited from this scenario, knowing, however, that its relative power was uncertain in the long run. Despite its active power, the passive power of the church was still unclear to all concerned, that is, the church leadership, the people, and the policy makers.

At the end of the 1940s it appeared that the policy makers had attained sufficient power to initiate extensive changes. The intention was not merely to restrict the influence of the church, nor simply to advance certain ideological goals, but rather to realize the passive power of the regime in order to establish a new set of rules. Thus, during the Stalinist period, the regime's three major aims were to limit the power of the church, to advance its own ideological goals, and to institutionalize the rules of the game. Although the restrictive policies of the Bierut period were not, as sometimes portrayed, excessively radical, it seems that the regime did, after all, take them quite far. Policy became extremely harsh in late 1953, and the increasingly hard line which followed Stalin's death actually continued until the onset of the new era. This can be explained by the fact that the very death of Stalin created conditions of instability and exposed the vulnerability of the leadership. Under the new circumstances the latter found it appropriate to attack its principal enemy, the church, which had the potential either to organize or support political opposition. However, the church's invincibility and developments in the East European system caused the regime to withdraw from the battle with the church; hence the shift of Polish October. Furthermore, the excessive limitations placed on the active power of the church increased its latent power.

From the standpoint of the policy makers, Gomułka's second period in power provided them with feedback regarding lessons relating to the power of the main environment and the government's attempts at realizing ideological goals in the two previous periods. It became clear that the maneuverability of policy opponents could be limited to a greater extent than had been acceptable in the first period. On the other hand, the regime understood the dictates of political realism: driving the main environment to the wall was liable to be dangerous. All-out conflict between the regime and the church might be devastating to them both. Hence, in the second period, both sides sought to shape and institutionalize the conflict.

The year that followed in the wake of October was an exceptional one in terms of the power of the environments, which afterwards went into decline. Therefore, the suggestion made by a number of scholars shortly after Gomułka's return, namely that his return restored matters to their previous state, is misleading. Beginning with the end of 1958, one can track a renewed tightening of the reins, which was nevertheless a substantial improvement relative to the Stalinist period. After 1956 the intra-period fluctuations were evident in the open, powerful, and institutionalized conflicts that arose between the episcopate and Poland's leaders. These fluctuations were so prevalent that they appear to be cyclical.

To sum up, the 'retreat from October' did not harm the church's position in any considerable way—at least not in terms of its passive power. To use the concepts of Etzioni and Lehman, the sources of the church's power have been essentially normative. Despite the change in the mosaic of values, beliefs, and attitudes of the Polish population, especially among the younger generation, such developments did not alter the basic nature of the circumstances. Furthermore, the church was nourished not only by static elements but also by dynamic ones. Each blow to the church—on the level of the balance of active power—resulted in an increase in its passive power.

The church's role in the formation of the opposition movement and in the building of a civil society in Poland—which first began to emerge under Gomułka and ended with the victory of 1989—proves the basic theses of this study and shows beyond doubt the stature of its power.

The final section of this book will offer a brief look at the development of the state-church balance of power in the post-Gomułka era. However, we wish to make two comments before proceeding with our epilogue.

First, it seems likely that the applicability of our type of analysis to the Polish system may be an indication of its usefulness in explaining the character of Communist-Socialist systems in general. The version of the systems approach adopted here, together with our emphasis on the analysis of the balance of power between environments and policy makers, have proved the ability of the environments (including those that were the objects of government policy) to influence not only the basic features of policy but also the composition of the elite, and, indirectly, the attitude of the Soviet Union. These demonstrate that East European societies had alternative political mechanisms to those studied by political scientists in Western democracies. The existence of such mechanisms enabled the moderation of ideological conflicts and meant that pragmatic solutions could be found. The tendency of the policy makers to adhere to these mechanisms, to mix 'positive' and 'negative' policies towards the environments, and to adopt incremental strategies based on historical lessons—despite the dogmatic and totalitarian features of the system—most likely prove the universal nature of political existence.

Second, despite Gomułka's limited personal role in the 'trial and error' process of Poland's recent history, the conclusions of our study not only confirm the existence of a Polish path to socialism, but also prove the mark of the man on its evolution. On the other hand, it is difficult not to be impressed by the tremendous personal impact of 'the thousand years primate', Cardinal Wyszyński. With his persistent struggles and activities, his adherence to goals, and his unequivocal belief and consistency, Wyszyński, more than any other person, should be identified with, and credited for, the seeds of the political drama of the late twentieth century—the seeds of triumph.

5. EPILOGUE: THE POST-GOMUŁKA ERA

The church has succeeded in maintaining its power, and in many ways has even increased it, in the post-Gomułka era. However, when studying continuity and change in the balance of power between the church and the state one must distinguish between two main periods: 1) the Communist period up until the 1989 upheaval—the 1970s and 1980s; and 2) the post-Communist era—the 1990s.

5.1 THE COMMUNIST ERA (THE 1970S AND 1980S)

5.1.1 GENERAL POINTS

Essentially, there are two main sub-periods: 1) the Gierek period of the 1970s; and 2) the Jaruzelski period of the 1980s.

In both of these sub-periods we witness the continuity of the church's power, the continuity of its traditional roles in Polish society, the continuity of the patterns and dynamics of church–state power relations, and continuity in the mechanisms and channels of influence of these relations (as demonstrated above). These characteristics of continuity do not imply absolute stability. Their ups and downs derive from changing circumstances and changes in leadership (on both sides). Thus we see the continuity of the benefits-restrictions pattern of policy on the one hand, and of militancy versus cooperation on the part of the church on the other; of mechanisms for the de-intensification of conflicts (by way of joint commissions); and of cooperation and 'deals' for the sake of the common denominator, and payoffs to the church—mainly in times of emergency and crisis. There was continuity and consistency in the competition for national representation—for example, in his sermon of 7 February 1974 in Warsaw Cathedral Wyszyński stubbornly stressed, as in the past, that "the church has been the genuine representative of the people".[1] Against the background of the ongoing ideological conflict lay a consistency in the church's strategy. Occasionally, this drew criticism from various groups, ranging from the church to the population, but in the final count this particular strategy, pioneered by Wyszyński, in fact proved itself.

On the other hand, the church in the 1970s and 1980s acted under different circumstances and realities. The most significant internal change had its roots in the 1960s: the strengthening of the protest and opposition movement in Poland and Eastern Europe, which gained momentum in the 1970s and 1980s, took a sharp downturn in the early 1980s before emerging victorious in 1989. The internal changes that occurred were closely connected to changes in the international arena— first and foremost in terms of superpower relations. These developments included the détente in the 1970s, the Soviet invasion of Afghanistan, the Star Wars Program (SDI), and Gorbachev's rise to power in the Soviet Union in 1985. The election of a Polish pope brought with it far-reaching consequences for opposition–government relations in Poland specifically, and in Eastern Europe in general.

The impact of these changes on church positions and status created a complex, multidirectional, sometimes paradoxical, picture. The church, with Wyszyński at the helm, made itself adaptable to the changes—at its own pace and in accordance with its own principles. It remained loyal to its cause, to the basic principles that had guided it in the past. However, while this made it the main force behind the opposition movement (and behind the victory of 1989), its support for the opposition was not unequivocal. The converse was also true: the opposition's support for the church was not wholehearted either, and there was evidence of cracks.

In light of the crises that arose between society and government— opposition and government, which seriously threatened the stability of the political system, the mediating role of the church (which acted as mediator and arbitrator) grew increasingly important. Against this background we also witness greater use of the joint episcopate-PZPR commissions. The crises forced the party to make important concessions to the church, which was expected to help solve the problems that had arisen. These concessions strengthened the church, awarding it special status and public recognition as the troubleshooter of the nation and as having the capacity to bring 'industrial peace'. The government rewarded the church for its help in calming the atmosphere and maintaining stability, and in so doing enlarged the 'living space' enjoyed by the church, as well as its ability to influence. Thus we witness an absolute and proportional increase in the number of bishops, priests, nuns etc. compared with the inter-war period,[2] as well as an increase in the quantity of parishes, churches, and catholic periodicals and publications. In the 1980s the government granted approximately 1,500 permits for building churches and chapels.[3] As part of the 'deals' struck between the church and the government, the church gained far-reaching benefits and concessions, although restrictive policies continued to be enforced.

A crucial factor in relation to the church's power, which was not undermined despite the threat of its erosion over time (and despite predictions by sociologists and social scientists who spoke of détente and the heightened secularization that was expected to accompany it[4]), was the Polish population, the mainstay of the church's strength. The church continued to enjoy tremendous prestige and high moral status (i.e., the Polish people identified with its moral goals), which clearly tied in with the human rights struggle and the church's social activity. Altogether, the population, of which 90 percent remained Catholic, continued to be loyal to the episcopate and to the church.

The throngs of people flowing to the churches on Sundays and religious festivals continued unabated. Churches were frequented not only by believers, but also by the secular and those opposing the regime, as in the past.

This is what was said by S. Kania, a man who became highly influential in policies *vis-à-vis* the church (and, through this, the party at a later stage), and who was in contact with church representatives before replacing Gierek in the leadership: "I am ashamed when Communists from other countries ask me why so many Poles still go to church..."[5]

In the first half of the 1980s—as the church walked a tightrope, trying to bridge the gap between the government and the opposition, and drawing public criticism for normalizing its relations with the state—the population's support for the church never wavered. It continued to enjoy the nation's trust and its position among believers remained strong.

Thus, in the last decade of PRL rule, the church enjoyed a status un-precedented even during the inter-war period.

As was previously mentioned, the church made a vital contribution to the opposition movement. In fact, the church preceded the opposition in its struggle for workers' and human rights. The human rights issue was made the church's first priority in its struggle against Communism in the 1970s and 1980s. Against this background began a decline in the op-position to Wyszyński and the episcopate within Znak and among the lay Catholics.

During this period, too (the 1970s and 1980s until his death) Wyszyński succeeded in preserving the unity of the church and in maintaining his unshaken leadership. He took a firm stand against ele-ments who continued to pose a threat to the power of the church and to himself. He took steps to prevent any harm to the chain of power through attack on its weak links, and continued to torpedo government efforts to bypass him in its relations with the Vatican. Wyszyński also acted to curb 'independent initiatives' by Znak and the lay Catholics, which had received momentum with Vatican II. The tension between Wyszyński and these elements (Znak and the lay Catholics) did decrease in the 1970s.[6]

So too, church unity was preserved despite the tensions that haunted the church organization—between the young and low-level and the higher levels; between radical and conservative trends; between active followers of the opposition and those that were more cautious. Within the young and lower-ranking clergy there developed a tendency to sup-port the opposition, occasionally even more actively, without authoriza-tion from above. (In the case of Popiełuszko, the church leadership did not like his initiatives, and their position toward him changed only after he was murdered.)

However, as mentioned earlier, Wyszyński was wise enough to pre-serve the unity of the church, and its walls remained unbreached.

Cardinal Wyszyński still retained his personal power, and even had it reinforced. His charismatic personality, together with admiration for him within the population, remained a potent combination, despite the rising strength of Cardinal Wojtyła, the future pope. Different research-ers have tended to cast a shadow on the greatness of Wyszyński com-pared to that of Wojtyła. They highlight the influence and popularity of the latter (the designated pope) among the lay Catholics and the opposition, while criticizing Wyszyński's continued conservatism in the context of the implementation of the Second Vatican Council's decisions in Poland. It seems that despite the understandable difference between the two (see below), dissimilarities between them have been exaggerated. Moreover, even at a later period the criticism in the church voiced against the conservatism of Pope John Paul II (also mistaken)[7] quite resembled the earlier criticism of Wyszyński, which compared him unfavorably with Cardinal Wojtyła.

Nor is there any justification for the credit given to John Paul II for the '1989 victory' at Primate Wyszyński's expense. The pope himself testified to this (and not for the first time) in his address to his Polish brothers in Saint Peter's Square on 16 October 1998, during the twentieth anniversary celebration of his pontificate: *"There never would have been a Polish pope in Rome, in Holy Peter's chair, without belief, without the primate [Wyszyński], without Jasna Góra."*(!!)[8]

It is no wonder then that Cardinal Glemp encountered many difficulties when the time came for him to step into Wyszyński's shoes after the primate's death in May 1981.

If we take a general look at the Gierek era until the end of the People's Republic of Poland (PRL), with all the ups and downs that took place, we find a relative improvement in church-state relations and in the position of the Roman Catholic Church, as well as signs of a partial solution to the controversial issues between the church and the state. The antagonism and harsh altercations that characterized the second Gomułka period would not be repeated until the end of the PRL.

As previously mentioned, the difference between the Gomułka era and the post-Gomułka era was rooted in the development of the opposition movement in Poland (1968, 1970, 1976, 1980) and Eastern Europe. This was a political opposition which took gradual shape and which was not identified exclusively with the church. This compares with the previous period when the church had been the rival force and the sole organized and threatening opposition to the government (apart from the brief period preceding 1947).

Paradoxically, it seems that during the post-Gomułka period the common ground between the church and the state increased as new groups and forces came to threaten the two older pillars. Some of these elements threatened both the church and the state, although in a different manner. The system ceased to be 'bipolar' (church versus state, with a 'cold war' between them), and the new equation to emerge was quite complex. Although the church and the opposition shared common interests and offered one another support, there were reservations, criticisms, and mutual disagreements between them. On the other hand, however, between the church and the government there was the common ground of protecting existing gains, national survival, and organizational and institutional preservation for each side. However, the common ground between the church and the opposition was clearly greater than the interest shared by the church and the regime, with church antagonism to the government being much greater. Here we need to reiterate that Wyszyński was wise to support the opposition and its struggle for freedom and for human and civil rights, and that, as noted earlier, he had even preempted the opposition in these struggles. It is in this light that we should also consider his position and that of the church in the 1976 constitutional affair, where the intended changes aroused many reservations on the part of Wyszyński and the church.

Far-reaching in particular were the decisions of the episcopate in that same year (1976), which *already then* included demands not just for respect of human rights and the guarantee of freedom of religion and conscience, but also included the condition for a normally functioning government—*free elections to Parliament.*[9]

There is no doubt about the importance of the church's contribution to the protest and opposition movement and to its victory in 1989, although its support for the opposition groups and organizations was neither automatic nor unequivocal. The church opened its gates, offering a haven to the opposition during the 1970s and 1980s. It did this by granting a home to clandestine universities and providing a roof for activists from the outlawed Solidarity movement (Solidarność, outlawed in 1982). It also provided a platform for opponents of the regime in the Catholic press—the only place they had to express themselves. Church organizations, social bodies, and movements all laid the foundations for the establishment of civil society.

However, the disagreements and antagonistic trends that existed between the opposition and the church did not disappear, but were only postponed for the time being. These differences on issues of secularization, modernization, the separation of church and state, and the criticism of the institutional egoism of the church, would surface once more in the 1990s as the church sought to 'cash in' on its role in the 1989 revolution—behaving as though it ruled the roost, in a manner somewhat reminiscent of its 'offensive' after October 1956—and it would receive a strong slap in the face (see below).

5.1.2 SELECTED PROBLEMS—MILESTONES ALONG THE WAY

5.1.2.1 The Change of Government (December 1970) and the Beginning of the Gierek Era

Existing documents (e.g. Dudek) seem to indicate that already as a result of the events of March 1968 a 'deal' existed between the church and the state. For the first time in many years the church was not considered the main political opponent but an independent social force. The church took no part in the revolt, remaining silent during the anti-Zionist campaign; and in the face of the youth protest exhibited friendly neutrality at most. Essentially, the church saw itself as the preserver of stability in the country.

The Gomułka regime rewarded the church. In the government propaganda campaign tied to the events of March 1968, there was basically no anti-church or anti-hierarchy slant, and all propaganda attacks landed squarely on the heads of the Znak representatives. However, on the threshold of the next decade, deadlock reigned in church–state relations. This would only change with the deep crisis in the political system, a crisis that would bring an end to Gomułka's rule in December 1970.

5.1.2.1.1 Benefits Policy: A Demonstration of Goodwill and a Positive Attitude with the Alternation of Power, and the Position of the Church

The change in government in December 1970 was marked by positive signals and gestures and a desire to reach full normalization in church–state relations. As in the past (the first Gomułka period; the Polish October) the government leadership displayed a high level of awareness of the importance of the church at times of vulnerability and in periods of confrontation with society. Already on 20 December 1970, the day of Gierek's election as first secretary following the December 1970 events,

Gierek announced plans to improve relations with the church. In his 23 December 1970 address to the Sejm regarding the direction that the new government would be taking, Piotr Jaroszewicz, the new prime minister, announced: "We will work for full normalization in church–state relations, with the expectation that government efforts will face true understanding on the part of the Catholic clergy and the lay Catholic circles."[10] These words were as good as a declaration of peace and a statement of a desire to cooperate during a time of distress for the PZPR and the new leadership and at a critical juncture in the destiny of the nation.

The church, for its part, anxiously watched developments on the Baltic coast in December 1970. According to Dąbrowski's account, the quick use of force by the government left no room for church mediation and another peaceful solution.[11] As in similar situations in the past, the church leadership, with Wyszyński at the helm, felt the full weight of national responsibility on its shoulders due to the inherent dangers of the situation. The church also feared spontaneity. It was afraid of losing control of the state, which would lead to violent and destructive outcomes. At the head of its concerns the church placed the issue of *raison d'état*, which, together with its understandable concern over its own fate, led it to act with restraint and caution.

Thus, among other things, we find the personal decision taken by Cardinal Wyszyński to prevent the reading of a sharp pastoral letter on the subject of abortions. The letter, written in September 1970, had been intended to be read from the pulpits on 27 December 1970. The church called upon all sides to demonstrate responsibility and reach an agreement. Accordingly, it turned to cooperation with the new government to calm the situation, responding to government calls and gestures in a positive and placatory manner, desirous of beginning the new period on the right footing. It too called for full normalization of church–state relations, together with respect for freedom of religion and conscience and the preservation of the status of the church.

The episcopate called for just and responsible behavior, for an end to suffering, and for restoration of order that together would allow all citizens to live safely in their common homeland. It also stressed that the responsibility lay with both the government and the citizens.

The church's stance was reflected in the words of the episcopate on 29 December 1970.[12]

The state reacted with satisfaction to the episcopate's willingness to establish relations on the basis of the recognition of the superiority of the national interest (the common denominator) and that of the state, and respect for the legitimate socialist basis of the Polish regime.

Thus the new regime, from the time it came to power and with an eye on the future, saw the need to repay the church for its behavior during the crisis, expecting that it would contribute to national stability as time went by. We need to remember that it was with this goal in mind and in order to achieve 'social and industrial calm', that Gierek chose to make concessions to the workers, farmers, and other elements.

Due to the unstable situation and lack of industrial calm that persisted through early 1971, it was important to the party that the church demonstrate a positive stance *vis-à-vis* its policy. This explains the readiness to make numerous concessions. Among the problems it sought to resolve, the government now displayed a readiness to address church real estate issues in the western and northern territories—that is, the settlement of church ownership of these properties—and praised the important contribution of the church to the incorporation of these territories (the western and northern) into (the mother country) Poland.[13] This contrasts with the accusations made on this subject during the Stalinist era. In an earlier conversation with Dąbrowski on 23 December 1973, Kania expressed the government's appreciation for the primate's efforts on the issue of the western and northern territories, and for the episcopate's vital and patriotic contribution on this issue.[14]

The episcopate, in a letter sent on 28 January 1971 to Piotr Jaroszewicz, chairman of the Council of Ministers—against the background of a mutual desire for normalized relations—called for a meeting with the highest-level government representatives, in order to determine the *modus operandi* of the joint commission of government and episcopate representatives. Moreover, the church decided to take advantage of the government's placatory tone and presented the regime with a number of demands. Thus, in the meeting between Wyszyński and Jaroszewicz on 3 March 1971, Wyszyński demanded that the government improve living conditions, develop national culture, maintain the rule of law, and safeguard civil rights.

At that meeting, a joint platform of contact and action was worked out that stressed the common denominator—the joint responsibility of the two sides for the fate of the nation. The parties also discussed the principle of separation between spiritual and secular authority, which would prevent a confrontation between the two. They also stressed mutual recognition of existence between the sides. The state acknowledged the unquestionable fact of the influence of the church on the Polish nation and its bond with the people, while the church recognized the current regime in Poland in accordance with the conclusions of the Second Vatican Council.

The principle of freedom of religion and respect for civil rights was stressed within the framework of normalization. The judicial basis for normalization consisted of the 1950 and 1956 agreements, which obligated the two sides. The joint government–episcopate commission would work toward resolving controversial problems.

5.1.2.2 Turning Point: Deteriorating Relations

Naturally, the 'honeymoon' between the two sides (church and state) could not continue indefinitely. The conflict areas and the controversial issues could not disappear. The government's contingency plans regarding the church stood firm, and the restrictions policy remained in force. Against this background the government created difficulties in 1972 in the important and sensitive area of education, in response to Cardinal Wojtyła's request for the establishment of a theological faculty in Kraków. The further we get from December 1970, the larger we find the gap between the benefits policy and the restrictions policy, in favor of the latter. The contradictions began to be noticed, while deep-rooted tension stemming from irreconcilable ideological differences dictated the recurring restrictions. Thus the government secularization drive continued, agreements were not implemented, and the process of rapprochement was curbed already in 1973 under a cloud of mutual allegations.

The government went mainly for Primate Wyszyński and certain of the bishops (mainly Tokarczuk), attacking their political stance and accusing them of hostile activity.

On the other hand, relations with the Vatican were more positive and the government took pains regularly to remind church representatives of this fact.

Again, as in the Gomułka period, despite positive declarations the party worked to divide the church from within and intervened in church appointments and other internal church affairs. In a manner reminiscent of his militant position in 1953 (the *non possumus*), Wyszyński vehemently opposed the government's attempt to intervene 'actively' in the appointment of a replacement for Cardinal Bolesław Kominek, who died in March 1974, and threatened to cease cooperation, to put an end to the 'deal', and to torpedo the normalization agreement. Henceforth he would have the upper hand in this chapter of appointments.

While there was not much progress in the normalization of relations with the Polish Church, relations between the government and the Vatican began to make more significant and satisfying headway. While there was progress on the subject of establishing permanent contacts between the PRL and the Vatican, Wyszyński did not allow anyone to circumvent him and the Polish Church in relations with the Vatican, and succeeded in subordinating Vatican–PRL relations to the status of the church in Poland. Thus, on 1 December 1977, Paul VI granted Gierek a private audience as a result of Primate Wyszyński's efforts.

A significant deterioration in state–church relations and the tipping of the balance in favor of the restrictions policy occurred in 1975.[15] By this time, Gierek and his colleagues in the government were feeling more secure in their position and were less attentive to public sentiment and to public opinion as they toughened their policy *vis-à-vis* the church. We witness increasing accusations leveled against the church hierarchy. The regime created administrative difficulties (among others, making it difficult for senior church officials to visit Rome), and restrictions were imposed in education. The state also intervened in church appointments, as we have noted, and in this matter the regime revealed its determination to prevent the appointment of individuals whose views were hostile to the government. At the same time, government representatives were heard declaring their *vigorous support for Wyszyński's continuation in office* and expressing the importance they attributed to his role in church–state relations: "We are not looking for anyone else...despite these and other claims...Wyszyński is a reasonable Pole and bishop, who has never acted outside his country's interests..." (Kania's words to Dąbrowski in 1975).[16]

Dąbrowski, on the other hand, spoke of the demonization of the primate by the security apparatus, adding: "The primate cannot and will not give in to your dictates."[17]

The government's complex attitude towards Cardinal Wyszyński is clearly evident, and the impression is that the regime had serious fears about the replacement of the man against whom it was fighting, preferring him to retain his position as primate of Poland.

5.1.2.3 The KOR (The Workers' Defense Committee)

In the 1970s the Roman Catholic Church backed the opposition movement by joining its voice in protest and taking action behind the scenes. The church, led by Cardinal Wyszyński, made up the main force that stood behind the activities of the KOR and the opposition movement.

It cooperated with the intellectuals and other protest groups on many occasions (such as in the 'letter of thirty-four' of March 1964) before the June events, in whose wake the KOR was established on 27 September 1976. Now, however, this cooperation began to be expressed in a bolder, more open and concerted manner than ever before.

In contrast to the revisionist phenomenon of previous years (from the Polish October until March 1968), which was tainted with the odor of 'true Marxism', this time the movement was based on the popular masses, and in their name and the name of human rights spoke in favor of "dialogue with the nation"[18] Ideologically, this allowed the church to grant the movement greater patronage and support than it had in the past.

From the outset, the church had given the KOR its complete backing, including backing for KOR demands and protests against the government. Moreover, the further we get from the events of June, the more we find that the voice of the church was raised with increasing force and stridency against the actions of the government, and that its relative role within the protest movement grew. So too, as government policy *vis-à-vis* the KOR hardened in April 1977, the church came out against the actions of the government, which for its part displayed a restraint that could have been interpreted as weakness.

In the initial phase of the crisis and the June events, church fears of possible disaster were evident. These were expressed (as in many analogous situations in the past and later on) in a call for public order and expressions of trust in government attempts to solve the problems resulting from the economic crisis. The voice of protest by the church against the verdicts of

Ursus and Radom was heard better under what seemed to be less sensitive conditions. Simultaneously, the church turned to behind-the-scenes diplomatic activity in order to sweeten the verdict on the workers.

The church called for the government fully to respect civil rights and to conduct a true dialogue with the nation. Thus, for example, in the Kania-Dąbrowski talks of 20 July 1976, Dąbrowski said: "One must speak to society in a communicative and objective language... punishments and dismissals from work do not calm anyone...dialogue with citizens must be conducted in a practical manner...There is a need to talk with the workers."[19] Furthermore, the church issued a demand for amnesty for workers and joined in condemning police brutality.

Only in November 1976 did church support for the KOR become overt and plain. At the same time it took independent initiatives to assist workers and their families.

Already at an early stage, on 16 July 1976, Wyszyński came out, in his letter to prime minister Piotr Jaroszewicz, in support and defense of the striking workers. In fact, as already noted, church activity on behalf of the workers and concern for their affairs preceded those of the opposition movement.

Thus Bishop Dąbrowski, in a conversation with Stanisław Kania on 26 January 1971, said: "The church has the responsibility of caring for the workers and supporting their needs."[20] The government was horrified and furious over the political alliance between the church and the opposition, and over the political support that the church gave the latter. The government later showed great concern over the possibility that the church had consciously cooperated with the political opposition (and had not been exploited by the opposition without its knowledge), and that it had opened its gates to, and provided a haven for, the opposition.[21] The government made serious efforts to prevent this alliance with the opposition.

The fact that the KOR membership included a Warsaw priest (Jan Zieja) angered the Communist leadership (especially Kania), which suspected that this had been agreed with Wyszyński, who had then authorized the priest to act. The government also protested to Wyszyński over the activities of Bishop Tokarczuk and with respect to the latter's open support for the aspirations of the political opposition—accusations that Wyszyński totally denied in July 1977. Already in 1973 Stanisław Kania had complained to Dąbrowski that the church had begun to serve as a stronghold for the fringe elements of society, such as Jews and the political opposition. According to Dąbrowski's documents, Kania was, to no small degree, a racist and an anti-Semite. For example, he called Tokarczuk 'Ukrainian' in 1976.[22]

The alliance between the church and the opposition, however, was not complete. There was, despite the alliance, a suspicion of the KOR and anxiety regarding the "leftist lay Catholics".

The new documents published by Andrzej Micewski demonstrate these apprehensions and also the church's fear of Soviet intervention in the 1980 to 1981 period (Śpiewak also relies on these testimonies).

Thus, in the meeting between Wyszyński, Michnik and Kuroń, already in May 1976, the two latter favored cooperation between the political opposition and the church, whereas Wyszyński argued that the *church had always protected the interests of the nation and would not allow herself to be exploited for the conjunctural ends of different political groups.* On another occasion, in 1977, Dąbrowski replied to Kania: "No attempt at the instrumentalization of the church by any political element will succeed in provoking it and in making it deviate from its evangelical mission."[23]

To conclude this section, we can say that, against the background of the June events and the establishment of the KOR, the church demonstrated immense power and even managed to increase that power compared with the past—more than ever under a Communist government. The church's power was unparalleled in any other Eastern European country, or any other state for that matter. Support for the church rose among the student population, the intellectuals, and the workers, as it continued to enjoy the traditional, unswerving support of the peasants. Secular opponents of the regime also rallied around the church. The support of the workers was a key element as Poland underwent industrialization and urbanization, and the church managed to gain this support once it adopted their cause and worked for their benefit.

5.1.2.4 Facing the Solidarity Crisis

5.1.2.4.1 The Role of the Church as Mediator

In his book *Jak to sie stało* (How it Happened. Warsaw, 1991), Mieczysław Rakowski wrote that the church, in its mediatory capacity, became a very important and possibly decisive political element on the country's political map, and that, during the 1980s, it was transformed into a real political force. All the same, the church did not choose the strategy of establishing a Catholic party or movement, despite being invited to do so by certain government circles. Minutes of meetings and reports found in Archbishop Dąbrowski's archive confirm the importance of the church as a mediating factor and moderating force during the crises of the 1970s and 1980s, as well as its impact on the dialogue that took place between the antagonistic parties and on Poland's bloodless transition to democracy. Micewski[24] has emphasized Wyszyński's role as a mediator during the Solidarity crisis of 1981, and that of the church later on in the 1980s (1981-1989). He believes that it was at this juncture that the church "changed from an opposing force into a sought-after arbitrator". This is also how the regime viewed the church. However, we must bear in mind that the church had assumed the role of mediator in the past as well, albeit under different conditions.

5.1.2.4.2 The 'Deal'

The social crisis of 1980 reached such proportions that it became cause for concern to the party authorities. They felt very threatened and began to look to the church for assistance, as they had in the past. Consequently, they began making far-reaching concessions to the church. Thus we witness an intense flurry of dialogue between the regime and the church leadership. On 24 September 1980, after a long period of inactivity, the joint government–episcopate commission renewed its activity, with a new membership format.

At the Joint Commission meetings of 1981, the government was willing to discuss returning Caritas to the church, and for the first time since the Second World War was prepared to deal with the controversial issue—between church and state—of freedom of belief and conscience.[25] The military coup of December 1981 did not put an end to the cooperation, and by 18 January 1982 the Joint Commission had convened once again.

A process of normalization between church and state began to take shape, despite the fact that in practice none of the concrete issues were actually resolved.

In exchange for its good will and gestures, the government naturally expected that the church would halt the radicalization of Solidarity, and should a confrontation with the latter arise, would side with the government and assist in solving the problems.

In a speech following his election as first secretary in September 1980, a large portion of which was dedicated to church–state relations, Stanisław Kania expressed appreciation and gratitude to the primate for his words and "constructive (i.e., helpful) appearance" in Jasna Góra.[26] Also, during the Joint Commission meeting of 1 April 1981, the government thanked the episcopate for its contribution to a peaceful solution of the social conflict.[27]

This 'deal' was utterly rejected by the liberal freedom fighters and other elements, who refused to see it as expedient collaboration designed to save the country from chaos and national disaster. They railed against institutional egoism on the part of the church, a claim that was basically an over-simplification. Wyszyński and the church had a genuine fear of Soviet intervention and tried by every means to calm matters down and prevent any bloodshed.

As already noted, Micewski's new documents confirm the anxiety experienced by Wyszyński and the church *vis-à-vis* confrontation between the government and the opposition (society) in 1980, and the trend toward less and less restraint on the part of Solidarity extremists.

Throughout 1981 Wyszyński kept reiterating in his sermons and speeches the danger of "external intervention", calling for calm, sound judgment and responsibility.

On 5 June 1981, some days after Wyszyński's death, the chief council of the Polish episcopate called upon Solidarity only to use those means that would not endanger the country's independence.

Within the church itself as well, not everyone was in agreement with cooperation with the government. The 1980s witnessed an overall (oppositional) radicalization of society that was especially marked in Catholic circles. This was true too for the lower ranks of the church. The government pressured the church hierarchy to clamp down on the phenomenon of oppositional priests supporting Solidarity, since it interfered with the process of normalization between church and state and damaged church–state relations.

Against this backdrop a number of priests were murdered by the secret service, turning them into freedom martyrs of the church. Of these, the murder of the radical priest Jerzy Popiełuszko on 19 October 1984 (see above) is a well-known case. The church had indeed taken steps to restrain him and after his murder worked to prevent the funeral from being transformed into a public political demonstration for Solidarity. According to Śpiewak, the bishops in fact despised Popiełuszko and were anxious to send him to Rome. The church, which was indeed afraid of involvement in anti-establishment activity, only rallied behind him after his death.

5.1.2.4.3 Support for Solidarity

It would be wrong to assume from the above that the new alliance of the 1980s was between the church and the government. The policy of restriction still continued, and with it the struggle to eliminate crosses from schools and factory halls (e.g., between 1983 and 1984).[28]

In the case of Solidarity, the church indeed played a central role, with Solidarity being nurtured by the power of the church. The Gdańsk workers' strike in the 'burning August' of 1980 enjoyed the blessing of the church and the pope. Pope John Paul II's visit to Poland in 1979 provided a crucial impetus to the establishment of Solidarity, and once the organization was formed (August–September 1980) the church supported it and its struggles: it granted its umbrella to Solidarity's human rights struggles, gave shelter to the movement's persecuted, and called for an amnesty for those serving sentences in camps and prisons. As noted earlier, some clergy were even active within the ranks of Solidarity (albeit against the wishes of Wyszyński and the episcopate).

The strong bond between the church and Solidarity was demonstrated in an unprecedented manner, symbolized on the personal level by the devotion, loyalty, and close ties between Solidarity leader Lech Wałęsa, the Polish episcopate, and the pope.

Moreover, in parallel with his significant role regarding Workers' Solidarity, Wyszyński also played a key part in the creation of Rural Solidarity.[29]

Yet, as noted above, church support for Solidarity was neither unequivocal nor automatic. The episcopate decided against direct involvement in organizational activities and called on priests to concentrate primarily on their pastoral functions. The church was cautious, choosing to exert a moderating influence, and acted to bring the sides to a constructive level of dialogue. The church, which also perceived Solidarity as having trends opposed to its own principles, was unwilling to be swayed away from its policy of caution and be dragged in by the extremists within Solidarity.

After the mid-1980s the church's attitude of distrust toward elements within underground Solidarity actually grew more fierce. The church rejected attempts on the part of the so-called leftist intelligentsia to exploit the church to its own ends.

5.1.2.5 Facing Martial Law

Deeply conscious and appreciative of the church for its unique role within society, the government gave church leaders advance warning of the possibility of the temporary imposition of martial law as a means of dealing with the threat posed by Solidarity.[30] The church responded with a warning against the use of such extreme measures.

In a similar vein, the regime even took pains to inform Primate Glemp directly of the announcement of martial law about an hour before Jaruzelski broadcast this to the nation (6 a.m., 13 December 1981). This contrasts sharply with the delay in relaying this information to the pope and possibly demonstrates, yet again, a certain discrepancy between the church in Poland and the Vatican (even when the pope was Polish!) when national interests were at stake.

From the moment the church learned of the introduction of martial law, its leadership took an active mediating role, frequently conferring with regime representatives, granting assistance to internees and their families, trying to free anyone who could be freed, and inviting representatives of both sides to discussions in an effort to mediate between them. The regime needed the church's assistance and acknowledged this explicitly. The church has consistently represented a vital pillar within Polish reality, with a traditional–historical dual role of safeguarding the national interest on the one hand, and human and civil rights on the other.

5.1.2.5.1 Criticism and Reservations Regarding the Imposition of Martial Law

In a speech made several hours after martial law was declared, Primate Glemp criticized its imposition, the means of oppression, and the severe violation of civil freedom. On 16 December 1981 the secretary to the episcopate, Dąbrowski, delivered a letter demonstrating that the Council of State decree of 13 December 1981 constituted a violation of the constitution. The episcopate pressured the new regime not to violate the August agreements, saying: "We believe that the nation will not retreat and cannot retreat from the democratic renewal that has commenced in the country."[31] The bishops called for the discharge of all internees, demanded that they be treated humanely, and called for the reinstatement of Solidarity.

5.1.2.5.2 A Call for Restraint and the Prevention of Bloodshed

In contrast to its firm position with regard to martial law, the church agreed to bow to pressure from the regime not to read the communiqué of 15 December 1981, and owing to the dangers and seriousness of the hour called, for the sake of the entire nation (and not only of certain groups), for all sides to avoid extremism and confrontation and to prevent any steps that might cause bloodshed. Opposition to the military regime at this particular time might result in deaths and the church saw avoiding this as its top priority. As the primate stated: "There will be those who will accuse the church of cowardice, but...the church will act against a civil war. There is nothing more valuable than human life."[32] The Polish bishops continued to work to ease tensions, emphasizing repeatedly the need for dialogue between the government and the governed and calling on the sides involved to find a way to the negotiating table.

Despite the ideological conflict and the ongoing tension and confrontation that existed between the church and the state, a certain amount of normalization (pragmatic accommodation) was achieved following the imposition of martial law.

The mechanism of the joint state–church commission helped to smooth out difficult controversies. The Polish Church, consistent with its policies in the past, has tended to cooperate with the government (as in the case of the 1950 and 1956 agreements), while fighting at the same time against it (as in the case of the episcopate memorandum during the dark days of May 1953).

Micewski and Peter Raina confirm my view that the church cannot be accused of 'betraying' the very society it claimed to represent; Casanova, however, criticizes the church for the ease with which it resumed its traditional role as mediator between state and society following the imposition of martial law. Casanova implies that the church ought to have assumed a more militant stance and should have given greater backing to the opposition. I would say, however, that this viewpoint overlooks the situation that then existed and the constraints of the time. Thus, too, he minimizes the church's contribution to the re-emergence of Solidarity, the 1989 revolution, and the transition to democracy.

5.1.2.5.3 Views Regarding the Outlawing of Solidarity

Casanova ignores the thin line trodden by the church when he implies that the church's position emanated from selfish institutional considerations. He criticizes the church's preservation of the *status quo*—also reflected in the outlawing of Solidarity (7 October 1982)—but admits that martial law was necessary in saving the Polish nation.[33] Chrypiński also argues that the church accepted the outlawing of Solidarity.

Indeed, although the church was interested in avoiding civil war and open confrontation, it did not give up Solidarity and genuinely hoped for its resurgence as an independent labor union. It is true that the church wished to see a more responsible Solidarity, one that was less threatening to Poland's political stability and to the church as an organization. Thus, already in 15 December 1981, it called for a resumption of trade union (Solidarity) activities in accordance with the law.

Even after the blows suffered by Solidarity, the Holy See and the Polish Church continued to support it, if only formally. They continued to support the original unions and refrained from recognizing the new official unions established by the government after January 1983. Earlier, in August 1982, Glemp had called for the release of Lech Wałęsa (he was released on 16 November 1982), insisting on his right to the human freedom of self-expression, and for—even gradually—the work of the labor union to be resumed. Micewski emphasizes time and again that the primate, in his meeting with Jaruzelski and the episcopate in the forum of the Joint Commission, stood firm on the issue of free labor unions.[34] Moreover, throughout 1983 the episcopate voiced its disappointment that no understanding had been reached regarding the reinstatement of the free labor unions.

The church, now headed by Glemp, did lend its support to the government in the face of the Soviet threat and the impending disaster; but again, not everyone in the church accepted this type of cooperation. The opposition forces heaped difficulties in Glemp's path, part of the opposition perceiving a danger in his allegedly weak leadership. John Paul II, however, supported Glemp, especially during the papal visit of June 1983 (see below).

5.1.2.5.4 Concessions Related to the 'Deal' with the Generals (the Junta)

The benefits gained by the church as a result of martial law were quite impressive. Although some church demands were not met within the framework of the 'deal', the government, which was concerned about good relations with the church and in desperate need of church support, was ready to make significant concessions. The 'agreement' not only upheld all existing benefits, it even increased them, and the church's position improved even further under martial law. Through the official organ of the PZPR, General Jaruzelski expressed his appreciation of the church, praising its constructive role in Polish history. The government did not revoke any of the concessions gained by the church as a result of the Gdańsk agreements (concessions made between August 1980 and December 1981). The strident tone of the ideological struggle against church influence was now muted. Moreover, the ruling elite respected the right of the church to speak on all national issues as a result of an agreement reached between Gierek and Cardinal Wyszyński at the latter's initiative. The government now also refrained from *de facto* intervention in church appointments (made possible by the decree of 31 December 1956). The 'organizational' consolidation of the church was not disturbed by the regime, nor was the building of new churches. On the contrary, the government granted new permits for construction and renovation without posing problems. The Catholic press also underwent expansion at this time.

5.1.2.5.5 The Defense of the Persecuted and Imprisoned, and the Representation of Society

During the period of martial law, the episcopate actually intervened with great diligence in hundreds of individual cases. Various party circles referred to the church at that time as 'Solidarity's substitute'. The church maintained, and even enhanced, its traditional role of representing society in the vacuum left by Solidarity.

The church now made humanitarian issues a top priority at the expense of strictly religious issues. It took broad steps in support of prisoners, detainees, and other victims of persecution and violence. From the first day that martial law was declared, the episcopate managed to free sick people who had been detained. A meeting was also held between Bishop Dąbrowski and Wałęsa, after which—and after intervention from the episcopate—Wałęsa was assured better conditions. The government allowed the church, on the basis of an agreement, to give aid to the needy on a wide scale. The church assisted secular people to organize material help in the form of clothing and food for prisoners and detainees. The episcopate strove to reduce the length of detention and offered religious services to the imprisoned. Increased religious activity among the latter and aid in other areas naturally also served the interests of the church itself.

In his speech during Corpus Christi celebrations, Cardinal Glemp condemned government oppression and spoke out against the violation of human rights and the use of such methods as those which caused the death of nineteen-year-old Grzegorz Przemyk.[35] The plea for the release of all political prisoners was heard repeatedly from church pulpits and from Cardinal Glemp personally. In 1983 the church repeatedly called for a general amnesty for Solidarity activists.

Throughout this period the Church actively strove to put an end to the 'state of war'. Following the pope's visit in the summer of 1983, martial law was indeed suspended. Before 22 July (the Polish national day during the Communist era), the government also declared an amnesty for prisoners (excluding Solidarity, and KSS KOR leaders, who were granted amnesty at a much later date).

5.1.2.6 The Polish Pope: Homecoming Visits and Contribution towards the Fall of Communism

The Polish pope continued to be a figure of key importance and a symbol of the spiritual strength of Polish Catholicism—it is believed that the pope defeated the Soviet divisions.[36] This was indeed the case. Wojtyła's effect on the church's contribution to the downfall of Communism inside Poland and overall, as well as in the transition to democracy, was felt greatly both before and after his election as pope. After Vatican II, and already during his term in office in Poland, Wojtyła represented the main force behind the movement for post-Council reform in Poland. He was close to reform-minded intellectuals, to Znak and the *Tygodnik Powszechny* circles. It was easier for him than it had been for Wyszyński. Micewski's new documents confirm Wojtyła's active role in supporting opposition groups during the 1980s.

Wojtyła built on the conditions created by Vatican II for a "modern type of Catholic public religion" in Poland.[37] Yet, as mentioned earlier, we cannot draw any far-reaching conclusions from this with regard to the differences between Wojtyła and Wyszyński.

Poland was overjoyed and became swept up in a surge of national and religious pride when one of its own was crowned bishop of Rome. John Paul II—elected to office in October 1978—made his first visit to his homeland in 1979. His contribution to the *establishment of Solidarity* in 1980 was significant, and he gave the organization his backing and support. Lech Wałęsa's visit to Rome on 13 January 1981, at the head of a Solidarity mission to the Holy See,[38] may also be viewed as evidence of the pope's support. This visit also served to *strengthen Solidarity in the international arena*.

The imposition of martial law worried the holy father, who, as previously mentioned, had lacked information during the opening phases of this period. On 18 December 1981 he sent Archbishop Poggi to Warsaw with a letter for Jaruzelski, calling on him—as did the Polish episcopate—to take steps to prevent bloodshed and to return to the path of dialogue, difficult as this might be. He spoke on behalf of the entire people, in the name of human rights and the people's rights, and called for respect for the people's wish to see an end to martial law in Poland.[39]

The government responded negatively, viewing the letter as 'insulting' and unfriendly toward the Soviet Union due to the compari-

son drawn between it and the Nazi occupation. Since it was not interested in warring with the church and the pope, the government requested that the letter not be formally delivered in order to avoid a sharp
backlash against the pope.

The pope made a second visit to Poland in June 1983. This strengthened the spiritual aspirations of Polish society for freedom, and stirred
up patriotic feelings among the populace. John Paul II came to his
homeland to bolster the Polish spirit and to demonstrate his moral support for its struggle for freedom and human rights. He came to boost
their hope and courage, bearing the old message that the Polish spirit
could not be stifled, even though its body be killed (Poland and Christ
are analogous).[40]

The pope indeed fanned the flame of Polish hope, which had begun
to fade. He spoke of *human rights* and the nation's right to sovereignty.
However, he did not ignore political reality. He restrained himself and
the huge crowds that rallied around him, in an effort to prevent violent
riots that might have endangered the country. The pope called for dialogue between the regime and Polish society. The Polish government,
for its part, did its best to maximize the potential return on the pope's
visit. Through his visit, the pope strove to bolster the church, from
whose power his own universal organization was nourished. He also
called for respect for freedom of conscience and religion. Primate
Glemp was also personally strengthened by the visit. The pope supported Glemp *vis-à-vis* those within the church who had questioned his
authority. Previously, already in early 1983, the pope had placed the
cardinal's cap upon Glemp's head.

During his visit, John Paul II spoke strongly in favor of the banned
Solidarity and Rural Solidarity, departing from the route of caution and
alarming the Polish government. The Vatican, like the Polish Church,
had never accepted the fact that Solidarity was outlawed, nor did it cease
its support for the original organization.

The pope's request to meet Lech Wałęsa during his visit was one of
the bones of contention with the regime. In the end, the pontiff took
matters into his own hands and met with Wałęsa. This turned into a
victory for Wałęsa.

The news agency TASS accused the Holy See of being responsible
for the situation in Poland, and described the pope as the leading sup-
porter of Solidarity. Everywhere, the pope expressed his sympathy for

the oppressed and the persecuted. Most significant was his statement at the holy shrine of Jasna Góra on behalf of political prisoners. He was firmly consistent in his demand for a general amnesty for all those imprisoned under martial law. About a month prior to his visit the pontiff had issued a powerful call for a general amnesty. The government had firmly rejected his demand.

To sum up, during his second visit to Poland (for details of the third visit, see below) John Paul II once again aroused—as in 1979—a wave of deep religious emotion. He clearly added an important chapter to the history of Catholicism in Poland and prepared the ground for 1989.

5.1.2.7 From Gorbachev to the 1989 Revolution

The church had not anticipated the rapid chain of events that occurred during the second half of the 1980s. No major policy change emerged from the PZPR congress of July 1986, and although it was decided to free any remaining political prisoners this was not extended to Wałęsa and the other Solidarity leaders.

Gorbachev's rule in Moscow and the new route he had chosen had not yet borne fruit, and as yet no signs of liberalization were apparent. *The church continued steadily in its role of representing the people and their suffering.* In 1987 the Polish episcopate and others protested against rising prices. The lack of basic reforms again caused an economic crisis in the country. The bishops complained (and rightly so, according to Micewski)[41] that for years the only measure adopted by the government to control economic crises had been to raise prices. On 8 June of that year, John Paul II started his third visit to his homeland.[42] In Gdańsk, at the mass celebrated in front of a million people, the pope said: "I am with you, and I am speaking to you."[43] On this visit he demanded changes relating to Polish society and its problems and also touched upon the subject of Solidarity—despite government protest. In the face of the weakening of the PZPR, the words of the pope took on extra force, giving the government food for thought.

The role of the church as mediator and preserver of social calm also continued, of course. The Solidarity strike in the Gdańsk shipyards, called by Wałęsa on 30 April 1988, ended on 10 May 1988 thanks to the mediation of Bishop Tadeusz Gocłowski and Tadeusz Mazowiecki.[44]

5.1.2.7.1 Round-Table Discussions

Church representatives played an active and important role in the round-table discussions and their preparation. Two priests, Bronisław Dembowski and Alojzy Orszulik, assisted in the talks held between 6 February and 5 April 1989, in which both government representatives and Solidarity (opposition) representatives took part. The church refused to allow a delegation of lay Catholics to participate. Stanisław Stomma and Jerzy Turowicz represented Solidarity.

5.1.2.7.2 The Elections of June 1989

The government's 'collapse' in the historic elections of June 1989 worried the church. Especially worrying was the failure of the National List, which included the Prime Minister, the Minister of Defense, and other public figures. Throughout the transitional period following the elections of June 1989, as in the months preceding them, the church attempted to arbitrate between the various sides and to alleviate tension and friction.

On 19 July 1989 the National Assembly unanimously elected Jaruzelski as president. Despite Solidarity's victory, all sides were afraid to rock the boat with a dramatic transformation. The events of Tiananmen Square had lit a red light and proved to be a restraining factor; the opposition, too, was in no hurry to cash in on its strength.

The church, following its traditional approach, influenced the voting, this time through church-affiliated senators. Despite its own preference for Solidarity, the church aided in the election of Jaruzelski to the presidency. Later, when it was convinced of the supremacy of Solidarity, it supported the latter's government. In any case, the church sought to have a religious man at the head of the government.

Throughout that time Gorbachev and the Soviet Union observed developments in Poland without attempts at intervention. During his last days in office as prime minister in August 1989, General Kiszczak was questioned regarding the reasons for his resignation (other than the reasons related to internal policy). His candid response was: "The Soviet comrades do not wish anything from us any longer, except that peace reign in Poland."[45]

5.1.2.7.3 The Regularization of the Legal Status of the Church

The church began exerting pressure for the regularization of its legal status already in 1978 (see Wyszyński's speech in Warsaw Cathedral on 6 January 1978).[46] This unique position was achieved only in 1989, as a result of decisions taken by the Mieczysław Rakowski government and agreed upon by government and episcopate delegates to the Joint Commission. Cardinal Franciszek Macharski, the joint chairman and representative of the church, had much influence on the decisions taken on this issue, as did Kazimierz Barcikowski, the vice-chairman of the Council of State.

The crucial negotiations on the subject of the church's status within the Joint Commission framework occurred at the same time as the round-table discussions, and one must conclude that the government rewarded the church handsomely in this significant and critical transitional period. Between 26 and 27 April 1989, the Rakowski government presented the Sejm with three bills related to the regularization of the church's legal status. The first dealt with the attitude to the state, to the Catholic Church in the People's Republic of Poland. The second safeguarded freedom of conscience and faith. The third secured social insurance for believers.

These three bills were passed and became law on 17 May 1989, two weeks before the elections.[47] According to the law, the government, among other things, would return Caritas to the church (from which it had been taken in January 1950). Equal rights were declared for all citizens of all religions—believers and non-believers alike; all sides were to respect each other's rights; church and state were separated; the church won freedom for its officials to fulfill their religious duties; and equality was given to all churches and religious denominations. In addition, the civil rights of believers were reinstated with regard to allowances, pensions, and health provision.

The laws of May 1989 closed a circle that had begun in 1945 with the conflict between church and state. Micewski rightly states that, at the time, no one anticipated that within a few weeks an upheaval would occur that would shake the political system in Poland.[48]

Thus we have learned of the important role played by the church in 1989 as in earlier times, and its influence in effecting the gradual ('velvet') bloodless transition into the 1990s and into a system of democracy. General Wojciech Jaruzelski met with Primate Józef Glemp four-teen times between 1981 and 1989,[49] in an effort to reduce the conflict between society and the state, and to further the interests of the church.

It seemed in 1989 that the church stood to gain the most from the fall of the People's Republic of Poland and the establishment of the Third Republic. This is the impression entertained by various research-ers,[50] and was probably also the feeling of the church functionaries and clerical circles who then felt the taste of victory—as if the time had come to cash in on their share of the victory. Actual events, however, did not exactly follow expectations.

5.2 THE 1990S

5.2.1 DIFFICULTIES FACED BY THE CHURCH IN POST-COMMUNIST POLAND IN GENERAL

During the 1990s the church's ability to adjust and conform to the times was again put to the test. The 1990s posed a new set of challenges, and the church experienced great difficulty adjusting to the new reality. Contrary to expectations, and in spite of the fact that Polish Catholics continued to comprise 90 percent of the population, the church faced the danger of losing control and influence.

Since the beginning of the 1990s there has been a real decline in popular support for the church and a fall in participation in religious life. Over half of those who consider themselves Catholic support euthanasia and abortion.[51] There has been a decline in the authority of the church and in overall confidence in its role in public life. Whereas in 1989 a to-tal of 90 percent believed that the church played a serious and important role, six years later this percentage had dropped by more than half. The proportion of Poles who do not wish the church to interfere in political issues has also grown steadily. Public opinion polls point to the fact that most people object to the clericalization of public life, and 70 percent think that the church should not intervene in politics.[52]

The church has had difficulty in defining its position with regard to the developing democracy and has been unable easily to accept the changes that have brought about a relaxation of traditional affinities and norms. In some respects it appears to have been easier for the church to face a despotic regime lacking any moral base than to face democracy, which it has found threatening and potentially dangerous. Paradoxically, freedom from Communism was inextricably accompanied by the movement toward freedom from the church's yoke (a kind of Siamese twins syndrome). The church, by its very nature, found it difficult to accept pluralism, in just the same way as the Communists themselves.

The church's function in post-Communist Poland is fraught with conflict and disputes that Gowin[53] traces to the "late confrontation of Polish Catholicism with values and institutions connected with modernity". Modernity entails the development of a free market and a capitalist economy, and the church cannot easily adjust to the uncertainties associated with the transition toward democracy and the establishment of a free market economy, in which the rules of the game have not yet been fully clarified. The church's firm positions of the early 1990s, which arose from a false sense of almost unlimited power, later gave way to confusion and ambivalence following the 'blow' that it suffered. Consequently, despite its reservations, the church supported capitalist reforms in its statements. However, it neglected to try and slow the rate of reform in its efforts to ensure social justice.[54]

It seems that despite the label 'conservative' applied to Primate Wyszyński by his critics in post-Communist Poland, the present-day church lacks his charismatic figure, broad vision, and methods of operation.

5.2.2 The Clerical 'Offensive' Following 1989

The church was the first stable institution of the post-Communist era. Its point of departure certainly placed it in an advantageous position. However, under the conditions of transition and uncertainty, the church, basking in the victory of 1989 and the overthrow of Communism, and conscious of its advantages, was insufficiently aware of the new limits to its power. It behaved like a self-assured landlord, while resembling a bull in a china shop. (Already in the 1988 document opposing the demand for neutrality, the church had presented a set of unrealistic demands[55].) It thus undermined its own interests by arousing unforeseen opposition.

Ironically, the rules of the game had been clearer during the Communist era. The new rules were not sufficiently clear, and the intoxication of victory gave rise to action lacking in due caution. We must re-member the past church 'offensives' that had spurred the counter-reactions that undermined its active power.

The church is beginning to be seen as an institution replacing the Communist establishment, and has thus become the target of criticism and hostility. Its preferential economic status and the privileges enjoyed by the priesthood are also in evidence, antagonizing broad sections of society.

Many authors have accused the church of indoctrination in schools and in the media, of hostility toward democracy, and of many other mis-deeds. They claim that the fall of Communism has left a void, which has been filled by the competing ideological doctrine of Catholic fundamen-talism. They accuse the church of opposing Communism out of a simple ambition to gain an ideological monopoly; and, after the fall of Com-munism, of systematically transforming Poland into a theocratic state with a single privileged religion and church.

Polish society is struggling with the question of the place occupied by the church and religion in public life, and their role in post-Communist Polish society. The debate both reflects and stimulates public fears re-garding the possible emergence of a theocratic state. Gowin sees devel-opments in post-Communist Poland as a "religious Cold War", charac-terized by bitter strife between two camps—one camp being the church and Catholicism (which is divided within itself) and the other being democratic public opinion. One may add (to Gowin's most perceptive observation) that here, too, as in the Cold War, differences emerged only after the defeat of the common enemy, with erstwhile allies becom-ing transformed into bitter opponents. In both cases the issue has been the upholding of democratic values.

The 'religious Cold War' includes the use of similar jargon and methods as those used in the Cold War against political opponents. The church's criticism of what has been termed 'demo-liberal culture' has not included explicit opposition to democratic rules. This would be against the position of the pope, who demands respect for the rules of democracy. However, the church continues to claim that natural laws, Catholic moral precepts, and human rights are above majority will and the rules of democracy. This provokes Catholics and theologians who do not agree with such trends, and who regard fundamentalist views as ex-tremely dangerous and damaging.

5.2.3 GROWING POLITICIZATION: THE ELECTIONS OF 1990 AND 1991

The clerical offensive of the early 1990s entailed a growing politicization on the part of the church, which included pressuring the new political leadership, intervening with political appointments, and openly and aggressively intervening in the elections. As a result of pressure from bishops and catholic groups, Prime Minister Mazowiecki reintroduced religion into schools and kindergartens in 1990.

In the presidential elections of November/December 1990, the church supported Lech Wałęsa. It also accorded a clear preference (which was mandatory on voters) to candidates identified exclusively with the right wing and openly loyal to the episcopate and its policies. Any criticism of the episcopate was dubbed leftism both at this time and later. The Polish bishops declared that the church encouraged, and even obliged, lay Catholics to vote for candidates who expressed the wishes and beliefs of religious people. A good candidate, according to them, was one who openly supported the church's political program.[56]

Following the bishops' declaration that the church would support candidates representing Catholic values, liberal Catholics, social democrats, and ex-Communists joined together against the clerical tendency. Cries arose for the separation of church and state, and the polemic over abortion became fiercer and included an attempt to legislate the right of freedom of decision to abort.

The parliamentary elections of October 1991 witnessed aggressive and importunate action on the part of the church. This was reflected in its campaign against abortion (a campaign which the church made its top priority) and for Christian values in education and the mass media. The episcopate went so far as to intervene in the appointment of high state officials.

In the 1991 elections the episcopate supported the establishment of a party named Akcja Wyborcza Katolicka (Catholic Electoral Action) and encouraged priests to support Catholic candidates. Thus, in this transition period, the church went beyond its militancy of the earlier Communist era and was vigorously active, even at the risk of violations of the law such as preaching election propaganda from the pulpits on the eve of elections and on election day itself. The church also identified friendly parties, 'worthy' of support. However, 'Akcja', as it was known, had little success in the elections, gaining only 9 percent of the votes.

5.2.4 The 1993 Elections and the Change in the Episcopate's
Position after Defeat

It would be true to say that, before the elections of September 1993, the
church failed to adjust to the new reality and behaved in an anachronis-
tic manner. Moreover, it tried to gain points and new victories in a weak
regime—the new and as yet unconsolidated democracy—after its victory
in 1989. This arrogant and dominating behavior brought the church
down painfully, forcing it to examine itself and search for new positions
and a fresh strategy.[57]

The 1993 elections reflected the failure of the path taken by the
church and had the effect of an earthquake. The defeat of several
Catholic parties and the victory of the Left served as a vote of no confidence toward the church. This brought about a change in the position of
the episcopate and in the strategy of the church. The new episcopate
spokesman, Bishop Tadeusz Pieronek (general secretary of the Polish
Bishops' Conference and representative of the moderate wing of the
church), said of the outcome of the elections that the defeated parties
had only themselves to blame for the results.

The church indeed internalized the defeat, drew its conclusions, and
has lately changed its path. One of the main lessons derived from the
defeat was reflected in the church's withdrawal from political involvement and from the support of any political party. The view that the
church must help create a political consensus regardless of religious affiliation has grown stronger. Even the pope, visiting Poland in 1997,
refused to meet with political leaders.

The church now tries to concentrate on its responsibility toward the
people in the new Poland, as another link in the long chain of its historical roles. It does not aspire to a new 'religious war'. It has also relented
on the subject of abortion, no longer making it a *casus belli*—although it
is consistent in its stand.

Its new path is not an easy one for the church, which has difficulty in
letting go of old patterns of behavior. It still demands Catholic obedience to its stand, and those opposing it are again branded as 'leftists'
(those following the Communist 'successor' parties).

The Catholic priesthood was horrified once again when Aleksander
Kwaśniewski was elected president in November 1995. After the election, Bishop Tadeusz Pieronek again asked the church to examine its

actions in the election campaign. Pieronek indirectly criticized Cardinal Glemp for describing the choice between the candidates as a choice between Christianity and paganism.[58] Thus, in May 1998, former Polish prime minister Józef Oleksy complained (on the seventeenth anniversary of the attempt on the pope's life): "Will the church forever see in the Polish Left an enemy, Satan's son? We must arrive at an understanding. Although we shall not forego secularity..."[59]

The change is nevertheless quite marked. Thus, in the bishops' sermons on 3 May 1998 (at the 3 May celebrations) a completely new spirit could be felt.

Let us only remark that the church continues to be a powerful force in Poland and beyond.

5.2.5 THE CONCORDAT AND THE HOLY SEE

Relations between the Polish government and the Apostolic See continued to provide a source of tension for church–state relations in post-Communist Poland. The crucial issue was the concordat, the signing and ratification of which were not automatic even in the Poland of the 1990s, and conditions in the transitional era contributed to preliminary procedures and lengthy interactions between the Polish government and the Vatican.

In the early 1980s negotiations aimed at reaching an international agreement between Poland and the Vatican were already underway. However, only after the elections of June 1989 were full diplomatic relations established between them (on 17 July 1989). The agreement (concordat) was 'hurriedly' signed on 28 July 1993, during Hanna Suchocka's regime. The signatories to the concordat—the government and the church—regarded the stabilization of church–state relations as advantageous to both sides and to Polish society. The concordat only needed ratification by the president. However, there was still the need for a preliminary procedure on this issue.

The fall of Suchocka's government after the upheaval of the September 1993 elections caused the ratification issue to be passed on to Waldemar Pawlak's government. A dispute in the new government coalition delayed ratification once more, with the SLD against ratification and the PSL (Polish Peasant Party) supporting it. On 1 July 1994 the Sejm adopted a resolution calling for the formation of a special committee to examine whether the concordat was in accordance with the constitution. The committee was to complete its examination after the referendum on the constitution, and no later than 31 December 1995. The Sejm decision was viewed unfavorably by church circles and increased tension between church and state, while the left-wing government was regarded as a threat to the church.

From the point of view of the church, the concordat was intended to gain the church the stable conditions it needed freely to carry out its evangelical mission. As an international agreement, the issue would attain a more forceful standing. The controversy over the concordat emphasized the conflict between the opposing sides. Critics claimed that the government should wait with the concordat until after the ratification of the new constitution (see below).

The delay in the ratification of the concordat became part of the political tactics used by the SLD, which mobilized a large section of its electorate under the banner of the struggle against the church. The church learned that only a small segment of Polish society favored the ratification.

In any event, once the constitution had been approved in the referendum of May 1997, ratification of the concordat finally took place.[60]

In the September 1997 parliamentary elections the left-wing coalition lost power to a coalition of the AWS and the UW. With the new regime in place, the Holy See took steps in 1998 to further the implementation of the concordat. At the end of April 1998 the Vatican's secretary of state, Cardinal Angelo Sodano, made a four-day visit to Poland to discuss the concordat. (It was Cardinal Sodano who signed the concordat with Poland in the pope's name.) The pope also appointed Bishop Tadeusz Pieronek to head the commission for the implementation of the concordat and for church-state affairs. The government, for its part, decided to set up a commission of its own.[61] Finally, in May 1998, the concordat was put into effect.

On 15 November 1998, on the basis of the concordat, the new codex on civil marriage and divorce came into effect—a single-act procedure for church and state.

* * *

Pope John Paul II has greatly influenced the direction that the church has taken in the 1990s, as part of what Gowin (1995) calls "the papal program for Poland in our short post-Communist history". According to Gowin, the pope has not turned his back on the Second Vatican Council, as some would claim. It was John Paul II, he argues, who went further than others in accepting democracy and a free market—the two pillars of modernity. It is true, however, that he advocates an evolutionary path for the application of the Vatican II decisions in Poland.

Indeed, the pope, in his last encyclical "Faith and Reason", sharply criticizes those who rely too strongly upon faith and neglect reason.

5.2.6 THE NEW CONSTITUTION

Another controversial issue that arose between church and state was the new constitution, which placed Polish society in turmoil and divided opinion in the political camps during the 1990s. The new constitution was intended to replace the 1952 constitution, which had since undergone some amendments. The issue was brought to the public vote in a referendum on 25 May 1997. In this referendum on the new constitution, 52.71 percent voted in favor of the constitution and 45.89 percent voted against it (with a turnout of only 42.86 percent of the total electorate).[62]

The new constitution was designed to promote Poland's aspiration to full integration in Europe. It is based on democratic principles, the rule of law, and the separation of powers (paragraph 1 of the constitution states that the Republic of Poland is a democratic state under the rule of law). According to the constitution, Poland will have a 'social' market economy assuring its citizens human rights—an additional stipulation for acceptance to the EU—without ignoring social rights in health, education, or employment. It sets down the separation of church and state (paragraph 25 of the constitution deals with state–church relations), and also ensures control by the civilian-elected leadership over the army—a condition of NATO membership.[63]

The church closely followed the formulation of the constitution, partly through its official observer on the drafting commission, and exerted its influence with regard to several important provisions. The draft new constitution aroused opposition from the church and the right-wing parties. The draft, formulated by the Left-dominated parliament headed by the former Communists (SLD), was not acceptable to the church or the right-wing parties, who called for its rejection.

The episcopate and its associated political parties firmly demanded that God and Christian roots be mentioned in the introduction to the constitution. Polish society was actually divided on this issue. The church feared that Poland would lose its character of traditional Catholic culture, and that the church would become marginalized politically. Jerzy Turowicz, the veteran editor of *Tygodnik Powszechny* (who died on 27 January 1999 of heart failure at the age of eighty-six), expressed the church's fears by stating that the church in Poland "is extremely allergic to this separation of church and state".

The church argued that the new constitution had no regard for religious tradition. While none of the constitution's sections forbids abortion, the authors did include, as a gesture to the church, a ban on same-sex marriages. In fact, the left-wing president, Aleksander Kwaśniewski, did show flexibility and a willingness to reach agreement on these issues. Kwaśniewski, who chaired the parliamentary commission that prepared the draft of the constitution over two years, did not wish to antagonize the church, and strove for a compromise. He claimed that it was possible to reach a compromise on each provision, and that the new constitution would contribute toward stability in the country.[64]

In contrast to Kwaśniewski, former president Lech Wałęsa opposed the draft of the new constitution and referred to the outcome of the referendum as a tragedy. (The new constitution enhances the separation of authority between prime minister and president, and allows Parliament to veto a presidential decision by a 60 percent vote instead of the former requirement of 75 percent—largely as a result of negative experiences under Wałęsa's presidency.)

The UW, then an opposition party, agreed to compromise, as did the SLD. On the other hand, Solidarity threatened to prevent the compromise and called on the public to reject it in the referendum. Its main demand, similar to that of the church, was to include a much stronger religious element in the final draft of the constitution, which emphasized Catholic values and what those behind the demand termed 'Natural Law'. They also demanded that abortion be made illegal. Compromise and social reconciliation gained the upper hand, however. Tadeusz Mazowiecki, the first prime minister of post-Communist Poland and one of the chief authors of the constitution, warned the Poles that by rejecting the constitution they would prove to the world that they were a quarrelsome people, not capable of forming a new state.[65] The Poles proved otherwise.

In October 1997 the new constitution went into effect, enhancing Poland's acceptance into Europe.

5.2.7 THE POLISH CHURCH'S POSITION TOWARD EUROPE AND THE INTEGRATION OF POLAND WITHIN IT

Nowadays, with Poland's membership of the EU and NATO on the agenda and actually in effect (formal integration in NATO took place on 12 March 1999), the church endeavors to be part of this top-priority national objective. The negative, arrogant position that was typical of the church during the early years of post-Communist Poland has given way to a more positive attitude.

Two opposing cultures were at war with one another over the ruins of Polish Communism: the long-standing culture of Christian Europe, that is, the culture of the church; and modern European culture. The church's earlier position was that Poland had no need for European integration, as it was already a central pillar within Europe. The church was affected by phobias and deep anxiety over exposure to the West and secular Western influence. Its critics claimed that in its 'post-Communist rhetoric' the church was expressing opposition to 'permissiveness' and the consumer society, as well as its reservations regarding the mores of an 'open society', liberalism, civil society, and 'European citizenship'.[66]

Following the 1993 elections a change occurred in the attitude of the church towards a United Europe. Bishop Pieronek openly criticized the nationalistic views expressed by Catholics and certain church media circles, which he regarded as fostering anti-European phobias. (In May 1998 the European Commission gave Bishop Pieronek an award for his Catholic activities on behalf of European integration.[67]) For the first time, the episcopate supported Poland's membership of super-national organizations such as the EU and NATO.[68] The church also began to accept the political norms of modern democracies.[69]

It is evident that the church chose to make a genuine effort towards integration, in the national endeavor to grasp, and under no circumstances to miss, Poland's historic opportunity to return to the ranks of Europe.

The church seeks to achieve this not as a minor, but as a major, player, while emphasizing that this does not actually mean a return to the European fold. The church (together with Poland) had always been part of Europe, from which it had never been cut off. Thus its contribution has been crucial not only to Poland, but to the whole of Europe as well.

In the Conference on European Integration held in June 1998, Primate Józef Glemp referred to the importance to the European Union of a common value base.[70] He emphasized that economic issues are not sufficient to unite Europe, as many now recognize, adding that European integration cannot exist without a religious basis. It must be based on a culture of Christian evangelism. Glemp's expression was another link in the chain of Catholic Poland's historical view of its special mission in Europe and in the world. Nonetheless, today the church is more open to the idea of a 'joint partnership' between church and state (as a continuation of Vatican II), and it seems that its chances have improved in the context of the European Union, due to a re-evaluation of the term 'sovereignty'.

5.2.8 CONCLUSION

Cardinal Glemp was invited to make a New Year's speech and to reply to the public's questions on the TV Polonia program "w Centrum uwagi" (At the Center of Attention) on 30 December 1998. The cardinal used this opportunity to advocate reform and change, claiming not to be afraid of them. "Every change entails pain", he said. The influence of the papal encyclical "Faith and Reason" was evident in his statement that reform is reasonable and pluralism possible.

The challenges of adjusting to democracy have in fact led to various divisions within the Catholic Church in Poland. These go beyond divisions between high and low rank, and take the form of splinter groups challenging the pope, for example the St. Joseph (Józef) Movement versus the Eighth of May Movement. However, these are marginal groups that are not the true cause of the splits in the church. The true reason for the splits lies in the problems of coping with the democratic system.

As Marcin Król, dean of the Faculty of History at Warsaw University, rightly puts it, "The church has always had a problem with democratic order that is not hierarchic...The Polish bishops refuse to adopt democracy, as they fear the question marks and reforms...and that democracy may destroy their main stronghold...These struggles create two types of Catholicism in Poland...The bones of contention between the church and democracy will always remain, especially those concerned with decisions between divine law and majority opinion."[71]

Albeit with great difficulty, and with the aid of the Polish pope, the Polish Church has taken a stride toward adjusting to the new Poland and the new times it confronts. With the new millennium, the episcopate shows willingness to integrate and to continue exerting its influence on the nation. Its impressive past certainly affords the church much credit for the future and provides a basis for many expectations. However, only time will tell the extent to which the church has responded to the challenge of building a 'civil Catholic society', and with what substance it has imbued the formula of 'establishing the Christian democracy of the Third Republic'.

NOTES

1. THE FIRST PERIOD OF GOMUŁKA'S RULE

1. There is, however, no doubt that the fact that the external enemies had a different religion was for the church sufficient reason to come out against them. In any case, the concept of 'a state church manqué' used by Casanova, is certainly relevant to the Polish case (see Casanova, 1994, p. 71).
2. Lucjan Blit, among others, stresses the church's suffering as a factor that augmented its strength throughout Polish history (Blit, 1965, p. 22). The way in which Casanova confronts the 'martyrdom of Saint Stanisław' with the *raison d'état*, while ascribing to the church an inclination to relegate the latter to the former (Casanova, 1994, p. 106), does not reflect the historical reality. Furthermore, this argument contradicts Casanova's own thoughts elsewhere (Casanova, 1994, p. 93).
3. For details see Dinka, 1963, pp. 33, 34; Secrétariat Général du Gouvernement, 1959, p. 4.
4. *Secrétariat Général du Gouvernement*, 1959, p. 7.
5. Nowak, 1951, pp. 1–3; Inter-Catholic Press Agency, No. 27, 1946; Pirożyński, *Homo Dei*, No. 21, 1946, No. 11, 1947; No. 9, 1948.
6. Nowak, 1951, p. 20–21.
7. Barnett, 1958, p. 72.
8. *Keesing's Contemporary Archives*, 1948–1950, 9758/D.
9. Sapieha's contribution to the people and to the church was praised in Wyszyński's eulogy at the newly dug grave. (See note 7 of part 2, "The Stalinist Era").
10. *Tygodnik Powszechny*, 14 July 1946.
11. List Pasterski Episkopatu, marzec (March) 1946, *Gamarnikow Files*, RFE.
12. Nowak, 1951, p. 8.
13. *Ibid.*, p. 32.
14. List Pasterski, 23 September 1948; Nowak, 1951, p. 34.

15. This was expressed, *inter alia*, in the subjects on which *Tygodnik Powszechny* concentrated. See also in this context Barnett, 1958, p. 73.
16. See also Gsovski, 1955; Morrison, 1968, p. 46.
17. The content of the letter appears in Nowak, 1951, pp. 26–27.
18. See 1.1.1.7.
19. *Religious News Service Bulletin*, 22 September 1946; Dinka, 1963, p. 60. On the positions held by the church with regard to the 1947 elections and the referendum of June 1946, see also Dudek, 1995, pp. 9–10.
20. See, for example, the pastoral letter of 23 May 1946 (Nowak, 1951, p. 38).
21. See *Tygodnik Powszechny*, 7 July 1946, 17 August 1946, 20 October 1946; as well as *Tygodnik Warszawski*, 13 October 1946.
22. Shuster, 1954, p. 142.
23. Nowak, 1951, p. 41.
24. Cardinal Hlond wrote his 1948 New Year greeting in this spirit. See *Przegląd Powszechny*, No. 1, January 1948; Secrétariat Général du Gouvernement, 1959, p. 12.
25. Thus, *inter alia*, the pastoral letter read out in all churches on 28 September 1947, which complained about the pressure exerted on Catholics to join political parties and the severe censorship of the Catholic press, in addition to other protests. See *Tablet* (London), Vol. 190, 4 October 1947, pp. 215–226.
26. See Piwowarczyk, *Tygodnik Powszechny*, 8 September 1946; and Narzutowski, *Tygodnik Powszechny*, 22 September 1946.
27. *Tygodnik Warszawski*, 27 April 1947; see also in this respect Kaczyński, *Tygodnik Warszawski*, 7 September 1947.
28. See *Tygodnik Warszawski*, 16 November 1947.
29. This threat was expressed, for example, in the government decision concerning the establishment of an umbrella organization for all youth movements. This was a matter of great concern to the hierarchy, which stressed its right and its duty to participate in the education of Polish youth. (See Inter-Catholic Press Agency, Vol. 3, June 1948, pp. 4–9; *New York Times* [hereafter *NYT*], 24 May 1948.)
30. See Naurois, 1956, pp. 152, 153; Secrétariat Général du Gouvernement, 1959, p. 12; as well as Nowak, 1951, pp. 35, 36.
31. Nowak, 1951, p. 35.
32. In this spirit one must view the article "Church Affairs" by Father S. Wawryn, and the proclamation to the population in the liberated territories by Cardinal Hlond on 24 May 1948 (*Przegląd Powszechny*, No 6, 1948; Secrétariat Général du Gouvernement, 1959, p. 19).
33. See *Tablet* (London), Vol. 192, 20 November 1948; Nowak, 1951, pp. 26–27.
34. Secrétariat Général du Gouvernement, 1959, p. 7.
35. Dinka, 1963, p. 22. According to Jan Nowak (1951, p. 19), the number of devout Catholics in 1946 reached 21,632,000, and in 1947 reached 22,799,000. Among those who refer to the unprecedented religious homogeneity in Poland, are Halecki (1957, p. 202) and Blit (1965, p. 133). It is worth noting that the majority of the repatriates who returned to Poland from the Soviet Union and other places were Catholic. Secrétariat Général du Gouvernement, 1959, p. 7.

36. According to the 1921 census, 18,814,000, or 69.2 percent, of the population in Poland were Polish, while the remaining 30.8 percent were from minorities (according to the census those who spoke Polish at home were considered Poles). (Dinka, 1963, p. 9; Schmitt, 1947, p. 85).

37. Halecki, 1957, p. 45; Dinka, 1963, p. 20.

38. Blit, 1965, p. 133; See also Bromke, 1965, p. 57.

39. Pirożyński, *Homo Dei*, I.C., No. 35, 1948; Nowak, 1951, p. 14.

40. Dinka, 1963, p. 78.

41. Barnett, 1958, p. 67; Szczepanski, 1970, p. 118.

42. See, for example, Rose, 1974 and, of course, Lipset, 1960.

43. Almond and Verba, 1965.

44. Below, Pax is discussed as an instrument used in policy towards the church.

45. Stehle, 1965, p. 108.

46. For details see Blit, 1965, pp. 19, 20, 22, 102, 103, 107, and 118; Tyrmand, *Świat*, 8 November 1956 (the details of Piasecki's story were published here for the first time in Poland); Mikołajczyk, 1948 (B), p. 206; Secrétariat Général du Gouvernement, 1959, p. 27. (The source refers, *inter alia*, to the conversion of Witold Bieńkowski into Serov's tool, according to Swiatło's revelations.)

47. See section 1.2.4.4.

48. Blit, 1965, p. 136.

49. See Blit, 1965, p. 161.

50. For additional details on the ideological basis of Pax, see Stehle, 1965, p. 108; Blit, 1965, p. 147.

51. See Radziwill, *Cahiers Franco-Polonais*, BIP, December 1946, pp. 45–47; Secrétariat Général du Gouvernement, 1959, p.26.

52. See Markiewicz, 1974, p. 21; Rosada and Gwóźdź, in Gsovski (ed.), 1955, p. 72; Boim, 1971, p. 12.

53. Markiewicz, 1974, p. 21.

54. Sources interested in presenting the Vatican favorably in Polish eyes interpret this position as a clear message that the initiative must come from the Polish government. Thus, for example, Nowak, 1951, p. 18.

55. See Nowak, 1951, pp. 17–18; *NYT*, 15 July 1946; Dinka, 1963, p. 52.

56. Dinka, 1963, p. 52; *NYT*, 16 September 1945.

57. Markiewicz, 1974, p. 21. Markiewicz is wrong in presenting this article as the first attempt by Vatican circles—with the exception of the pope's aforesaid response—to respond to the annulment of the concordat (see Markiewicz, 1974, pp. 20–21).

58. Markiewicz, 1974, p. 22, based on *Tygodnik Warszawski*, January 1946; see also Carrol, *America*, Vol. 78, 20 December 1947, p. 320. Carrol presents a slightly different formulation of the pope's response in this letter and is quoted, *inter alia*, by Frank Dinka, 1963, p. 50.

59. The announcement by the Holy Father appeared in April 1948 in the Berlin periodical *Der Tag*. The text was also published by the London *Tablet*, 28 August 1948, quoting *NYT*, 16 April 1948.

60. Markiewicz, 1974, p. 24, based on Klafkowski, 1958, p. 205.

61. *NYT*, 2–3 April 1947; Dinka, 1963, p. 63.

62. Sections 1.1.5.1 and 1.1.5.2 include comments on the Soviet Union as an environmental sphere relating to the church as well as to the agricultural system.
63. See section 1.2.3.
64. Lucjan Blit (1965, p. 21) reports Stalin's profound consciousness of the subject.
65. Interview in June 1977.
66. On the Kremlin's decision calling on the Polish Communists to adopt such a path for the above purpose see, *inter alia*, Dziewanowski, 1959, p. 112.
67. See Nowak, 1951, p. 3.
68. See Secrétariat Général du Gouvernement, 1959, p. 8; and Halecki, 1957, p. 204.
69. Additional laws and formal acts that deal with policy towards the church in various fields will be presented, along with the general legal background, in the sections following this chapter. The same pattern will be used in all chapters dealing with policy.
70. *Dziennik Ustaw* (hereafter Dz.Us., the legal code), 1944, No. 1, Item 1; the manifesto was also published by Wydawnictwo Prawnicze, 1958, p. 8.
71. See *Dz. Us.*, 1945, No. 6, Item 259; *Dz. Us.*, 1947, No. 59, Item 316; Małkiewicz and Podemski, 1960, pp. 8, 9.
72. See documents in Nowak, 1951, p. 122; and Małkiewicz and Podemski, 1960.
73. See *Dz. Us.*, 1925, No. 72, Item 501; also published by Cybichowski, *Encyklopedja Podręczna Prawa Publicznego* (1929); and also in the work by Świątkowski, 1960, pp. 31–32.
74. Secrétariat Général du Gouvernement, 1959, p. 4. For comments relating to the concordat, see also Dinka, 1963, pp. 26–28.
75. See *Dz. Us.*, 1927, No. 1, Item 9.
76. *Dz. Us.*, 1947, No. 18, Item 71.
77. Professor Stefan Rozmaryn (professor of law at Warsaw University) speaks of the importance of normal legislation in the implementation of the 1921 Constitution— against the background of the adoption of the 'Little Constitution'—in an article in the monthly *Państwo i Prawo*, January 1948. (Quoted also by Gsovski (ed.), 1955, p. 173; and Dinka, 1963, p. 55).
78. Dinka, 1963, p. 73; Polish Research and Information Service, 1949, p. 2.
79. Miłosz states that the tactics adopted towards the different sections of the population were determined by the Polish Communists while they were in Moscow, taking into account the country's specific conditions (Miłosz, 1953, p. 99). See also Blit's comment on Stalin's similar perception of the issue (section 1.1.5).
80. Nowak, 1951, pp. 6–7.
81. For details, see section 1.2.3.1.
82. The characteristics of this government policy are discussed, *inter alia*, by Beneš and Pounds, 1970, p. 285; Secrétariat Général du Gouvernement, 1959, p. 9; Barnett, 1958, p. 73; Nowak, 1951, p. 12; Halecki, 1957, p. 202; Halecki, 1966, p. 337; Roos, 1966, pp. 238–239; and Dziewanowski, 1959, p. 241.
83. Stehle (1965, p. 29) builds his assertions around this point.
84. See, *inter alia*, Miłosz, 1953, p. 212.
85. See sections 1.1.4 and 1.2.4.3.
86. See section 1.1.3, and section 1.2.4.4.

87. The nature of this body and the failure of these efforts are discussed by Nowak, 1951, p. 13. See also section 1.2.1, and Boim, 1971, pp. 25–26.
88. This ambivalence is stressed, *inter alia*, by Stehle, 1965, p. 102.
89. Dziewanowski, 1959, p. 242.
90. See section 1.2.4.2.
91. Dinka, 1963, pp. 81–82; *Religious News Service Bulletin*, 14 February 1948; *NYT*, 10 February 1948.
92. See Bierut's interview, 20 November 1946; section 1.2.4.2.
93. See Secrétariat Général du Gouvernement, 1959, p. 10, based on *Robotnik* from the beginning of 1946.
94. Dinka, 1963, p. 76; *Tablet* (London), Vol. 190, 8 November 1947; cf. *America*, Vol. 78, 20 December 1947.
95. Skowroński, 1953, p. 48.
96. Inter-Catholic Press Agency, Vol. 2, 5 November 1947.
97. A document from the Labor Movement Archive, Dudek, 1995, pp. 8–9.
98. See Barnett, 1958, p. 356.
99. Nowak, 1951, p. 40.
100. *Rzeczpospolita*, 23 November 1946; quoted also in *NYT*, 24 November 1946.
101. *NYT*, 6 January 1947; Dinka, 1963, p. 61.
102. Nowak, 1951, p. 44; and Secrétariat Général du Gouvernement, 1959, p. 10.
103. See section 1.1.1.5.
104. See section 1.1.4.
105. Rosada and Gwóźdź, in Gsovski (ed.), 1955, p. 172; and Nowak, 1951, p. 16.
106. See Dinka, 1963, pp. 49–50; Mysłek, *Polish Perspectives*, August-September 1959, p. 67.
107. Secrétariat Général du Gouvernement, 1959, p. 8; Nowak, 1951, p. 16.
108. See also Świątkowski, 1960, p. 47; and Halecki, 1957, p. 203.
109. Markiewicz (1974, p. 20) and others refer to this privileged base granted by the concordat.
110. Boim, 1971, p. 19; based on Zakrzewska and Sobolewski, 1963, p. 188.
111. Halecki, 1957, p. 204; see also Nowak, 1951, p. 17.
112. For details see, *inter alia*, Barnett, 1958, p. 73.
113. See section 1.2.4.2.
114. See Secrétariat Général du Gouvernement, 1959, p. 8; and *Tablet*, Vol. 189, 17 May 1947, p. 246.
115. For the response of the Vatican to these flirtations, see section 1.1.4.
116. Blit, 1965, p. 111; see also section 1.1.3.
117. The establishment of the organization was, therefore, received with greetings and satisfaction by the organ of the Central Committee of the PPR, *Trybuna Wolności*, 1 March 1946.
118. See Blit, 1965, p. 103.
119. For details of the economic strength and the privileges enjoyed by Pax during this period, see, *inter alia*, the following works: Blit, 1965, pp. 22, 151; Weit, 1971, pp. 118–119.
120. Section 1.1.3.

121. *NYT*, 9 February 1945; Dinka, 1963, p. 46.

122. *Religious News Service Bulletin*, 10 July 1945.

123. See also Secrétariat Général du Gouvernement, 1959, p. 7; Blit, 1965, p. 132; Nowak, 1951, p. 38.

124. *Dz. Us.*, 1947, No. 9, Item 43; Boim, 1971, p. 20; see also Secrétariat Général du Gouvernement, 1959, p. 8.

125. *Dz. Us.*, 1944, No. 3, Item 13.

126. Jan Nowak adheres to the version that the government, time and again, granted material benefits to the church between 1945 and 1948 so as to exert more effective pressure on the church and the clergy during the next stage by threatening to cancel these privileges (Nowak, 1951, p. 15). It is doubtful that the existence of such a plan can be proved.

127. See Roos, 1966, p. 283.

128. Halecki, 1957, p. 203.

129. *Religious News Service Bulletin*, 9 September 1946.

130. *Ibid.*, 9 September 1946.

131. Dudek, 1995, p. 7.

132. See Secrétariat Général du Gouvernement, 1959, p. 9; Stehle, 1965, p. 61.

133. Halecki, 1957, p. 207.

134. On benefits in the field of education, see section 1.2.4.5.5.

135. A full list of the publications appears in *Tygodnik Powszechny*, 13 July 1947. Additional details on freedom of the press are provided by Halecki (1957, p. 208) and Dinka (1963, p. 48).

136. Dziewanowski, 1959, p. 241.

137. *Dziennik Urzędowy Ministerstwa Oświaty* (hereafter *Dz. Urz. Min. Oświaty* [the official gazette of the Ministry of Education]), 1945, No. 4, Reg. 189; cited also by Rosada and Gwóźdź, in Gsovski (ed.), 1955, p. 187; and Dinka, 1963, p. 205.

138. McEoin, 1951, p. 199.

139. See Nowak, 1951, p. 11; and also Valkenier, *Review of Politics*, Vol. 18, July 1956, p. 306.

140. An attack on the law in the drafting stage is included in the pastoral letter published by Archbishop Sapieha. See *Tygodnik Powszechny*, 19 August 1945. For the protest by the church hierarchy against the law after its passage, see Carrol, *America*, Vol. 77, 20 December 1947, p. 320. Another source (Secrétariat Général du Gouvernement, 1959, p. 9) characterizes the response by the episcopate regarding the law as feeble on the whole.

141. *Dz. Us.*, 1948, No. 55, Item 434.

142. Boim, 1971, p. 24; based on *Polska Ludowa*, 1965, p. 433.

143. Secrétariat Général du Gouvernement, 1959, p. 8; and Rose, 1948, pp. 208, 210.

144. *Dz. Us.*, 1947, No. 52, Item. 267.

145. See section 1.2.4.2.

146. Secrétariat Général du Gouvernement, 1959, p. 11; Dinka, 1963, p. 79; *Tablet*, Vol. 190, 8 November 1947.

147. Secrétariat Général du Gouvernement, 1959, p. 11.

148. Inter-Catholic Press Agency, Vol. 2, 15 October 1947, pp. 1–2.

149. McEoin, 1951, p. 198; Inter-Catholic Press Agency, Vol. 2, 5 November 1947.
150. Fragment of Bishop Choromański's letter to the minister of public administration, Wolski, 4 February 1950. See Nowak, 1951, p. 55.
151. For legal persecution on a much narrower scale, but by no less severe means, on the eve of the 1947 elections, see section 1.2.4.2.
152. Secrétariat Général du Gouvernement, 1959, p. 11; based on *Rapport sur la Situation du Pays*, November 1949, p. 184.
153. See sections 1.1.3 and 1.2.4.4.
154. Bilas, 1950, pp. 111–112; Dinka, 1963, p. 206.
155. *Christian Science Monitor*, 5 September 1946.
156. Secrétariat Général du Gouvernement, 1959, p. 10.
157. Rosada and Gwóźdź, in Gsovski (ed.), 1955, p. 204.
158. Halecki, 1957, p. 206.
159. McEoin, 1951, p. 199.
160. In this context, see sections 1.2.2 and 1.2.3.
161. Interview, June 1977.
162. See section 1.2.2.
163. Interview, May 1977.
164. See below.
165. See, for example, section 1.2.2.
166. See, for example, section 1.2.4.6.2.
167. See section 1.2.4.5.1.
168. See also note 68 above.
169. *RFE*, Item No. 4243/III, 5944, 19 July 1957.
170. Nowak, 1951, p. 23; based on *Tygodnik Warszawski*, No. 29, 1947.
171. *Ibid.*
172. A similar tendency is also evident in the party's theoretical publications, such as *Nowe Drogi*, between 1947 and 1948, where there is no attempt to evaluate church-state relations on the ideological level, and only a slight and scattered treatment of the very subject.
173. *Artykuły i Przemówienia*, 1946–1948, pp. 246, 247.
174. *Ibid.*, p. 247.
175. *Ibid.*, p. 247.
176. Such a positive approach by Gomułka is also revealed in the interview granted by Piasecki's deputy to Shneiderman (1959, p. 205).
177. In addition to the context of the Italian arena (below), Gomułka refers to the Vatican in one other place (*Artykuły i Przemówienia*, 1946–1948, p. 543), with regard to its support for US policy on the German issue.
178. *Artykuły i Przemówienia*, 1946–1948, pp. 564–565.
179. Stehle (1965, p. 29) emphasizes Gomułka's adoption of the 'safety-valve' technique within the framework of the postponement of the overall confrontation.
180. Peter Raina (1969) indeed tendentiously presents an extreme picture of the situation.

2. THE STALINIST ERA

1. Bieńkowski similarly stresses the fact that the Stalinist era clearly contributed to reinforcing the religious factor as a source of identity and a sanctuary for humanitarian objectives (for example, Bieńkowski, 1957, p. 110).
2. The reconstruction project in the liberated territories was almost complete by 1950 (see Roos, 1966, p. 218).
3. *Tygodnik Powszechny*, 16 February 1951.
4. See section 2.2.3.4.5.
5. See Szuldrzyński, 1953, pp. 37–38.
6. Additional biographical details on Wyszyński will be given in section 3.1.1.2.2.
7. See Wyszyński's eulogy for Sapieha at the burial ceremony (27 July 1951). A document is affixed to Zawadski's tract (Zawadski, 1953, pp. 194–201).
8. An announcement of the appointment was published in *L'Osservatore Romano*, 29 November 1952.
9. Published under the title "The Church Is Conscious of the Mission of Catholics in Poland and in the World".
10. *Tygodnik Powszechny*, 3 February 1952.
11. Wyszyński's pastoral letter of 10 October 1949 had already discussed the ideological emptiness and the spiritual poverty of materialism (see Dziewanowski, 1959, p. 245; Boim, 1971, p. 36).
12. Inter-Catholic Press Agency, 1 October 1953, p. 16.
13. The *Promemoria*, composed soon after the primate's return from Rome, emphasized, *inter alia*, the clergy's role in educating the young in the spirit of Catholic morality (*Tygodnik Powszechny*, 13 May 1951).
14. The memorandum enumerates rights which the new constitution should guarantee and which the church considered as basic demands (Zawadski, 1953, pp. 40–41).
15. The editorial which appeared under the title "The New Proposed Constitution", related positively to the proposed article, but clarified that as far as the Catholic position was concerned it could not be considered a solution to the problem (*Tygodnik Powszechny*, 16 March 1952).
16. For the text of the telegram see Nowak, 1951, p. 81.
17. See Nowak, 1951, p. 82; Boim, 1971, p. 37.
18. See Secrétariat Général du Gouvernement, 1959, pp. 14–15.
19. Szuldrzyński, *Kultura* (Paris), 1953, p. 24; quoted also in Secrétariat Général du Gouvernement, 1959, p. 17.
20. See Rosada and Gwóźdź, in Gsovski (ed.), 1955, pp. 192–193.
21. The episcopate's communiqué regarding the new appointments in the liberated territories was published in *Tygodnik Powszechny*, 18 February 1951.
22. Inter-Catholic Press Agency, 1 October 1953.
23. Dziewanowski, 1959, p. 251; see also Barnett, 1958, p. 77.
24. Boim, 1971, p. 34; Syrop, 1957, pp. 140–141.
25. See section 2.2.3.4.4.
26. See section 1.1.1.

27. See also section 2.1.1.3.
28. Rosada and Gwóźdź, in Gsovski (ed.), 1955, p. 248.
29. On the church's resignation regarding the nationalization of its lands, see *Poland Today*, Vol. 5, May 1950, p. 15.
30. For example in the article by Stanisław Stomma and Jerzy Turowicz, in *Tygodnik Powszechny*, 10 December 1950, p. 4.
31. Since the agreement recognized the pope as the exclusive authority in this area.
32. See the episcopate's protest of 8 May 1953 (Inter-Catholic Press Agency, 1 October 1953).
33. See Zawadski, 1953, p. 51.
34. *Tygodnik Powszechny*, 16 December 1951.
35. See "Komentarz Biskupów Do Porozumienia" (*Dokument*), Nowak, 1951, pp. 262–264; and also Secrétariat Général du Gouvernement, 1959, pp. 45–46.
36. *Przegląd Powszechny*, April 1950; quoted also by Secrétariat Général du Gouvernement, 1959, pp. 16–17.
37. Inter-Catholic Press Agency, 1 October 1953, pp. 11–12.
38. *Tygodnik Powszechny*, 3 August 1952; quoted also by Zawadski, 1953, p. 44. The article appeared under the title "The New Constitution".
39. Secrétariat Général du Gouvernement, 1959, p. 22; quoting Griffith, 1959.
40. *Tygodnik Powszechny*, 29 November 1951.
41. See section 2.1.1.5.
42. *Tygodnik Powszechny*, 16 December 1951.
43. *Tygodnik Powszechny*, 27 April 1952. See section 2.1.1.5.
44. See, for example, Boim, 1971, p. 32.
45. See, *inter alia*, Shuster, 1954, p. 146.
46. See Zawadski, 1953, p. 35.
47. See Nowak, 1951, pp. 72–73; Zawadski, 1953, p. 27; as well as Secrétariat Général du Gouvernement, 1959, p. 27.
48. See the episcopate's protest on 8 May 1953 (mentioned above). (Inter-Catholic Press Agency, 1 October 1953, p. 4.)
49. Secrétariat Général du Gouvernement, 1959, p. 27.
50. *Słowo Powszechne*, 2 March 1953.
51. Blit, 1965, p. 134.
52. Stehle, 1965, p. 102.
53. See, for example, the negative position on Pax in *Tygodnik Powszechny*, 21 September 1947.
54. Occasionally called the *Dziś i Jutro* group by members of the Polish episcopate (see, for example, the aforementioned protest by the episcopate in Inter-Catholic Press Agency, 1 October 1953, p. 4).
55. Inter-Catholic Press Agency, 1 October 1953, p. 4.
56. For example, their attacks on Bishop Choromański, detailed in Zawadski's tract (Zawadski, 1953, section 29).
57. See also Blit, 1965, p.169.
58. See section 2.2.3.1.

59. Halecki and Murray, 1954; Markiewicz, 1974; and also *Keesing's Contemporary Archives*, 1948–1950, 10267/A.
60. Markiewicz, 1974; Halecki and Murray, 1954; and also *Keesing's Contemporary Archives*, 1950–1952, 10827/B.
61. Blit, 1965, p. 179.
62. Boim, 1971, p. 54; Shuster, 1954, p. 149.
63. Published in *L'Osservatore Romano*, 9 September 1951. Government censorship in Poland did not permit publication of the missive in the local Catholic press.
64. Zawadski, 1953, ch. 8.
65. Nowak, 1951, p. 108.
66. See, for example, the famous article by J. Makarenko in *Pravda*, 9 June 1950, translated in *Trybuna Ludu*, 11 June 1950, against the background of the initiative linked to the Stockholm Peace Declaration.
67. Barnett, 1958, p. 77.
68. Additional formal decisions backing the various restrictive measures introduced by the government will be given below.
69. *Dz. Us.* 1949, No. 54, Item 334.
70. A translation of the text into English appeared in *NYT*, 14 May 1950.
71. On the agreement from the church's point of view, see section 2.1.1.
72. See section 2.2.3.4.
73. *Dz. Us*, 1952, No. 33, Item 232. The text was also published in the following: Secrétariat Général du Gouvernement, 1959, p. 21; Zawadski, 1953, p. 39; and *Keesing's Contemporary Archives*, 1952–1954, 12442/A.
74. See section 2.1.5.
75. Section 2.2.1.
76. See section 2.2.3.4.1.
77. On this deterioration from the church's point of view see the episcopate protest of 8 May 1953, cited above. (Inter-Catholic Press Agency, 1 October 1953, p. 2.)
78. This spirit is reflected, for example, in J. Górski's article, "The National Debate on the Constitution", published in *Nowe Drogi* (1952/1–2), which called for strengthening patriotic unity.
79. See "Chronicles of the Church in Poland, 1952–1953", *Gamarnikow Files* (Collection), RFE, p. 2.
80. On the other hand, on the attacks against the Vatican as an indirect method of blaming and undermining the Polish Church already in the first period of Gomułka's rule, see section 1.2.3.2.
81. *Rzeczpospolita*, 27 July 1949; see also Secrétariat Général du Gouvernement, 1959, p. 13; and also Dziewanowski, 1959, p. 243.
82. See section 2.2.1.
83. On the Vatican in the service of US imperialism, see also *Trybuna Wolności*, 24 February 1952.
84. *Nowe Drogi*, No. 6, 1952; Zawadski, 1953, p. 48.
85. *Trybuna Ludu*, 8 and 10 December 1952; *Głos pracy*, 9 December 1952.
86. For additional comments on this subject, see also the discussion of Pax as an environmental factor (section 2.1.3).

87. Blit, 1965, p. 173.
88. Inter-Catholic Press Agency, 1 October 1953, p. 7.
89. See section 2.1.3.
90. See section 2.2.3.1.
91. *Nowe Drogi*, 1949/1, pp. 47–48; Secrétariat Général du Gouvernement, 1959, pp. 12,13.
92. Boim, 1971, p. 29; Shuster, 1954, p. 145.
93. Dinka, 1963, p. 88.
94. *Nowe Drogi*, 1949/2; Nowak, 1951, pp. 57,58.
95. *Nowe Drogi*, 1952/6; Zawadski, 1953, p. 48.
96. *Dz. Us.*, 1950, No. 34, Items 308, 309.
97. The efforts at secularization in other spheres—the education system, health service, and prisons—will be examined in subsequent sections.
98. Zawadski, 1953, p. 74.
99. Section 2.2.3.4.4.
100. For the propaganda that accompanied the Kraków trial, see *Trybuna Ludu*, 1, 15–18, 22–27, 29, and 31 December 1952; and *Chłopska Droga*, 4 January 1953; *Trybuna Wolności*, 14 January 1953.
101. See *Trybuna Ludu*, 26, 27–30 September 1953. For example, in the above-mentioned article, dated 26 September, which appeared under the title "Who Hinders Normalization between the Church and the State?", the writer, Edward Ochab, attacks Cardinal Wyszyński.
102. Section 1.2.4.6.2.
103. For the arrests and the trials at this time, see Zawadski, 1953, pp. 1–3, 153–158, 164–169; Secrétariat Général du Gouvernement, 1959, pp. 21–23; Boim, 1971, pp. 21–23; see also *Keesing's Contemporary Archives*, 1952–1954, 12821/A. More than once additional accusations were leveled in these trials, including collaboration with the Germans during the war.
104. Boim, 1971, p. 51.
105. See *Trybuna Ludu*, 26 January 1951.
106. See Markiewicz, 1974, p. 24; Rosada and Gwóźdź, in Gsovski (ed.), 1955, p. 211; Nowak, 1951, pp. 103–107; see also *Keesing's Contemporary Archives*, 1950–1952, 11257/E.
107. *Dz. Us.*, 1953, No. 10, Item 52. The decree was also published as an addendum to the following source: Secrétariat Général du Gouvernement, 1959, p. 46.
108. The text of the oath was also published in *Dziś i Jutro*, 3 January 1954.
109. Section 2.2.2.
110. *Dz. Us.*, 1949, No. 40, Item 292.
111. *Dz. Us.*, 1950, No. 9, Item 87. For details on this matter, see Nowak, 1951, pp. 87–89; Dinka, 1963, pp. 98–100; Boim, 1971, pp. 38–41.
112. See *East Europe*, Vol. 7 (1958), No. 9, p. 22.
113. See Secrétariat Général du Gouvernement, 1959, pp. 14–15; see also *Keesing's Contemporary Archives*, 1948–1950, 10508/D.
114. Nowak, 1951, p. 69.

115. See "Kronika Kościoła w Polsce, 5 October 1952–15 February 1953", *Gamarnikow Files* (Collection). Faithful echoes and a detailed survey of the restrictions under discussion are included in the episcopate's protest of 8 May 1953, referred to several times above (see Inter-Catholic Press Agency, 1 October 1953, pp. 5–6, 15).
116. The text of the speech was published in *Rzeczpospolita*, 18 December 1948.
117. Markert, 1959, p. 362; Dinka, 1963, p. 156.
118. See Dinka, 1963, p. 155; and also Secrétariat Général du Gouvernement, 1959, p. 25.
119. Stehle, 1965, p. 64.
120. See section 2.1.1.5.
121. Nowak, 1951, p. 92.
122. Halecki, 1957, p. 219.
123. See section 2.2.3.4.1.
124. Nowak, 1951, pp. 47, 48.
125. Boim, 1971, p. 29.
126. Secrétariat Général du Gouvernement, 1959, pp. 25, 26.
127. Secrétariat Général du Gouvernement, 1959, p. 15. For comments on preliminary contacts between Wolski and Choromański before the establishment of the commission, see section 1.2.4.6.2.
128. Inter-Catholic Press Agency, 1 October 1953.
129. Syrop, 1957, p. 68.
130. See above.
131. *Dz. Us.*, 1950, No. 9, Item 87.
132. Section 2.2.3.4.6.
133. Dinka, 1963, pp. 100–101.
134. For details see Zawadski, 1953, pp. 8–10.
135. *Keesing's Contemporary Archives*, 1948–1950, 9880/A.
136. Heyman, 1966, p. 14.
137. *Keesing's Contemporary Archives*, 1950–1952, 11259/A. The fate of the Yugoslav cardinal, Stepinac, is of interest in this context.
138. Section 2.2.3.4.

3. THE SECOND PERIOD OF GOMUŁKA'S RULE

1. *Kuźnica Kapłańska*, 1 November 1955; Kownacki, *Polish Affairs*, April 1959, p. 9; Secrétariat Général du Gouvernement, 1959, p. 29. The entire text is given by Wasung (1958, Doc. No. 8).
2. Secrétariat Général du Gouvernement, 1959, p. 29.
3. Also published in *L'Osservatore Romano*, 26 September 1956.
4. Syrop, 1957, p. 134.
5. Hiscocks, 1963, p. 235.
6. Lewis, 1958, p. 223.
7. Details of these developments are given below, see section 3.2.

8. Roos, 1966, p. 284.
9. *Tygodnik Powszechny*, 4 January 1959; see also RFE, Item No. 4954/57, 23 August 1957.
10. Terry, *Sunday Times*, 29 March 1959.
11. Dudek, p. 233; based on the *Statistical Yearbook of 1991*.
12. For biographical material on Wyszyński, see also E. Celt, RAD, *Background Report*/179, 18 August 1976; Rosenthal, *NYT*, 7 September 1958; *Słowo Powszechne*, 3 August 1976.
13. See section 1.1.1.2.
14. A concept quoted by Bader (*Frankfurter Allgemeine Zeitung*, 31 July 1976).
15. For the extraordinary nature of this strong leadership within the context of the Catholic political map in those years, see section 3.1.1.3.
16. Dudek, appendix no. 6, pp. 244–246.
17. *Życie Warszawy*, 23 October 1956. For information on this subject see also Bromke, 1967, p. 234; and Hiscocks, 1963, p. 237.
18. For details of this viewpoint, see, for example, the article by Znak member Gołubiew (*Tygodnik Powszechny*, 13 January 1957).
19. Kisiel, *Tygodnik Powszechny*, 17 March 1957.
20. *Ibid.*
21. Stomma, *Tygodnik Powszechny*, 21 June 1959.
22. Turowicz, *Tygodnik Powszechny*, 19 July 1959.
23. *Kultura* (Paris), June 1957, p. 32.
24. Bromke, *East Europe*, Vol. 11, No. 2, February 1962, p. 15.
25. For details regarding Zawieyski's role, see, *inter alia*, *Zawieyski*, interview with *Le Monde*, RFE, *Gamarnikow Files* (Collection); RFE *Pers. File*, 197/Lo-9441, 31 January 1964; Halperin, 2 October 1958, RFE, *Pers. File*, 2806; RFE, *Pers. File*, 2174/Pa-13157D, 22 November 1968; *Trybuna Ludu*, 14 November 1964; RFE, *Polish SR/50*, 20 June 1969, p. 4.
26. Stehle, 1965, p. 82.
27. Griffith, W. E., *Background Information*, 11 June 1958, p. 13. The source quotes Kisielewski's famous interview with the Parisian *Kultura*, which appeared in 1963 and resulted in the imposition of restrictions on Znak's activities.
28. See his interview in *Le Monde* (January 1964).
29. For details, see RFE, SR/Poland, 18 July 1966; and also RFE, PPS, No. 389 (1590).
30. For a discussion of Pax and the Frankowski group, see section 3.1.3.
31. This position was expressed in an interview that Bishop Klepacz granted to *Ekspres Ilustrowany* (see Secrétariat Général du Gouvernement (1959, p. 34; Wasung, 1958, p. 20).
32. See Bishop Klepacz's interview above.
33. *Słowo Powszechne*, 5 November 1956.
34. *Trybuna Ludu*, 8 December 1956; Małkiewicz and Podemski, 1960, p. 129. The words also appear in Secrétariat Général du Gouvernement, 1959 (App. VI), pp. 46–47.
35. See, for example, Hiscocks, 1963, p. 64.
36. On the function of the church as a mediator and its contribution in moderating conflicts, see, *inter alia*, Casanova, 1994, p. 107. Dąbrowski's documents in Raina's

book (1995) provide some evidence of a similar function of the church in the post-Gomułka era.

37. *Słowo Powszechne*, 19 November 1956.
38. Secrétariat Général du Gouvernement, 1959, p. 30; Wasung, 1958, Doc. no. 13.
39. *Życie Warszawy*, 31 December 1956.
40. RFE, BMCG/A 1537, 29 July 1958.
41. For election results according to the official reports, see *Trybuna Ludu*, 23 January 1957.
42. Bethell, 1969, p. 232.
43. *Słowo Powszechne*, 16 January 1957; *Trybuna Ludu*, 16 January 1957.
44. *East Europe*, March 1957, p. 10; Dinka, 1963, p. 174.
45. Barnett, 1958, p. 108.
46. See section 1.1.1.5.
47. Dinka, 1963, p. 173; Mestrovic, *Commonweal*, 13 January 1961, p. 405.
48. Hiscocks, 1963, p.282.
49. Dinka, 1963, p. 197, basing himself on *Look*, Vol. 26, 14 August 1962, p. 25.
50. See section 1.1.4.
51. For the contribution of the primate and the church regarding the liberated territories and the Vatican's recognition of People's Poland, see section 3.1.1.5.5.
52. Section 1.1.4.
53. See Dąbrowski's documents in Raina, 1995, pp. 19, 21.
54. See the protocol of Dąbrowski's conversation with A. Skarżyński, 10 December 1970 (Raina, 1995, p. 37).
55. To be discussed below, section 3.1.1.5.
56. Hiscocks, 1963, p. 299.
57. See the joint announcement by the mixed commission established at the end of July 1958 and reported by Warsaw radio on 2 August 1958 (Radio Warsaw III, RFE, #1225), and by *Trybuna Ludu* on 3 August 1958.
58. See also section 3.1.1.5.2.
59. Terry, *Sunday Times*, 29 March 1959.
60. See section 2.1.1.4.
61. Dudek, pp. 229–230.
62. For this intolerance see, *inter alia*, Roos, 1966, p. 285; and RFE, *Background Report* (Poland), 2 October 1958.
63. See the communiqué from the cardinal's secretariat, *Tygodnik Powszechny*, 12 May 1957; and Turowicz's article, *Tygodnik Powszechny*, 26 May 1957.
64. See the editorial, *Tygodnik Powszechny*, 8 September 1957.
65. *Tygodnik Powszechny*, 1 June 1958 (the article "In the Light of the Millennium of Polish Christianity").
66. Dinka, 1963, p. 199.
67. Casanova, 1994, p. 97.
68. See section 2.1.1.3.
69. Signed by Wyszyński and sixty-four Polish bishops. Sztachelski's report to the Politburo in January 1960, implying a wish to avoid open confrontation with the government, coincided with the clerical offensive. It also demonstrates the Politburo's

policy, in response to this offensive, of obstructing the church in all arenas (see Dudek, appendix no.1, p. 237).

70. *Keesing's Contemporary Archives*, 1961–1962, 18961/A.

71. Also *Keesing's Contemporary Archives*, 1961–1962, 18179/A.

72. Dinka, 1963, pp. 191–192; *Keesing's Contemporary Archives*, 1961–1962, 1879/A.

73. *Keesing's Contemporary Archives*, 1965–1966, 21372/A.

74. See section 3.2.5.5.2.

75. Dinka, 1963, p. 185; *Polish Affairs*, August 1958, pp. 14–16.

76. See section 3.1.1.4.6.

77. Dinka, 1963, p. 185; *East Europe*, September 1958, p. 41; Rosenthal, *NYT*, 28 July 1958; RFE S/R, 29 July 1958, BMCG/A 1537.

78. *Le Monde*, 6 October 1959.

79. *Keesing's Contemporary Archives*, 1959–1960, 17134/A.

80. See, *inter alia*, Dinka, 1963, pp. 218–219.

81. Stehle, 1965, p. 83.

82. RFE, *S/R Poland*, 19 December 1961.

83. RFE, *S/R Poland*, 24 May 1962, p. 4.

84. *Keesing's Contemporary Archives*, 1961–1962, 18596/A.

85. *Ibid.*, 18961/A.

86. RFE, *S/R Poland*, 22 December 1961.

87. *East Europe*, September 1958, p. 42; Rosenthal, *NYT*, 12 August 1958; Dinka, 1963, p. 187.

88. Dinka, 1963, p. 183; Assembly of Captive Nations, March–October 1958, p. 88.

89. Korotyński, *Życie Warszawy*, 15 June 1959.

90. See section 1.1.1.3.

91. *Słowo Powszechne*, 15 December 1956.

92. See Secrétariat Général du Gouvernement, 1959, p. 38.

93. Catholic News Agency, 19 August 1957 (published in RFE under the reference Jupers F 47 Series).

94. Hamm, *Deutscher Zeitung*; RFE (Trans.), 5 August 1957.

95. See, for example, on convening a conference of such teachers at Jasna Góra, *Głos Pracy*, 21–22 September 1957.

96. See section 3.2.5.5.8.

97. *Keesing's Contemporary Archives*, 1961–1962, 18961/A.

98. See RFE, #1626, August 1958; RFE, M-66, 22 September 1958; RFE, #1054 (CNR/NCWC) 26 September 1958.

99. *Münchner Merkur*, Halperin; trans. in RFE, 23 September 1959.

100. Hiscocks, 1963, p. 304.

101. *Keesing's Contemporary Archives*, 1961–1962, 18596/A.

102. See section 3.1.4.

103. Secrétariat Général du Gouvernement, 1959, p. 37.

104. *Daily Telegraph*, 6 May 1959. The article was published under the title "The Special Interest of the Pope in Poland".

105. *Daily Telegraph*, 6 May 1959.

106. He was also helped in this by Stanisław Stomma (see comment in note 29 above), who accompanied him. (See Halperin, *Münchner Merkur*, 7 January 1959.)
107. *Dziennik Polski*, 23 December 1958.
108. According to Barnett, less than 5 percent of the Polish population were not Roman Catholic (1958, p. 82). Stehle reports that in the mid-1960s, some 90 percent of the population were active Catholics (1965, p. 68). Ross Johnson, presenting the church's version, also claims that more than 90 percent of the population continued to show loyalty to the church (RFE, *Background Report*, August 1968, p. 12). On this, see also *Słowo Powszechne*, 6 January 1958; 11 January 1958.
109. Thus, for example, when describing the 1960s, Ross Johnson (see note 108 above) emphasizes the high percentage of active believers in Warsaw itself.
110. Adam Ważyk (author of the famous "Poem for Adults") described this conflict between modern atheism and Catholic society, dominated by deep religious feelings, to an American journalist several years after writing the poem. His words are quoted by Shneiderman (1959, p. 38).
111. S. Korboński, 1959, p. 296; Secrétariat Général du Gouvernement, 1959, p. 30.
112. *East Europe*, September 1958, p. 41.
113. RFE (trans.), #0130, *Die Welt*, 27 August 1958.
114. See RFE, ASB/F 2317, Warsaw, 28 May 1959.
115. Blit, 1965, p. 209.
116. Markert, 1959, p. 363; Dinka, 1963, p. 173.
117. See, *inter alia*, Bieńkowski, 1971, pp. 41–42.
118. Moats, *National Review*, 23 May 1959, pp. 81–83; Dinka, 1963, p. 188.
119. Terry, *Sunday Times*, 29 March 1959; Rosenthal, *NYT*, RFE, 30 March 1959.
120. See *NYT*, 8 April 1960; RFE, RAD/Celt, 16 May 1977, 1650/n/Fi. On the affair see also Blit, 1965, pp. 209–210; Hiscocks, 1963, pp.300–301; Stehle, 1965, p. 88.
121. Section 1.1.2.3.
122. *Kultura i Społeczeństwo*, 10/No. 1, 1966, p. 138.
123. Kozakiewicz, quoted in Jaroszewski, *Kultura i Społeczeństwo*, 10/No 1, 1966, p. 137.
124. Pawełczyńska, *Argumenty*, 18 September 1960, pp. 83–86.
125. Blit, 1965, p. 133.
126. Blit, 1965, p. 134.
127. Józefowicz, Nowak, and Pawełczyńska, *Polish Perspectives*, No. 3–4, 1958; Wilder, *Public Opinion Quarterly*, No. 1, Summer 1964, p. 449.
128. See Pawełczyńska, *Studia Socjologiczno-Polityczne* (*SSP*), No. 10, 1961; Jaroszewski, *Kultura i Społeczeństwo*, 10/No.1, 1966; Staciwa, *SSP*, No. 24.
129. An estimate of the number of Patriotic Priests attending various congresses and conferences gives a figure of approximately 2,000 prior to the Polish October, and only 800 to 1,000 afterwards (see Dinka, 1963, p. 218). According to Blit (1965, p. 213), of the 17,000 priests in Poland in the 1960s (according to Rosenthal, in his *NYT* article of 7 September 1958, there were only 15,000), the number who were subservient to the government and Pax was 600 at most. Thus, for example, in March 1961 it was announced that 300 priests belonging to government-sponsored circles had abandoned Caritas and disbanded their groups (see *Keesing's Contemporary Archives*, 1961–1962, 18179/A; see also Żurawski, 1962, p. 144). Thus the data

reflect both a numerical reduction and a lack of success and weight for the Patriotic Priests' movement in the later periods (as, also, in the first period).

130. See, *inter alia*, Secrétariat Général du Gouvernement, 1959, p. 31.

131. For the background to his thinking, see also the following note. On the continuation of Pax's economic privileges and its impressive economic success, see Bromke, *Survey*, December 1961, p. 32; and also Kidel, 4 September 1957, RFE, *Gamarnikow Files*.

132. These attacks began in May (see Zimmerer, *Die Welt*, 7 May 1957, RFE #1140).

133. Bromke, 1967, p. 215.

134. See, for example, Jan, *Słowo Powszechne*, 26 March 1958.

135. Piasecki, *Słowo Powszechne*, 18–19 October 1958. A careful examination of Pax's "ideological approach" is presented by Chrypiński, 1958.

136. See section 3.2.5.3.

137. See section 3.2.5.3.

138. See section 3.1.1.3.

139. See the editorial in *Tygodnik Powszechny*, 8 September 1957.

140. Bromke claimed that the group lacked a unified program and that Frankowski supported the plan for maintaining "perennial values" in Pax's program (Bromke, 1967, p. 229; based on Frankowski, *Trybuna Ludu*, 12 November 1956).

141. See, *inter alia*, RFE, Item No. 4954/57, 23 August 1957.

142. *Neues Deutschland*, 26 September 1958.

143. Dinka, 1963, p. 180; Markert, 1959, p. 365.

144. Markiewicz, 1974, p. 34.

145. Stehle, *Survey*, January 1968, p. 111; Boim, 1971, p. 95.

146. See section 1.1.4.3.

147. RFE, trans. of Alessandrini editorial in *L'Osservatore Romano*, 6 August 1958.

148. Blit, 1965, p. 211.

149. See section 3.1.1.5.5; see also *Daily Telegraph*, 6 May 1959.

150. For the official announcement, see *L'Osservatore Romano*, 5 January 1959; see also *The Times*, 27 December 1958. The émigré delegation to the Vatican was fully dismantled in 1972.

151. See, *inter alia*, RFE S/R, Poland, 19 March 1962; 18 October 1962.

152. See Dąbrowski, in Raina, 1995, p. 114.

153. See section 3.1.1.3.5.

154. Additional details can be found in Dąbrowski's document ("The issue discussed with Prime Minister Piotr Jaroszewicz, 3 December 1971, *Pro Memoria* concerning the visit of the holy father Paul VI to Poland", Raina, 1995, p. 71).

155. See section 1.1.5.

156. As during the 1960s, also in the opposite direction. Concerning the aggravation of the policy towards the church, see below.

157. See below, in this paragraph.

158. See section 1.1.5.

159. For testimony on this, see, for example, RFE, *Pers. File* (Gom.)/Lo-9860, 10 December 1964; Lo-1109, 9 June 1967.

160. See, *inter alia*, RFE, *Pers. File* (Gom.), No. 133, 28 January 1969.

Notes

161. The reference is to evidence presented in Weit's book (1971).
162. Weit, 1971, p. 120.
163. Weit, 1971, p. 233.
164. See Krahn, *Neues Deutschland*, 26 September 1958.
165. Weit, 1971, pp. 120–121.
166. See section 3.2.7.
167. Published in *Trybuna Ludu* on 8 December 1956 under the title "Communiqué of the Joint Commission of the Government and the Episcopate". Also published in Małkiewicz and Podemski, 1960.
168. See section 2.2.3.4.5.
169. *Dz. Us.*, 1957, No. 1, Item 6.
170. See section 1.2.4.3.
171. See, *inter alia*, Secrétariat Général du Gouvernement, 1959, p. 33.
172. Małkiewicz and Podemski, 1960, pp. 57–59.
173. *Ibid.*, p. 59.
174. Gomułka, *Przemówienia*, 1956–1957, p. 304.
175. *Nowe Drogi*, 5/1957.
176. Gomułka, *Przemówienia*, 1957–1958, p. 328.
177. See Gomułka, *Przemówienia*, 1959, p. 183.
178. See section 3.1.1.5.1 and section 3.2.5.5.
179. See section 3.2.7.6.
180. See section 1.2.3.
181. See Bieńkowski, 1971, p. 43, and, on the other hand, Mijał's Natolin, neo-Stalinist group, which accused Gomułka of lacking class consciousness and of having inconsistent policies. RFE, *Pers. File*, No. 516/Lo-9925, 30 March 1965.
182. See Nowak (1958, p. 53), who claims to base himself on a reliable report by a foreign correspondent in Warsaw, dated 3 July 1957.
183. See section 3.1.5.
184. See 3.2.7 below.
185. See section 3.1.5.
186. Section 3.1.5.
187. Weit, 1971, p. 115.
188. Weit, 1971, p. 121.
189. See Siemek, *Dziennik Polski*, 4 December 1960.
190. Gomułka, *Przemówienia*, 1961, p. 473. See section 3.2.4.4 for Gomułka's statement in the same context at the Ninth Plenum, which reflected his conception of the religious factor in Poland even better. There, the operational conclusions are much more unequivocal.
191. *Times*, 28 June 1960.
192. Weit, 1971, p. 114.
193. *Nowe Drogi*, 5/1957.
194. Terry, *Sunday Times*, 29 March 1959.
195. *Ibid.*
196. Gomułka, *Przemówienia*, 1958, pp. 137–138.
197. RFE, *Pers. File*, No. 10408/II/4646.

198. Gomułka, *Przemówienia*, 1956–1957, p. 305; *Nowe Drogi*, 6/1957, pp. 27–28.
199. *Artykuły i Przemówienia*, 1956–1957, p. 305, published also in *Nowe Drogi*, June 1957, pp. 27–28.
200. Gomułka, *Przemówienia*, 1956–1957, p. 179.
201. Secrétariat Général du Gouvernement, 1959, p. 39. The source is based on an interview granted to *Tygodnik Polski* and published under the auspices of the Polish embassy in Paris on 21 September 1958.
202. Gomułka, *Przemówienia*, 1959, pp. 137–138. Part of the text also appears in *Trybuna Ludu*, 11 March 1959.
203. Dąbrowski, in Raina, 1995, p. 37.
204. See Nowak, 1958.
205. For an overview of the forces pressuring Gomułka at that time see section 3.2.4.
206. Thus, for example, the apprehension that arose as a consequence of Gomułka's increasingly hard-line policy, with regard to Wyszyński's re-arrest, was not realized. Regarding this apprehension see *Tablet* (London), 1 August 1958.
207. In Brown's words (Brown, 1966, p. 61). In this context Weit speaks about the 'salami' tactics used by the government (Weit, 1971, p. 113).
208. Bieńkowski was appointed by Gomułka after his return to power and also served as a representative in the Sejm. He was associated with Gomułka during the war and in the period between 1945 and 1948, and served as the director of the National Library in Warsaw between 1949 and 1956.
209. Stehle, 1965, p. 68.
210. *Nowa Kultura*, 7 November 1957.
211. Stehle, 1965, p. 68. See also the article published under the title "Two Paths to Secularizing Society" (*Argumenty*, 26 July 1959; *PPS* No. 702 (1905), p. 5.
212. See also a letter to the editor ("Is religion an ideological phenomenon?"), *Polityka*, 29 March 1958.
213. For example, Gomułka, *Przemówienia*, 1956–1957, p. 304.
214. See, for example, Mrowczyński, *Nowe Drogi*, 5/1957. In the article the author explains that administrative measures are "poor weapons for the formation of a secular world outlook among the young generation".
215. Stypułkowski, *Polish Affairs*, February 1958, p. 4.
216. Gomułka, *Przemówienia*, 1957–1958, p. 329.
217. Hiscocks, 1963, p. 320.
218. Reuters, 14 May 1960, RFE, *Pers. File*, 606; and also *Trybuna Ludu*, 15 May 1960.
219. See H. Diskin, *Medina, Memshal Ve Yehasim Benleumi'im*, No. 12, 1978, p. 88, based on statements made on Polish television on 27 June 1976 and on *Polityka*, dated 10 and 17 July 1976.
220. Dinka, 1963, p. 219.
221. See *Gamarnikow Files*, 1957–1959, "Kampania Propagandów..."
222. See Dudek, Appendix no. 5, pp. 242–243.
223. *Trybuna Ludu*, 25 May 1958.
224. Nowak, May 1959, p. 10.
225. For attempts by Polish diplomacy to promote the appointment of another cardinal, see, *inter alia*, RFE, *Pers. File* (Poland) No. 448/ST-10187, 18 March 1965.

226. See, *inter alia*, RFE, *Pers. File* (Poland) 1883/RO-4538, 26 August 1963.

227. Weit, 1971, p. 97.

228. See RFE (Poland), ASB/F-2317, Warsaw, 28 May 1959.

229. Dinka, 1963, pp. 173,174; Mestrovic, 13 January 1961, p. 405.

230. UP, Warsaw, 16 March 1965, RFE (Pd), *Pers. File*, (Poland) 4402/1.

231. Bromke, 1967, p. 170.

232. Instytut Literacki, 1962, p. 112.

233. *Nowicz*'s definition, *Polityka*, 2 June 1962.

234. (Zk), *Życie Warszawy*, 10 January 1959.

235. See section 3.1.4.

236. RFE, *S/R Poland*, 13 June 1962; *S/R Poland*, 2 May 1963; Stehle, 1965, p. 99.

237. RFE, *Pers. File* (Gom.) st-10064, 10 September 1964; RFE, *S/R Poland*, 13 December 1962.

238. *SR/Poland*, 2 May 1963.

239. RFE, *Gamarnikow Files*, UPI, Warsaw, 18 April 1959; Rosenthal, *NYT*, 16 April 1959.

240. Reported by, *inter alia*, UP, Warsaw, 18 April 1959.

241. See, for example, RFE, *S/R Poland*, 26 November 1962.

242. RFE, 2284/Lo-10694, 23 December 1966.

243. See, for example, RFE, *S/R Poland*, 6 May 1963.

244. RFE, *S/R Poland*, 29 November 1962; RFE, *Pers. File*, 621/VI—12655/a, 9 April 1965.

245. See Archbishop Kominek's promise to Gomułka to raise the Oder–Neisse issue with the Vatican (RFE, [Pd], *Pers. File* [Gom.], GND/10 February 1967); and also attempts by Gomułka and Kliszko to placate the primate (RFE [Pd], *Pers. File*, 279/Lo-10770, 7 February 1967).

246. Blit, 1965, p. 168.

247. See the article published in *Słowo Powszechne* on 16 October 1956, in which Piasecki's fate is linked to that of the Natolin faction and its struggle against the liberal faction of the PZPR.

248. In an interview granted by Hagmajer, Piasecki's deputy, to Shneiderman, he disclosed that during the January 1957 meeting with Gomułka, the Pax leaders reminded Gomułka of his previous positive stance towards their movement (Shneiderman, 1959, p. 205).

249. Nowak, 1958, p. 63.

250. Blit, 1965, pp. 141,142.

251. Gomułka, *Przemówienia*, 1959, pp. 137–138.

252. RFE, *Pers. File* (Gom.) No. 2899III/7498/0, 11 July 1959; RFE, *Audience Report*, Item No. 3694/59, 2 September 1959.

253. RFE, *Pers. File* (Gom.), No. 5076/C, 7755/C, 8 December 1959.

254. RFE (Pd), *Pers. File*, 2396/R—8513, 28 July 1961.

255. See, *inter alia*, Bromke, 1967, p. 225; Blit, 1965, p. 120; and Stehle, 1965, p. 110.

256. RFE (Pd), Item No. 4119/60, 16 November.

257. See Bromke, 1967, p. 229. For Kliszko's special support for the Frankowski group, see RFE (Pd), *Pers. File* (Gom.), VI-13044/n, 12 January 1966.

258. RFE, *Pers. File* (Gom), 657/D-11070/d, 27 March 1963.

259. RFE, *Pers. File* (Gom), 1657/Lo-11364, 16 September 1969.

260. As, for example, when Piasecki was received by Gomułka on 25 November 1965 (RFE [Pd], *Pers. File* [Gom.], VI-13151/hd, 9 December 1965).

261. RFE, *Pers. File* (Gom.), 2457/Z-10017, 30 November 1962; Secrétariat Général du Gouvernement, 1959, p. 30.

262. *Trybuna Ludu*, 8 December 1956.

263. See section 3.2.2.

264. His statement is quoted in Secrétariat Général du Gouvernement, 1959, p. 36, and sections of the statement appeared in *Tygodnik Powszechny*, 28 July 1957.

265. Bromke, 1967, p. 234. See section 3.1.1.3.

266. See Ministry of Interior circular dated 25 June 1957 (Nr.D II, 4/30/24/57); Secrétariat Général du Gouvernement, 1959, p. 35; and also Małkiewicz and Podemski, 1960.

267. See section 2.2.3.4.2.

268. RFE, *Background Report*, No.409 (1325), p. 1.

269. *Keesing's Contemporary Archives*, 1961–1962, 18179/A. According to Frank Dinka, after the war the state allocated 65 million zlotys for church reconstruction and repair (Dinka, 1963, p. 101). For Gomułka's reaction to the realities of church construction in Poland, see section 3.2.7.

270. RFE, *Pers. File* (Gom.), M-19 July 1969, 2806.

271. *Dz. Us.* 1958, No. 62, Item 309; see also section 3.2.5.5.7.

272. Already discussed above, section 3.2.5.4.2.

273. Markiewicz, 1974, p. 32.

274. Gomułka, *Przemówienia*, 1956–1957, pp.304–305.

275. Gomułka, *Przemówienia*, 1957–1958, pp. 55–56.

276. Gomułka, *Przemówienia*, 1959, p. 137.

277. Gomułka, *Przemówienia*, 1959, p. 138.

278. Gomułka, *Przemówienia*, 1957–1958, p. 322.

279. Secrétariat Général du Gouvernement, 1959, p. 39.

280. See section 1.2.4.6.2.

281. See *Trybuna Ludu*, 4 November 1956.

282. Mainly from the United States. On this, see, *inter alia*, *Keesing's Contemporary Archives*, 1957–1958, 16404/A.

283. See, for example, the meeting between Gomułka and Wyszyński in February 1958, reported by Stehle (*Frankfurter Allgemeine Zeitung*, 30 January 1960). Based on church sources, Stehle reported another meeting in January 1958 and one on 23 April 1958. The problem of religious education was discussed on each occasion, but no agreement was reached: *Keesing's Contemporary Archives*, 1957–1958, 16404/A. A meeting took place in January 1960 and was reported by Halperin on 16 and 17 January 1960: *La Croix* (19 January 1960) and *Le Monde* (21 January 1960).

284. On 30 July 1958 *Frankfurter Allgemeine Zeitung* reported a meeting with Jerzy Zawieyski a day after the raid at Jasna Góra (indeed, without any results).

285. On discussions with Kisielewski in July 1959, see RFE (Pd), *Pers. File* (Gom.), No. 4286/XII 7681, 16 October 1959.
286. See, for example, *Okólnik Nr Po 5/57 Ministra Finansów*, 26 January 1957; *Wiadomości Archidiecezjalne Warszawskie*, 1957, No. 4; and Secrétariat Général du Gouvernement, 1959, p. 35.
287. *Okólnik Nr Po 3/57 Ministra Finansów*, 5 June 1957; *Wiadomości Archidiecezjalne Warszawskie*, 1957, No. 8.
288. See section 3.2.5.5.5.
289. *Okólnik Nr URU 2/15/57 Ministerstwo Rolniczy*, 19 June 1957; *Wiadomości Archidiecezjalne Warszawskie*, 1958, No. 1.
290. See section 3.2.5.4.2.
291. See section 3.2.4.4.
292. Bromke, 1965, p. 57.
293. Bieńkowski, 1971, p. 42.
294. Dinka, 1963, p. 176; Markert, 1959, p. 365.
295. Secrétariat Général du Gouvernement, 1959, p. 36; Rosenthal, *NYT*, 26 September 1958.
296. Gomułka, *Przemówienia*, 1957–1958, p. 320.
297. *Ibid.*, p. 328.
298. *Sztandar Młodych*, 13 October 1958.
299. Stehle, 1965, p. 101.
300. Indeed, outside the walls of the schools in Poland.
301. Bromke, 1965, p. 57.
302. See below for echoes of the Jasna Góra affair in the government press.
303. See *Życie Warszawy*, 15–16 April 1959.
304. Nowak, May 1959, p. 10.
305. Wróblewski, *Życie Warszawy*, 16 May 1958.
306. The article was translated into English in RFE, 10 August 1958, and marked #1001, F-48 X/8/15.
307. Stehle, *Frankfurter Allgemeine Zeitung*, 29 July 1958. English translation RFE, OK-PAO (2240).
308. See below.
309. See Radio Warsaw, III, 2 August 1958, RFE #1225; *Economist*, 8 August 1958, RFE #1507.
310. Siemek, *Nowe Drogi*, July 1958.
311. Dobrowski, 17 September 1958.
312. Korotyński, *Życie Warszawy*, 8 and 9 August 1958.
313. Mainly laws relating to marriage and birth control. For this, see also *Keesing's Contemporary Archives*, 1957–1958, 16404/A.
314. See also Barnett, 1958, p. 81; and also *Keesing's Contemporary Archives*, 1957–1958, 16404/A.
315. Quoted in *East Europe*, 1/59.
316. See, *inter alia*, Parzyńska, *Życie Warszawy*, 10 December 1959.
317. See Weit, 1971, pp. 91, 94–104; and also *Keesing's Contemporary Archives*, 1965–1966, 21372/A.

318. *Fakty i Myśli*, 14 March 1959; Dinka, 1963, pp. 190–191.

319. PAP 3, RFE, 10 September 1958, #1343.

320. Section 3.2.5.5.1.

321. RFE, Reuters, 23 May 1958, #2344; Gruson, *NYT*, 24 May 1958, RFE #0630.

322. RFE, Reuters, 30 July 1958, ASB/F; *Keesing's Contemporary Archives*, 1957–1958, 16404/A. Words quoted, as said, by the official press.

323. The statements were also published in *Trybuna Ludu*, 25 September 1958.

324. Mekarski, *Polish Affairs*, June 1959, p. 2; Gomułka, *Przemówienia*, 1959.

325. Mekarski, *Polish Affairs*, June 1959, p. 2.

326. Section 3.2.5.5.1.

327. Blit, 1965, p. 218; Stehle, 1965, p. 95; *Keesing's Contemporary Archives*, 1961–1962, 18179/A.

328. RFE, *S/R Poland*, 11 October 1961.

329. *Dz. Us.*, 1958, No. 72, Item 358.

330. *Dz. Us.*, 1959, No. 11, Item 62.

331. Bromke, 1967, p. 144; *Rocznik Polityczny i Gospodarczy*, 1960, p. 220.

332. See Secrétariat Général du Gouvernement, 1959, pp. 36–37; and also Hiscocks, 1963, p. 301.

333. See, for example, Jaroszewski, *Nowe Drogi*, June 1958, pp. 93–106; Guranowski, *Nowe Drogi*, March 1959, pp. 162–173. The steps towards secularization in education will be discussed extensively below (section 3.2.5.5.8).

334. See section 3.2.5.5.1.

335. Barnett, 1958, p. 78.

336. See RFE, Reuters, 26 May 1958, ASB/S 1916; RFE, trans. Halperin, *Münchner Merkur*, 8 August 1958.

337. Nowak, May 1959, p. 11; *Trybuna Ludu*, 18 March 1959; Secrétariat Général du Gouvernement, 1959, p. 3.

338. These even include accusations of infringing the freedom of conscience of non-believers. See Bromke, 1967, p. 145; see also Father Piroszyński's trial (Halperin, *Münchner Merkur*, 21 January, *Gamarnikow Files*, 1957–1959, RFE #0830). For the same accusations, only in the media, see section 3.2.5.5.1.

339. See section 1.2.3.2.

340. See "The propaganda campaign in the struggle against the church in Poland", RFE, 1957–1959.

341. See section 3.2.5.4.

342. Hiscocks, 1963, p. 299; Sherman, *Scotsman*, 8 July 1958, RFE #1852; Stehle, *Frankfurter Allgemeine Zeitung*, 10 July 1958, RFE #1150.

343. See *Dz. Urz., Min. Finansów*, 1959, #4, Item 9. The text of the circular also appears in Małkiewicz and Podemski, 1960, pp. 89–90; see also *Głos Pracy*, 25 October 1960; *Münchner Merkur*, 25 April 1959; Nowak, May 1959, pp. 34–35 (and App. no. 3); and also *NYT*, RFE, #630, 29 April 1959.

344. Hiscocks, 1963, p. 301.

345. *Dz. Us.*, 1959, #23, Item 150. Also appears in Małkiewicz and Podemski, 1960, pp. 88–89; see also Secrétariat Général du Gouvernement, 1959, p. 35.

346. *Tablet* (Brooklyn), 1 April 1961; Dinka, 1963, p. 196.

347. See Ministry of Finance circular, dated 10 August 1959 (Małkiewicz and Podemski, 1960, pp. 97–102); and Ministry of Finance circular, dated 28 October 1960 (No Po. 25742/3/60) (Małkiewicz and Podemski, 1960, pp. 106–107).

348. *Keesing's Contemporary Archives*, 1961–1962, 18179/A.

349. *Ibid.*, 18596/A.

350. Nowak, 1958, p. 62; Sejm minutes for 12 July 1957, p. 200.

351. Nowak, 1958, p. 62.

352. Nowak, 1958, p. 62; Sejm minutes for 12 July 1957, p. 198.

353. *Trybuna Ludu*, 31 July 1958; Secrétariat Général du Gouvernement, 1959, p. 38; Halperin, *Münchner Merkur*, 8 August 1958.

354. Secrétariat Général du Gouvernement, 1959, p. 36.

355. Nowak, May 1959, p. 10.

356. Bromke, 1967, p. 249.

357. *Ibid.*

358. Section 3.2.5.1.

359. RFE, *S/R Poland*, 19 December 1961.

360. *Keesing's Contemporary Archives*, 1961–1962, 18961/A; RFE, *S/R Poland*, 2 April 1962.

361. Mrowczyński, *Nowe Drogi*, 5/1957; Sokorski, *Nowe Drogi*, 6/1957.

362. Inter-Catholic Press Agency, 22 September 1958.

363. *Ibid.*

364. *Ibid.* Also Halperin, when writing in *Münchner Merkur* on 8 August 1958, referred to the new prohibitions mentioned above (the English translation of the report appears in RFE under the reference OK-PAO 1525).

365. Rosenthal, *NYT*, 26 September 1958.

366. Kozakiewicz, *Życie Warszawy*, 24 August 1960.

367. See Assembly of Captive Nations, March–October 1958, pp. 90–91.

368. Bieńkowski, 1971, pp. 41–42.

369. See section 1.2.4.6.4.

370. Gomułka, *Przemówienia*, 1957–1958, pp. 318–319; *Trybuna Ludu*, 25 September 1958.

371. Gomułka, *Przemówienia*, 1957–1958, p. 320.

372. See the statement by *Bieńkowski*, as reported by Reuters, Warsaw, 1 September 1959 (at the beginning of the new school year) (RFE, OK-PAO, DG/F 23).

373. For data on the increase in the number of schools without religious instruction at the end of the 1950s, see also Stehle, 1965, p. 91.

374. Bieńkowski, 1971, p. 42. According to French government documents (Secrétariat Général du Gouvernement, 1959, p. 36), the society was established on 21 January 1957, and by the end of the year had spread throughout Poland. In 1958 the society had over 20,000 members, and in 1959 numbered 32,000 members. According to Hiscocks (1963, p. 301), in 1960 the membership rose to 60,000. For the activity of the Society for Secular Schools, see also Jezierska, *Nowe Drogi*, 4/1958, pp. 126–130.

375. Nowak, May 1959, Appendix III.

376. *Polish Perspectives*, November 1960, p. 42.

377. *L'Unita*, 24 January 1961; Dinka, 1963, p. 195.
378. *America*, 29 July 1961, p. 558; Stehle, 1965, p. 93.
379. *Trybuna Ludu*, 10 September 1961.
380. Stehle, 1965, p. 93.
381. See section 3.2.7.
382. It is worth noting the restrictions imposed on ecclesiastical appointments: see sections 3.2.2 and 3.2.4.
383. Restrictions of this type were imposed, for example, in everything linked to the Congress on European Culture and the Conference of Catholic Youth in August 1962 (see RFE, *SR/Poland*, 30 August 1962).
384. This, of course, in addition to the environmental changes cited above.
385. See section 3.2.4.1.
386. Gomułka, *Przemówienia*, 1959, p. 24.
387. RFE, *Pers. File* (Gom.), Z-9020, 6 October 1960.
388. RFE, *Pers. File* (Gom.), No. 10408/II/4646.
389. See section 3.2.4.4.2.
390. See section 2.2.2.
391. Though the subject itself continued to be of supreme importance in policy.
392. See the comment on those personal relations in section 1.2.6.
393. See, for example, the article "Cardinal Wyszyński Not Allowed to Leave Poland within the Next Few Years?", *Audience* (Poland), Item No. 613/68 JP-28 March.
394. See RFE, *Pers. File* (Gom.), No. 1871/LO-10565, 28 October 1966.
395. According to a certain source, the Central Committee attached less and less weight to his opinions and statements (RFE, *Pers. File* [Gom.], Lo-10511, 3 June 1966).
396. See, *inter alia*, Brown, 1966, p. 52.
397. As it appears, for example, on the basis of the following source: RFE, *Pers. File* (Gom.), III/6909, 17 September 1958.
398. Such as, for example, Kliszko's support for the position not to allow visits by bishops from abroad during the millennium celebrations (RFE, *Pers. File* [Gom.], Lo-10447, 12 April 1966).
399. RFE, *Pers. File* (Gom.) 804/MI/512, 1 March 1960.

5. EPILOGUE: THE POST-GOMUŁKA ERA

1. For the contents of this sermon see, *inter alia*, Casanova, 1994, p. 97.
2. Casanova, 1994, p. 96.
3. Micewski, 1994, p. 82.
4. See, *inter alia*, Casanova, 1994, p. 9.
5. Dąbrowski (in Raina, 1995, p. 228). Kania's words are quoted in *La Documentation Catholique* (Paris).
6. See Gowin, 1995, p. 22.
7. *Ibid.*, pp. 285–288.
8. TV Polonia, 16 October 1998.

9. Dąbrowski, 1995, p. 226.

10. Dudek, 1995, p. 231, based on *Trybuna Ludu*, 24 December, 1970.

11. Dąbrowski, 1995, p. 43.

12. See *ibid.*, p. 44.

13. See the conversation between Kania and Dąbrowski on 26 January 1971; Dąbrowski, 1995, p. 51.

14. Dąbrowski, 1995, p. 145.

15. See *ibid.*, p. 191.

16. *Ibid.*, p. 224.

17. *Ibid.*

18. Diskin, 1978, p. 81.

19. Dąbrowski, 1995, p. 261.

20. *Ibid.*, p. 51.

21. See *ibid.*, p. 317; Śpiewak, 1997, p. 1.

22. Dąbrowski, 1995, p. 228.

23. *Ibid.*, p. 289.

24. Micewski, 1994, p. 70.

25. *Ibid.*

26. Dąbrowski, 1995, p. 376.

27. Micewski, 1994, p. 69.

28. See *ibid.*, p. 78.

29. For details, see *ibid.*, pp. 60, 70.

30. Dąbrowski, 1995, p. 386.

31. Communiqué of the Head Council of the episcopate, 15 December 1981, *ibid.*, p.388.

32. *Ibid.*, pp. 387–388.

33. Casanova, 1994, p. 107.

34. Micewski, 1994, p. 76.

35. Diskin, in Black and Strong, 1986, p. 138.

36. Śpiewak, November 1997, p. 2.

37. Casanova, 1994, p. 72.

38. Micewski, 1994, p. 67.

39. Dąbrowski, 1995, p. 390.

40. Diskin, in Black and Strong, 1986, p. 137.

41. Micewski, 1994, p. 81.

42. For this visit see M. Janicki, "Wolność zadania" (The tasks of freedom), *Polityka*, No. 23 (2092), 7 June 1997. The pope's later visits to his homeland were in post-Communist Poland. His fourth visit took place in the summer of 1991 (June, August), his fifth in the summer of 1997 (end of May/beginning of June). The pope made a triumphant visit to Poland again in June 1999.

43. Micewski, 1994, p. 81.

44. See *ibid.*, p. 82.

45. Interview by Micewski, 1994, p. 84.

46. Dąbrowski, 1995, p. 321.

47. *Dz. Us.*, No. 29, 23 May 1989.

48. Micewski, 1994, p. 87.
49. See Rakowski's speech before the Sejm, 26 April 1989.
50. E.g., Dudek, 1995, p. 235.
51. Śpiewak, November 1997, p. 9.
52. *Ibid.*, p. 10.
53. Gowin, 1995, p. 12.
54. See the criticism of Father Pieronek in Gowin, 1995, p. 188.
55. See Śpiewak, November 1997, p. 2.
56. See Śpiewak, November 1997.
57. On the defeat of the right-wing clerical parties and the victory of the Left in 1993, see, for example, Gowin, 1995.
58. *Ha'aretz*, 7 August 1996, from *Die Welt*.
59. *TV Polonia*, 13.5.98.
60. See *Gazeta Wyborcza*, 23 June, 1997, p. 4.
61. TV Polonia, 11 May 1998.
62. *Polityka*, No. 23 [2092], 7 June 1997, pp. 12,20.
63. For further details on the constitution, see *Gazeta Wyborcza*, 24 June 1997, p. 6.
64. On Kwaśniewski's efforts toward reaching a compromise, see, for example, Jane Perlez, "Shrinking Gap between Church and Polish State", *NYT*, 17 July 1995.
65. "A Cross in the Wheels of the Constitution," *Ha'aretz*, 15 April 1997, translated into Hebrew from *The Economist*.
66. Gowin, 1995, p. 42.
67. TV Polonia, 8 May 1998.
68. At the end of 1997 the Hungarian bishops also expressed their support for efforts to achieve economic reform related to joining the EU and NATO. In Romania, criticism has been raised against the Romanian patriarch for obstructing efforts toward reform and integration in NATO.
69. Śpiewak, November 1997, p. 11.
70. TV Polonia, 18 June 1998.
71. From an article written for Project Syndicate in December 1998, quoted in *Ha'aretz*, 14 December 1998, under the Hebrew title "Not a Catholic Wedding".

BIBLIOGRAPHY

Adamowicz, A. K. (1964). "Polski Handel Zagraniczny w 20-Leciu." *Sprawy Między-narodowe* (July), pp. 101–120.

Alessandrini (1958). RFE, No. 1423, a full translation of Alessandrini's editorial in *L'Osservatore Romano*, Rome, 6 August.

Alessandrini (1959). RFE, N.Y., 3 April 1959, No. 2011. NCWC, Gomułka-Vatican, Alessandrini in *L'Osservatore Romano*, Rome, 2 April.

Almond, G. and S. Verba (1965). *The Civic Culture*, Boston: Little Brown.

Ambrosini, M. L.(1995). *Tajna Archiwa Watykanu* (The secret archives of the Vatican). Warsaw: Pax.

America, 105 (29 July 1961).

Andrzejewski, J. and A. Paczkowski (eds.)(1986). *Gomułka i inni. Dokumenty z archiwum KC 1948–1982*. Warsaw.

A. R. (1959). "210 Szkół Swieckich". *Sztandar Młodych*, 23 March.

Argumenty, 26 July 1959. ("Two Ways for Secularization of Social Life".)

Assembly of Captive European Nations. *A Survey of Recent Developments in Nine Captive Countries*, (March–October, 1958; March–October, 1960).

Atkins, T. (1949). *Polityka Watykanu*. Warsaw: KiW.

Audience Report, RFE, 1956–1959.

Audience, RFE, "Outcome of the Piasecki–Gomułka Talks", Item No. 3694/59 I X/F 8302/a, 2 September 1959 (source Vienna).

Audience, RFE, "Weakening of Pax", Item No. 4119/60 C-8074/E, 16 November 1960.

Audience, RFE, "Cardinal Wyszyński Not Allowed to Leave Poland within the Next Five Years?", Item No. 613/68, JP, Vi/P 14396, 28 March 1968.

Background Information, RFE, 1958–1960.

Background Report, RFE (Poland), "The Olkusz Trial—A Clash of Rival Regime Priests", 2 October 1958.

Background Report, RFE, 1958–1975.

Barnett, C. R. (1958). *Poland, Its People, Its Society, Its Culture*. New Haven: HRAF Press.

Basiński, E., and T. Walichnowski (1974). *Stosunki Polsko—Radzieckie 1944–1974*. Warsaw: Ministerstwo Obrony Narodowej.

Beck, C., et al. (1973). *Comparative Communist Political Leadership*. New York: D. McKay Co.

Beneš, V. L., and N. J. Pounds (1970). *Poland*. New York: Praeger.

Bergman, A. (1966). "Gomułka's Long Hot Spring". *East Europe* 15 (August).

Bernstein, C. and M. Politi (1997). *His Holiness: John Paul II and the History of Our Time*.

Bethell, N. (1969). *Gomułka, His Poland and His Communism*. London: Longman.

Bieńkowski, W. (1957). *Rewolucji Ciąg Dalszy/Dokumenty*. Paris: Instytut Literacki.

Bieńkowski, W. (1958). "The Political and Economic Sitution in Poland since October 1956". *International Affairs*, 34 (April), pp. 137–144.

Bieńkowski, W. (1969). *Motory i Hamulce Socjalizmu/Dokumenty*. Paris: Instytut Literacki.

Bieńkowski, W. (1971a). *Socjologia Klęski, Dramat Gomulskiego Czternastolecia/Dokumenty* Paris: Instytut Literacki.

Bieńkowski, W. (1971b). *Drogi Wyjścia/Dokumenty* Paris: Instytut Literacki.

Bierut, B. (1952a). *O Partii*. Warsaw: KiW.

Bierut, B. (1952b). *Pod Sztandarem Frontu Narodowego, Wybrane Artykuły i Przemówienia 1952r*. Warsaw: KiW.

Bierut, B. (1952c). *Wskazania i Nauki XIX Ziazdu KPZR Przemówienia Wygłoszone na Naradzie Aktywu PZPR w Warszawie Dnia 4 XI 1952 r*. Warsaw: KiW.

Bierut, B. (1952d). *O Konstytucji Polskiej Rzeczypospolitej Ludowej*. Warsaw: KiW.

Bierut, B. (1954). "Dziesięc-Lat Polski Ludowej". *Sprawy Międzynarodwe* (July–September), pp. 17–18.

Bierut, B., and J. Cyrankiewicz (1952). *Podstawy Ideologiczne PZPR*. Warsaw: KiW.

Bierut, B., and J. Cyrankiewicz. *Socialist Unity in the Polish People's Democracy*. Merhavia: Ha'kibbutz Ha'artzi, Ha'shomer Ha'tzair (in Hebrew).

Bierut, B., and H. Minc (1951). *The Polish Nation in the Struggle for Peace and the 6-Year Plan*. Kraków: Czytelnik.

Bilas, B. S. (1950). *Organizacja Szkolnictwa w Polsce*. Kraków: Czytelnik.

Blau, P. M. (1964). *Exchange and Power in Social Life*. New York: Wiley.

Blit, L. (1959). *Gomułka's Poland*. London: Hutchinson.

Blit, L. (1965). *The Eastern Pretender. Bolesław Piasecki: His Life and Times*. London: Hutchinson.

Bociurkiw, B. and W. J. Strong (eds.) (1975). *Religion and Atheism in the USSR and Eastern Europe*. London: Macmillan.

Bodnar, A. (1968). "Współpraca Gospodarcza Polski i Związku Radzieckiego". *Sprawy Międzynarodowe* (January), pp. 34–45.

Boim, M. (1971). *The Development of Church-State Relations in Poland: 1944–1971*. M.A. dissertation. Jerusalem: Department of Political Science, the Hebrew University of Jerusalem, November.

Brecher, M. (1972). *The Foreign Policy System of Israel: Setting, Images, Process*. London: Oxford University Press.

Bromke, A. (1961). "From 'Falanga' to 'Pax'". *Survey*, (December) pp. 29–40.

Bromke, A. (1962a). "The Znak Group in Poland". *East Europe*, 11 (1 and 2).

Bromke, A. (1962b). "Nationalism and Communism in Poland". *Foreign Affairs* (July), pp. 635–643.

Bromke, A. (ed.) (1965). *The Communist States at the Crossroads: Between Moscow and Peking*. New York: Praeger.

Bromke, A. (1967). *Poland's Politics: Idealism vs. Realism*. Cambridge, Mass.: Harvard University Press.

Bromke, A. (1971). "Beyond the Gomułka Era". *Foreign Affairs*, 49 (April).

Brown, J. F. (1966). *The New Eastern Europe, the Khrushchev Era and After*. New York: Praeger.

Brown, J. F. (1976). "Hungary and Poland Twenty Years Ago: Thoughts in Retrospect". RAD, *Background Report*, 207 (Eastern Europe), 5 October.

Brzeziński, Z. K. (1957). "Wrażenia z Polski". *Kultura* 11/121. Paris.

Brzeziński, Z. K. (1959). "Gomułka's Road to Socialism". *Problems of Communism*, 8 (May–June).

Byrski, Z. (1971). "Legenda Pierwszego Sekretarza". *Kultura* (March). Paris.

Carrol, W. (1947). "The Church in Poland". *America*, 78 (20 December).

Casanova, J. (1994). *Public Religion in the Modern World*. Chicago: The University of Chicago Press.

Celt, E. (1976). "Cardinal Wyszyński Turns Seventy-Five". *Background Report*, RAD (Poland), 18 August.

Celt, E. (1977). "Nowa Huta Consecrates Its First Catholic Church". *Background Report*, RAD (Poland), 16 May.

Central Statistical Office (1930). *Concise Statistical Yearbook of Poland*.

Central Statistical Office (1949). *Statistical Yearbook of Poland* 1947, 1948. Warsaw.

Chłopska Droga, 4 January 1953.

Christian Science Monitor, 5 September 1946.

Chrypiński, V. C. (1958). *The Movement of 'Progressive Catholics' in Poland*. Unpublished Ph.D. dissertation. University of Michigan.

Chrypiński, W. (1989). *Kościół a Rząd i Społeczeństwo w Powojennej Polsce*. London.

Cianfarra, C. M. (1950). *The Vatican and the Kremlin*. New York: Dutton.

Ciupak, E. (1968). "Katolicyzm Warszawiaków". *Polityka*, 27 January.

Conquest, R. (1962). *Power and Policy in the USSR*. London: Macmillan.

Current History (1957). "Text of Polish–Soviet Agreement on Status of Soviet Troops in Poland", March, pp. 179–182.

Current History (1964). "The Gomułka Proposals", August, pp. 107–108.

Cybichowski, Z. (ed.) (1929). *Encyklopedja Podręczna Prawa Publicznego* (2 vols.). Warsaw: Biblioteka Polska.

Dąbrowski (1995). *See* Raina, 1995.

Daily Telegraph, 11 August 1958.

Daily Telegraph, "Pope's Special Interest in Poland", 6 May 1959.

Dan, L. (1973). "Moje Czternaście Lat, Zwierzenia Władysława Gomułki". *Nowini Kurier* (16, 20, 27 April; 4, 11, 18, 25 May; 1, 8, 15, 22, 29 June; 6, 13 July).

Daszkiewicz, W. (1970). "Stosunki Polsko–Radzieckie w Latach 1945–1970". *Sprawy Międzynarodowe* (October–November).

Daszkiewicz, W., T. Kowalski, and S. Łopatniuk. "Próba Periodyzacji Historii Stosunków Polsko-Radzieckich, 1917–1968". Polish Academy of Sciences (hereafter

PAN), *Z Dziejów Stosunków Polsko-Radzieckich, Studia i Materiały*, vol. VI. Warsaw: KiW, pp. 3–22.

Deklaracja Episkopatu w Sprawie Wyborów do Sejmu 19 Września 1952. In T. Zawadski (1953). *Walka z Kościołem 1951–1953/Dokumenty*. RFE, mimeo., p. 257.

Dekret "O Ochronie Wolności Sumienia i wyznań", 5 August 1949. In J. Nowak (1951). *Walka z Kościołem w Polsce 1945-1951/Dokumenty*. RFE, mimeo., pp. 201–203 (*see also*: Małkiewicz, E., Podemski, S., 1960, p. 20).

"Dekret z Dnia 31 Grudnia 1956 r. o Organizowaniu i Obsadzaniu Stanowisk Kościelnych". In E. Małkiewicz and S. Podemski (1960). *Położenie Prawne Kościołów i Związków Wyznaniowych w PRL*. Warsaw: Ars Christiana, p. 54.

Deutsch, K. W. (1963). *The Nerves of Government*. New York: The Free Press of Glencoe.

Dinka, F. (1963). *Church and State in Poland: Political Conflict between the Catholic Church and the Communist Regime*. Unpublished Ph.D. dissertation. Washington University, Department of Political Science (May).

Diskin, H. (1978). "The KOR against the Background of the June Riots and in Historical Perspective". *State, Government and International Affairs*, 12, pp. 78–96 (in Hebrew).

Diskin, H. (1986). "The Pope's Pilgrimage to Jaruzelski's Poland: A Test of Power Revisited". In J. L. Black and J. W. Strong (eds.), *Sisyphus and Poland (Reflections on Martial Law)*, pp. 133–144. Winnipeg: Frye.

Downs, A. (1957). *An Economic Theory of Democracy*. New York: Harper and Row.

Dudek, A. (1995). *Państwo i Kościół w Polsce 1945–1970*. Kraków: PiT.

Dudek, A. and G. Pytel (1990). *Bolesław Piasecki. Próba Biografii Politycznej*. London.

Dziennik Polski, "czy Amb. Papée Pozostanie w Stolicy Apostolskiej?", 23 December 1958.

Dziennik Urzędowy Ministerstwa Oświaty, 1945, No. 4, Reg. 189.

Dziennik Ustaw Rzeczypospolitej Polskiej, 1925, No. 72, Item 501.

Dziennik Ustaw Rzeczypospolitej Polskiej, 1927, No. 1, Item 9.

Dziennik Ustaw Polskiej Rzeczypospolitej Ludowej (PRL). Warsaw, 1944–1970.

Dziewanowski, M. K. (1957). "Gomułka and the Polish National Communism". *Problems of Communism*, 6 (January–February).

Dziewanowski, M. K. (1959). *The Communist Party of Poland: An Outline of History*. Cambridge, Mass.: Harvard University Press.

Dziewanowski, M. K. (1961). "Stalin and the Polish Communists". *Soviet Survey* (January–March).

Dziś i Jutro, 3 January 1954.

East Europe, 1957–1966.

East Europe, 6 March 1957, "The Polish Elections".

Easton, D. (1965). *A Framework for Political Analysis*. Englewood-Cliffs: Prentice Hall.

Economist, "The Fall and Rise of Comrade Gomułka", 20 October 1956.

Economist, 8 August 1958; 1 April 1961.

Fakty i Myśli, 14 March 1959.

Faliński, Z. (1968). *Polityka Partii i Rządu i Jej Przeciwnicy*. Łódź: Książka.

Farrell, B. R. (ed.) (1970). *Political Leadership in Eastern Europe and the Soviet Union*. Chicago: Aldine.
Fischer-Galati, S. (ed.) (1963). *Eastern Europe in the Sixties*. New York: Harper and Row.
Fletcher, W. C. (1973). *Religion and Soviet Foreign Policy, 1945–1970*. London: Oxford University Press.
Frankowski, J. (1956). "W Związku z Artykułem B. Piaseckiego". *Trybuna Ludu*, 12 November.
Gamarnikow Files (Collection), RFE, 1946–1959.
Gamarnikow Files, RFE, 1958–1963.
Gamarnikow, M. (1967). "Poland: Political Pluralism in a One-Party State". *Problems of Communism*, 16, July–August.
Garlicki, A. (1993). *Z Tajnych Archiwów*. Warsaw.
Gazeta Wyborcza, 23 June 1997; 24 June 1997.
Gibney, F. (1959). *The Frozen Revolution in Poland: A Study in Communist Decay*. New York: Farrar, Strauss and Cudahy.
Głos Ludu, 8 January 1947, Biografia Gomułki; 8 September 1947.
Głos Nauczycielski, 1 June 1958.
Głos Pracy, 16–17 November 1952; 9 December 1952; 21–22 September 1957; 21 April 1959; 25 October 1960.
Główny Urząd Statystyczny (hereafter GUS). *Rocznik Statystyczny*. Warsaw, 1947–1949; 1955–1969.
Godawa, M. (1972). "Stosunki Gospodarcze Między Polską a Związkiem Radzieckim". *Sprawy Międzynarodowe* (November), pp. 14–25.
Gołubiew, A. (1957). ("Why do we take part in politics?") *Tygodnik Powszechny*, 13 January.
Gomułka, W. (1945a). *Polska wobec Nowych Zagadnien*. Warsaw: Książka.
Gomułka, W. (1945b). *Nowa Karta Dziejów Polski*, Warsaw: Państwowe Wydawnictwo Literatury Politycznej.
Gomułka, W. (1945c). *Ku Nowej Polsce: Sprawozdanie Polityczne i Przemówienia Wygłoszone na I Zjeździe PPR*. Katowice: Literatura Polska.
Gomułka, W. (1946). *Nasza Gospodarka na Ziemiach Odzyskanych: Przemówienia na Drugim Zjeździe Przemysłowym Ziem Odzyskanych w Wrocławiu*. Warsaw: Książka.
Gomułka, W. (1947a). "Jednością Silni". *Nowe Drogi* (1), pp. 4–14.
Gomułka, W. (1947b). *W Walce O Demokracje Ludową*, 2 vols. Warsaw: Książka.
Gomułka, W. (1948a). "Na Nowym Etapie". *Nowe Drogi* (3), pp. III–XII.
Gomułka, W. (1948b). "Jaką Jedność Budujemy". *Nowe Drogi* (5-6), pp. 1–6.
Gomułka, W. (1948c). "Przemówienie na Sierp. Plenum". *Nowe Drogi* (9-10).
Gomułka, W. (1956). *Przemówienie Wygłoszone na VIII Plenum KC PZPR*. Warsaw: KiW.
Gomułka, W. *Przemówienia*. Warsaw: KiW, 1956-1957 (1957); 1957-1958 (1959); 1959 (1960); 1960; 1961; 1962.
Gomułka, W. (1957). *Sytuacja w Partii i w Kraju: Referat na X Plenum KC PZPR 24.10.57 r.* Warsaw: Dom Słowa Polskiego.
Gomułka, W. (1958). "O Wspólnocie Państw Socjalistycznych i Kampanii Propagandowej Reakcyjnych Kól Zachodnich". *Sprawy Międzynarodowe* (July–August) pp. 3–8.

Gomułka, W. (1959). *Polska Zjednoczona Partia Robotnicza: Referat Sprawozdawczy Komitetu Centralnego PZPR, Wygłoszony na III Zjeździe Przez I Sekretarza KC Tow Gomułkę*. Warsaw, KiW.

Gomułka, W. (1960). "The Policy of the Polish People's Republic". *Foreign Affairs*, 38 (April), pp. 402–418.

Gomułka, W. (1962, 1964). *Artykuły i Przemówienia*. Vol. 1: 1943–1945; Vol. 2: 1946–1948. Warsaw: KiW.

Gomułka, W. (1964). "The International Situation and Poland's Foreign Policy". *Polish Perspectives* (7–8), pp. 3–35.

Gomułka, W. (1968a). *Z Kart Naszej Historii*. Warsaw: KiW.

Gomułka, W. (1968b). *O Naszej Partii*. Warsaw: KiW.

Gomułka, W. (1977). "Polemika z Archiwum Ruchu Robotniczego". *Zeszyty Historyczne*, No. 39. Paris: Instytut Literacki.

Gomułka, W., H. Minc, and R. Zambrowski (1945). *Przemówienia Na Rozszerzonym Plenum Komitetu Centralnego Polskiej Partii Robotniczej w Lutym 1945r*. Warsaw: Książka.

Góra, W. (1966). *Z dziejów Polski Ludowej: Zbiór Artykułów*. Warsaw: Państwowe Zakłady Wydawnictw Szkolnych.

Góra, W. (1967). *W Walce o Utrwalenie Władzy Ludowej w Polsce 1944–1947*. Warsaw: KiW.

Góra, W., *et al.* (1973). *PPR Rezolucje Odezwy Instrukcje i Okólniki Komitetu Centralnego, I.1947–XII.1948*. Warsaw: KiW.

Gowin, J. (1995). *Kościół Po Komunizmie (Demokracja, Filozofia i Praktyka)*. Kraków: Znak (Fundacja Im. Stefana Batorego, Warsaw).

Graham, R. A. (1954). "Catholic Press in Poland". *America*, 90 (6 February), pp. 477–478.

Graham, R. A. (1955). "Progressists Mix Marx and Christianity". *America*, 93 (23 July), pp. 407–408.

Greenstein, F. I. (1967). "The Impact of Personality on Politics: An Attempt to Clear Away Underbrush". *American Political Science Review*, 61 (September) pp. 624–641.

Griffith, S. (1959). *Lying in State*. New York.

Griffith, W. E. (1958). *Gomułka and the 1948 Cominform Resolution*. Munich: RFE, July (mimeo).

Groth, A. J. (1972). *People's Poland: Government and Politics*. San Francisco: Chandler.

Grudzień, J. (1969). *Zasady Polityki Wyznaniowej PRL*. Warsaw: KiW.

Gruson (1958). "Morawski Attacks Church". Gruson Reports from Warsaw in Sat. *NYT*, RFE 0630 (24 May). New York.

Grzybowski, K. (1947). *Zarys Historyczno-Polityczny 1-ego Rządu Demokratycznego w Polsce 1944–1946*. Warsaw: Książka.

Grzybowski, K. (1952). "Uwagi o Stosunku Państwa do Kościoła". *Państwo i Prawo*, vol. 2 (April).

Grzybowski, K. (1958). "Reforms of Government in Poland". *Slavic Review*, 17, pp. 454–467.

Gsovski, V. (ed.) (1955). *Church and State Behind the Iron Curtain*. New York: Praeger.

Gsovski, V. (ed.) (undated). *Digest-Index of East European Law: Poland, Churches and Religion*. (Mimeo.) Washington.

Gsovski, V. and K. Grzybowski (1959). *Government, Law and Courts in the Soviet Union and Eastern Europe* (2 volumes). London: Stevens.

Guranowski, J. (1959). "Youth Problems on the Pages of *Tygodnik Powszechny*." *Nowe Drogi* (March), pp. 162–173.

GUS. *Biuletyn Statystyczny*, No. 10 (1957); No 4 (1958); January, October, December (1962).

GUS. (1962). *Polska w Liczbach* 1944–1961. Warsaw.

GUS. (1963). *Mały Rocznik Statystyczny*.

Gwuźdź, A. and J. Zakrzewska (eds.) (1958). *Konstytucja i Podstawowe Akty Ustawodawcze Polskiej Rzeczypospolitej Ludowej*. Warsaw: Wydawn, Prawnicze.

Ha'aretz (Hebrew daily), 7. August 1996 (from *Die Welt*).

Ha'aretz (Hebrew daily). "A Cross in the Wheels of the Constitution", 15 April 1997 (from the *Economist*).

Ha'aretz (Hebrew daily). "Not a Catholic Wedding", 14 December 1998 (from an article written for Project Syndicate in December 1998).

Halecki, O. (1956). *A History of Poland*. New York. (Also 1966, 1978.)

Halecki, O. (ed.) (1957). *East-Central Europe under the Communists: Poland*. New York

Halecki, O. (1966). *Pierwsze Tysiąclecie Katolickiej Polski*. London: Veritas.

Halecki, O. and J. F. Murray (1954). *Pius XII: Eugenio Pacelli, Pope of Peace*. London: Weidenfeld and Nicolson.

Halperin. *Münchner Merkur*, 8 August 1958; 16 January 1960; 17 January 1960.

Halperin. "Piroszyński Trial". Halperin's article in *Münchner Merkur*, 21 January, RFE, Munich (CNR), No. 0830.

Halperin. Translation of Halperin's article in *Münchner Merkur*, RFE, Munich, September 23(CNR), No. 1130.

Hamm. Translation of Hamm's Dispatch in *Deutscher Zeitung*, Gamarnikow Files, RFE, Munich, 5 August 1957.

Hemmerling, Z. (1990)."Bitwa o Dusze. Polityka W. Gomułki wobec Kościoła w Okresie Millenium". *Konfrontacje*, no. 8.

Heyman, F. (1966). *Poland and Czechoslovakia*. Englewood Cliffs N.J.: Prentice.

Hiscocks, R. (1963). *Poland: Bridge for the Abyss?*. London: Oxford University Press.

Hlond, A. (Kard.) (1946). "Do Kobiety Warszawy". *Tygodnik Powszechny* (14 July).

Hoffman (1967). "Studies in Comparative Analysis". In L. J. Edinger (ed.), *Political Leadership in Industrialized Societies*. Studies in Comparative Analysis, New York: Wiley.

Instytut Literacki (1956). *Przemówienie 1-ego Sekretarza KC PZPR Władysława Gomułki na VIII Plenum 21.10.1956/Dokumenty*, Vol. II. Paris.

Instytut Literacki (1962). *6 Lat Temu...Kulisy Polskiego Października/Dokumenty*. Paris.

Instytut Literacki (1971). *Poznań 1956—Grudzień 1970/Dokumenty*. Paris.

Inter-Catholic Press Agency Inc. Documents. *Protest Episkopatu Polskiego Złożony na Ręce Bol. Bieruta w Dniu 8 Maja 1953 roku w Warszawie*, 1 October 1953. New York (*also*: Vienna, 1 October 1953, under title: "Episkopat o Położeniu Kościoła w Polsce, Oświadczenie Biskupów Polskich").

Inter-Catholic Press Agency Inc. 23 October 1946; No. 27, 1946, vol. 3, June 1948, pp. 4–9; vol. 2, 15 October 1947; vol. 2, 5 November 1947; 22 September 1958.

Ionescu, G. (1967). *The Politics of the European Communist States.* New York: Praeger.

Jan (1958). "What Can We Expect?". *Słowo Powszechne* (26 March), RFE, PPS, No. 369 (1570).

Janicki, M. (1997). "Wolność Zadania". *Polityka*, no. 23 (2092), 7 June.

Jarocki, R. (1990). *Czterdzieści Pięć Lat w Opozycji (O Ludziach "Tygodnika Powszechnego").* Kraków: Wydawnictwo Literackie.

Jaroszefowicz, Z., *et al.* (1958). "Students: Myth and Reality". *Polish Perspectives* (3–4).

Jaroszewski, T. M. (1958). ("Secularization of Social Life".) *Nowe Drogi* (June), pp. 93–106.

Jaroszewski, T. M. (1959). "Postępowe Katolicy Wobec Przemian Ustrojowych". *Polityka* (30).

Jaroszewski, T. M. (1966). "Dynamika Praktyk Religijnych i Postaw Światopoglądowych w Polsce w Świetle Badań Sociologicznych". *Kultura i Społeczeństwo* (10/No. 1, January–March).

Jaroszewski, T. M. (1970). "Kryzys Władzy w Kościele Rzymsko-Katolickim" (Refleksje Po II Synodzie Watykańskim). *Nowe Drogi* (March).

Jaroszewski, T. M. (1976). "Perspektywa Rozwinięte Społeczeństwo Socjalistyczne". *Nowe Drogi* (2), pp. 55–69.

Jasiukiewicz, M. (1993). *Kościół katolicki w Polskim życiu politycznym 1945–1989. Podstawowe uwarunkowania.* Wrocław.

Jeleński, K. A. (1958). "Revisionism—Pragmatism—Gomułkaism". *Problems of Communism*, 7 (May–June), pp. 5–13.

Jezierska, M. (1958). *Nowe Drogi* (April), pp. 126–130.

John XXIII (1964). *Encyklika o Pokoju ("Pacem in Terris")* (John XXIII, Encyclical on Peace). London: Veritas.

Johnson, A. R. (1968a). "Poland: The End of the Post-October Era". RFE, *Backgrounds*, Poland (5 April).

Johnson, A. R. (1968b). "Polish Communist History and Factional Struggle". RFE, *Backgrounds*, Poland/20 (2 July).

Johnson, A. R. (1968c). "Poland: The End of the Post-October Era". *Survey*, July.

Johnson A. R. (1968d). "Political Tensions in a Post-Liberalization Communist Stystem: Poland since 1956". RFE (August). Prepared for delivery at the 1968 annual meeting of the American Political Science Association.

Johnson, A. R. (1970). "Poland: The End of an Era?" *Problems of Communism*, 19 (January–February).

Johnson, A. R. (1971). "Polish Perspectives, Past and Present". *Problems of Communism*, 20 (July–August), pp. 59–72.

Jordan, Z. (1957). "Odwrót od Października". *Kultura*, 12/122 (December).

Józefowicz, Z., S. Nowak, and A. Pawełczyńska (1958). "Students: Myth and Reality". *Polish Perspectives*, (3–4). (Reprinted from: *Przegląd Kulturalny*, 17 July 1958.)

Jurkiewicz, J. (1958). *Watykan a Polska w Okresie Międzywojennym 1918–1939.* Warsaw.

Jurkiewicz, J. "Konkordat z Roku 1925 na Tle Polityki Kurii Rzymskiej w Okresie Międzywojennym". *Kwartalnik Historyczny*, 60/4, pp. 57–85.

Kaczyński, Z. (1947). "Nasza Własna Droga". *Tygodnik Warszawski* (7 September).

Kamiński, M. (1959). "Radzieckie Kredyty". *Polityka* (5 December).

Kapuscik, Z. (1989). "Rumieniec Wstydu. Kościół Katolicki w Czasach Bieruta". *Tygodnik Kulturalny* (18 April).

Keesing's Contemporary Archives, 1946–1970.

Kertesz, S. D. (ed.) (1962). *East and Central Europe and the World: Developments in the Post-Stalin Era*. Notre Dame (Ind.): University of Notre Dame Press.

Kidel, B. (1957). "Poland's Third Man". (4 September.) Included in Gamarnikow Files without any specification of the periodical.

Kisiel (1957). ("Nails in the Brain".) *Tygodnik Powszechny* (17 March).

Kisielewski, S. (1962). "Mój Testament". *Kultura*, 10/176.

Kisielewski, S. (1990). *Na Czym Polega Socjalizm? Stosunki Państwo—Kościół w PRL*. Poznań.

KiW (1958). *Polska Zjednoczona Partia Robotnicza. Materiały XII Plenum KC PZPR*. Warsaw.

KiW (1964). *IV Zjazd PPR 15-20 Czerwca 1964, Podstawowe Materiały i Dokumenty*. Warsaw.

Klafkowski, A. (1958). *Granica Polsko-Niemiecka a Konkordaty z Lat 1929, 1933*. Warsaw: PWN.

Kliszko, Z. (1958). *Z Problemów Historii PPR*. Warsaw.

Klugman, A. (1970). "Zerowy Bilans 5172 Dni—Wzloty i Upadki Władysława Gomułki". *Nowiny Kurier* (25 December). Tel Aviv.

Kołomejczyk, N. (1966). *Ziemie Zachodnie w Działalności PPR*. Poznań: Wydawnictwo Poznańskie.

Kołomejczyk, N. (1968). *Polska w Latach 1944–1949, Zarys Historii Politycznej*. Warsaw: Państwowe Zakłady Wydawnictw Szkolnych.

Kominek, B. (1958). "List Pasterski o Tolerancji". *Tygodnik Powszechny*, 28/494.

"Konkordat Polski". In Z. Cybichowski (ed.), *Encyklopedia Podręczna Prawa Publicznego*.

"Konstytucja PRL". In E. Małkiewicz and S. Podemski, *Położenie Prawne Kościołów i Związków Wyznaniowych w PRL*. Warsaw: Ars Christiana, 1960, p. 19.

Koper, A. (1972). "Współpraca Polski i ZSSR w Latach 1945–1965". *Sprawy Międzynarodowe* (January), pp. 113–117.

Korboński, S. (1954). *W Imieniu Rzeczpospolitej*. Paris: Instytut Literacki.

Korboński, S. (1956). *W Imieniu Kremla*. Paris: Instytut Literacki. (English translation: *Warsaw in Chains*. London and New York: George Allen and Unwin, Ruskin House, 1959.)

Korboński, S. (1963). *W Imieniu Polski Walczącej*. London: B. Swiderski.

Korboński, S. (1969). *Między Młotem a Kowadłem*. London: Gryf.

Korotyński, H. (1958a). "On Church-State Relations". *Życie Warszawy* (8 August.)

Korotyński, H. (1959b). "Unfulfilled Agreement". *Życie Warszawy* (9 August).

Korotyński, H. (1959). "Cui Bono, or Who Needs This". *Życie Warszawy* (15 June).

Kot, S. (1963). *Conversations with the Kremlin and Dispatches from Russia*. London: Oxford University Press.

Kowalski, W. T. (1971). *Polityka Zagraniczna RP 1944–1947*. Warsaw: Instytut Polske Sprawy Międzynarodowe.

Kownacki, L. (1959). "A new Phase of Communist Campaign against the Church in Poland". *Polish Affairs* (April), pp. 7–9.

Kozakiewicz, M. (1960). ("School and Religion".) *Życie Warszawy* (24 August).
Kozub-Ciembroniewicz, W. and J. Majchrowski (1993). *Najnowsza Historia Polityczna Polski, Wybór źródeł*. Kraków.
Krahn, K. (1958). *Neues Deutschland* (26 September).
Krukowski, J. (1992). "Kościół wobec Reżimu komunistycznego w Polsce". *Kościół i Prawo*, vol.10.
Krukowski, J. (1993). *Kościół i Państwo. Podstawy Relacji Prawnych*. Lublin.
Kurkiewicz, W., *et al.* (1971). *25 Lat Polski Ludowej*. Warsaw: Ludowa Spółdzielnia Wydawn.
Kuroń, J. (1990). *Wiara i Wina. Do i Od Komunizmu*. Warsaw: Nowa.
Kuroń, J. and K. Modzelewski (1966). *List Otwarty Do Partii*. Paris: Instytut Literacki.
Kuźnica Kapłańska, 1 November 1955.
La Croix, 19 January 1960.
Lane, D. and G. Kolankiewicz (1973). *Social Groups in Polish Society*. London: Macmillan.
Lange, O. (1957). *Some Problems Relating to the Polish Road to Socialism*. Warsaw: Polonia Publishing House.
Lange, O., *et al.* (1960). *Węzłowe Zagadnienia Budownictwa Socjalizmu w Polsce*. Warsaw: PWN.
Lasswell, H. D. and A. Kaplan (1950). *Power and Society: A Framework for Political Inquiry*. New Haven: Yale University Press.
Lehman, E. W. (1969). "Toward a Macrosociology of Power". *American Sociological Review*, 34 (August), pp. 353–365.
Le Monde, 6 October 1959; January 1964.
Leonhard, W. (1962). *The Kremlin since Stalin*. New York: Praeger.
Lewis, F. (1958). *The Polish Volcano: A Case History of Hope*. New York: Garden City.
Linden, C. A. (1967). *Khrushchev and the Soviet Leadership, 1957–1964*. Baltimore: The Johns Hopkins Press.
Lipset, S. M. (1960). *Political Man*. New York: Doubleday.
Lipski, J. J. (1994). *Katolickie Państwo Narodu Polskiego*. London.
Listy Pasterskie Episkopatu Polski 1945–1974. Paris, 1975.
Listy Pasterskie Prymasa Polski 1946–1974. Paris, 1975.
L'Osservatore Romano, 27 July 1949; 9 September 1951; 29 November 1952; 26 September 1956; 5 January 1959.
Lubojanski, J. (1970). "Władysław Gomułka Minister Ziem Odzyskanych". *Życie Literackie* (26 July).
L'Unita, 24 January 1961.
Lyon, S. (1958). "Radio Moscow on Gomułka's Specific and General". RFE, *Background Information*, Poland (29 September).
Makarenko, J. in 'Pravda'. 9.6.1950. in Nowak, J: *The Struggle with the Church/Documents*, 1951, pp. 265–266.
Makarenko, J. in 'Pravda'. 17.7.1951. in Zawadski, T., *The Struggle with the Church/Documents*, 1953, pp.190–193.
Maksymilan, J. (1961). ("Problems of Laicization".) *Żołnierz Wolności* (27 April).

Malara, J. and L. Rey (1952). *La Pologne d'une Occupation à l'autre, 1944–1952*. Paris: Editions du Fuseau.

Małkiewicz, E. and S. Podemski (1960). *Położenie Prawne Kościołów i Związków Wyznaniowych w Polskiej Rzeczypospolitej Ludowej (Zbiór Przepisów i Dokumentów W/g Stanu na Dzień 1.10.60)*. Warsaw: Ars Christiana.

Malmuth, Ch. (1965). "Gomułka: Head of People's Poland". *Communist Affairs* (September–October), pp. 19–30.

Manchester Guardian. "Gomułka: A Profile" (28 October 1956).

March, J. G. (1955). "An Introduction to the Theory and Measurement of Influence". *American Political Science Review*, 49.

Markert, W. (1959). *Osteuropa—Handbuch: Polen*. Cologne: Böhlau Verlag.

Markham, R. (1950). *Communists Crush Churches in Eastern Europe*. Boston.

Markiewicz, S. (1963). "Stosunek Watykanu do Granicy na Odrze i Nysie". *Sprawy Międzynarodowe* (June), pp. 77–86.

Markiewicz, S. (1974). *Kościół Rzymsko-Katolicki a Państwo Socjalistyczne*. Warsaw: KiW.

Mason, D. S. (1977). *Elite Change and Policy in Communist Poland*. Indiana: Unpublished Ph.D. dissertation.

McEoin, G. (1951). *The Communist War on Religion*. New York: Davnir Adair (*also* 1959).

Mekarski, S. (1959). "The Communists and the Church". *Polish Affairs* (June).

Mekarski, S. (1960a). "The Campaign against the Church". *Polish Affairs* (September).

Mekarski, S. (1960b). "The Struggle against the Church". *Polish Affairs* (7 December).

Mestrovic, M. M. (1961). "Poland under the Cross". *Commonwealth* (January).

Meyer, A. (1967). In L. J. Edinger (ed.), *Political Leadership in Industrialized Societies*, Studies in Comparative Analysis, pp. 84–107. New York: Wiley.

Meysztowicz, V. (1966). *La Pologne dans la Chrétienté*. Paris: Nouvelles Editions Latin.

Mianowicz, T. (1994). "Kardynał Sapieha a 'modus vivendi' z 1950 r." *Zeszyty Historyczne*, No. 108. Paris.

Micewski, A. (1982). *Kardynał Stefan Wyszyński, Prymas i mąż stanu*. Paris.

Micewski, A. (1984). *Wyszyński: A Biography*. New York: Harcourt Brace.

Micewski, A. (1987). *Kościół wobec Solidarności i Stanu Wojennego*. Paris.

Micewski, A. (1994). *Kościół—Państwo 1945–1989*. Warsaw.

Michnik, A. (1976). *Kościół, Lewica, Dialog*. Paris: Instytut Literacki (*also*: Paris, 1977; Warsaw, 1983; and Chicago, 1993).

Michnik, A., J. Tischner, and J. Zakowski (1995). *Między Panem a Plebanem*. Kraków: Znak.

Mikołajczyk, S. (1948). *The Pattern of Soviet Domination*. London: Sampson Low, Marston.

Miller, M. (1963). "Poland and Khrushchev's Russia". *World Today*, 19 (October), pp. 422–431.

Miłosz, Cz. (1953). *The Captive Mind*. New York: Alfred A. Knopf.

Minc, H. (1948). *Nowe Drogi* (7–8), pp. 83–106.

Moats, A. L. (1959). "Gomułka's Poland: Who Will Win Out, the Cardinal or the Commissar, in the Battle for Poland?" *National Review*, 7 (23 May).

Monticone, R. (1986). *The Catholic Church in Communist Poland 1945–1985.* Boulder (Col.): East European Monographs.

Morris, B. (1959). "Soviet Policy Toward National Communism: The Limits of Diversity". *American Political Science Review,* LIII (March).

Morrison, J. F. (1968). *The Polish People's Republic.* Baltimore: The Johns Hopkins Press.

Mrowczyński, T. (1957). ("Comments on Religion".) *Nowe Drogi,* 5.

Münchner Merkur, 25 April 1959.

Mysłek, W. (1959). "Church and State". *Polish Perspectives* (August–September), pp. 67–71.

Narzutowski, K. (1946). "Mocna Manifestacja Jasnej Góri". *Tygodnik Powszechny* (22 September).

Naurois, C. (1956). *Dieu contre Dieu? Dames des Catholiques Progressistes dans une Eglise du Silence.* Fribourg.

New York Times (hereafter *NYT*), 9 February 1945; 16 September 1945; 15 July 1946; 24 November 1946; 6 January 1947; 2–3 April 1947; 10 February 1948; 16 April 1948; 24 May 1948; 14 May 1950; 8 April 1960; 17 July 1995.

NYT. "A Stubborn Pole: Władysław Gomułka" (20 October 1956).

Niebuhr, R. (1957). "The Cardinal and The Commissar: Poland's Curious Alliance". *New Leader,* 40 (21 October), pp. 5–6.

Norretranders, B. (1960). *Gomułka's Poland.* Copenhagen.

Nowak, J. (1951). *Walka z Kościołem w Polsce (1945–1951)/Dokumenty.* Munich: RFE (mimeo).

Nowak, J. (1957). "One Year of Gomułka: Illusion and Reality in Poland". *World Today,* 13 (December), pp. 528–538.

Nowak, J. (1958). *Analysis of Developments in Poland since October 1956.* Munich: RFE (mimeo), May.

Nowak, J. (1959). *Analysis of Developments in Poland since January 1959, Including the Party Congress.* Munich: RFE (mimeo), May.

Nowe Drogi, 1948/9–10, pp. 40–43; 156–183.

Nowe Drogi, 1952/8, pp. 3–18.

Nowe Drogi, October 1956; June 1957; July 1958.

Nowicz, W. (1962). ("The Vatican and Peace".) *Polityka* (2 June).

Olsen, A. J. (1961). "The Polish Faithful in Spite of Marx". *NYT* (18 June).

Olszewski, K. (1966). "Znaczenie Współpracy Ekonomicznej z ZSRR dla Polskiej Gospodarki". *Sprawy Międzynarodowe* (April), pp. 12–33.

Olszewski, K. (1976). "Współpraca Gospodarcza Polski i Związkiem Radzieckim". *Nowe Drogi,* 4, pp. 26–33.

Osóbka-Morawski, E. and W. Gomułka (1946). *Walka o Jedność Narodu.* Łódź: Książka.

Ossokowski, Z. (1957). "Poland under Stalinism and Gomułkaism". *Christian Democratic Review* (March), pp. 7–11.

Papée, K. (1954). *Pius 12 a Polska 1939–1949, Przemówienia, Listy, Komentarze.* Rome: Editrice Studium.

Parzyńska, M. (1959). ("A Bad Silence".) *Życie Warszawy* (10 December).

Pawełczyńska, A. (1960). ("The Students and Religion".) *Argumenty* (18 September).

Pawełczyńska, A. (1961). "Dynamika i Funkcje Postaw Wobec Religii". *Studia Socjologiczno-Polityczne (SSP)*, 10.
Personality File, RFE (Gom.), 1957–1969.
Piasecki, B. (1954). *Zagadnienia Istotne*. Warsaw: Pax.
Piasecki, B. (1958a). *Słowo Powszechne* (18-19 October).
Piasecki, B. (1958b). *Patriotyzm Polski*. Warsaw: Pax.
Piasecki, B., priest (1982). *Ostatnie Dni Prymasa Tysiąclecia*. Rzym.
Pietrowski, S. (1947). "Konkordat Zawarty ze Stolicą Apostolską w 1925 roku. Przestał obowiąziwać Jako Wewnenczna Ustawa krajowa". *Państwo i Prawo*, 2 (December), pp. 3–8.
Pirożyński, *Homo Dei*/I.C.: 1946/21; 1947/11; 1948/9; 1948/35.
Piwowarczyk, J. (1946). "Manifestacja Jasnej Góri". *Tygodnik Powszechny* (8 September).
Podgórecki, A. (1976). "The Global Analysis of Polish Society (A Sociological Point of View)". *Polish Sociological Bulletin*, 4, pp. 17–30.
Poland Today, vol. 5 (May 1950).
Polish Affairs. "The Outrage at the Monastery of Jasna Góra" (August 1958), pp. 14–16.
Polish Perspectives, 3 (November 1960).
Polish Research and Information Service (1949). *Documents and Reports on Poland, the Provisional Constitution of February 20, 1947, and the Declaration of Rights*. New York.
Polish Research and Information Service (1950). *Sprawa Caritas*. New York.
Polityka, (Editorial), "W Perspektywie III Zjazd PZPR" (4–10 September 1957), pp. 1, 4.
Polityka, 29 March 1958.
Polityka, no. 22 (2091) (31 May 1997); no. 23 (2092) (7 June 1997).
Pomykało, W. (1967). *Kościół Milczenia? Kościół Rzymsko Katolicki w Polsce Ludowej*. Warsaw: KiW.
Pomykało, W. (1971). *10 Razy o Problemach Laicyzacji*. Warsaw: KiW.
Prymas Tysiąclecia, praca zbior. pod red. (ed. by) F. Kniotka, Z. Modzelewskiego i (and) D. Szumskiej. Paris, 1982.
Przegląd Powszechny, 1 January 1948. (Hlond's New Year message.)
Przegląd Powszechny. "Komunikat Episkopatu Polski do Wiernych", 229 (April 1950).
Putrament, J. (1957). "Polski Eksperiment". *Polityka* (6–12 March).
PWN (1964). *Wielka Encyklopedia Powszechna* (Gomułka).
PWN (1975). *Polityka Wyznaniowa: Tło, Warunki, Realizacja*. Warsaw.
"PZPR wobec Religii i Kościoła w 1953 r." *Więz*, no. 10, 1992.
Radecki, W. (1968). "Swoboda Wyznania w Tezach V Zjazdu PZPR". *Prawo i Życie* (25 August).
Radio Free Europe (hereafter *RFE*). PPS, No. 389, (1590), pp. 3–4.
Radio Warsaw III. "On Church Publication" (2 August 1958) *RFE*, No.1225.
Radziwill, Ch. (1946). "Catholiques et Patriotisme". In *Cahiers Franco-Polonais* (December). Paris: Bureau d'Informations Polonaises.
Raina, P. (1969). *Gomułka*. London: Polonia Book Fund.
Raina, P. (1979). *Stefan Kardynał Wyszyński Prymas Polski*. London.
Raina, P. (1991). *"Te Deum" Narodu Polskiego Obchody Tysiąclecia Chrztu Polski w Świetle Dokumentów Kościelnych*. Olsztyn.

Raina, P. (1993a). *Kardynał Wyszyński. Droga na Stolice Prymasowską* (1). Warsaw: Książka Polska.

Raina, P. (1993b). *Kardynał Wyszyński. Losy Więzienne* (2). Warsaw: Książka Polska.

Raina, P. (1994a). *Kościół-Państwo w Świetle Akt Wydziałów do Spraw Wyznań 1967–1968.* Warsaw.

Raina, P. (1994b). *Kościół w PRL. Dokumenty*, vol. I: 1945–1959. Poznań.

Raina, P. (1994c). *Kardynał Wyszyński. Czasy Prymasowskie 1956–1961*, 3. Warsaw.

Raina, P. (1994d). *Kardynał Wyszyński. Czasy Prymasowskie 1962–1963*, 4. Warsaw.

Raina, P. (1995a). *Rozmowy Z Władzami PRL. Arcybiskup Dąbrowski. W Służbie Kościoła I Narodu*, vol. I: 1970–1981. Warsaw: Książka Polska.

Raina, P. (1995b). *Kardynał Wyszyński. Orędzie Biskupów a Reakcja Władz*, 6. Warsaw: Książka Polska.

Rakowski, M. (1991). *Jak to się stało.* Warsaw.

Rastawicka, A. and priest B. Piasecki (ed.), *Czas Nigdy Go Nie Oddali (Wspomnienia o Stefanie Kardynale Wyszyńskim* ('Time will never fade his memory'. Memoirs on Cardinal Stefan Wyszyński). Flo Press.

Reale, E. (1968). *Raporty: Polska 1945–1946 ("Seria Dokumenty").* Paris: Instytut Literacki.

Religious News Service Bulletin, New York, 10 July 1945; 9 September 1946; 22 September 1946; 14 February 1948.

RFE. "Jasna Góra Search". (29 July 1958) BMCG/A.

RFE. "Minister Criticizes Wyszyński". Warsaw (30 July 1958), Reuter ASB/F.

RFE. "Letter of Protest from the Secretary of the Polish Episcopate". Warsaw (9 August 1958), 1626.

RFE. "Dziennik Ludowy—Church Estates". PAP 3 (10 September 1958), 1111, Lo, 1343.

RFE. "In Thousands of Schools There Will Be No Religious Instruction" (22 September 1958).

RFE. "Bishops Protest about Religion Classes". New York (26 September 1958), No.1054.

RFE. "Wyszyński's Speech". Warsaw (28 May 1959) ASB/F 2317.

RFE. OK-PAO/Monit., Confirms Broadcast School Policy DG F2300, Reuter (1 September 1959).

Robinson, W. F. (1977). "Selected Demographic and Economic Data on Eastern Europe". RAD, *Background Report*, 19 (Eastern Europe) (29 April).

Roos, H. (1966). *A History of Modern Poland, from the Foundation of the State in the First World War to the Present Day.* New York: Alfred A. Knopf.

Rosada, S. and J. Gwóźdź (1955). "Church and State in Poland". In V. Gsovski (ed.), *Church and State behind the Iron Curtain.* New York: Praeger.

Rose, J. W. (1948). *Poland: Old and New.* London.

Rose, R. (1974). *Electoral Behavior: A Comparative Handbook.* New York: Free Press.

Rosenthal, A. (1958). "Conflict of Church and Communism in Poland. Cardinal versus Commissar". *New York Times Magazine* (7 September). (*The Reporter*, 27 November 1958.)

Rosenthal, A. In *NYT*: 28 July 1958; 26 September 1958; 12 August 1958; 16 April 1959.

Rosenthal, A. (1959). "Warsaw Worships". (Rosenthal Reports to Monday's *NYT* from Warsaw) *RFE*, New York (3 March), FM/1214A.

Rothschild, J. (1964). *Communist Eastern Europe*. New York: Walker.

Rozmaryn, S. (1948). "W Jakim Zakresie Obowiązuje Dziś Konstytucja z 17 Marca 1921". *Państwo i Prawo*, 2 (January).

Rozmaryn, S. (1961). *Konstytucja Jako Ustawa Zasadnicza PRL*. Warsaw: PWN.

"Rozmowa ze Stefanem Kisielewskim". *Kultura*, 6/11 (June 1957).

Ruszczyc, J. (1974). "Źródeł Programu Polski Ludowej". *Życie Warszawy* (10 July).

Rzeczpospolita, 23 November 1946; 18 December 1948; 27 July 1949.

Secrétariat Général du Gouvernement (1959). *Rapports entre l'Etat et les Eglises en Pologne 1945–1959*. Paris: La Documentation Française.

Seton-Watson, H. (1951). *The East European Revolution; the Pattern of Communist Revolution*. New York, Praeger.

Sherman, G. (1958). In *The Scotsman* (8 July) (RFE #1852).

Shneiderman, S. L. (1956). "The Four Days that Shook Poland". *The Reporter*, XV (13 December).

Shneiderman, S. L. (1959). *The Warsaw Heresy*. New York: Horizon Press.

Shuster, G. N. (1954). *Religion behind the Iron Curtain*. New York: Macmillan.

Siciński, A. (1963). "Public Opinion Surveys in Poland". *International Social Science Journal*, 1.

Siemek, J. (1958). ("We Need Collaboration between the Believers and the Non-Believers") (I, II). *Nowe Drogi* (July), PPS Nos. 451 (1652); 452 (1653).

Siemek, J. (1960). ("The Mitre and the Myth"). *Dziennik Polski* (4 December).

Situation Report (hereafter *SR/Poland*). RFE, 1961–1976.

Skilling, H. G. (1964). *Communism National and International: Eastern Europe after Stalin*. Toronto: University of Toronto Press.

Skilling, H. G. (1966). "Interest Groups and Communist Politics". *World Politics* (April), pp. 435–451.

Skilling, H. G. (1967). *The Governments of Communist Eastern Europe*. New York: Crowell.

Skowroński, J. (1953). *Polityka Episkopatu w Polsce*. Warsaw.

Słowo Powszechne, 2 March 1953; 16 October 1956; 5 November 1956; 15 December 1956; 16 January 1957; 6 January 1958; 11 January 1958; 3 August 1976.

Sobolewska, B. (1966). "Z Problematyki Ewolucji Doktryny Katolickiej w Kwestii Stosunku Kościoła i Państwa". *Państwo i Prawo*, 6.

Sokorski, W. (1957). "IX Plenum a Zadania Propagandy". *Nowe Drogi*, 6.

Śpiewak, P. (1997a). Lecture given at the international conference "The Impact of Religion on Politics at the End of the Twentieth Century", 10–12 November. Jerusalem: The Konrad Adenauer Foundation and B'nai Brith World Center.

Śpiewak, P. (1997b). "Church and Democracy in Poland". A paper presented at the international conference "The Impact of Religion on Politics at the End of the Twentieth Century", 10–12 November. Jerusalem: The Konrad Adenauer Foundation and B'nai Brith World Center.

SR/Poland (1961). RFE (11 October), "Gomułka Interview". (An interview given to Hubert Beuve-Mery, editor-in-chief of *Le Monde*.)

SR/Poland (1963). *RFE* (2 May), "Gomułka Interview". (An interview given to Victor Vinde, editor-in-chief of *Stockholm Tidnigen*.)

SR/Poland (1964). RFE (8 December), "Gomułka's Speech in Zabrze".

Staar, R. F. (1960). "Third Congress of the Polish Communist Party". *ASEER*, 19 (1).

Staar, R. F. (1962a). "The Central Apparatus of Poland's Communist Party". *Journal of Central European Affairs*, XXII (October), pp. 337–348.

Staar, R. F. (1962b). *Poland 1944–1962: The Sovietization of Captive People*, Baton Rouge, Louisiana: State University Press.

Staar, R. F. (1965). "Gomułka: Head of People's Poland". *Communist Affairs* (November–December), pp. 17–26.

Staar, R. F. (1966). "Destalinization in Eastern Europe: The Polish Model". In A. Gyorgy (ed.), *Issues of World Communism*. Princeton: Van Nostrand.

Staciwa, Cz. "Społeczne Aspekty Religijności Młodzieży Poborowej". *Studia Socjologiczno-Polityczne (SSP)*, No. 24.

Stalin, J. W. (1949). *Wybór Dokumentów w Sprawie Polski*. Warsaw.

Starewicz, A. (1959). "Po III Plenum KC PZPR". *Polityka*, 43.

Staron, S. (1969). "State–Church Relations in Poland". *World Politics*, XXI (July/4), pp. 575–601.

Staszewski, M. T. (1969). "Państwo Socjalistyczne Wobec Kościołów i Ludzi Wierzących". *Prawo i Życie* (13 July; 27 July).

Staszewski, M. T. (1994). *Państwo–Kościół w Europie Środkowo–Wschodniej (Aspekty instytucjonalno–prawne)*. Warsaw: Instytut Studiów Politycznych (ISP), Polskiej Akademii Nauk (PAN).

Stefanowski, R. (1974). *Urban Demography: Past Developments and Projections*. RFE (Poland), 7 (20 May).

Stehle, H. (1958). "Gomułka's Combined Actions". (Stehle's article: "Poland Represses Stalinists and Catholics…" *Frankfurter Allgemeine Zeitung*, 29 July), RFE, Munich, 29 July.

Stehle, H. In *Frankfurter Allgemeine Zeitung*, 10 July 1958 (*RFE* #1150); 29 July 1958; 30 January 1960.

Stehle, H. (1964). "Polish Communism". In W. E. Griffith (ed.), *Communism in Europe*. Cambridge, Mass.: The MIT Press.

Stehle, H. (1965). *The Independent Satellite, Society and Politics in Poland since 1945*. London: Pall Mall Press.

Stehle, H. (1968). "Vatican Policy Towards Eastern Europe". *Survey*, 10 (January).

Stehle, H. (1993). *Tajna Dyplomacja Watykanu. Papiestwo wobec Komunizmu (1917–1991)*. Warsaw.

Stillman, E. (ed.) (1959). *Bitter Harvest*. London: Thames and Hudson.

Stomma, S. (1959). "Czień Winkelrieda". *Tygodnik Powszechny* (21 June).

Stomma, S. (1960). *Myśli o Politice i Kulturze*. Kraków.

Stomma, S. and J. Turowicz (1950). *Tygodnik Powszechny* (10 December).

Stomma, S. and J. Turowicz (1952). *Tygodnik Powszechny* (3 February).

Stroynowski, J. (1962). "Vaticanum II". *Polityka* (20 October).

Stypułkowski, Z. (1958). "The Church in Poland". *Polish Affairs* (February), pp. 4–6.

Świątkowski, H. (1946). "Z Zagadnien Nowego Prawa Małżeńskiego". *Państwo i Prawo*, 1 (March), pp. 24–29.

Świątkowski, H. (1960). *Państwo i Kościół w Świetle Prawa (Wybrane Zagadnienia)*. Warsaw: KiW.

Świątkowski, H. (1962). *Wyznaniowe Prawo Państwowe, Problematyka Prawna Wolności Sumienia w PRL*. Warsaw: PWN.

Syrop, K. (1957). *Spring in October: The Polish Revolution of 1956*. London: Weidenfeld and Nicolson.

Szczepański, J. (1966). *Empirical Sociology in Poland*. Warsaw: PWN.

Szczepański, J. (1970). *Polish Society*. New York: Random House.

Szczypka, J. (1989). *Jan Paweł II Rodowód*. Warsaw.

Sztandar Młodych, 14 November 1952; 13 October 1958; 14 November 1958.

Szuldrzyński, J. (1953). *Situacja Kościoła w Polsce*. Paris: Instytut Literacki.

Tablet (London). 189 (17 May 1947); 190 (4 October 1947, 8 November 1947); 192 (28 August 1948, 20 November 1948); (1 August 1958).

Tablet (Brooklyn). "Polish Reds Seek to Tax Church out of Existence" (1 April 1961).

Tatu, M. (1964). "Le Camp Socialiste et la Crise Sino–Soviétique". *Le Monde* (17 April).

Terry, A. (1959). "Poles Throng the Churches, Clash with State Feared". *Sunday Times* (29 March).

Times. "Vatican Makes Gesture to Warsaw" (27 December 1958).

Times, 28 September 1960.

Times (London). An interview with Gomułka (4 February 1963).

Trybuna Ludu, 1950–1968.

Trybuna Ludu, "Tylko Polska Socjalistyczna Może Być Wolna, Niepodległa i Suwerenna, Przemówienie Gomułki" (30 November 1956).

Trybuna Wolności, "Kościół Katolicki a Obóz Demokracji" (1 March 1946).

Trybuna Wolności, "O Kogo Dba Watykan" (24 February 1952).

Trybuna Wolności, 14 January 1953.

Turowicz, J. (1957). In *Tygodnik Powszechny* (26 May).

Turowicz, J. (1959). In *Tygodnik Powszechny* (19 July).

TV Polonia, 8 May 1998; 11 May 1998; 13 May 1998.

TV Polonia. Program: "W centrum uwagi" (In the center of attention), 30 December 1998.

Tygodnik Powszechny, 1946–1970.

Tygodnik Warszawski, 27 April 1947; 16 November 1947; No. 29, 1947.

Urban, W. (1966). *Ostatni Etap Dziejów Kościoła w Polsce Przed Nowym tysiącleciem*. London: Veritas; Rome: Hosianum.

Valkenier, E. (1956). "The Catholic Church in Communist Poland 1945–1955". *Review of Politics*, 18 (July), pp. 301–326.

Veritas (1966). *Listy Biskupów Polskich i Inne Dokumenty*. London.

Washington Post, editorial, 13 August 1958.

Wasung, A. (1958). *L'Eglise Catholique en Pologne 1954–1957, Faits et Documents*. Fribourg: Centre de Documentation pour les Affaires de l'Eglise en Pologne.

Wawryn, S. (1948). ("Church Affairs".) *Przegląd Powszechny*, 6.

Wawryn, S. (1950). "Sens Porozumienia Między Państwem a Kościołem". *Przegląd Powszechny*, 229 (May).

Weigel, G. (1995). *Ostateczna Rewolucja, Kościół Sprzeciwu a Upadek Komunizmu*. Poznań: W drodze.

Weit, E. (1971). *Dans l'ombre de Gomułka*. Paris: Editions Robert Laffont, S.A.

Wiadomości Archidiecezjalne Warszawskie, 1957/4 and 8; 1958/1.

Wiatr, J. (ed.) (1967). *Studies in the Polish Political System*. Wrocław.

Wiatr. J. (1970). "Political Parties: Interest Representation and Economic Development in Poland". *American Political Science Review*, LXIV (4 December), pp. 1239–1245.

Wilder, E. (1964). "Impact of Poland's Stabilization on Youth". *Public Opinion Quarterly*, 28 (Summer/1).

Wisłocki, J. (1993). *Konkordat Polski, 1993. Tak Czy Nie*. Poznań: SAWW.

World Today (1957). "Gomułka's Road to Socialism, the May Meeting of the Polish United Workers' Party". 13 (August), pp. 350–431.

World Today, "Revisionist Poland Charting a Difficult Course" (June 1958), pp. 247–259.

Wróblewski, A. (1958). "Swięta Wojna w Olkuszu". *Życie Warszawy* (16 May).

Wydawnictwa Zachodnie (1960). *Straty Wojenne Polski w Latach 1939–1945*. Warsaw.

Wydawnictwo Prawnicze (1958a). *Konstytucja, Podstawowe Akty Ustawodawcze Polskiej Rzeczpospolitej Ludowej*. Warsaw (and 1966).

Wydawnictwo Prawnicze (1958b). "Manifest Polskiego Komitetu Wyzwolenia Narodowego". *Konstytucja i Podstawowe Akty Ustawodawcze Polskiej Rzeczypospolitej Ludowej*. Warsaw.

Wyszyński, S. (1958). ("A Millennium of Polish Christianity"). *Tygodnik Powszechny* (1 June).

Wyszyński, S. (1966). *Polska Droga Krzyżowa*. London: Veritas.

Wyszyński, S. (1981). *Kościół w Służbie Narodu*. Poznań: Pallotinum.

Wyszyński, S. (1983). *A Freedom Within: The Prison Notes*. New York: Harcourt Brace.

Z Pola Walki. "60-lecia Urodzin Towarzysza Władysława Gomułki" (1965/1).

Zakowski, J. (1990). *Trzy ćwiartki wieku. Rozmowy z Jerzym Turowiczem*. Kraków.

Zakrzewska, J. and M. Sobolewski (1963). *Wolność Sumienia i Wyznania*. Warsaw: Iskry.

Zawadska, B. (1959). "Kościół Przestaje Być Atrakcyjny". *Polityka*, 27.

Zawadski, T. (1953). *Walka z Kościołem 1951–1953*. Munich: *RFE* (mimeo), vol. II.

Zawadski, T. (1958a). "W Sprawie Obrazy Wierzen Oraz Tolerancji i Polityki". *Polityka*, 35.

Zawadski, T. (1958b). *Gomułka and Yugoslavia in 1948*. Munich: *RFE* (mimeo). *Gamarnikow Files* (30 June).

Zawadski, T. and K. Wager (1977)."Gomułka i Historia PPR". Polish Broadcasting Department, RFE (19–22 July).

Żełobowski, A. (1989). *Episkopat Kościoła Rzymskokatolickiego w Polsce wobec Przemiań Społeczno—Politycznych w Kraju w l. 1944–1974*. Warsaw.

Zieliński, H. (1954). *Population Changes in Poland 1939–1950*. New York.

Zimmerer, L. (1957). "Zimmerer Reports Wednesday from Warsaw to *Die Welt*". Hamburg (7 May), RFE, No. 1140.

Zinner, P. E. (ed.) (1956). *National Communism and Popular Revolt in Eastern Europe*. New York: Columbia University Press.

III Zjazd Polskiej Zjednoczonej Partii Robotniczej Stenogram. Warsaw, 1959.

Zk (1959). "Złudzenia i Fakty o Cofnięciu Akredytacji Przedstawicielowi Polskiego Rządu Emigracyjnego K. Papée". *Życie Warszawy* (10 January).

Żurawski, J. W. (1962). *Poland the Captive Satellite: A Study in National Psychology*. Detroit: Endurance Press.

Życie i Prawo, 10 August 1958.

Życie Warszawy, 19 November 1952; 31 December 1956.

Życie Warszawy (1956). "Oświadczenie Pisarzy i Działaczy Katolickich" (23 October).

Życie Warszawy (1959). "W Watykanie Bez Zmian" (12 May).

Życie Warszawy (1965). "Katolicy wobec Polskiej Współczesności: Rozmowa 'Życia' z Jerzym Zawieyskim" (25 May).

Życie Warszawy (1966). "Państwo, Kościół, Społeczeństwo, Rozmowa 'Życia' z Prof. Konstantyn Grzybowskim" (4 March).

Zyzniewski, S. J. (1959). "The Soviet Economic Impact on Poland". In RFE, *Background Information (USSR)* (18 July). ("Khrushchev and Poland/II".)

Interviews (1977–1997)

Chava, A. Recruited by Gomułka as a non-partisan member to the Polish underground in 1942; worked with him during the war, and later with Loga-Sowiński.

Bielecki, F. Senior official at the Polish Ministry of Education from 1945 to 1960; director general of the Ministry during the 1950s; worked with W. Bieńkowski between 1956 and 1959.

Boim, L. Professor of political science and law; a member of the executive of the regional committee of Kielce; a member of the municipal council of Częstochowa (1945–1952); chairman of the judicial committee of the council; held contacts with church officials in Częstochowa.

Czaplicka, F. A KPP activist; a member of the Communist underground; a relative of Loga-Sowiński.

Gilart, A. Party (youth movement) member already before the war; official at the Polish Ministry of Foreign Affairs from 1949 to 1961; employee of the Institute of the History of Soviet-Polish relations from 1961 to 1968.

Grajewski, W. Polish Press Agency employee from 1949 to 1956; party member from 1948. He was responsible for the transfer of Khrushchev's "secret speech" to the West (CIA).

Klugman, A. Former editor of *Nowiny Kurier*; worked with Mrs. Gomułka.

Krakowski, Sz. Member of a Communist organization in the Łódź ghetto; a member of the Institute of Jewish History in Warsaw; held contacts with senior party officials.

Kratko, Z. Trade union activist already before the war; deputy director and director of the party's department of trade unions; as a member of the organization department of the Central Committee of the PPR he worked with Mrs. Gomułka and under her supervision.

Mazur, E. A personal friend of the Gomułka family following underground ties with Mrs. Gomułka; most of her contacts were during Gomułka's house-arrest. (Two interviews.)

Nusbaum, K. Senior officer of the Polish army; his wife—a member of the Central Committee of the PZPR—was chairwoman of the Women's League; deputy mayor of Warsaw until 1953. (Two interviews.)

Smoler, H. Chairman of the Central Committee of the Jewish community; later, chairman of the Institute of Social and Cultural Affairs of the Polish Jewish community; editor of the Yiddish newspaper *Falksshtime*; author of a number of famous books; had personal contacts with Gomułka. (Two interviews.)

Śpiewak, P. Professor of sociology at the University of Warsaw; editor of, and contributor to, *Życie Warszawy*; a member of the editorial board of *Republika Nowa*.

Wygodski, S. The famous Polish poet and author; had close contacts with Gomułka's aides and within government circles.

INDEX